Theory, Policy, Practice

AF849426

This book explores the meanings and perceptions of development and the dialectics of theory, policy and practice. It looks at how theory translates into policy, and the disconnections in its design and implementation in the Indian context.

The book focuses on the influence of capitalist globalisation, democratisation, decentralisation and neoliberal economic reforms on the development discourse in India and how these have challenged the traditional role of the 'state', the meaning of citizenship, and public participation. Through an analysis of case studies from various parts of the country, it bridges the gap between policy prescriptions and practices and unpacks the institutional, political and policy-led compulsions and incompatibilities which most often remain unreported. It also discusses the intersections between policymaking and the politics of class, caste and gender, and emphasises the role bureaucracy plays in institutional governance.

The volume includes articles from professionals ranging from academics, practitioners and activists. It will be of interest to scholars and researchers of public policy, development studies, South Asian politics, and economics as well as policy makers and practitioners in government and civil society.

Suman Nath received his PhD jointly under faculties from the Indian Institute of Management Calcutta and the University of Calcutta in Anthropology. He teaches anthropology as Assistant Professor at Dr A. P. J. Abdul Kalam Government College, Kolkata, India. Since 2007, he has been researching on issues of politics of resource allocation, which includes a stint as Research Associate at Public Policy and Management Group, Indian Institute of Management Calcutta, India. His books include a monograph, titled *People-Party-Policy Interplay in India* (2020) and a co-authored volume on *Sexuality, Identity and Health* (2014). He has published in international journals on issues of politics, corruption and governance. He was awarded to participate in different research programmes organised by the UNDP, Planning Commission and SaciWATERs. Apart from his academic publications, Suman runs a couple of internationally recognised blogs and writes popular articles in Little Magazines and Bengali dailies. His forthcoming research monograph *Democracy and Social Cleavage in India* is scheduled to be published next year.

Debraj Bhattacharya is with the Azim Premji University, Bengaluru, India. An alumnus of Presidency College, Kolkata, he is working in the development sector of India since 2000. He has published on a wide range of themes and topics - colonial modernity, urban crime in colonial Calcutta, rural development, migration, local government, Marx, and Marxist West Bengal. His books include a monograph *Exploring Marxist Bengal* (2016) and a couple of edited volumes entitled *Of Matters Modern* (2008), and *Karl Marx: 19th Century Memories and Reflections* (2018).

Theory, Policy, Practice

Development and Discontents in India

Edited by Suman Nath and
Debraj Bhattacharya

Routledge
Taylor & Francis Group
LONDON AND NEW YORK

First published 2022
by Routledge
2 Park Square, Milton Park, Abingdon, Oxon OX14 4RN

and by Routledge
605 Third Avenue, New York, NY 10158

Routledge is an imprint of the Taylor & Francis Group, an informa business

© 2021 selection and editorial matter, Suman Nath and Debraj Bhattacharya; individual chapters, the contributors

The right of Suman Nath and Debraj Bhattacharya to be identified as the authors of the editorial material, and of the authors for their individual chapters, has been asserted in accordance with sections 77 and 78 of the Copyright, Designs and Patents Act 1988.

All rights reserved. No part of this book may be reprinted or reproduced or utilised in any form or by any electronic, mechanical, or other means, now known or hereafter invented, including photocopying and recording, or in any information storage or retrieval system, without permission in writing from the publishers.

Trademark notice: Product or corporate names may be trademarks or registered trademarks, and are used only for identification and explanation without intent to infringe.

British Library Cataloguing-in-Publication Data
A catalogue record for this book is available from the British Library

Library of Congress Cataloging-in-Publication Data
A catalog record has been requested for this book

ISBN: 978-0-367-63454-4 (hbk)
ISBN: 978-0-367-74867-8 (pbk)
ISBN: 978-1-003-15994-0 (ebk)

Typeset in Sabon
by Deanta Global Publishing Services, Chennai, India

To all those who lost their lives and livelihoods due to Covid19

Contents

Figures

Tables

Contributors

Bhaskar Chakrabarti is a professor of the Public Policy and Management Group at the Indian Institute of Management, Calcutta, West Bengal, India. With a core competency in the evaluation of policy and institutional environment for implementation of local government projects, Bhaskar Chakrabarti synthesises knowledge from various disciplines to foster innovation in "people's participation" as applied to practical challenges of governance. He has worked as a consultant to the provincial and the national government in India on the effectiveness of local governments, evaluation of development programmes, restructuring of handloom cooperatives, evaluation of microfinance programmes for marginal groups, and to international agencies like UNICEF on gap analysis of cluster-level resource centres. His recent research is on local bureaucracy in West Bengal and on the challenges of the nascent democracy in Bhutan. Chakrabarti is also working on a mega research project on inclusivity, cross-boundary cooperation and institutional interconnectedness funded by the Ministry of Education and Science, Government of Japan. He has published, amongst others, in the *Journal of South Asian Development*, *Commonwealth Journal of Local Governance*, *Review of Development and Change*, *Government Information Quarterly*, and the *Economic and Political Weekly*. He is a member of the Board of Commonwealth Local Government Forum, UK.

Manish Thakur is a professor at the Public Policy and Management Group, Indian Institute of Management Calcutta, West Bengal, India. He is the recipient of the prestigious Prof. V.K.R.V. Award in sociology. He is the author of two books, *Indian Village: A Conceptual History* (2014) and *The Quest for Indian Sociology* (2014). He has also co-edited two volumes: *Management Education in India: Perspectives and Practices* (2017) and *Doing Theory: Locations, Hierarchies and Disjunctions* (2018).

Jeetesh Rai is teaching as an assistant professor at the Department of Geography, Kirori Mal College, University of Delhi, New Delhi, India. Having done his M.Phil. from the University of Cambridge he did his PhD from the University of Delhi. He is working on the issues of Urban Poor and Right to the City.

Aparajita De is a professor at the Department of Geography, Delhi School of Economics, University of Delhi, New Delhi, India. Aparajita is currently working on the middle class and imaginations and formulations of the global city in South Asia.

Anjan Chakrabarti is a professor-director at the UGC Human Resource Development Centre of the University of North Bengal, West Bengal, India. His research interest includes agriculture in Bengal, development discourse with special emphasis on ecology, gender and the northeastern region of India. He has published many research papers in national/international journals and edited volumes. He also presented research papers and delivered lectures in premier institutions in India and aboard. He also acted as visiting scientist at Indian Statistical Institute, Bangalore. He is also visiting professor at Raiganj University. He completed seven research projects (International and National). He authored *Economic Development and Employment in Sikkim*, 2009 and edited, a volume titled *Interrogating Development: Perspectives on the Economy, Environment, Ethnicity, and Gender*, 2017. He is also the co-author of the book titled *Introduction to Microeconomics and Statistics*, 2019.

Abhijit Guha is currently a senior fellow, Indian Council of Social Science Research attached with the Institute of Development Studies Kolkata, West Bengal, India. Formerly faculty in the Department of Anthropology during December 1985–August 2016 and retired as professor. He has published more than 100 articles, comments and book reviews in various international and national level peer-reviewed journals, and edited volumes. He has published, among others, a book *Land, Law and the Left: The Saga of Disempowerment of the Peasantry in the Era of Globalisation* in 2007 (with a Foreword by Michael Cernea). UGC Visiting Fellow at the Department of Sociology, Delhi School of Economics, Delhi University during 29 August–12 September 2006. He was invited to give suggestions as an expert on the 2007 Land Acquisition and Resettlement Amendment Bills by the Standing Committee on Rural Development of the Lok Sabha. He has peer-reviewed articles for *Current Anthropology* (Chicago), *Journal of the Indian Anthropological Society* (Kolkata) and *Development and Change* (The Hague), *The Journal of Anthropology* (New York), *Anthropological Forum* (Perth), *The European Journal of Development Research* (Palgrave), *Forum for Development Studies* (Taylor & Francis) and *Contemporary South Asia* (Taylor & Francis) and is the associate editor of the *Journal of the Indian Anthropological Society*,

Kolkata. His forthcoming book is called, *Encountering Land Grab: An Ethnographic Journey.*

Arnab Roy Chowdhury is an assistant professor in the school of sociology at the Higher School of Economics (HSE), Moscow, Russia. Prior to this, he was a postdoctoral fellow in the department of public policy at HSE. He has received his PhD in sociology from the National University of Singapore (NUS). His research interests cover social movement studies, environmental sociology, sociology of development, forced migration and refugee studies, historical and comparative sociology, state society relations and post-colonial studies.

Late Sanjay Kumar Rajhans was a senior lecturer and vice chair of the department of public policy, Higher School of Economics, Moscow, Russia.

Sarasij Majumder is an associate professor of Anthropology and director of India Studies at the University of Houston, Houston, USA. His research primarily looks at the politics of land and industrialisation in South Asia. Sarasij's research interests include critical political economy, development, anthropology of work and rural change. He has published in renowned anthropology journals, such as *Dialectical Anthropology, Focaal: Journal of Historical and Global Anthropology, Critique of Anthropology, Environment and Society*. Sarasij has also contributed to the *Economic and Political Weekly of India*, and *American Anthropologist*. Sarasij has also contributed chapters to important edited volumes on South Asia, such as *Industrializing Rural India*. The title of his first single-authored book based on five years of ethnographic work in West Bengali villages is *People's Car: Industrial India and Riddles of Populism*. Sarasij's research in India was supported by the United States National Science Foundation and the American Institute of Indian Studies. Sarasij's current research project looks at corporate cultures of identifying, archiving and using tacit knowledge for the purposes of knowledge management.

Debarati Sen is an associate professor of anthropology at the University of Houston, Houston, USA. Her research takes place at the confluence of cultural anthropology, gender studies and conflict studies. For the past 14 years, she has examined gendered mobilisations around sustainable development and subnational conflict in rural India, specifically Darjeeling, drawing keen attention to issues of social sustainability at the community level. This work has culminated in her book, *Everyday Sustainability: Gender Justice and Fair Trade Tea in Darjeeling*. Wenner-Gren Individual Research Grant, National Science Foundation DDIG Grant, Princeton University, and Columbia University's Marion Jemmott grant funded her research. In 2018, this monograph won two major national-level book awards: The International Studies Association's book award for the Global Development Section and the Gloria E. Anzaldúa Book Prize from National Women's Studies Association. In 2019, her book also received an honorable mention for the Michelle Rosaldo Book Prize of the Association for Feminist Anthropology(American Anthropological Association). Her other publications have appeared in refereed journals such as *Anthropology in Action*, *Critique of Anthropology*, *Feminist Studies*, *Society and Natural Resources*, *Environment and Society* and *Anthropology of Work Review*. She contributed to anthologies like *New South Asian Feminisms* and *Indigenous Conflict Management Strategies*.

Rahul Bhaumik is an assistant professor in the Department of History at Women's College, Calcutta, West Bengal, India. He has written articles on the history of medical-zoological management of snakebite in British India.

Nandini Sen is an anthropologist who has done her PhD (social anthropology) from Goethe University, Frankfurt , Germany, and masters from the University of St Andrews (Social Anthropology), Scotland, UK. Nandini had published her paper titled Women and Gender in Short Stories by Rabindranath Tagore in *Anthropological Journal of European Cultures* in 2016. Her book chapter, How Bollywood Filmdom Operates in India and the International Arena, Consumption of Bollywood, was published in *Anthropological Approaches to Understanding Consumption Patterns and Consumer Behavior*, in 2020. In 2021 she has co-authored 'Gender-based Violence in India in Covid-19 lockdown'. It is published in the *Journal of Comparative Literature and Aesthetics*. In 2020, she had published an essay, 'Pandemics, Covid-19, and literary studies, past and present' in Covid-19 Perspectives, University of Edinburgh. She has also co-authored few essays on Indian situations in Covid-19 lockdown in different academic blogs, Department of Law and Anthropology, University of Edinburgh, 2020. Her anthropological experience with the waste pickers "Urban Marginalisation in South Asia: Waste Pickers in Calcutta" was published by Routledge in 2018. Now it has been turned into a paperback edition since August 2020 after being well acclaimed by academicians and peers.

Subhasish Ray is working at the Jindal School of Government and Public Policy, O.P. Jindal Global University, Haryana, India. His current research interests include studies of historical legacies in modern ethnic conflict, the political psychology of nationalism, and party system development in post-civil war contexts. He serves as an editor for the Journal of Genocide Research. His articles have appeared in leading journals, such as the International Studies Quarterly, Political Psychology, Journal of Peace Research, and Critical Asian Studies.

Anit Mukherjee is a policy fellow at the Center for Global Development (CGD), Washington DC, USA, where he works on issues of governance, public finance and service delivery in developing countries. His current research focuses on the impact of biometric ID and digital payment systems to reform public subsidies, improve financial inclusion and promote gender empowerment. Prior to joining CGD, Mukherjee was an associate professor at the National Institute of Public Finance and Policy, New Delhi from 2005 to 2013, where he designed and implemented innovative citizen-led public expenditure tracking surveys in education and health. As a policy advisor to the world's largest biometric ID programme, Aadhar, he was involved in the direct benefit transfer of subsidies in India. He studied economics at the Presidency College, Calcutta and Jawaharlal Nehru University, Delhi, and obtained a PhD in policy and planning sciences from the University of Tsukuba, Japan. He has published extensively in peer-reviewed journals and his latest book is *Social Sector in Decentralized Economy: India in the Era of Globalization* (2016).

Mohit Kumar Gupta is a PhD scholar at the Centre for the Study of Law and Governance, Jawaharlal Nehru University, Delhi, New Delhi, India. Earlier, he has worked as a project associate in the research project on "The State, Globalization and Industrial Development in India: The political economy of regulation and deregulation" at Ambedkar University Delhi in collaboration with the Norway Institute of International Affairs (NUPI). He had also served as a research associate at the Indian Institute of Foreign Trade, Delhi. Currently, he is working at the intersection of law and economics and his research interests are corporate governance, taxation, political economy and the role of institutions. He has presented his work highlighting the peculiar aspects of family-owned business groups in India in various International conferences on Law and Economics. He has co-authored a paper on 'The *Hindu Undivided Family* in Independent India's Corporate Governance and Tax Regime' published in *South Asia Multidisciplinary Academic Journal*. He has also co-authored a Chapter titled "Capitalism and Un-Paid Work in India" in an edited volume *"Labouring Women Issues and Challenges in Contemporary India"* which was published by Orient Blackswan in 2020. He is the recipient of the ICSSR Institutional Doctoral Fellowship in Social Science for the year 2019.

Acknowledgements

This volume is an outcome of a long-term friendship and intellectual partnership between us and a handful of others. The idea of a book was born out of our conversation over rounds of drinks on a windy Kolkata summer evening. The idea was incomplete, fragmented and full of confusions then. When we were discussing the idea of this book an overlooking sun was setting at one corner of the built-in city of New Town Kolkata. Underneath the dazzling skyscrapers there stood daily labourers exhausted after their day's work was over. The city of New Town often drove off the hawkers from the wide footpaths of the city to give it a makeover. They were the displaced people, initially because of the land acquisition and then they were displaced regularly because the city didn't quite appreciate their existence. The definition of development as a planned social change that is supposedly progressively inclusive is not what our lived experience suggests, neither in New Town, nor in the old city of Kolkata, or for that matter anywhere in the country where we did most of our empirical works. Our discussion on such discontents of development led us to question the very notion of the development as experienced by the academicians and practitioners. Although our work fronts do not let us meet every day, the idea of the discontents in the development paradigm kept haunting both of us, and our contributors as the idea we shared over a series of emails with them. Our contributors did a wonderful job not only by contributing with their experiences but also by helping us to improve the idea and the manuscript. We are really thankful to everyone. It is their constant effort to improve that the idea of the discontent in different facets of development discourse came alive. Many of our articles are empirical and involve a lot of research participants. We on behalf of our entire team wish to express our heartfelt thanks to each of the research participants who agreed to participate in each of the issues that this book deals with.

While the idea was still half baked we started receiving chapters, it was the Routledge team of editors and their reviewers who gave an unusual effort to give it a shape. The freedom that we have enjoyed, and the feedback we have received from them is highly appreciable. We extend our heartfelt thanks to the team especially to Aakash Chakrabarti, Brinda Sen and Shloka Chauhan for their relentless effort for a perfect volume.

We would like to thank our wives Anwita and Amrita for their constant support in many different ways. We are hopeful that this volume will add to the puzzle and paradox of development discourse.

Suman and Debraj

Introduction

Suman Nath and Debraj Bhattacharya

During 2007–2008, Suman was working as a Research Associate after his Masters and Debraj was working as Research and Studies Coordinator with a project on Strengthening Rural Decentralisation, a project of the Government of West Bengal supported by the British government. They met in a white Ambassador car on the way to a Gram Panchayat office at Chatuhansa, in Purulia district of West Bengal. This was in 2007. After the usual introductory sessions, Debraj said, "perhaps we are going to witness the poorest of the poor part of the state, as per our sample this Panchayat is the not going through its best times." As the car took the dusty country roads, half-naked kids started cheering seeing a "sarkari gari." Debraj didn't forget to mention while getting down from the car that this could indeed be labelled as elitism. Suman felt it was too alienating! In most of his research, Suman had used a bicycle to collect data. Getting down from a car to collect data was beyond what young anthropologists could imagine back in 2007! This was the beginning of a long friendship between an academician and a practitioner which has culminated in this book.

Today as both Debraj and Suman do their fieldwork in different parts of rural India, they discuss often how things are changing. Indian villages, much like Indian cities, are transforming over the years (Gupta, 2005). Unlike a classic ethnographic monograph written in the ethnographic present for which Suman had to undergo rigorous university training, what they observed was quite different (Hastrup, 1990). Even a revisit to Chatuhasa was not the same in 2014. The Panchayat office building had a makeover, streets and lanes were metalled and kids no longer ran after the vehicle half-naked. Did the trick happen because of implementation of the coveted mid-day meal scheme, or wage employment through Mahatma Gandhi National Rural Employment Guarantee Scheme, or Pradhan Mantri Gram Sarak Yojana or was it because of the direct impact of the much-celebrated neoliberal "success" story of the country (Das, 2006, 2015; Aiyar, 2008)? Debraj went on to expand his rural fieldwork experience to different states of India from 2009, specialising in local governance, while Suman immersed himself into the customary teaching and research. As they kept meeting and

DOI: 10.4324/9781003159940-101

discussing they could apprehend convergence and divergence in their ways of understanding the development discourse. Both knew for example that development-related decisions are political decisions, but Suman found everyday politics as a driving force while Debraj insisted that bureaucracy has an important role to play apart from politicians, a fact often missed in academic literature. Suman is keen on knowing policy paradox in its epistemology, Debraj points out that there are differences between what is said and what is done. Apart from their life courses what accounts for such divergences? Over time, through many addas, this led to a mutual realisation – it is not enough to understand India's attempt at development only through the lens of this or that theoretical paradigm; a much more complicated dialectic between theory, policy and practice is required.

This book aims to open up a discussion of, rather than say the final word on, [dis]connections between "theory," "policy" and "practice" of India's development. As Suman teaches development-related issues, he ponders on policy regimes, which are a typical set of policies favoured by states and their financial allies. In the classroom he uses concepts like Keynesianism, neo-classical, neoliberal frequently, while Debraj maps how a policy gets implemented, including a practical understanding of why they succeed or fail. Their experiences led to a joint book project for which they invited other scholars, experts in their own field, to contribute. Fortunately, the core idea resonated with some scholars who agreed to participate in the project.

Development in standard connotation

The trajectories of development as change is viewed both as a "natural" law of progress through evolution in the 1950s and 1960s, and also as an essentially unequalising process of materialistic domination of the South by the North with an underlying philosophy of ideological domination of East by the West (Said, 1978; Escober, 1995; Haynes, 2005). This is rooted in a rather sudden labelling of vast areas of the south as underdeveloped with President Truman's use of the term. This is essentially a hotly debated "evolutionary" philosophy to the question of social-cultural change as "progress" (Esteva, 1993). The development discourse, especially in developing nations, has a twin problem – first, the common sense notion which shapes much of the policy discourse even today sees development broadly as a "modernising" trend where infrastructure development and technology transfer is a key problem solver. The second, and even more nuanced, dimension is a lack of concrete understanding of the "what," "how" and "why" questions of the discontent of theory–policy–practices of the development discourse that have surprisingly been rather understudied. People gathered essentially rich experience in working with the development discourse which sees paradigm shift over the years. The notions of development have began with the post-war infrastructure building and technology transfer through fund injection led *modernisation* (Long and Long, 1992) approach. The critical engagements with the modernisation approach revealed its essentially unequalising and *dependency* process (Frank, 1967; Wallerstein, 1974). In recent years development discourse is revolving around the rise of local and bottom-up *postmodern* trends of welfare and basic needs (Gardner and Lewis, 1996, 2015). With the ever-increasing expansion of market-led globalisation through neoliberal policies, increasingly shrinking avenues for the state and the rise of new powers from erstwhile developing nations have made development discourses more complex than ever before. Such a geopolitical complexity brings forth fluidity in the conceptualisation of the traditional notions of the third world, aid agencies and development practitioners. In response to that, theories, policies and methodologies of development studies are undergoing rapid changes. While scholars have increasingly engaged with critical standpoints, new subjectivities and newer informal economic avenues challenging the hegemonic discourses of globalisation have also come to the forefront. In this context the book (a) explores the three domains in different sectors as experienced and studied by different stakeholders, (b) unravels the multiple meaning of the concept of development, its perception and practices, (c) bridges the gap between and exploring the cultural possibilities of policy prescriptions and practices, and (d) unpacks the institutional, political and policy-led compulsions and incompatibilities which most often remains unreported.

Theory–policy–practice paradox

The word "development" simply put is an attempt by nation-states to bring about changes so that an increasing proportion of a nation's citizens can attain a higher material standard of living, healthier and longer lives, and more importantly, an increasing control over how they live. Such an endeavour depends heavily on a particular form of economy. In turn it is an outcome of thousands of decisions by selfish actors which collide to form a decision, in short a market decision. Markets according to Polanyi (1944) are social constructs where states have a great role to play in making, shaping and directing them. How a state shapes markets has lot to do with its policy and practice. So, ideally, a well-functioning state is not expected to run the economy by the production of goods and services but also by generating employment and distributing public goods and services to the people. Such questions of growth and welfare have been dealt with quite differently in two policy-linked grand narratives that characterised much of the development discourse with the advent of post-colonial democracy. These include the Keynesian Social Democratic policy regime which was a dominant paradigm till 1980 and the neoliberal policy regime which is dominating since 1980. India, being one of the often-cited success stories of neoliberal policy, has seen the devaluation of the rupee, increase in interest rates, reduction of public investment, reduction in public sector food and fertiliser subsidies, restructuring of the industrial sector, increase in imports and foreign investment in capital-intensive and high-tech activities, and the abolition of the cash compensatory support for exports since 1991. With the abolition of what is known as centrally controlled "Licence Raj" states were expected to encourage private capital (Das, 2006, 2015; Aiyar, 2008; Peet, 2011). The most conspicuous presentation of India's success is shown in terms of its growth in the gross domestic product (GDP), which supposedly has shown a steady growth and then a decline (Figure I.1). It was declining steadily even before the COVID-19 pandemic led to a country-wide lockdown (see e.g. Guruswami, 2019). The other narrative to project the success of neoliberalism is the late capital projection of a sophisticated "cultural" industry.

Such an industry is pervasive and most often goes unnoticed while it leaves a substantive impact on our minds. Urban-centred people in their everyday living cannot comprehend the depth of deprivation that makes India standing on what is termed by Dreze and Sen as *Uncertain Glory* (Dreze and Sen, 1995; see also Dreze and Sen, 1995). Apart from Dreze and Sen, Palmer-Jones and Sen (2001), Paul (2009), Banerjee and Duflo (2011) have also questioned India's celebrated growth story both in terms of its inclusiveness and its methodology. These questions with huge data showing how India has ignored if not deliberately its vast majority from the growth trajectory and that there is hardly any real change in the number of

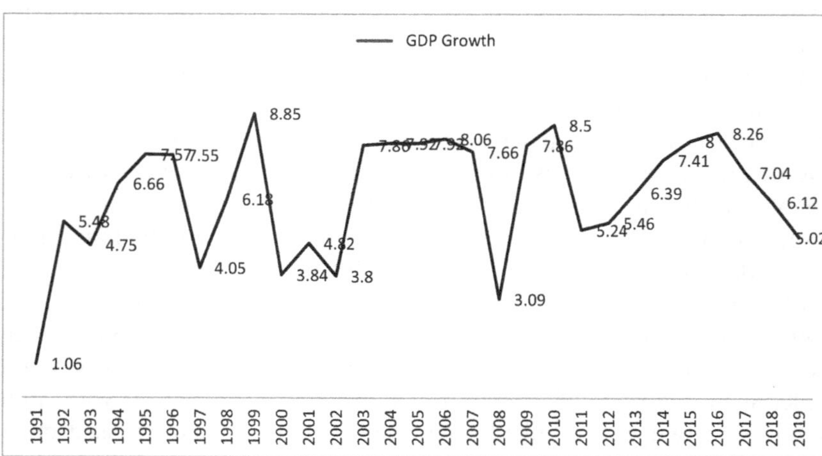

Figure I.1 GDP Growth in India since the adoption of neoliberal policy (1991–2019). Source: Computed from https://www.macrotrends.net/countries/IND/india/gdp-growth-rate and GoI 2007

poor or quality of life of the marginal. Dreze and Sen (1995) discuss how India is lagging behind its neighbours in several human development indices simply because it failed to reach the vast majority lagging behind the "middle class." However, neither scholarly publications nor available data could challenge the glossy cultural industries that provide visual evidence of people doing well feeling aided by high rises at built in cities, well dressed young people busy in their phones, streets full of cars and crowded shopping mall. These visuals have actually overwhelmed statistical data. From a Marxian perspective this is a result of more wealth being extracted from labour. What David Harvey (2005, p. 178) calls "accumulation by dispossession" through privatisation, indebtedness, environmental degradation, the loss of traditional rights to common property requires intervention by the state. The powerful theoretical model still remains *modernisation* in terms of the inevitability of progress, the necessity for "development," minus the question of "for whom" and at "what cost" Peet (2011) aptly describes this as powerful "anti-poverty discourse." Such a denial of data that speaks about the rising gap between rich and poor can be seen as a paradox in perception (see also Basu, 2008).

The paradox of perception is theorised and discussed in academia through the *dependency* theory of development having Marxian and neo-Marxian perspectives. Despite its influences by the 1980s it was clear that grand theories like Modernism, Structuralism or Marxism were increasingly contested by more localised accounts of reality. While the academic world began to celebrate the diversity of experiences rather than homogeneity (Lyotard, 1984), the development paradigm started taking fragmentary experiences of the entire discourse centrally. Thus issues concerning specific categories of people like women, ethnicity or landless are given their due importance with the recognition that these categories are themselves problematic (Gardner and Lewis, 1996, 2015). The rhetoric of "bottom up," grassroots initiatives with stress on "basic needs" became more relevant than macro planning (e.g. UNDP, 1990). In turn, development became seen as full of contradictions, conflicts and unintended consequences happening not only at the practising level but also very much within the aid agencies (Ferguson, 1990; Axelby and Crewe, 2013; Apthorpa, 2011; Gould, 2004). Development and related policies are increasingly recognised as not an external mechanism for betterment but also as a central and dominant organising principle of contemporary society affecting virtually every aspect of human life (Shore and Wright, 1997; Wedel et al., 2005). The second paradox arises from this twin recognition (a) that development needs micro-perspectives and (b) that development policies operate quite differently as a social construction of organising principles like myths or fables in so-called "pre-industrial" societies. The central question that this book deals with is linked to this second paradox. If international and national policies, much like myths and folktales in traditional societies are governing much of the late capital and postmodern subjectivities, often through self-governance and self-surveillance, why shouldn't we look at dialectics of the theory–policy–practice interplay as they shape our society at large? This book therefore explores how the three interplay in different problematised areas as reflected in the essays by the contributors.

The book begins with a section on organisational mechanisms of development governance. In Chapter 1, Suman captures the ways in which an institutional environment determines much of the organisational responses at the grassroots. Using a longitudinal, multi-sited ethnographic research he unearths the dynamics of Gram Panchayat (GP), India's rural local government, and agricultural co-operatives interfacing local politics in West Bengal. He shows that despite postmodern inclination towards the local and bottom-up approach, institutional building has remained secondary. Consequently, these organisations experience incompatibilities, overlaps, corruption and result in poor functioning in terms of institutional effectiveness and performance. Because of the lack of institutional effectiveness, the implementation of different policies through decentralised institutions face difficulties from local power groups. Even with political change and relatively a more empowered administrative wing, he argues, decentralised institutions have failed to look after the interest of the weaker sections. The organisations could never go beyond the control of the local elites and political leaders. Debraj, along with co-authors Bhaskar Chakrabarti and Manish Thakur, addresses the issues of the institution by looking at the Community Developments of the Block, a tier of Government that was added after independence to develop rural areas. Chapter 2 traces the history of the concept of block development office and shows in what ways with increasing emphasis on decentralisation the block office loses its discursive importance but remained an important organisation for rural development. This chapter indicates the problems of implementation despite complex bureaucratic mandates and guidelines. It shows the intricacies of block offices at the practice level through empirical cases. The authors show that, with a motive strikingly different from colonial administration, block offices have largely failed to cater to the need of rapid development of postcolonial India because of reasons like institutional incompatibilities, role confusion, democratic-bureaucratic interface and task overload on Block Development Officers.

While the focus on institutional issues unearths several incompatibilities, both intra- and inter-organisational and organisational societal, a focus on policy formulation and implementation also shows paradox. Aparajita De and Jeetesh Rai in Chapter 3 using a case study of Bawana resettlement Colony, Delhi show how the poor and marginal people are carving out their rights to space and resources of the city when the dominant "developmental" narrative sees and projects them as hindrances to developing world-class cities. They bring out painful narratives of sudden displacement, police brutality and a complete ignorance by the state and present the dynamics of the civil society movement that paved a way for their resettlement. Their study is an example of the inherent contradictions of "modernisation"-led development policies that have the potential to adversely affect the poor; it also presents how the ignored and marginalised people find out an effective solution to combat the "almighty government."

Anjan Chakrabarti gives a historical outline to the concept of the Indian "North-East" as an exclusive place that entails a challenge of governance in Chapter 4. He contextualises the much-celebrated Look East policy in colonial and post-colonial legacy. He argues that let alone implementation, there are macro-economic imbalances in framing policies for the North-East since independence. Consequently, look east policy for transforming this region as the historical genesis goes looks elusive. Anjan dwells and unearths the domains of path dependency in policy formulation, especially in the much neglected Indian North-East.

From Chapter 5 onwards the book attempts to address perennial and emerging issues from fresh perspectives. Based on his decades long ethnographic field experiences on land acquisition policies and practices Abhijit Guha uses a self-reflexive account of the complex issue of land grab. He has used multi-sited ethnography to unravel the entire spectrum of land linked policies and politics. His work ranges from studying the dynamics of small farmers as they face displacement in the liberalised policy context to interaction with the policymakers in the Parliament. The ethnographic eye, in this chapter, searches for clues and effectively glues people's experiences, law-making parliamentarians' perceptions and assembly debates to unravel rare insights into the ways in which policies are made, implemented and their impact on the most marginal section of the population.

Water being another perennial issue of development discourse, Arnab Roy Chowdhury and Sanjay Kumar Rajhans use Wittfogel's idea of Hydraulic Society to trace the management of water resources from pre-colonial through colonial to post-colonial India in Chapter 6. This chapter unearths the centrality of water to the continuation of human civilisation, politics and policy discourses and at the same time shows the inherent messiness of its management strategies. It heuristically maps the continuity of water through ages and presents cases that can best be seen as a "patchy history" to arrive at a comprehensive idea of the extent of water mess throughout the much known period of human history in the subcontinent. This chapter shows how historically formulated dominant policy narratives actually shape further courses of policies and actions even if a paradigm shift in governance has taken place over the years.

In Chapter 7, Sarasij Majumder and Debarati Sen argue that a much-preferred policy alternative in financing and entrepreneurship development through microcredit brought the local and regional scales closer to the global metropolis bypassing the state. They show how the excitement of changing the lives of the rural and urban poor has been rather short lived. They show that despite its success stories microcredit loans also pushed rural women and youth into further indebtedness and it entails caste-based and class-based rural differentiations which is perpetuated by NGOs. The chapter shows the lopsided policy prescription and unforeseen consequences of policy interfacing in the existing social-cultural milieu.

One of the perennial problems for countries like India has been in the health sector. Rahul Bhaumik takes on the discourses of health as an essentially power-ridden matrix where a serious health crisis resulting from snakebite has been ignored for decades in Chapter 8. He shows how a snakebite is ignored by agencies like the World Health Organisation in a process of global politics of othering. The chapter shows the ways in which seriousness, care and management of a particular health crisis is linked to existing class and regional divisions and that policies and practices are very much culturally engrained. Poverty and marginalisation have been at the forefront of issues related to development.

In Chapter 9, through her study of the waste pickers in Kolkata, Nandini Sen shows that an extreme form of ignorance and marginalisation by the state makes the weaker section carve out an alternative space of existence. This alternative, as Nandini shows, is a result of the negotiation skills of the waste pickers which challenges the existing stereotypical understanding of power dynamics. Through a longitudinal ethnographic research she shows hitherto unknown dimensions of marginal existence of waste pickers facing waste retailers, civic society, state and NGOs. The chapter also reflects on development policies and practice in mapping the possibilities of how policymakers and other stakeholders like the NGO personnel can link the marginalised community to individual and community-based rights, needs and desires.

Since this particular form of development theory, policy and practice revolves around the notions of power, in Chapter 10 Subhasish Ray addresses two dimensions of the sudden rise of BJP in West Bengal. First, he assesses how far this rise has ruptured the party society which has been the prominent feature of the state in determining much of the delivery of public services during the Left and much of TMC's period. Second, he explores the ways in which RSS and Sangha led social services organisations are tapping popular sentiments for political mobilisation. This chapter brings back the notion of service delivery–oriented politics in democracy and shows how rifts within such delivery mechanism result in power alteration at the grassroots. India, like any other country around the world, is transforming its public governance and development mechanism rapidly with digitisation. Over the years it has shown limitations and also brilliant outcomes.

Anit N. Mukherjee in Chapter 11 takes on this issue with a focus on Rajasthan. He studies schemes like liquid petroleum gas (LPG) subsidy distribution and public distribution system (PDS) to show that despite problems of connectivity and poor data management a large section of people find the e-governance mechanism as useful. Anit shows that key development challenges like improving the delivery of public services, subsidies and transfers, addressing social inequalities and improving accountability, choice and voice of citizens as they interact with the state has the potential to get revolutionised by the use of Information Communication Technology (ICT). Neoliberal India embracing ICT has opened up potentials for entrepreneurship experimentations, especially among the upwardly mobile middle class.

Mohit Gupta focuses on entrepreneurship among the family-owned business groups in Chapter 12. The chapter shows how family business groups in India acquire multi-entity character by attaining an optimum mix of entities in the fold of group structure in a particular spatial, temporal and institutional context. He reflects on the ineptness of existing theories of corporate governance to explain such family-based close business groups and argues that the gap between theory, policy and practice in corporate governance and taxation could be bridged when a "firm" as a central unit of decision-making is revisited. Additionally, "business groups," as a combination of firms under common control need to be considered as a unit of analysis in policies pertaining to corporate law, taxation and anti-trust law.

The essays together therefore hope to bring out some of the complexities which can explain why India has failed to develop as much as it was perhaps expected to. Instead of looking only through mono-causal explanations such as budget allocation for various sectors or GDP growth or Human Development Index, it is perhaps more useful to dig deep into specific development efforts and try to explain what went right or wrong at the level of theory, policy and practice. It is Suman and Debraj's contention that only when the effort is successful in all three dimensions development can be achieved. Through in-depth research using this paradigm, it is possible to generate lessons for the future. Neither arm-chair theorising nor theoretically unsound field practice is likely to result in the achievement of the desired goals of development. We also argue that there is no magic formula – a shift from socialism to neoliberal capitalism or the reverse for example – that can ensure the development of India. In this sense we agree with Banerjee and Duflo (2019), although we are not dismissing theoretical analysis, nor are we propagating a dogmatic adherence to randomised trials and "plumbing." Our approach to theory should be dialectical, not dismissive.

References

Aiyar, S .S. A. (2008). India lets success happen. *The American Spectator*, July 1. Retrieved November 21, 2020, from https://spectator.org/43388_india-lets-success-happen/

Apthorpa, R. (2011). Coda – with Alice in aidland: A seriously satirical allegory. In D. Mosse (Ed.). *Adventures in aidland: The anthropology of professional international development* (pp. 199–219). Oxford: Berghahn.

Axelby, R. and Creqe, E. (2013). *Anthropology and development: Culture, morality and politics in a globalised world.* Cambridge: Cambridge University Press.

Banerjee, A. V. and Duflo, E. (2011). *Poor economics: Rethinking poverty and ways to end it.* Noida: Random House.

Banerjee, A. V. and Duflo, E. (2019). *Good economics for hard times.* New York: Juggernaut.

Basu, K. (2008). India's dilemmas: The political economy of policymaking in a globalised world. *Economic and Political Weekly*, *43*(5), 53–62.

Das, G. (2006). The India model. *Foreign Affairs*, July/August. Retrieved November 21, 2020, from https://www.foreignaffairs.com/articles/asia/2006-07-01/india-model

Das, G. (2015). *India unbound: From independence to global information age.* London: Penguin.

Dreze, J. and Sen, A. (1995). *India: Economic development and social opportunity.* Oxford: Clarendon Press.

Escober, A. (1995). *Encountering development: The making and unmaking of the third world.* Princeton, NJ: Princeton University Press.

Esteva, G. (1993). Development. In W. Sachs. (Ed.). *The development dictionary: A guide to knowledge as power* (pp. 6–26). London: Zed.

Ferguson, J. (1990). *Anti-politics machine: Development, depoliticisation, and bureaucratic power in Lesotho.* Cambridge: Cambridge University Press.

Frank, A. G. (1967). *Capitalism and underdevelopment in Latin America.* London: Monthly Review.

Garnder, K and Lewis, D. (1996). *Anthropology, development and the postmodern challenge.* Chicago: Pluto.

Garnder, K. and Lewis, D. (2015). *Anthropology and development: Challenges for the twenty first century.* Lodong: Pluto.

GoI (Government of India) (2007). *Economic survey.* New Delhi: Ministry of Finance.

Gould, J. (2004). Introducing aidnography. In J. Gould and H. S. Marcusen (Eds.). *Ethnographies of aid: Exploring development texts and encounters* (pp. 1–14). Roskilde, Denmark: Graduate School of International Development Studies, Roskilde University.

Gupta, D. (2005). Whither Indian village: Culture and agriculture in "rural" India. *Economic and Political Weekly*, *40*(8), 751–758.

Guruswami, M.(2019). India's plunging economy: Why 2010–2020 will be remembered as the lost decade. *Scroll.* Retrieved December 17, 2020, from https://scroll.in/article/946864/indias-plunging-economy-why-2010-2020-will-be-remembered-as-the-lost-decade#:~:text=The%20nominal%20GDP%20in%20September,its%20lowest%20in%20the%20decade.&text=When%20India's%20economic%20history%20is,%2D'20%20will%20be%20highlighted

Harvey, D. (2005). *A brief history of neoliberalism.* Oxford: University Press.

Hastrup, K. (1990). The ethnographic present: A reinvention. *Cultural Anthropology*, *5*(1), 45–61.

Haynes, J. (2005). Introduction. In J. Haynes. (Ed.). *Palgrave advances in development studies* (pp. 3–25). London: Palgrave Macmillan.
Long, N. and Long, A. (1992). *Battlefields of knowledge: The interlocking of theory and practice in social research and development*. London: Routledge.
Lyotard, J. (1984). *The post-modern condition*. Manchester: Manchester University Press.
Palmer-Jones, R. W. and Sen, K. K. (2001). On India's poverty puzzles and the statistics of poverty. *Economic and Political Weekly*, *36*(3), 211–217.
Paul, C. (2009). Count puts poverty at 50%, riles govt. *The Telegraph (Calcutta)*, p. 1, September 21.
Peet, R. (2011). Neoliberalism, inequality, and development. In W. Ahmed, A. Kundu and R. Peet. (Eds.). *India's new economic policy: A critical analysis* (pp. 11–32). London: Routledge.
Polanyi, K. 1944. *The great transformation*. Boston: Beacon Press.
Said, E. (1978). *Orientalism*. Harmondsworth: Penguin.
Shore, C and Wright, S. (Eds.). (1997). *Anthropology of policy: A critical perspectives on governance and power*. New York: Routledge.
UNDP (1990). *Human development report*. New York: United Nations Development Programme
Wallerstein, I. (1974). *The modern world-systems: Capitalist agriculture and the origins of the European world-economy in the sixteenth century*. New York: Academic Press.
Wedel, J., Shore, C., Feldman, G. and Lathrop, S. (2005). Toward an anthropology of public policy. *Annals of the American Academy of Political and Social Science*, *600*(1), 30–51.

Chapter 1

Institutional environment and organisational responses in changing decentralised governance systems in India

An ethnographic study

Suman Nath

Introduction

West Bengal, one of the 29 states in India, has seen the longest dominant party rule of the world by the democratically elected Communist Party of India (CPIM)–led Left Front (LF). Trinamool Congress (TMC) in 2011 put an end to the rule, reaffirmed it in 2016 but started losing its popular support with a distinctive rise of Bharatiya Janata Party (BJP) in the 2019 Parliamentary election. Clearly, LF had a hegemonic (in Gramsci's sense) dominant party system that has been changed over time by TMC. There is a clear difference between the two forms of politics: the LF adopted what is termed as the "bhadralok model" (Ruud, 1999; Franda, 1971; Mallick, 1993), and for TMC it is the profile of a "lumpen" or "subalternised" party – indicating its close link with the "subaltern" and lower-caste groups (Chandra, 2017; Samaddar, 2016). However, even in 2006 the "bhadralok" LF had a strong support base among the lower castes, tribes and also the Muslims. Scholars like Dasandi and Esteve (2017), Iyer and Mani (2012), Jourde (2008) and Turner and Hulme (1997) show that there is a possibility of a policy paralysis with the end of a dominant party system. It happens because in a dominant party system bureaucracy increasingly attaches itself to the regime. During regime change a series of power uncertainty, a crippling chain of command and role confusion arise. Mitra (2010) shows how, anticipating a political change in 2011 Assembly, several key bureaucrats sought transfer from their positions and often from the state as well. The LF allowed a political "deep probe" into the administration, which resulted in the percolation of party politics into the administration. They allowed the bureaucrats into administration and supervision. They were not the decision makers. The decision making and implementation were left for the party (Svara, 1994; Fredrickson, Smith, Larimer and Licari, 2014; Rakshit, 2011). Consequently, even though some of the important bureaucrats sought transfer and left the state or their positions, TMC inherited large sections of bureaucrats who had developed working under a distinct political

DOI: 10.4324/9781003159940-1

culture, and a considerably large portion were involved within the hegemonic structure of the LF. While work on the bureaucracy–politics interface is rather limited, Rakshit (2011) and Nath (2018b) show that TMC has been able to make people and administration relatively free of the iron-fist of the party. Ray (2020), drawing on such research, posits two propositions to explain how TMC could avoid such policy paralysis and actually managed a considerable improvement to the public service delivery. The West Bengal Public Services Act that fixed up the timeline for the delivery of several public services indicates the effectiveness of such a delivery mechanism (GoWB, 2013). Ray (2020) argues that West Bengal is an exception because (a) "the nature of the mandate against the erstwhile dominant party ... triggered by mass unrest," hence the bureaucracy had no choice but to look at policy implementation and (b) because of TMC's weak party institution it could not afford to disrupt the existing bureaucratic stability. While existing literature shows that the dominant party system seeps into bureaucracy, I have studied the structural and interactional mechanisms of such seepage to show (a) in what ways similar institutional environment affects different decentralised institutions differently and why and (b) what happens to the institutional environment and how do different organisations respond to it at the time of political transition. I have concentrated on two sectors of governance: (a) the Gram Panchayat (GP), the strictly public sector; and (b) agro-cooperatives, the quasi-public sector registered under the Societies Registration Act of the state. Before going to the ethnographic details of the governance institutions, I will focus on the theoretical perspectives related to institutions and organisations to situate the present work.

Theorising the present perspective

Institutions, organisations and their interface have a vast history of being studied by scholars from Economics, Political Science and Sociology. Each of them theorises over the debates of the structure-agency dilemma. Consideration of institutions as a structuring mechanism for early institutionalists is debated with neo-classical economics, which justifies pragmatic models with more agency orientation (Jaccoby, 1990). For Political Science much emphasis is on structural models as they explored formal political institutions or charters, legal codes and administrative rules during the nineteenth century (Eckstein, 1963). An expected alternative is the behaviouralist approach, which looks at the informal distribution of power both outside and inside the government institutions that influences the attitudes and political behaviour of the stakeholders (Thelen and Steinmo, 1992). Traditional sociologists like Spencer (1910), Sumner (1906) and Durkheim (1893) begin with an organic analogy to explain institutions as organ systems comprised of subsystems and analyse the mechanisms that maintain equilibrium. It soon became broad and included a set of organising principles (mores, folkways, laws, etc.) to perform particular functions. While Marx (1844/1972) focused on economic structural parameters, he also embraced the fact that these are products of human ideas and activities that gave early expression to the social constructions of reality. Weber's work on bureaucracy (1946, 1947) and then the Parsonian view on "Cultural-institutional" (Parsons, 1960) have dominated the idea of institutions as a socio-cultural mechanism until the 1970s. Later on the neo-institutional theories in Economics stressed neo-classical economics. It theorised institutions from *transaction cost* perspective (Coase, 1937). Organisation structures as they explain is responses to the functional requirement of the institutional choice (Williamson, 1994, 2005). In Political Science, neo-institutional theories put significant emphasis on social arrangements and structures as creating a template of the institutional environment, ultimately shaping the organisations containing both formal and informal rules and procedures (Thelen and Steinmo, 1992; Evans, Rueschemeyer and Skocpol, 1985). The social constructionist position is quite apt here as Krasner (1988, p. 72) argues "capabilities and preferences ... the very nature of the actors, cannot be understood except as part of some larger institutional framework." The analysis therefore is a complex one that involves historical analysis, institutional building processes and path dependency (Ertman, 1997; Karl, 1997). Practical, everyday questions on the ways in which organisations run have also been explained through the rational choice theory (Pierson, 2004; Peters, 1999). Sociological enquiries with neo-institutional theories look at the cognitive aspect of human organisms as information processors (Markus and Zajonc, 1985). The Durkheimian idea of humans being influenced by social and cultural forms dominates a significant part of sociological enquiry through Mead, Parsons and Bourdieu till present times (Bergeses, 2004). Cultural anthropology plays an important conceptual as well as methodological role in so far as institutions are seen as crystallisation of culture and that humans have infinite possibilities even within institutions (Ridley, 2003). The debate of individual free agency and structural–cultural constraints are far from being resolved, but enquiries through phenomenology and ethnomethodology on cultural-cognitive dimensions of institutions put emphasis on *externalisation* of symbolic structures stemmed through institutions, *objectification* of constructs and finally *internalisation* of objectified constructs including institutional environment (Berger and Luckmann, 1967; DiMaggio and Powell, 1991). Such an idea of institutional environment consisting of cultural predispositions including rituals, codified bodies of knowledge and cultural artefacts (Wuthnow, 1987) has resulted in a generation of scholars enquiring the ways in which cultural items are produced, distributed, selected and institutionalised (Becker, 1982; Caves, 2000; Lampel, Shamsie and Lant, 2006). With this "cultural turn" scholars like DiMaggio and Powell (1991) emphasise on cognitive and not the evaluative-normative, components of behaviour, thereby questioning neo-classical economic model of rational decision making. Instead they emphasised on the tacit, routine nature of "choice" in organisational settings. To put things in perspective it is worth defining institutions after Scott (2008, p. 48): institutions "are comprised of regulative, normative and cultural cognitive elements that, together with associated activities and resources, provide stability and meaning to social life."

Evidently, with such complexity of ideas and scholarly works on nature, methodology and functioning of institutions there is increasing recognition of institutional environments as part of a given culture and society that shapes much of the nature of organisations. The need for a comprehensive understanding of the culture as a powerful organising principle has been recognised by institutions like World Bank and World Trade Organisation (Sridhar, 2008a, b). It is necessary to look at institutions as parts of culture and not as an isolated enterprise. Such a view requires ethnographic engagements. Taking the cue of the scholarly works it is important to unearth the institutional components through the normative and regulative frameworks, and their internalisation as part of cultural-cognitive domain of the people to explore how incompatibilities emerge between rural governance organisations, how do they function and in what ways institutional environment influences their mode of operation (Scott, 2008). Gellner and Hirsch (2001) show that access to organisations, gaining consent and mediating the insider/outsider relationship are most prominent in doing ethnographic research in organisations. Taking Bate (1997) and Gellner and Hirsch (2001) as benchmark ethnographic works in organisations requires (a) participation, (b) multivocality and (c) a focus on people's everyday working and how it differs from the prescribed rules.

West Bengal represents an interesting case. With its 34-year-long CPIM-led LF regime, it is expected that different organisations have developed a dependence on the regime itself. A particular nature of the institutional environment was nurtured during the earlier regime. It was an environment which shaped much of the informal norms and regulations that were internalised by the functionaries of administrations. Perhaps the strongest influence of the regime was on the three-tier Panchayat system. As Bhattacharyya (1998) notes through his study of CPIM party documents, it was a plan of the regime to make the Panchayat function according to the ideals of the party. Through a number of field-based studies it is seen that such machinery was indeed successful in continuing the regime (Bardhan, Mitra, Mukherjee and Sarkar, 2009; Chatterjee, 2009; Dasgupta, 2009; Majumdar, 2009; Chakrabarti, Chattopadhyay and Nath, 2011). As an extension of such an institutional environment, the machinery has also percolated in the farming systems, most conspicuously through cold storage networks (Nath and Chakrabarti, 2011; Nath, 2017). However, relatively little is known regarding the organisational mechanisms of such control and how did it transform over the years of regime change. I have carried out ethnographic works on two kinds of organisations over the period of such political transformation.

The two sets of ethnographies

I have explored two different sectors of governance, viz. Panchayat and agro-cooperatives in West Bengal to make sense of the ways in which institutional environment actually influences the organisational outcome. The timeframe of my ethnographic study is from 2008 to 2018, a period which has seen the fall of the 34-year-long Left regime and a consecutive second term of the TMC. While in 2016 TMC gained a massive popular mandate to assume the Assembly for the second time, the 2018 Panchayat election and 2019 Parliamentary election have shown a definite rise of the BJP as a challenging opposition force of the state. This political background reflects the nature of the political instability of the state at the moment. Moreover, there appears to be a definite inclination of the governance mechanism from the earlier party-based public transaction (as explored by Chatterjee, 2004; Bhattacharyya, 2009, 2016; Nath, 2018b) to identity-based mass mobilisation (Nath, 2018b, 2019a,b). In this section I will first reflect on the nature of the institutional environment framed by the local and state political dynamics and then will explore in what ways it affects the service delivery through these institutions at local and micro levels.

My first sets of ethnographies are done in the GP – the lowest of the three-tier governance system in India. I concentrate on two adjacent GPs under Khatra Panchayat Samiti (block) of Bankura Zilla Parishad (district). In the second set I concentrate on two agro-cooperatives working in connection with a couple of cold storages falling under the Baghnapara region of Purba Bardhaman district.

The political clout

Each of the two fieldwork sites has been undergoing a continuous political transformation since 2009, and electoral evidences suggest it will continue for a while. The LF used to have a localised form of three-tier political hierarchy in rural Bengal. The lowest of the three tier was the Booth Committee, which ensured political control at the very booth level. I have seen this level roughly corresponds to the vote-casting booths and often quite undefined in nature. A booth usually consists of 700 to 1300 electorates, accounting for a relatively small area. Booth Committee was tasked with collecting and passing on the information to its upper tiers, which included the Branch Committee and on top of it a Local Committee (henceforth LC). Additionally there were zonal, district- and state-level hierarchies. At the grassroots the most powerful tier used to be the LC. The LC was designed to have control over several GPs and their functioning. The committee secretary and influential members decided the course of action for the GP, and virtually every decision ranging from an entitlement for wage-earning schemes to the allotment of houses was made after the committee "sanctioned" them. A person looking for access to GP had to go to the nearby party office first and then follow the hierarchy to finally get (or get rejected from) the assistance (Nath, 2018b). One of the criteria for getting the assistance was to support the LF parties. According to Chatterjee (2009) it happened to be a major form of clientele base of the LF parties. This political clout, needless to say, percolated in every sphere of the society ranging from micro-level economic activities to people's personal lives including even their marital decisions and resolution of familial disputes. As Bhattacharyya (2009, 2016) argued the partisan nature of public transactions has resulted in a distinctive form of society known as "party society."

After 2009 the nature of political clout began to change at villages. This change took place in a variety of ways in different parts of the state. For example the Maoist-affected western forested districts of the state experienced a series of violence and counter-violence, which made the LF leaders flee from their homes, creating a local leadership vacuum, which allowed the TMC to assume control over the GPs from backstage. In places where farming is still profitable, like Purba Bardhaman, Hooghly and parts of Purba Medinipur and 24 parganas north and south, LF leaders lost their control over the agro-cooperatives and eventually the GP-based local politics as well. While the actual mechanisms were local and micro, the outcome was a definite rise of locally powerful leaders to replace the party-based mobilisation. These leaders often belong to the landed local elite class with considerable monetary resources at their disposal. Their counterpart is the hardworking party workers who often find it beneficial to have an ally with a person with considerable economic resource and command over some part of the rural economic resources. This form of local-leader-dependent politics largely continues till date, with a substantive rise of a distinct form of identity-mobilising organisation at the grassroots spearheaded by the BJP. Ray and Dutta (2017), through ethnographic research, gave a hint to an organisation vacuum, and it appears the vacuum has been mobilised effectively by the BJP instead of the LF who used to be the champions of organisation-based mobilisation.

The long-lasting organisation-based political clout and later on a radically different form of individual dependent political mobilisation have generated a distinct form of institutional environment and allied organisation responses.

The Gram Panchayat responses

The architecture of the Panchayat organisations blends administrative staffs and elected representatives in such a way that all three tiers at the village, block and district levels have an office headed by the elected representatives under whom bureaucrats work. In block and district levels parallel to the elected representatives there is Block Development Officer (or BDO), from West Bengal Civil Service (WBCS) Cadre and at the district there is District Magistrate (usually a senior WBCS or Indian Administrative Service Cadre officer). The elected representatives of block – the Sabhapati and in the district – the Sabhadhipati works parallel and ideally in a compatible way with the administrative personnel. Both office heads often use the same human resources to discharge their responsibilities.

Both the GPs during the LF period were under the exclusive control of the LC. The members including the Pradhan themselves used to work under Sudarshan Mahato, the LC Secretary and his party machineries. The distribution of development-related service deliveries (including the targeted schemes like housing and pension schemes) were based on a calculation of the voting percentage. A member securing maximum votes used to get the highest portion of the resources, and it dropped according to the percentage of votes secured by others. Interestingly, the person securing the highest mandate did not necessarily become the Pradhan. In an interview in 2008 Mahato revealed

> "one has to have total devotion to the party including its decisions to become a Pradhan ... it doesn't mean that one cannot question or challenge the party decisions, it does mean that once a decision is made internally s/he cannot debate it anymore and is bound to implement it!

Mahato added to the fact "earlier getting such devoted persons was not difficult for us, since 2008 with the rise of TMC such party dedication is increasingly becoming a rare find." It was also the time when places like Khatra experienced an extreme form of violence, and counter-violence resulted from a fight between the CPI Maoists and the informal armed mercenaries popularly termed as "harmads." West Bengal saw one of the bloodiest phases in its history because of Maoist–counter-Maoist violence during the period. Statistics from satp.org[1] show that out of 528 civilians being killed by Maoists from 2000 to 2019 there were 18, 137, 326 and 24 civilians killed in 2008, 2009, 2010 and 2011, respectively, which amounts to 95.6% of the total Maoist killing for 19 years. Most of the targets were the CPIM and other Left party leaders. By the beginning of 2010 most of the local LF leaders were absconded because Mahato was gone missing and then his body was found, allegedly killed by the CPI Maoists. This followed a phase of confidence building of the LF leaders by involving the harmads who left the place permanently in early 2011 after the Netai incident (Bose, 2011). Consequently, the leadership vacuum was capitalised by the TMC to assume control over the two GPs from backstage. In several group discussions both the elected representatives and GP bureaucrats argued that they have faced an extreme phase of uncertainty and disagreements regarding the decision making because of the sudden disappearance of the "guiding force" of the party. GP secretary in 2010 reflected:

> We have an Annual Action Plan to follow, but we do not know where to start the work. That decision was in the hands of the local politicians. They used to instruct us where to implement projects and we followed those instructions ... with the absence of such leaders our office becomes paralysed ... We tried to talk to the elected members [at the upper echelons] but they are also clueless. There are other problems too. We do not know who will take the contract [in case of a housing scheme]? Who will provide the material? What amount of extortion money will go to the party fund and to leaders? Until these questions are settled nothing can be done.

Such confusion and halt in development-related decision making continued until 2011 Assembly election when TMC along with Congress put an end to the 34-year-long LF rule. When TMC assumed control over the GPs from backstage the decision making came under the exclusive control of a couple of local elites. Both of them were veterans of the Indian National Congress (INC) and joined TMC in 2006. With their money and muscle power they could exercise significant control over the GP. Both of them belong to local landlord families, and they had to give away land to the local tribal people during the land reform movement, which was carried out by the LF.

Gram Sabha, the annual meeting of the GP with its electorate where most of the decisions related to the development governance are supposed to be taken, is increasingly abandoned by the people over these years (Figure 1.1), and after 2013 there was no meeting held.

Although it violates the Planning Commission of India guideline (PCI, n.d.), which states that if Gram Sabha, the only permanent unit of a GP, is non-functioning, it can invite a suspension to the GP. Over the years of my fieldwork I have asked for the reasons that make people (N = 782) avoid Gram Sabha and gathered numerous responses which can be classified into the five major categories. Figure 1.2 shows that people have a reluctant attitude towards the Gram Sabha primarily because they find nothing significant happening there. Only 8% say preoccupation as the major reason, which means if they were free they might have attended. Lack of canvassing (26%), lack of activities (30%) and lack of space to express one's opinion (12%) largely denote a failure on GP's part to ensure successful conduct of the forum. It is interesting to note that about 20% of the village women identified Gram Sabha as a place for village men. In terms of exact number it is about one-third of the village women. Gram Sabha over the years has failed to reach a significant percentage of women as a gender-neutral forum.

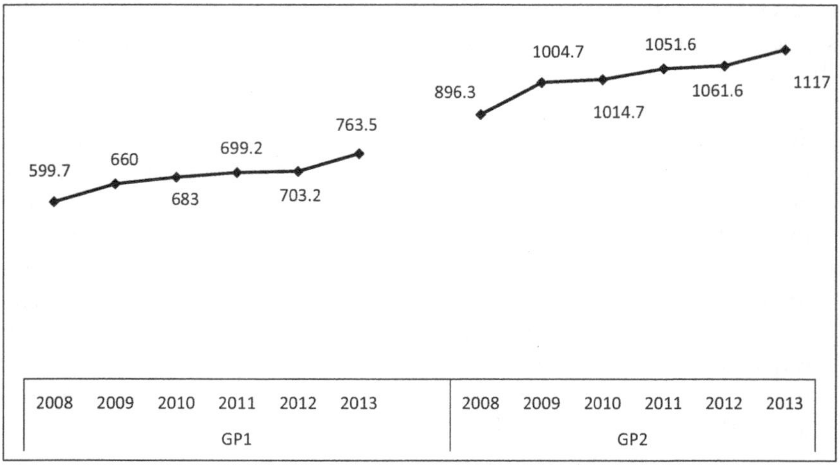

Figure 1.1 Increasing gap between people required and people attended in the two GPs under study (Source: field data)

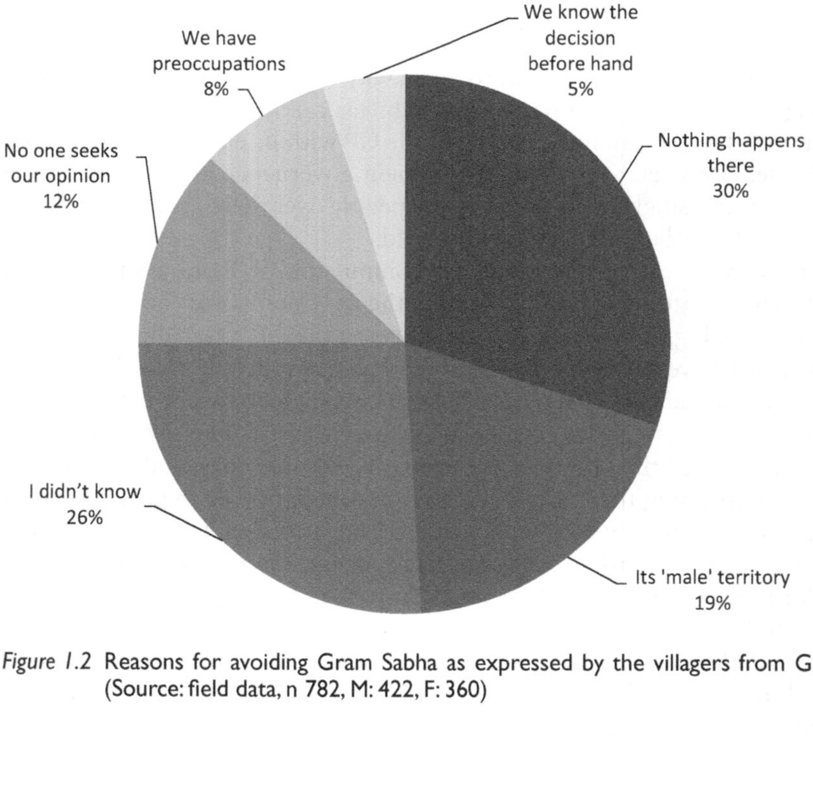

Figure 1.2 Reasons for avoiding Gram Sabha as expressed by the villagers from GP1&2 (Source: field data, n 782, M: 422, F: 360)

While Gram Sabha lost its vibrancy and was largely abandoned by the people, local leaders collect signatures and GPs prepare Annual Action Plans as per the instruction from LC during the LF period and since 2011 largely under exclusive dictation of a couple of locally influential TMC leaders.

In June 2012 one of them reflected

> we consider CPIM [and the LF] as our main enemies ... they have diverted all development related benefits to the tribal "belt" because they constitute their vote-bank and have ignored our sansads [ward] completely ... they have taken away land and our control over these junglis [derogatory term denoting tribals] ... this is the payback time.

The couple of GPs continued to run under the exclusive control of these powerful elites till the next Panchayat election in 2013. TMC after assuming the office made policy changes to free the Panchayat system from the strong grip of the party. First, they made the Executive Officer of the GPs the fund sanctioning authority; second, they reduced the GPs' involvement in the decisions related to the Local Area Development Fund of the Members of Parliament and Legislative Assembly by giving the authority to the BDOs (Bakshi, 2011). It can be seen as a desperate attempt to reduce the GP dependence over the local political institutions.

With such changes and onslaught of Institutional Strengthening of Gram Panchayat Programme, TMC could ensure relatively smooth delivery of development-related resources. Its aim of loosening the party grip over the Panchayat arguably was rather successful (Nath, 2018b), but corruption and extortion money related to the delivery of such resources remained visible (Nath, 2017). In 2019 it rocked the entire political spectrum of the state (Mondal, 2019). Moreover, as Ray and Dutta (2017) argued that strengthening the administrative arm of the Panchayat resulted in "hyper development" and ignorance of people's participation in decision making. Both the GPs remained under the exclusive control of the local elites, and a distinct form of money-laundering mechanism through Panchayat developed. Starting from entitlement to employment generation schemes to housing projects beneficiaries are bound to pay a certain percentage of the money which they get from the scheme. In the employment generation scheme it ranges from 10% to 25% of the wage, and for housing scheme a beneficiary is asked to deposit Rs. 5000 for getting empanelled and then another Rs. 10,000 to 12,000 at the time of work. The amount is often negotiable based on the beneficiary's nature of association with TMC and economic background. For example a family historically known to be a TMC supporter can effectively negotiate the deal while a family whose loyalty is in question has to pay more.

West Bengal sees a change in the institutional environment – a shift from party-mediated decisions to a comparatively "swift" delivery through the use of administrative arms. Although the delivery of services became quicker and West Bengal could climb up several positions in terms of the delivery of services especially in schemes like employment generation in 2018 and housing in 2019 (*The Hindu*, 2018; Guhathakurta, 2019), it has resulted in the complete disappearance of the party organisation grip over the Panchayat organisation, though a handful of elite control continued. The institutional environment took little time to become entangled with the corrupt nexus of the local party bosses. In the two GPs in Khatra block a relatively simple but detailed corrupt nexuses developed. From 2013 onwards the local landed elites already expanded their network with the district- and state-level TMC leaders and were asked to send about 80% of the extortion money through the "channel." As some of the recent reports show, the extortion money now popularly termed as "cut money" was often levied on the poor and helpless (Bhattacharya and Chowdhury, 2019). In a group discussion in 2018 both the local elites in the presence of other workers argue:

> The major revenue comes from the contractors who are allotted specific jobs of construction including roads, bus stands, water reservoirs and the like. We usually conduct a meeting along with the district secretary's representatives regarding which schemes to take up ... whom to give contract at what rate of [extortion] money ... for housing schemes the money is collected by booth level cadres who then deposit the whole amount to me ... for [MG]NREGA [employment generation scheme] supervisors are asked to collect the money from them before allotting the work to the beneficiaries ... there is hardly any pressure being exerted. ... Frankly people know party needs money and they pay to speed up the process.

Quite clearly, with the change in the political spectrum there has been an alteration in the institutional environment and GP's organisation behaviour responded accordingly. Even though the financial authority has been delegated to the Executive Officers, they are not in a position to challenge or intervene in the corrupt nexus. Over the years of my association with the Executive Officers of the two GPs I have seen them completely immersed with paper works and they are not in a position to challenge the Pradhan, let alone talking against the local party workers. One of them reflected:

> earlier paperwork was relatively easier for us ... primarily because CPIM party workers used to stay with the GP and helped us out with such a daunting task of managing the processes of documentation ... since 2009 there is hardly any help from any of the party cadres ... GPs used to function smoothly because of party cadres who involved themselves almost selflessly to reduce the office loads.

In response to the issue of corruption another Executive Officer reflected:

> See we really do not have the authority to do something about it. If the givers and takers are agreeing and are happy with the system who are we to even judge? People during the LF regime were frustrated with the lengthy process of decisions and implementations, now people have the option to pay some money and speed up the process ... so be it! Moreover now we have no space where we can even discuss these issues ... earlier we had the co-ordination committee [CPIM-led employees association] which used to listen to us, now there is none. Even doctors and professors like you are not spared from party goons, are we even exist?

The agro-cooperative responses

Since 2014, the Ministry of Agriculture, Government of India, is giving thrust for better marketing and economic return to the farmers through "bottom up" policies executed through cooperatives in a variety of names like registered Farmer Producer Organisations (FPOs), proprietary farms/companies/organisations, cooperatives, NGOs and Self Help Groups (SHGs), autonomous public bodies and state-run departments (GoI, 2014). The policy document covers everything related to the marketing of the farm produce and puts thrust to the micro-level governance. Since 2011 when TMC assumed power in the state primarily through anti-land acquisition (popularly anti-industry) movements most conspicuously in Singur and Nandigram, the state government also puts the emphasis on the betterment of the agriculture of the state (see Figure 1.3).

Increasing investment in the farm sector needs an organisation-level analysis to understand the institutional domain of farm sector development in post-Left period. To do so I have studied a couple of agro-cooperative

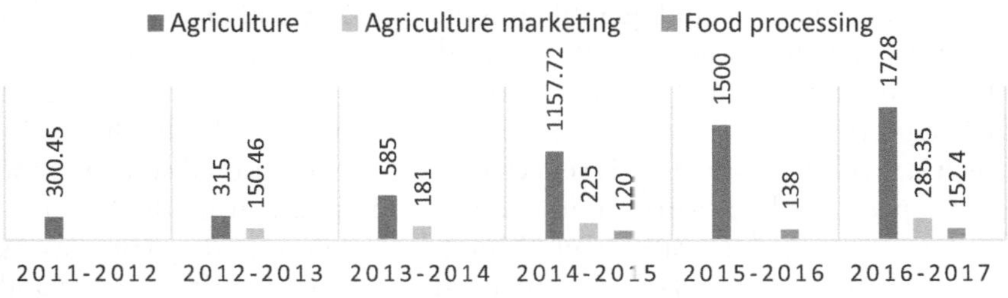

Figure 1.3 Over the year budgetary allocations (in crore rupees) in agriculture and allied sectors by the Government of West Bengal (Source: computed from state budget statements, accessed from http://www.wbfin.nic.in/Page/budget.aspx)

organisations in the Purba Bardhaman district. One is attached with a rice-mill and another one with cold storage.

When I started my fieldwork in the region I could find out three sources of structural dependence network between two sections of people. The first can be loosely termed as local elites. They possess more than 10 acres of land and usually have an extended family structure. Their participation in the storage or rice milling business has a kinship and/or friendship network base but hardly follows any caste pattern. I have seen the key players of both the cooperatives including people from Chakrabarti (Brahmin), Mondal (Dalit), Dutta (Kayastha) and Debnath (Yogi Brahmin belonging to Other Backward Classes) families. The small and marginal farmers having 0.5 to 5 acres of land also crosscut caste boundaries as the local elites do. The small and marginal farmers are dependent on the local landed elites primarily in three ways. First, although Purba Bardhaman gets adequate rainfall for winter and summer crops small and marginal farmers are bound to buy water from those having the deep tube-wells or shallow pump-sets, which could be used to pull water either from the ground or from the nearby water bodies. Landed elites provide water on credit. Even the pump-sets given as part of a one-time assistance programme in 2013–2014 by the state in this region were siphoned by the landed elites. Second, the small and marginal farmers find it important to have an alliance with elites because they get micro-credit (an exorbitant rate of interest) for cultivation and in the time of emergency. Third, for the marketing of the farm produce the small and marginal farmers are completely dependent on the local elites because they find it easier to push-sale their products at low price to avail the transportation arranged by the elites to the cold storage. It also minimises the insecurity regarding the price fluctuations (especially in the case of potato), alleviates immediate cash crisis and makes the small and marginal farmers free from the indebtedness until the next season. In consequence, over a crop cycle with the help of a variety of locally influential middlemen the cold storage owners and large-scale investors are able to assume monopolistic control over the region's farm produce. With their oligopoly of network in case of cold storages (as shown by Harriss-White, 2008), they exert considerable control over the timing and quantity of potato release and hence the market price. It ensures profit maximisation. Needless to say it gives nothing back to the small and marginal farmers who are bound to sale off their product often at a throwaway price to ensure their subsistence (see also Nath, 2021).

Such structural dependence is reflected in the organisational sphere of the agro-cooperatives like the rice-mill and cold storages. During the LF's tenure, members from Chakrabarti and Mondal families were the main players of the cold-storage-related cooperatives and representatives from Dutta and Debnath families used to control the rice-mill-related cooperatives. If one looks at the profile of the other members it becomes clear that none of them has land lesser than 10 acres and each has alternative sources of income in their families. Their other occupations range from acquiring government contracts under Public Works Department to school teaching. These core members occupy the highest position in the local agro-political economy and are exclusively networked with regional forces.

During CPIM-led LF phase the hierarchy was solidified and had direct linkage with local and district-level leaderships. The deal was to let a few political leaders participate and enjoy the privilege of gaining economic control over the products of the region by allowing them to invest in cold storage with minimum input and maximum returns. Such investments used to have informal security in a sense that even if there is a loss in the overall investment of the storage the political leaders would get his/her invested amount along with a 6–10% increment. For investments made by each of the general party cadres, the party was funded. The calculation was rather simple; the party would levy a flat 1–1.5% of the net profit. This percentage would increase if additional benefits are given to storage through the cooperative-like subsidies from the government or bulk purchase from the Food Corporation of India. This money in the 2000s amounted from a few lakhs to 50 lakhs or more. In a group discussion in 2009 when the CPIM was facing a strong contest from the rising TMC Mr. Chakrabarti argued

> Whatever government subsidies come are usually channelized by the Panchayats. We seek leaders' investment to ensure that the subsidies or other benefits reach to us. Moreover, having political players in the committee or as investors is important because it ensures "administrative" support at the time of conflict ... it doesn't matter who comes to power, we will establish our network with them ... you know TMC leaders are also investors ... political enemies cooperate here and even invest together!

Mr. Chakrabarti was an important Local Committee leader of the local CPIM hierarchy but prioritised his economic interest over the party. During 2009–2010 the agro-cooperative association related to the cold storages faced the toughest time regarding the disagreements on whether the association should formally affiliate itself with TMC by transforming the leadership equation or should it continue to operate as the CPIM-affiliating association. There was no easy answer to this question, and for Mr. Chakrabarti it was the most difficult call. He was loyal to the association and to the party and was under pressure from both organisations.

> We wanted to make the change ... by 2010 it was crystal clear that LF was losing and we needed to have the connections to the ruling party to continue our trade smoothly ... any disruption in the production cycle and supply chain would be extremely costly, especially with potato, because of its perishable nature ... we had the offer from local TMC

> leaders who were already important investors and the pressure was mounting (as told by another large investor to the storage)

The most decisive blow to the organisation came when a section of middlemen changed their camps from CPIM to TMC overnight. There was a fight between local people who wanted to become middlemen but couldn't enter into the network because of their TMC identity and existing middlemen who are also CPIM cadres. Middlemen play the critical role of establishing a connection between the storage association/investors to the small and marginal farmers. They negotiate with the small farmers to get the lowest price. Such a sudden change in party affiliation and related violence compelled Mr. Chakrabarti to step down from the position of the president of the storage association, and it was assumed by Mr. Dasgupta – a known TMC face in the region. In an interview with Chakrabarti and Dasgupta in 2013, Dasgupta emphasised:

> see, this is business. I was happy with Chakrabarti, despite the fact that he belongs to CPIM. I was also a CPIM cadre but then joined TMC sensing the possible power-shift in the region. It was Chakrabarti (looking at him with a smile) who requested me to assume the role of the secretary to formally convert the association to a TMC affiliated one.

As I was quite shocked to know the internal organisational-level adjustments of the cooperative, Mr. Chakrabarti smiled at me and said:

> see, party is important but economy is more important than party or for that matter my position. Our middlemen group was against me and I had to find peace and restore the chain of command which we have established over a long period of time!

The network quite effectively remained, and there was a marginal change in the middlemen layer of the three-tier structure, which includes the small and marginal farmers at the bottom, middlemen in the middle and the investors, owners and the association members on the top. Even though these organisations are highly influenced by party politics, the political change didn't bring any major alteration in their institutional environment.

In 2016 and 2017 it was seen that the production of potatoes increased about 22%. Earlier, because of overproduction farmers were forced to sell off farm produce at much lower prices. I have seen people letting the potatoes rot underground or dumped at places beside National Highways to destroy them without paying the additional cost of disposal. It used to result in economic disasters to the farmers, especially the small and marginal farmers. Since 2016 the state has provided subsidy in transportation and ordered the storages to keep open for additional 20–25 days than their original schedule

(Nath, 2018a). The transportation subsidy was strategically siphoned by the association as it got the information regarding such decision beforehand and asked relatively smaller investors to sell their potato bonds to the large investors. As Mr. Ghosh, one of the small investors, emphasised:

> We could sense the overproduction as information was coming from every corner and I was sure for the loss. I invested a little more than two lakh rupees and I was looking for whatever money I was offered to save myself from the coming disaster. One of the middlemen close to Mr. Dasgupta told me that Dasgupta was planning to release a large lot to the market to save his investment and I could sell mine if I wanted to. I thought it was the only opportunity to save myself from the bankruptcy ... I did that. I could only get about one and half lakh rupees ... later on government announced the subsidy and I know Dasgupta and his associates have utilised the subsidy and sold potato to Orissa!

Clearly, the uncertainty with overproduction and the alleged unfair flow of information have resulted in Mr. Ghosh's loss and maximised the profit of the key players of the association.

Decentralisation(?) – An institutional-level disjunction of theory-policy

We need to look at the two forms of governance mechanisms just discussed, their nature of differences during the political transition and the probable reasons for it. The overarching nature of party-mediated mechanisms during the LF and locally influential leaders during TMC have limited the extent to which decentralisation could involve people in decisions. During the LF period it was this process of planned creation of the institutional mechanism that successfully placed a template of normative and regulative institutional foundation. Such regulative instruments as the party network pushed away other forms of mediating institutions like ethnic, religious, village chief, kinship, age-grade and patron–client formulations. The decisions were almost exclusively channelized by the Local Committee members and the Secretary through an apparent decentralised channel via loosely formed booth committees and much organised brunch committees. It was systematic and provided a template for every decision that affects people. The network had its extensions in nearly every public sector offices, most conspicuously through the state-level association known as the Co-ordination committee. The party-based regulations were institutionalised directly through the local party, through elected representatives and/or independently and indirectly through a variety of Left-oriented associations like the Co-ordination committee. The regulative mechanism was so massive that it became a customary norm to look at the party before making any decision. The capacities for decision making, even when GP Annual Action Plan was available, was crippled, and officials were not empowered to go beyond the elected representatives and/or party or Co-ordination committee until the political change in 2011. Clearly the GPs in Bankura during the phase of leadership vacuum was suffering from indecision primarily because of the absence of decision making institutions, which for so long existed outside the porous but strictly legal boundary of the Panchayat system. Sensing the expanded base of the LF regime, TMC's critical policy change by empowering the administrative wing of the governance system played a crucial role. It went parallel to the processes that weaken the iron-fist of the Co-ordination committee at the employee level. Meanwhile the mighty LCs at the local level disappeared too. However, without careful building of the institutional mechanisms, which were the template for GPs to function, it was only a matter of time when the increasing dependence on locally influential leaders gave rise to the corrupt form of exchange.

At the level of agro-cooperatives, political change shows an adjustment in the existing organisation system. It doesn't bring much of a change in the existing political economy of the network. The topmost tier of the agro-cooperatives remains largely undisturbed, and relatively smaller reshuffling is noted among the middlemen belonging to the second tier. It shows that the informal governance institutions linked to the economic pursuit of a large section of the population didn't experience any structural alteration along with the political change. During the LF period party mechanism as institutional backdrop used to exercise significant control over the organisations like the Panchayat and agro-cooperatives. In post-Left period such institutional mechanism was dismantled and there was a rise of significant local leaders having direct contact with state-level leadership. As my ethnographic evidences suggests the two kinds of organisational responses are actually linked to the nature of institutional dependencies they have. Why did the GPs suffer from the indecision while agro-cooperatives continue to function smoothly? One answer to this is purely utilitarian; that is, cooperatives were not dependent on the political institutions for decision making. They work as a profit-maximising enterprise, and individual and institutional rational choices are compatible here. Looking at the transaction cost perspectives the two organisations respond differently because of the differences in their functional requirements of the actors involved, e.g. the Panchayat being a major platform to expand political control, with economic interest as secondary and agro-cooperatives on the other hand are more interested in expanding economic control. Hence, the informal rules for decision making as applicable in Panchayats and dependence network-based economic control exercised through agro-cooperatives, as neo-institutionalists argue, set completely different templates and cultural mechanisms (Thelen and Steinmo, 1992; Evans, Rueschemeyer and Skocpol, 1985). During the LF period, apparently, the structural template of political control had an influence over the agro-cooperatives but their involvement was linked to profit making and mostly at the level of individual players. Hence, even within the organisation-level people directly connected to different political parties existed and they climbed up their position along with the political change. Thus, when TMC brought a change in the institutional environment from an elaborate structural party network to an individual dependent network, it failed to affect the nature of functioning of the agro-cooperatives but gave rise to increasing corruption in the GPs. With such party organisation vacuum, self-interest maximisation of individual actors started to engulf the entire spectrum of public service delivery in such a way that the corruption with which once people were quite habituated became a major source of grudge in 2019 (Nath, 2017, 2019).

An institutional level of analysis of the two governance systems which exist parallel to each other results in an increasing understanding of the complex nature of the interface between politics and administration in Panchayats and elites and marginals in the agro-cooperatives. The continuous control and profit maximisation of the key players at the expense of the marginals within the agro-cooperatives even after political change seriously questions the effectiveness of the agriculture inputs, which the Government of India is planning to channelize through these institutions (GOI, 2014). Meanwhile, earlier party control and later the empowered Executives who work maintaining an "understanding" with the locally powerful individualistic party system and the absence of effective Gram Sabha could only take away the agenda of decentralisaiton and empowerment of people at the grassroots.

Note

1 https://www.satp.org/datasheet-terrorist-attack/fatalities/india-maoistinsurgency-westbengal

References

Bakshi, A. (2011). Weakening panchayats in West Bengal. *Review of Agrarian Studies*, *1*(2), 202–214.

Bardhan, P., Mitra, S., Mookherjee, D., & Sarkar, A. (2009). Local democracy and clientelism: Implications for political stability in rural West Bengal. *Economic and Political Weekly*, *44*(4), 46–58.

Bate, S. P. (1997). Whatever happened to organizational anthropology? A review of the field of organizational ethnography and anthropological studies. *Human Relations*, *50*(9), 1147–1175.

Becker, H. S. (1982). *Art worlds*. Berkeley: University of California Press.

Berger, P., & Luckmann, T. (1967). *The social construction of reality*. New York: Doubleday Anchor.

Bergeses, A. J. (2004). Chomsky versus Mead. *Sociological Theory*, *22*, 357–370.

Bhattacharya, R., & Chowdhury, S. (2019). In West Bengal, TMC men's cut money rate list: Rs 200 for last rites, Rs 25,000 for house. *The Indian Express*, July 04,

2019. Retrieved October 15, 2019, from https://indianexpress.com/article/india/trinamool-congress-workers-mamata-banerjee-cut-money-last-rites-west-bengal-5811928/?fbclid=IwAR3G3a4gfSX963PgASHymK2HruAsPnPTDYjVhfaxhMLXtL9P0nQtP4V5_cQ

Bhattacharyya, D. (2009). Of control and factions: The changing 'party-society' in rural West Bengal. *Economic and Political Weekly*, *44*(9), 59–69.

Bhattacharyya, D. (2016). *Government as practice: Democratic Left in a transforming India*. Delhi: Cambridge University Press.

Bhattacharyya, H. (1998). *Micro-foundations of Bengal communism*. New Delhi: Ajanta.

Bose, R. (2011). CBI files charge sheet in Netai case, 12 CPI(M) leaders named. *The Hindu*. Retrieved August 26, 2019, from https://www.thehindu.com/news/national/other-states/CBI-files-charge-sheet-in-Netai-case-12-CPIM-leaders-named/article14670713.ece

Caves, R. E. (2000). *Creative industries: Contracts between art and commerce*. Cambridge, MA: Harvard University Press.

Chakrabarti, B., Chattopadhyay, R., & Nath, S. (2011). Local governments in rural West Bengal, India and their coordination with line departments. *Commonwealth Journal of Local Governance*, *8/9*, 33–51.

Chandra, N. (2017). Lumpen. *South Asia: Journal of South Asian Studies*, *40*(2), 349–353.

Chatterjee, P. (2004). *The politics of the governed: Reflections on popular politics in most parts of the world*. New Delhi: Permanent Black.

Chatterjee, P. (2009). The coming crisis in West Bengal. *Economic and Political Weekly*, *44*(9), 42–45.

Coase, R. H. (1937). The nature of the firm. *Economica, N.S.*, *4*, 385–405.

Dasandi, N., & Esteve, M. (2017). The politics-bureaucracy interface in developing countries. *Public Administration and Development*, *37*, 231–245.

Dasgupta, R. (2009). The CPI(M) 'machinery' in West Bengal: Two village narratives from Kochbihar and Malda. *Economic and Political Weekly*, *44*(9), 70–81.

DiMaggio, P. J., and Powell, W. W. (1991). Introduction. In P. J. DiMaggio and W. W. Powell (Eds.), *The new institionalism in organisational analysis* (pp. 1–38). Chicago: University of Chicago Press.

Durkheim, E. (1893). *The division of labor in society*. Glencoe, IL: Free Press.

Eckstein, H. (1963). A perspective on comparative politics: Past and present. In H. Eckstein and D. E. Apter (Eds.), *Comparative politics* (pp. 3–32). New York: Free Press.

Ertman, T. (1997). *Birth of the Leviathan: Building states and regimes in medieval and early modern Europe*. Cambridge: Cambridge University Press.

Evans, P. B., Rusechemeyer, D., and Skocpol, T. (Eds.). (1985). *Bringing the state back in*. Cambridge: Cambridge University Press.

Franda, M. F. (1971). *Political development and political decay in Bengal*. Kolkata: Firma K.L. Mukhopadhyay.

Frederickson, G. H., Smith, K. B., Larimer, C. W., & Licari, M. J. (2014). *The public administration theory primer*. Boulder: WestView Press.

Gellner, D., & E. Hirsch. (Eds.). (2001). *Inside organisations: Anthropologists at work*. Oxford: Berg.

GoI (2014). *Integrated scheme for agriculture marketing*. Ministry of Agriculture. New Delhi: Government of India. Retrieved October 15, 2019, from http://agricoop.gov.in/sites/default/files/finalopguidelines.pdf

GoWB (2013). The West Bengal right to public services. *Kolkata Gazette*. Retrieved August 26, 2019, from http://wbja.nic.in/wbja_adm/files/The%20West%20Bengal%20Right%20To%20Public%20Services%20Act,%202013.pdf

Guhathakurta, G. (2019). Grameen awas yojnay Bangla shirshe (Bengal tops in housing sceme). *Anandabazar Patrika*, July 19, 2019. Retrieved October 15, 2019, from https://www.anandabazar.com/state/west-bengal-is-in-top-to-built-houses-under-pmay-1.1011618?fbclid=IwAR2u9byGRVKBwzV2CVSnvVRHy6kyre7u35FqkkTZgh9ToJf1ExkIjmiWWX8s

Harriss-White, B. (2008). *Rural commercial capital: Agricultural markets in West Bengal*. New Delhi: Oxford University Press.

Iyer, L., & Mani, A. (2012). Traveling agents: Political change and bureaucratic turnover in India. *Review of Economics and Statistics*, *94*, 723–739.

Jacoby, S. M. (1990). The new institutionalism: What can it learn from the old? *Industrial Relations: A Journal of Economy and Society*, *29*(2), 316–340.

Jourde, C. (2008). The master is gone, but does the house still stand?: The fate of single-party systems after the defeat of single parties in West Africa. In E. Friedman and J. Wong (Eds.), *Political transitions in dominant party systems: Learning to lose* (pp. 75–90). New York: Routledge.

Karl, T. L. (1997). *The paradox of plenty: Oil booms and pero-states*. Berkeley: University of California Press.

Krasner, S. D. (1988). Sovereignty: An institutional perspective. *Comparative Political Studies*, *21*, 66–94.

Lampel, J., Shamsie, S., & Land, T. K. (Eds.). (2006). *The business of culture: Strategic perspectives on entertainment and media*. Mahwah, NJ: Lawrence Erlbaum.

Majumdar, M. (2009). Democracy in praxis: Two non-left gram panchayats in west bengal. *Economic and political Weekly*, *24*(9), 82–93.

Mallick, R. (1993). *Development policy of a Communist Government: West Bengal since 1977*. Cambridge: Cambridge University Press.

Markus, H., & Zajonc, R. B. (1985). The cognitive perspective in social pshychology. In G. Lindzey and E. Aronson (Eds.), *Handbook of social psychology*, vol 1 (pp. 137–230). New York: Random House.

Marx, K. (1844/1972). Economic and philosophic manuscripts of 1944: Selections. In R. C. Tucker (Ed.), *The Marx-Engels reader* (pp. 52–106). New York: W.W. Norton.

Mitra, D. (2010). In a red funk: A pre-emptive flight of Bengal's bureaucracy. *Outlook*, September 27 . Retrieved August 12, 2018, from https://www.outlookindia.com/magazine/story/in-a-red-funk/267114

Mondal, Pranab (2019). TMC's cut money victims in West Bengal: Widows, poor and the aged. *The New Indian Express*. Retrieved July 01, 2019, from https://www.newindianexpress.com/thesundaystandard/2019/jun/30/tnie-exclusive--tmcs-cut-money-victims-in-west-bengal-widows-poor-and-the-aged-1997202.html.

Nath, S. (2017). Chasher joler dor ke thhik kore? (Who decides water price for farming?). *Anandabazar Patrika*, November 08, p. 4.

Nath, S. (2018a). Aalu chash o sorkari neeti (Potato cultivation and government policies). *Anandabazar Patrika*, April 09, p. 4.
Nath, S. (2018b). 'Cultural Misrecognition' and the sustenance of Trinamool congress in West Bengal. *Economic & Political Weekly*, *53*(28), 92–99.
Nath, S. (2019). Poschimbonge BJP: Akosmikota na dharabahikota (Rise of BJP in West Bengal: Is it sudden or in a continuum?). *Arekrakam*, 7(12), 17–24.
Nath, S. (2021). Farmers politics in West Bengal: Left Front and post-Left Front period. *Economic and Political Weekly*, *56*(15), 42–49.
Nath, S., & Chakrabarti, B. (2011). Political economy of cold storages in West Bengal. *Commodity Vision*, *4*(4), 36–42.
Nath, S., & Roychowdhury, S. (2019a). Manufacturing polarisation in contemporary India: The case of identity politics in post-Left Bengal. *International Journal of Conflict and Violence*, *13*, 1–8.
Nath, S., & Roychowdhury, S. (2019b). Mapping polarisation: Four ethnographic cases from West Bengal. *Journal of the Indian Anthropological Society*, *54*, 52–65.
Parsons, T. (Ed.). (1960). *Structure and process in modern societies*. Glencoe, IL: Free Press.
PCI (Planning Commission of India) (n.d.). Objectives - Panchayat Raj Institutions: Gram Sabha. Retrieved June 09, 2015, from http://planningcommission.nic.in/reports/sereport/ser/bihinter/st_bihch11.pdf
Peters, B. G. (1999). *Institutional theory in political science: The "new institutionalism."*. London: Pinter.
Pierson, P. (2004). *Politics in time: History, institutions and social analysis*. Princeton, NJ: Princeton University Press.
Rakshit, S. (2011). Capital intensification, productivity and exchange – a class-based analysis of agriculture in West Bengal in the current millennium. *Journal of Agrarian Change*, *11*(4), 505–535.
Ray, S. (2020). Bureaucracy unbound? The end of dominant party rule and the politics-administration interface in West Bengal. *India Review*, *19*(1), 1–32.
Ray, S., & Dutta, M. J. (2017). Insecure peace: Understanding citizen and local government relations in a Maoist-affected region in India. *Critical Asian Studies*, *50*(1), 37–57.
Ridley, M. (2003). *Nature via nurture: Genes, experience and what makes us human*. New York: HarperCollins.
Ruud, A. E. (1999). From untouchable to communist: Wealth, power and status among supporters of the communist party (Marxist) in rural West Bengal. In B. Rogaly, B. Harriss-White, and S. Bose (Eds.), *Sonar Bangla?: Agricultural growth and agrarian change in West Bengal and Bangladesh* (pp. 253–278). New Delhi: SAGE.
Samaddar, R. (2016). The verdict of politics. *Economic and Political Weekly*, *51*(24), 23–25.
Scott, W. R. (2008). *Institutions and organizations*. California: SAGE.
Spencer, H. (1910). *The principles of sociology*. London: Appleton-Century-Crofts.
Sridhar, D. (2008a). Hungry for change: The World Bank in India. *South Asia Research*, *28*(2), 147–168.
Sridhar, D. (2008b). Anthropologists working with and in organisation. In D. Sridhar (Ed.), *Anthropologists inside organisations: South Asian case studies* (pp. 1–12). Los Angeles: SAGE.

Sumnar, W. G. (1906). *Folkways*. Boston: Ginn & Co.
Svara, J. (1994). Dichotomy and duality: Reconceptualizing the relationships between policy and administration in Council-Manager cities. In H. G Frederickson (Ed.), *Ideal and practice in council-manager government* (pp 221–232). Washington, DC: International City/County Management Association.
The Hindu (2018). Bengal tops in rural job scheme, T.N. is second. *The Hindu*, March 11, 2018. Retrieved October 15, 2019, from https://www.thehindu.com/news/national/bengal-tops-in-rural-job-scheme-tn-is-second/article23041918.ece
Thelen, K., & Steinmo, S. (1992). Historical institutionalism in comparative politics. In S. Steinmo and K. Thelen (Eds.), *Structuring politics: Historical institutionalism in comparative analysis* (pp. 1–32). Cambridge: Cambridge University Press.
Turner, M., & Hulme, D. (1997). *Governance, administration and development: Making the state work*. Basingstoke: Palgrave.
Weber, M. (1946). *From Max Weber: Essays in sociology*. New York: Oxford University Press.
Weber, M. (1947). *The theory of social and economic organization*. New York: Oxford University Press.
Williamson, O. E. (1994). Transaction cost economics and organization theory. In N. J. Smelser and R. Swedbnerg (Eds.), *The handbook of economic sociology* (pp. 77–107). Princeton, NJ: Princeton University Press and Russell Sage Foundation.
Williamson, O. E. (2005). Transaction cost economics: The process of theory development. In K. G. Smith and M. A. Hitt (Eds.), *Great minds in management: The process of theory development*, (pp. 485–508). Oxford: Oxford University Press.
Wuthnow, R. (1987). *Meaning and moral order: Explorations in cultural analysis*. Berkeley: University of California Press.

Chapter 2

The Community Development Block and India's development discourse

Debraj Bhattacharya, Bhaskar Chakrabarti, and Manish Thakur[1]

The concept of Community Development Block as a unit of local governance became an important aspect of rural extension discourse from India's First Five Year Plan. These units became crucial for the implementation of different schemes of the Central and the state governments. In this chapter, we trace the role of the Community Development Block (or more colloquially the "Block") in the development discourse and policymaking of independent India, and argue that over time, its discursive significance has reduced significantly. Through a historical analysis of the policy context within which the Block has functioned, we search for the causes of the appearance and disappearance of the Block in the development discourse of India.

Introduction: Developmental dreams of a nation-state

Independent India inherited the colonial structure of administration at the sub-national level. The erstwhile provinces became "states," the district administration remained in the hand of the District Magistrate, followed by the Sub Divisional Officer (SDO). Local governments from the colonial period continued in a scattered manner, varying from state to state, till the 1993 Constitutional Amendment created a standardised three-tier system of the Panchayats. Various specialised departments continued to have their state and district level presence under the coordination of the District Magistrate.

The first major intervention within the administrative structure was the Block which came as a tier lower than the sub-division. Towards the end of the British period itself, there were some experiments with rural development at the district level (Venkatesan, 2002). In Bombay the Sarvodaya programme was started which sought to (i) introduce improved methods of agriculture; (ii) build cottage industries; (iii) eradicate illiteracy; (iv) improve health facilities; (v) improve village records. In Madras, Rajagopalachari started experiments with rural development programmes, which after the Second World War came to be known as the Firka Development Scheme.

DOI: 10.4324/9781003159940-2

Firka was a geographical area consisting of about 5–10 villages. This scheme sought to achieve the Gandhian ideal of Gram Swaraj by bringing about a holistic development of the villages. By 1952 the programme covered 74 *Firkas*. In Uttar Pradesh a separate rural development department was created which started to work in full earnest after the war. In 1947 Etawah district was chosen for the pilot programme of district-level planning.

Meanwhile in Haryana's Nilokheri a refugee camp of people coming from Pakistan became the beginning of a landmark experiment. Many idealistic volunteers came to work in this camp and this included a man named S.K. Dey. Within a short while Nilokheri emerged as a township from a marshy land based almost entirely on the effort of the people of the camp and the volunteers. It was an example of how people could build their own future. Jawaharlal Nehru, the first Prime Minister of India, visited Nilokheri in 1947, was highly impressed and invited S.K. Dey to join the Cabinet as the Minister of Community Development Programme. Dey agreed. He first joined as an administrator and later on became the minister when the Community Development Ministry was created. Nehru, according to Dey, was so impressed by Nilokheri that he said that "I want 9999 more Nilokheris" across India (Dey, 1962, p. 57).

Around this time the US Ambassador to India, Mr. Chester Bowles was also impressed by Nilokheri and he attracted the attention of the US Government towards India's ambition of community development programmes. He wrote a report called "The Indo American Aid Programme – the problems of opportunities." This report was favourably received by the US Government and resulted in the Indo-US Technical Agreement that was signed in July 1952. The United States pledged to support the Community Development Programme (CDP) with a grant of $50 million. Both the countries had high hopes about rural development through direct state intervention. S.K. Dey (1986, p. 34) in an article based on his memories, says:

> Chester Bowles and his wife came to Nilokheri, stayed there overnight and saw the place and people at work during the day and a drama was performed by the inmates in the evening. On his return to New Delhi Bowles said that the entire $50 million must be spent on community development and connected programmes.

Central to S.K. Dey's conceptualisation of the CDP was the concept of the Block. He wrote:

> The idea was the extension of services and facilities to rural areas delimited blocks which would grow into rural-cum-urban townships, radiating services to the surrounding areas. Through this reciprocal process a rural cum urban continuum would emerge. You cannot have two Indias, one rural and one urban.

(Dey, 1986, pp. 34–35)

He further explained,

> The idea of the Community Development Programme was to bring about administrative and technical coordination between the different agencies of government at the block level so that the block headquarters could ultimately become the repository of multi-polar knowledge integrated at that level. These will integrate the villages meeting at that level in a coordinated pattern.
>
> (Dey, 1986, p. 35)

What Dey had in mind was to replicate the core idea of Nilokheri in every Community Development Block. His idea of rural development has been explored by Ranbir Singh. According to Singh, Dey perceived Community Development

> not only as an instrument for the economic development of India's predominantly rural society but as a part of his strategy for the institutionalization of the ideal of social democracy embodied in the Preamble of the Constitution of India. It was also developed as a devise for tackling the economic and social problems in an integrated way. It aimed at awakening the dormant forces of progress in the rural society so that instead of looking towards the government as the Mai-baap people do things for themselves. The programme for its implementation placed emphasis on multi-purpose approach, on area development, and on the development of the individual and the community.
>
> (Singh, 2007, p. 8)

The idea of a Block was first proposed by the Grow More Food Enquiry Committee, whose Chairman was V.T. Krishnamachari. The report was submitted in 1952. The report analysed the defects in development organisations in the following words:

> for many years, there have been fairly well-organised development departments – Agriculture, Animal husbandry, Co-operation – in larger states. These however work independently of one another, following their own programmes and without a sense of common objectives.
>
> (Government of India, 1952, p. 53)

It therefore went on to say:

> What we have said points inevitably to the need of an organisation for intensive rural work which would reach every farmer and assist in the

> coordinated development rural life as a whole ... For such an organisation, the taluk or tehsil – the lowest administrative unit above a village, usually consisting of 100 to 120 villages would be a convenient unit ... The taluk would be a development block. It will be in charge of a Development Officer or "Extension Officer" who will be the revenue divisional officer ... The Extension Officer will be assisted by four technical officers – for agriculture, animal husbandry, co-operation and engineering – the last one to deal with minor irrigation works, drainage and anti-erosion measures.
>
> (Government of India, 1952, p. 53)

The report then went on to say how this would be different from the usual administration – "This organisation will function as a team, constantly consulting one another and exchange experience and will establish the closest links with agriculturalists and be their friend and guide." (Government of India, 1952, p. 53).

Community Development and the Block became an important aspect of India's first Five Year Plan. The Plan devoted a chapter to Community Development and Rural Extension (Planning Commission of India 1951, chapter 15). The chapter began by outlining the basic principles of Community Development:

> Community Development is the method and Rural Extension the agency through which the Five Year Plan seeks to initiate a process of transformation of the social and economic life of the villages. The Plan provides Rs. 90 crores for community projects and proposes the establishment over a period of about ten years of a network of extension workers throughout the country.

The Plan then went on to describe the key lessons learnt from previous experiments in rural development in India, which deserves to be quoted at length:

1. When different departments of the Government approach the villager, each from the aspect of its own work, the effect on the villager is apt to be confusing and no permanent impression is created. The peasant's life is not cut into segments in the way the Government's activities are apt to be; the approach to the villager has, therefore, to be a coordinated one and has to comprehend his whole life. Such an approach has to be made, not through a multiplicity of departmental officials, but through an agent common at least to the principal departments engaged in rural work, whom it is now customary to describe as the village level worker.
2. Programmes which have been built on the cooperation of the people have more chances of abiding success than those which are forced down on them.

3. While the official machinery has to guide and assist, the principal responsibility for improving their own condition must rest with the people themselves. Unless they feel that a programme is theirs and value it as a practical contribution to their own welfare, no substantial results will be gained.
4. Programmes largely dependent on expenditure by the Government, in which the elements of self-help and mutual cooperation on the part of villagers are present only in a nominal degree are short lived. The essential idea should be the reduction of chronic unemployment which is a feature of rural life—through the practice of scientific agriculture and cottage and small-scale industries.
5. Advice and precept are of no avail unless they are backed by practical aids – supplies of seed and fertiliser, finance and technical guidance for solving the farmer's immediate problems.
6. Whatever the measures of the effort which the Government wishes to make, the best results will be gained if the programmes are pursued intensively, and practically every agriculturist family has its own contribution to make through a village organisation.
7. The approach to the villager would be in terms of his own experience and problems, conceived on the pattern of simplicity, avoiding elaborate techniques and equipment until he is ready for them.
8. There has to be a dominant purpose round which the enthusiasm of the people can be aroused and sustained, a purpose which can draw forth from the people and those who assist them on behalf of the Government, the will to work as well as a sense of urgency. The aim should be to create in the rural population a burning desire for a higher standard of living - a will to live better.

The first Five Year Plan went on to explain that on the basis of these lessons from past experience the CDP was launched by the Government of India. For the purpose of the implementation of the CDP each project area was divided into about 300 villages with a population of about 200,000. This area was in turn divided into three development blocks, each consisting of about 100 villages and a population of about 70,000. The development blocks were in turn divided into groups of five villages each. Each group was placed under a village level worker. Therefore the development block became the administrative unit of the most important development initiative of the Government of India.

The CDP consisted of the following areas of intervention – (a) agriculture and related matters, (b) irrigation, (c) communication, (d) education, (e) health, (f) supplementary employment, (g) housing, (h) training and (i) social welfare. In other words, almost the entire responsibility of the rural development initiatives of the newly independent country was given to the Block.

In his memoir, *Destination Man*, S.K. Dey (1982, pp. 58–59) says,

> An altogether new organisation independent of the normal apparatus of government was unthinkable. For the old apparatus was far too deeply entrenched to permit the promotion of an upstart newcomer organisation from outside to threaten it. The new administration had necessarily to be woven from and into the existing structure of Government.
>
> (Dey, 1982, p. 59)

The hope however was, Dey said, a "spurt of vitality" could be introduced into the old system, it would activate the bureaucracy from within (Dey, 1982, p. 59). Within a year the programme grew from 60 Blocks to 165 and then to 400. In course of a few years the number of Blocks expanded to 5,400. (Dey, 1982, p. 62). Each Block was equipped with trained Block development and extension officers. These trained officers were supported by 50,000 village level workers (VLWs). Each Block also had a primary health centre supported by sub-centres to look after the health needs of the rural people. Animal Husbandry Centres were also formed in a similar manner (Dey, 1982).

The second Five Year Plan (Planning Commission of India, 1956) also continued to give importance to the block-based Community Development and National Extension Services. As in the case of the first plan, the second plan also devoted a chapter on this. At the beginning of the chapter the Plan said, "Community projects and the National Extension Service have a place of central importance in those sectors of development which bear most closely upon the welfare of the rural population." The Plan then noted with satisfaction that since the beginning of the programme in 1952, all 1,200 development Blocks have been taken up.

The second Plan, however also noted certain practical difficulties in this development strategy. It quoted an evaluation report to point out six important problems arising out of the community development experience. First, "considerable strengthening of the various technical departments is needed at all levels and in all branches." Second, research units nearer the field should be strengthened and there should be better flow of information from the field to the research unit. Third, "The dual control of specialists concerned with different subjects at the block level by the Block Development Officer (whose administrative control may sometimes go too far) and by technical officers at the district level is not yet working satisfactorily." Fourth, construction activities were taking up an "increasing proportion of time of the village level worker whose primary training is in agriculture and agricultural extension." Fifth, village panchayats are not receiving constant guidance and active assistance; and sixth, "in the operation of the programme there has been excessive emphasis on physical and 'financial' accomplishments ... and not enough on educating the people into new ways of doing things" (Planning Commission of India, 1956).

On the basis of the experience of the first Five Year Plan, the second plan (Planning Commission of India, 1956) proposed that

> the entire country should be served by the national extension service and that not less than 40 per cent of national extension blocks should be converted into community development blocks ... During the second plan 3800 additional development blocks are to be taken up under the national extension scheme and of these it is expected that 1120 will be converted into community development blocks.

Each national extension service Block was to be allocated Rs. 400,000 and each Community Development Block was to be provided Rs 12,00,000.

The expansion of the community development programme also necessitated a substantial mobilisation of personnel. The Plan envisaged that 200,000 workers in addition to those who were already in place will be required. It would also require training infrastructure, although some of this has been already made. In order to cope with the training needs, 25 basic agricultural schools and 16 agricultural wings for imparting basic agricultural training were to be set up. Thus altogether 61 extension training centres and 95 agricultural schools were planned (Planning Commission of India, 1956).

The second Plan also called for an integration of the activities of the development Blocks and the activities of the panchayats. It said that panchayats have two types of functions. First, those which are sponsored by the Government and those which are undertaken by the village community of its own volition and its own resources. The real test of the panchayats was to have a high proportion of the latter in comparison to the former. It is desirable, the Plan document said, that there should be assistance to the panchayats to undertake joint activities "to the maximum extent possible" (Planning Commission of India, 1956, chapter 7).

The chapter in the second Plan on Community Development ends by pointing towards what it saw as the central problem that the new rural development administration would have to solve. It said,

> It is necessary to stress that while the material conditions have to be assured; transformation of the social and economic life of rural areas is essentially a human problem. It is a problem, briefly, of changing the outlook of 70 million families living in the countryside, arousing in them the enthusiasm for new knowledge and filling them with the ambition and the will to live and work for a better life.
>
> (Planning Commission of India, 1956, chapter 11)

It is interesting to note here that the Plan document is imagining both a role for the Government as well as imagining a citizen who is to be transformed. The Government is no more the preserver of law and order and extractor of land revenue but has taken for itself the task of uplifting the downtrodden. Both the first and the second plan reflected a firm belief that the developmental state can make direct interventions in the economy and society and transform not only the structure of the society (through agriculture, irrigation etc.) but the individual human being as well. The key administrative intervention to achieve this was the establishment of the Community Development Block which was to be rapidly spread across the country. The developmental state's role was to instil in the citizen "enthusiasm for new knowledge" and "will to live and work for a better life." The state saw itself in an uncomplicated manner as a moderniser in the enlightenment tradition and believed that there was a method – installation of a will to live better – to transform the poor irrespective of the baggage of tradition. Once the citizen begins to aspire for a better future she will find her way with some help from the administration. It also follows that in the discourse on development generated by the first two plans the citizen of the newly independent country lacked the will to live better, and was held back because of this.

The administrative unit that was created for achieving this modernising dream was the Block headed by the BDO. Venkatesan (2002, pp. 58–59) has argued that the CDP was an important step in the "development of an institutional framework for agriculture and rural development." This was the first attempt to have an administrative framework consistent with the objectives of the programme. Previously the different line departments were hierarchically structured, each department having its chain of command from the district to the village. The CDP brought the line department functionaries at the Block level under the BDO.

The third Five Year Plan continued and further strengthened the emphasis on the Block. Meanwhile, the Balwantrai Mehta report was published, which we shall take up in the next section. Briefly speaking, the report paved the way for the first generation of Panchayati Raj system of local democracy to be installed. The third Plan also devoted a chapter to community development. It began by stating with a note of satisfaction that the CDP had spread over 3,100 development Blocks comprising 370,000 villages. By October 1963 the entire country was expected to be covered under the programme.

The third Plan (Planning Commission of India, 1961) pushed for a more ambitious dream regarding the Blocks. It sought to transform the Block into a unit of planning. It said:

> The third aspect of the community development work which has assumed considerable importance is the proposal that, along with the district, the block should serve as a unit of planning and development.

> It was suggested that in the following fields proposals for the third plan should be drawn up by the States on the basis of District and Block plans:
>
> 1. agriculture, including minor irrigation, soil conservation, village forests, animal husbandry, dairying, etc.;
> 2. development of cooperatives;
> 3. village industries;
> 4. elementary education, special provision of school building for local communities;
> 5. rural water supply and the programme of minimum rural amenities, including the construction of approach roads linking each village to the nearest road or rail-head; and
> 6. works programmes for the fuller utilisation of manpower resources in rural areas.

The third Plan then went on to say with modernist enthusiasm,

> The establishment of the democratic institutions at the district and block levels and the role assigned to the Gram Sabha and the Village Panchayat constitute fundamental and far-reaching changes in the structure of the district administration and the pattern of rural development.

The third Plan recognised the significance of the block level bureaucracy in making Panchayati Raj a success. It argued that "the manner in which the block extension team, comprising the Block Development Officer and Extension Officers in different fields of development functions is of the highest importance for the success of Panchayati Raj." The introduction of the Panchayati Raj, according to the Plan, greatly enhanced the responsibility of the technical departments at the state level. They were now expected to provide the necessary training and technical support to the elected members of the local governments. The Third Plan also emphasised the importance of fieldwork for the BDOs – "care should be taken to see that the Block Development Officer and the Extension Officers undertake extensive touring within the block and are not tied up excessively with discussions at headquarters."

The fourth Five Year plan stated emphatically that all villages of the country were by then covered by the community development blocks. Their total number amounted to 5,265. The fourth Plan however noted a certain problem within the overall strategy of building Community Development Blocks:

> The operation of the Blocks in five-year stages, with tapering financial provision from stage to stage, was based on the assumption that by the

> end of the initial ten-year period, there would be adequate mobilisation of resources by the local institutions and sufficient channel of other Plan funds to make any separate provision thereafter for the Blocks unnecessary. Community Development, in other words, would then no longer be assisted and schematic by self-reliant and locally rooted.

However, this assumption did not prove to be correct, noted the fourth Plan. The programmes were usually dependent on Government initiative and funds. Activities tended to languish when funds were lacking. Where financial support was adequate, the Plan said, Panchayati Raj and Community Development has had a significant impact.

Reality check 1: Balwantrai Mehta Report

In 1957 the second volume of the Balwantrai Mehta Report (Mehta, 1957a, b) did a detailed analysis of the Block and various aspects of its functioning. As part of the research that went into the final report the team carried out eight studies – (1) study of the working of the Block Advisory Committees; (2) study of the working of the community centres; (3) study on people's participation in community projects; (4) study on people's attitude to community projects; (5) study on the impact of community projects on the Harijans; (6) study of the BDO and the specialist staff; (7) study of the problems of administrative coordination at the Block and state levels and (8) study of programmes for women and children. Of these, the first six studies were incorporated within the main report.

The report noted that the first important characteristic of the Blocks is the "great variation in the geographical and physical features of each of these Blocks" (Mehta, 1957b, p. 37). While the variation between various states of India was well known, the report noted that the variations within Blocks of one state can be diverse as well. Within Uttar Pradesh (UP) itself there were Blocks that had rainfall less than 25 inches while there were others that had rainfall of about 85 inches. Similarly, in one Block, the main crop is a food crop while in another the main crop is a cash crop. The report also noted that apart from physical variations, there were variations in terms of population, magnitudes and densities. Thus one Block in UP had a population of 43,000 while another Block in Kerala had a population of five times that number. In terms of density also in one Block the density was as low as 148 per square mile while in another it was as high as 1,628 per square mile. The number of administrative village units also varied. In Kerala, a Block with a population of 81,000 was made up of only six villages while in Bihar a Block with a population of 60,000 was made up of 268 villages.

Even though there were such variations among the Blocks, when it came to staffing pattern, the report noted,

> the general tendency is for all the Blocks to have the same pattern of staffing, consisting of one Block Development Officer, one Extension Officer for Agriculture, and ADO for Social Education, one for Panchayat and Cooperation, one Engineer or Supervisor, one or two Health Visitors, varying number of skilled artisans working as instructors, one Veterinary Officer and some additional staff.
>
> (Mehta, 1957b, p. 38)

The report observed:

> While one can understand the imperative need to have a single Development Officer at the top, one cannot understand the wisdom of a policy of having just one agricultural or cooperative or engineering person attached to the block, irrespective of varying populations, physical conditions and crop economics of these areas.

The study of staffing patterns also showed that there is no specific staff for health and artisan training. The report observed:

> This seems to show that far from providing additional staff wherever the requirements of an area justify, many of the Blocks do not even have the minimum staff considered to be necessary. This situation is rather disconcerting when once notes that the majority of the Blocks studies for our purpose in the intensive stage of development.
>
> (Mehta, 1957b, p. 39)

Another problem that the study team noted was that the average duration of stay of the staff was rather short. The average length of time spent by the BDO in one Block was one year and three months. For the agriculture officers, the average was one year and ten months.

The study team also found the training of staffs to be a problem. 25% of the BDOs were yet to be trained. Among the agricultural officers, 32% were not trained and 22% of the social education officers were untrained. The situation was worse in the case of the post-intensive phase Blocks. Here 75% of the BDOs and 50% of the agricultural officers were untrained. The report observed that "the situation where the post-intensive phase is left in the hands of the untrained officers is not a very reassuring one." (Mehta, 1957b, p. 40)

The study team also observed that there were problems with the number of Gram Sewaks (GS). The average period of service for the GS in his particular Block was one year and nine months. In UP the number of villages per GS varied from 4 to 17 with an average of 9. In Bihar it was 17, in Madras 6, Bombay 6 and Assam 12. It was also not clear whether there was any definite relationship between the population in the Block and the number of GS. In UP, which has an average Block population of 61,000 the average number of GS was 9 but in Bihar where the average Block population is 52,000 the average number of GS is 12. In Kerala the average Block population was 1,26,378 the average number of GS was 10. The study team observed:

> This variation may again be due to other factors such as topography, accessibility, etc. But it is not clear as to whether there is any comparable basis that is used to work out the minimum staff requirements from one Block to another.
>
> (Mehta, 1957b, p. 40)

The study team carried out detailed interviews of 21 BDOs on various aspects of their work. Some of the important administrative difficulties mentioned by the BDOs were as follows:

(a) Lack of effective coordination between the community projects and the regular development departments of the state governments.
(b) Duplicate control under which the various schemes and projects had to be executed. There was an unnecessary division of schemes which required both a technical sanction and administrative sanction.
(c) There was no genuine acceptance of planning and development programmes on the part of the departmental heads.
(d) The BDOs did not have full administrative control over specialist staff. The Departmental heads deal directly with their specialists. Therefore the specialists were not available for extension work when required.
(e) Frequent transfer of specialist staff and extension officers without concurrence of the BDOs. This defeated all efforts at systematic planning of work.
(f) Difficulties in the receipt of supplies of materials and equipment.
(g) Lack of storage facilities which was a major bottleneck in the speedy implementation of development programmes.
(h) Lack of transport facilities.
(i) Inefficiency of technical officers.
(j) Delays in the sanction of short-term crop loans.
(k) Frequent visits of VIPs.
(l) Recruitment of Gram Sewaks based on political considerations. (Mehta, 1957, pp. 44–45)

The BDOs were of the opinion

> that the greatest difficulty in coordination at the Block level arises from the departmentalized outlook of the personnel of the regular departments ... So long as the individual officers have to make their careers in their respective parent department they will tend to upon their placements in the Block as short interludes which one has to get over within the course of one's career.
>
> (Mehta, 1957b, p. 47)

When the study team talked to the departmental specialists about their experience of community development projects, one-third of the agricultural officers and health and sanitation officers were uninterested in project work. One-fourth of social education officers and cooperative officers were not interested (Mehta, 1957b, p. 49). The specialists were also asked whether working in the community development projects helped their career. Seventy-eight per cent respondents said that their career was not affected positively or negatively; 19% said that their career was negatively affected; and only 3% said that their career was positively affected (Mehta, 1957b, p. 50). At the same time, 88% of the specialists who were interviewed said that they had a sense of participation in the planning and decision-making process relating to block work (Mehta, 1957b, p. 52).

The study team observed that a BDO should have three qualities. He should be technically sound, he should have the capacity to build a team and finally he should have the capacity and know-how to work with the community. According to the study team they were usually good at the first, had the greatest difficulty regarding the third. On the positive side, the report observed, BDOs have a general faith in the usefulness of the Block Advisory Committees and an awareness of the problems of their work. But many of them were unable to build a good relationship with their colleagues. They also did not have any well-defined system of selecting villages for particular projects; do not have a regular system of checking of the reports of subordinates and "the procedures adopted by them for finalising programmes are not always calculated to promote the objective of making the Block community democratically mature and self-reliant" (Mehta, 1957b, p. 52).

The Report observed that the staff of the Blocks is working as a self-contained unit. The highest post open to the Block staff is that of the BDO. However, the post of the BDO is usually filled by outsiders to the rank of the Block staff. Hence the Block staff did not have the opportunity to get promoted to the post of a BDO. The Report suggested that "unless avenues of promotion are found for the Block staff, it will affect the enthusiasm and the quality of work of the Gram Sewak and the other block staff" (Mehta, 1957b, p. 171). The report further noted that there were too many instructions issued to the GS and the Block staff as a result of which there was

> (a) no proper codification of instruction; and (b) even if they were codified there was little disposition to read them in view of the fact that many repeated each other and the number was large. The paper work in the Blocks seems to be gradually mounting.
>
> (Mehta, 1957, p. 171)

It was also observed that the GS has to make too many visits to the Block which was detrimental to their effective work (Mehta, 1957b, p. 172).

The most important recommendation that the Balwantrai Mehta report made was that "at the Block level, an elected self-governing institution should be set up with its jurisdiction co-extensive with the development Block" (Mehta, 1957a, p. 125) This was to be known as the Panchayat Samiti and was to be constituted by indirect elections from the village panchayats. The functions of the Panchayat Samiti recommended by the Report was the development of agriculture in all its aspects, improvement of cattle, promotion of local industries, public health, welfare work, administration of primary schools and collection and maintenance of statistics.

The Report pointed out the following sources of income for the Panchayat Samiti (i) percentage of land revenue collected within the Block; (ii) cess on land revenue; (iii) tax on professions; (iv) surcharge of duty on transfer of immovable property; (v) rent and profit accruing from property; (vi) net proceeds of tolls and leases; (vii) share of motor vehicle tax; (viii) pilgrim tax, entertainment tax, primary education cess; (ix) voluntary public contribution and finally (x) grants made by the government. Henceforth, the Report recommended, "all Central and State funds spent in a Block area should invariably be assigned to the Panchayat Samiti to be spent by it directly or indirectly excepting when the Samiti recommends direct assistance to an institution" (Mehta, 1957a, p. 127). However, the annual budget of the Panchayat Samiti was to be approved by the Zila Parishad and therefore the latter was given a supervisory role. The state government, it was recommended, was also to retain the power to supersede the Panchayat Samiti in public interest. The Panchayat Samiti was in turn to maintain a supervisory role vis-à-vis the Gram Panchayat.

However, the Balwantrai Report also made certain recommendations specifically on the Block. First, the Block should have its headquarters located centrally as existing facilities of communication would permit. Second, "as far as possible the Block should be treated as administrative unit of all development departments with one unified set up" (Mehta, 1957a, p. 133) Third, the BDO should be invariably a gazetted rank officer and should be a "drawing and disbursing officer in respect of all the Block area budgets of all the development departments" (Mehta, 1957a, p. 134). Fourth, "at the Block level the staffing pattern of the government departments and the staffing pattern of the local bodies should not overlap functionally" (Mehta, 1957a, p. 134). Fifth, "the Block should not have more than 20 circles, each circle not exceeding a population of 4000" (Mehta, 1957a, p. 135). Therefore, the population of a block should not be more than 80,000.

Reality check 2: Empirical studies on the BDO

In 1972 Kuldeep Mathur's book on the BDO was published. This was perhaps the first scholarly study of the BDO in independent India (Mathur, 1972). Mathur's work was set in the context of a widely held perception among academicians that the new administrators of India more or less continued the mindset of the colonial Indian Civil Service (ICS) officers. The British administrative legacy, according to such critics, consists of the functional orientation of the British Indian Civil Servants. The civil servants who ruled India during the colonial period was a select group who were often referred to as the "steel frame". They considered themselves as men of superior virtue than the common masses and took upon themselves the monopoly of understanding and providing for their public good. The belief resulted in the *mai baap* administration wherein they assumed the role of the parents and guardians of the population. This led to distrust in non-bureaucratic institutions that were willing to share in the responsibilities. Along with this an emphasis was placed on quick decision and independent and firm action. Finally for the ICS, maintenance of law and order was of the highest priority, not the development of the districts.

Nehru was certain such a mindset will not serve the purpose of an independent nation-state that has embarked on a path of modernist development. He said:

> I am quite sure that no new order can be built up in India so long as the *spirit of the ICS* pervades our administration and our public services. That spirit of authoritarianism ... cannot coexist with freedom ... Therefore it seems essential that the ICS and similar services must disappear completely as such before we can start real work on a new order.
> (Nehru, 1953, p. 282, cf. Mathur, 1972, p. 6) (emphasis added).

The new ideology that the new nation-state wanted its administrators to acquire was expressed by G.B. Pant. He said:

> To serve the villagers, you have to identify yourself with rural life; to find joy in the air you breathe and consciousness of the fact you are engaged in the act of building of a new society. You have to train people in the art of life and in the art of living. You have to see that they move, they move onward and they are not pushed onward artificially. Let them learn the art which will enable them to secure for themselves what we want them to possess.
> (Pant, 1967, cf. Mathur, 1972, p. 6)

The question that Mathur sought to answer was, a couple of decades after independence, how far was bureaucratic attitude different and in accordance with the new ideology? He wrote, "Enough systematic data to describe and analyze the perceptions, attitudes and behaviour of Indian bureaucrats is lacking" (Mathur, 1972, p. 7). He noted further that there are some studies of Indian Administrative Service (IAS) which succeeded the ICS. However, the purpose of his study was to "move the focus away from the

IAS" (Mathur, 1972, p. 8). Instead of the IAS, Mathur chose to study the BDOs. Explaining the decision to study the BDO, he said that the CDP is the most important development initiative of the Government of India which was implemented by the BDOs. The Block and the Panchayat Samiti were the "key functional institution" (Mathur, 1972, p. 10). The purpose of his study was to investigate the perceptions of the bureaucrats and "we are concerned with their evaluation of various bureaucratic situations and the kinds of meanings they attach and attribute to these events. We are interested in identifying their own self-images" (Mathur, 1972, p. 11). The reason behind studying the self-perception was that this determines how "energetic and hopeful any individual will be in assuming the tasks that confront him" as "development depends in the final analysis upon certain changes occurring in the realm of the subjective." The key research objectives were:

1. To delineate the major dimensions of bureaucratic thinking and perceptions.
2. To place the individual bureaucrat in his social and working setting.
3. To investigate the relationship between the social background of the bureaucrats and their perceptions.
4. To develop typologies of the bureaucrats in the total developmental context of two states (Rajasthan and Uttar Pradesh). (Mathur, 1972, p. 14)

Mathur attempted a quantitative analysis of the BDOs based on a survey of 89 BDOs that was roughly 10% of the total Blocks in Rajasthan and Uttar Pradesh, the two states that he chose to study. The Blocks were randomly selected and the interviews usually lasted about an hour and a half. He found that the average BDO was about 37.5 years of age, usually male, was born in the same state in which he was working and had about 12 years of government service behind him. The BDO was typically from a rural or small-town background, called himself Hindu and was usually from the upper castes. He felt that in terms of livelihood he was doing no worse than his father. In terms of educational qualifications, he was usually a graduate, studied in Government-aided schools in the Hindi medium and had switched over to English at the college level. These were of course the central tendencies but there were variations among the states as well as inside the states. In terms of religious composition for example, in Rajasthan 92.5% were Hindus and 2.5% were Muslims whereas in UP 83.6% were Hindus and 12.2% were Muslims. 93.6% of the Hindus were from the upper castes. 31.4% were Brahmans, 17.9% were Rajputs, 15.7% were Kayasths while low castes consisted of only 5.6%. Analysing the background of the BDOs Mathur came to the conclusion that in comparison to the IAS the BDOs were "less elitist." However, Mathur also found that the BDOs wanted their own children to get "English medium" education. They also did not want their children to become government servants but preferred to send them for Medicine and Engineering (Mathur, 1972, p. 29).

Following an analysis of the social background and aspirations, Mathur (1972, p. 33). studied the perception of the BDOs regarding the administrators and administrative system. The BDOs perceived that

> the bureaucracy as the only effective and efficient instrument of implementation and execution of programmes. They believed that this is possible only when they are free from the interference of the politicians. They considered their judgment to be superior to those of the elected representatives.
>
> p. 42

In fact they showed an hostile attitude towards the elected representatives and blamed the politicians and their way of doing things for the continuous rise of corruption and dishonesty in the administration. However, the BDOs also expressed their concern about the decrease in nationalistic values and ideals in the interviews. Following the data analysis Mathur (1972, p. 42) states:

> The central problem that emerges from the description of the data above reflects the classic bureaucratic myth. Administrators left to themselves without the meddling of the politicians, would be able to achieve the epitome of rationality – a well administered state ... Politicians are looked at with hostility and only the formal election process held on a periodic basis is considered a legitimate link between the elector and the elected ... The common people are perceived as lacking in the ability to discern their own good an in the capacity to make rational choices, for they are easily swayed by the politicking of the elected representatives.

How far was the mindset described above different from that of the ICS? Mathur concluded that there was not much of a difference. Both believed in the superior virtue of the administrator, pride in upholding honesty and integrity in government, insisted on efficiency and effectiveness, objectivity in the face of castism, familism etc.

The BDOs, according to Mathur's study were predominantly cynical and pessimistic about the present situation. They were not doing badly in terms of their personal economic life but were "nationally pessimistic." He concluded:

> Thus, the evidence in this study leads us to suggest that the BDOs have

> not imbibed the public service or democratic exhortations of the political leaders. Their commitment to the whole ideology is weak. They would not continue here if alternative employment were available.
> (Mathur, 1972, p. 91)

A few years later, in 1976, another study on the BDOs of Bihar by Awadhesh Prasad was published (Prasad, 1976). The study was conducted in eight Blocks of two districts of Bihar. Explaining the need for the study, Prasad explained that there are a lot of casual observations about the role that the BDOs were playing. Hence there was a need for a systematic study of the BDO that will add sound empirical evidence to our understanding of the BDO. The two districts that were selected were Gaya and Ranchi, the latter now in Jharkhand. The respondents included the 8 BDOs of the 8 sample Blocks, 5 extension officers from each Block (agriculture, animal husbandry, public health, co-operation, panchayats and statistics), 16 Mukhiyas of village Panchayats, MLA and MPs of the Blocks. Apart from these, one village from each of the eight Blocks was also studied. In each village four respondents were interviewed. The fieldwork was done in 1968.

The study found that there were different systems of recruitment to the post of a BDO in Bihar. Three types could be found in the eight Blocks – (1) those recruited directly to the Bihar civil services; (2) those recruited to these cadres by promotion; and (3) those who belonged to the Department of Agriculture. They were also men of different administrative experience, age group, educational qualification, family background, caste and status. The BDOs were found to be well educated. Four of them had an MA in different subjects of social sciences. Three had a BA Honours degree, and one was a BS in Agriculture. The BDOs were usually born in rural areas but were educated in urban areas and had been urbanised over time. They felt that they were more town dwellers than countrymen. In terms of caste background they were from the upper castes like Rajput, Brahmin and Kayasthyas. They had landed property and thought of themselves as superior to the lower castes. Prasad commented that "Perhaps the 'feudal blood' has not still dried up in their veins. This has inhibited a free mixing between the BDO and the masses in the majority of the Blocks" (Prasad, 1976, p. 34).

Prasad found mixed responses regarding the question as to whether BDOs should be recruited directly or whether they should be promoted to the post. However, a majority of the different types of respondents felt that direct recruitment was better than the promoted BDO. They were thought to be better educated, well trained, and they brought a fresh outlook to the job. Their education and training outweighed the experience of the promoted education officers. On the other hand, some felt that those who are promoted to the post of BDO often bring with them practical experience of village life and problems whereas a direct recruit is often an inexperienced person with little understanding of village life.

Prasad's analysis of the training method of the BDOs showed that they did receive various types of training; however, there was a gap in what they were taught and the responsibilities that they had to carry out:

> Most of the respondents, especially those who attended the ATS courses, felt that it had been of little help to them in working as BDOs. Not much time had, they disclosed, been devoted in that training to extension method and the development aspects.
>
> (Prasad, 1976, p. 66)

The BDOs also felt that the duration of job orientation and training was too short to be very effective. The trainings were imparted in a hurry just to finish the course in a short period. They also expressed their disappointment with the refresher course which according to them did not prove to be very useful. There were lectures, seminars etc but no opportunity to interact with BDOs from other states which they felt would have been useful to them. The BDOs also showed little interest in the publications of the Community Development Department such as Kurkshetra, Yojana and Panchayati Raj. Prasad concluded that "the CD literature has not contributed much to broaden the intellectual interest of the BDOs or to deepen their commitment to the programme" (Prasad, 1976, p. 71).

Prasad found that the BDOs were involved in a variety of tasks. He observed that their activities could be clubbed together under four types – (a) development tasks; (b) revenue tasks; (c) office tasks and (d) miscellaneous tasks. Prasad concluded that "it appears that only about fifty per cent BDOs devote forty to sixty per cent of their time to different facets of development programmes". He concluded that the "various facets of the CD programme are not the main concern of the present BDOs" (Prasad, 1976, p. 81). It was also found that the BDOs had little time for the development of village panchayats. One BDO explained, "There are twenty panchayats in this Block. It is not possible to inspect even one panchayat in a month" (Prasad, 1976, p. 86). He also found that the BDOs are largely restricted to their desks and are not able to go to the field. A large number of reports have to be written by them. In all 79 different types of reports had to be sent by the BDO office. In a year the total number of reports was 759. This causes a delay in sending the reports. Heavy desk work made it difficult for the BDO from getting close to the villagers and spending the night in the villages which they were expected to do under the CD programme. But it was also seen that they do visit villages and made night halts. On the whole, however, Prasad concluded that the BDO was more a miscellaneous officer – "the BDO, instead of devoting a major portion of his time and energy to the community development efforts, too often is engaged in revenue work and other miscellaneous tasks which could be well-done by a Circle officer under him" (Prasad, 1976, p. 95).

How did the BDO perform as a team leader? Prasad noted a conflict between the BDO and the Medical Officer (MO). The MOs felt that although they had spent more time and money to become doctors they were getting less payment than the BDO who was often a graduate. Sometimes there were conflicts between the BDO and the MO in terms of seniority. MOs were also found to be apathetic towards their job and continued their private practice although they were not supposed to do so as long as they were MOs. Similar problems were found between the BDO and the agricultural extension officer. Prasad wrote,

> what makes the relations between the two functionaries bad, firstly is that the BDO engages the AES in jobs other than agriculture. The latter has been engaged in procurement of grains levied by the government, relief operations, distribution of permits of sugar, inquiries, and distribution and collection of loans.
>
> (Prasad, 1976, p. 108)

Prasad also found that the relationship between the BDO and Block Animal Husbandry Officer (BAHO) was cordial but for an ironic reason. The BDOs were in general not interested in the work of the BAHO. Prasad (1976, p. 113) says, "While the indifference of generalist BDO towards the work of the BAHO has contributed towards a harmonious relationship between them, it has made the latter neglectful of his duty."

Prasad also observed caste politics at play in the relationship between the BDO and the VLWs. Some BDOs had preferred some VLWs of their own caste and some defaulting VLWs were not punished by them as they belonged to the same caste.

He also carried out a detailed analysis of the relationship between the BDO and different categories of elected representatives – Mukhiyas of Gram Panchayats, Presidents of Gram Panchayats, MPs and MLAs. He found that the BDOs and the Mukhiyas were more or less able to work with each other. The BDOs honoured and respected the Mukhiyas. However, it was not always a marriage made in heaven. There were areas of contention and conflict. One area of contention between the BDO and the Mukhiya was the recovery of loans in which the BDOs complained that the Mukhiyas did not help. There were also complaints about BDOs getting caught up in the battle between various village groups for the post of Pramukh and Up-Pramukh of the Panchayat Samiti. The relationship with the Pramukh or President of the Panchayat Samiti was also apparently cordial. The relationship was good when the BDO managed to maintain a good personal equation through his administrative experience. On the other hand, the Samiti depended on the BDO for fund disbursement. The Pramukh's election to some extent depends on the BDO conducting a fair election and hence the Pramukh remained grateful to the BDO. However,

Prasad also noted that the relationship between the non-tribal BDO and the non-tribal Pramukh was usually better than the non-tribal BDO and the tribal Pramukh. In some Blocks Prasad noted that the BDO and the Pramukh do not get along well under certain circumstances. This could happen if the Pramukh interfered too much in the day-to-day affairs of the BDO. Another area of conflict was the transfer of teachers of the middle and primary schools. Pramukhs sometimes misused their power to transfer a certain teacher or the BDO sometimes transferred a teacher without informing the Pramukh. There were also conflicts over status symbols like the jeep of the Block which some Pramukhs said were used for personal reasons by the BDOs.

Prasad found the presence of the MLAs in the popular bodies was harmful to the smooth functioning of the Block administration. The Pramukh and MLA were sometimes rivals. The relationship between the BDO and the MLA was cordial when the MLA was a man "with a spirit of service" and the BDO was "amiable." In the majority of the Blocks, however, there were frictions between the two. The BDO was duty bound to push certain programmes while the MLA wanted to earn cheap popularity by obstructing the levy collection programme of the BDO. One BDO said:

> The MLA, the other political leaders, likes to see that his wishes are carried out. They do not realise the difficulties with which we have been confronted. If his wishes are not fulfilled, the MLA gives political colour to the BDO's acts and approaches Ministers to get him transferred from the block.
>
> (Prasad, 1976, p. 167)

Prasad found that the MPs are usually disinterested in the affairs of the Block. Since the MPs are not involved in the block administration the relationship with the BDOs is usually cordial. Finally, the elected members of the Block Development Committee (BDC) were not much interested in the activities of the BDC. The Pramukh largely dominated the proceedings. They were usually supporters of the Pramukh and supported the Pramukh in case there was a conflict between the BDO and the Pramukh.

Regarding the relationship between the BDO and the higher authorities, Prasad observed that the BDOs worked under three different kinds of control mechanisms. He was answerable to the District Collector (DC) and the SDO, the state-level heads of the various line departments and also the Pramukh of the Panchayat Samiti. There were various methods of control exercised on the BDO – conferences, meetings, inspection, writing of confidential reports, instructions and directives, review of reports of performances and progress, fixation of targets and prior approval of actions and decisions. Prasad discussed in detail the problems associated with each of these forms of control. Let us consider the confidential report as an example. In the Panchayati Raj Blocks, the president of the Samiti gave a confidential report on the BDO to the Collector at the end of each financial year. However, on the administrative side generally the SDO initiated a report but he typically gave less importance to the development aspects of the work of the BDO. The BDOs were of the opinion that the reports of the SDOs often reflected their personal opinion rather than an accurate assessment. This sometimes resulted in the demotivation of the BDOs.

In the final two chapters Prasad analysed how people saw the BDOs and how the BDOs saw themselves. The respondents of Prasad's survey found that the BDO was perceived to be performing a traditional administrator's role rather than a catalyst or educator of people. He was seen as lacking in warmth in his responses towards the people and their problems. In consequence, he was not liked by the people; some even viewed him as a "new feudal lord" or "Zamindar" (Prasad, 1976, p. 203). As the BDO was evaluated by the SDO and DCs they preferred to do the regulatory and executive tasks assigned by the superiors. Prasad quoted a former Chief Minister, without naming him:

> With the inception of the community development programme a start was made to make the BDO a savior of the people, who could work with them for their development. But in our administrative system this role of the BDO remained a pious wish. He is today an administrative officer, who has been tied to regulatory tasks.
>
> (Prasad, 1976, p. 204)

As the BDO became tied down to the regulatory tasks his contact with the people became weak, says Prasad. He is often seen to use force and authority rather than persuasion. The interviewed villagers said they found that the BDOs were often unresponsive to the needs and difficulties of the local people (Prasad, 1976, p. 204). Prasad quoted a villager:

> My idea of the BDO is very poor. He is not a local development officer. He is not active in helping us. We appealed to the Mukhiya and the BDO to get the breaches in Ahar of this area repaired. The BDO says that the money is not at his disposal. At present we cannot store waters in our Ahars for irrigating the paddy fields. The Ahar is the only facility available to us for irrigation. But the BDO takes no step to repair it.
>
> (Prasad, 1976, p. 205)

There were also complaints of the BDO carrying out programmes of procurement of paddy levy irrespective of the quantum of yield in the Block. One Block was facing a drought-like situation but the BDO did not relent and insisted on the levy.

Some respondents found the BDO to be an ineffective captain of the Block staff. The Extension Officers saw the BDOs as post offices of different departments. Some felt that the BDO was an ineffective team leader as he could not control the extension officers of the line departments.

In spite of such negative remarks some respondents did feel that the BDO was playing an important role as a development officer. This was especially true of the agriculture specialist turned BDO who took interest in the agricultural aspects of the Block's works. Those BDOs who were development minded were sensitive to the demands of the villagers.

Regarding the explanation behind the unpopularity of the BDO, Prasad found one rather curious explanation. Most of the respondents felt that the BDO's image suffered because he was too close to the people. He was directly in touch with the rural people and was exposed to them more than any other bureaucrat. Although there were many government departments that were notoriously corrupt they did not face public anger as they were far away from the people. However, the BDO was too close to the masses and therefore was often considered to be responsible for the lack of development. Some respondents were also of the opinion that the disgruntled elected representatives and the extension officers also deliberately campaigned against the BDO.

Finally, Prasad sought to understand how the BDOs saw themselves. His conclusion was that "the BDOs in our sample blocks were unhappy and discontented men" (Prasad, 1976, p. 223). Some of the young BDOs who were of the rank of sub-deputy collector were satisfied with their jobs. This was because they started their career as a BDO and or as Anchal Adhikari and were specifically trained in the ideal of transforming rural India. But the majority was not motivated to serve as community developers nor did their assignment provide them scope for promotion and adequate material and social incentives. It was found that many of the officers were not able to find enough satisfaction in their job and in fact felt downgraded to work in this assignment. They considered it as a temporary jumping ground for higher posts or some other assignment in the government. There were many practical problems of being a BDO which made the job unattractive. For example, very few Blocks had proper education facilities for children, medical aid, recreation and other amenities. Therefore, the BDOs who were posted in the backward Blocks had to maintain two establishments simultaneously – one for themselves and another for their family in the town. Thus, the posting proved to be less attractive than some other government job based in the town. Prasad also found that there was very little praise for the good work that the BDO did which acted as a demotivating factor. One BDO said – "I worked continuously for fourteen hours in the Block. But the result: not even a single word of appreciation from any quarter." (Prasad, 1976, p. 231) It was said that the senior officers hardly ever tried to understand their difficulties. Unsuitable accommodation, personal and professional, was another problem faced by the BDOs. Leakage from the roof was a common complaint. (Prasad, 1976, p. 232) Some BDOs complained of a lack of recreational facility and scope for intellectual development and an absence of people of their rank with whom they can socialise as disincentives for the job (Prasad, 1976, p. 233).

Why did planning and development from below fail?

In an article published in 1985, Walter C. Neale attempted an analysis of what went wrong with the Community Development Project. After tracing the origins of the CDP, Neale pointed out several drawbacks of the CDP. He argued that the 1950s saw the expansion of community development from three Blocks in Etawah District in Uttar Pradesh to some 5,200 Blocks covering the whole of the country. This expansion, according to him, "was so rapid that growing disillusionment with the community development programs was as much due to the strains of such a rate of expansion as to any inherent weakness in the scheme itself" (Neale, 1985, p. 678). Neale then went on to discuss what went wrong with planning from below. He argued:

> The institution of Panchayati Raj never really had a chance to engage actively in local planning. Obviously the creation of local institutions capable of drawing up a plan required time, trials, error and practice if the members of the panchayats were to perfect techniques of planning. But time was not allowed, nor was error to be accepted. Those competent to help panchayat institutions in drawing up the plans, simply did not have the time, amongst all other duties, to spend the days and weeks needed. Panchayat planning faced the same obstacles as community development; too few people available to help village, block, and district panchayats to learn how to plan combined with the administrator's attitude of "we know best, so let's tell them.
>
> (Neale, 1985, p. 680)

As a result, the planning by panchayats, as envisaged by the Balwantrai Mehta Committee, could not develop into a robust practice. The real process of planning remained in the hands of the administrators. A VLW attended the annual meeting of the Gaon Sabha (meeting of all the villagers). He presented the programmes in which the development department was interested, explained their merits, and "by some mixture of persuasion, bullying, smiles, and frowns indued the meeting to pass resolutions adopting specific targets under at least some of the departmental programs." He then wrote the resolution on a piece of paper and got the members of the panchayat to give their signatures and thumbprints.

The villagers at first went along with such a form of planning because the villagers were afraid to refuse the government officials. They mostly agreed to the proposals made by the Extension Officers or VLWs. Similarly Block Plans contained a summation of the information recorded on the scraps of paper that the EOs and VLWs had collected, to which were added the programmes administered from Block headquarters.

> The Block plan was largely a creation of the Block office when it combined the statistical summary of village plans with its own schematic budgets for some departmental plans to be carried out by the BDO's office, and with the orders (often called "suggestions") from higher authorities.
>
> (Neale, 1985, p. 681–682)

In principle, the Block plan was drawn up in consultation with the Samiti but what really happened was that the administrators headed by the BDO prepared the plans and placed them before the Samiti members for approval and usually the Samiti members did not disapprove of the plans prepared by the BDOs.

At the district level also, a similar process took place, notes Neale:

> The Block plans became the raw data for a statistical summary that constituted a part of the district plan. The district planning officer (DPO) added the programs of the development departments, and that was the district plan. The process of submission by the officials, explanation and rapid passage through the legislative process paralleled that which occurred at the Block.
>
> (Neale, 1985, p. 682)

Neale explains that post-Balwantrai Mehta report and the introduction of the Panchayati Raj, the role of the BDO and other extension officers became more complicated:

> The DPO and BDO had dual and conflicting roles to play in their dealings with panchayats. This duality of role stemmed from the fact that the administrative organization merged the roles of "program officer" and "extension officer." As extension officers of community development they should have served as advisors to the local legislative bodies, explaining to these bodies how they could articulate felt needs within the framework of national planning and how they could alter the plan as it came from the government. But as government administrators the DPOs and BDOs had a duty to persuade the *Samitis* and *Parishads* to adopt plans at least more or less as drawn up by the administration.
>
> (Neale, 1985, p. 685)

In addition, there was a conflict between the hierarchical social structure of rural India and the egalitarian objectives of the national policy. Traditional rural leaders and some of the new leaders did not, according to Neale, want to become part of modern industrial society and actively opposed the process of introduction of modern technology in the villages. Others were glad to adopt modern technology but did not want to adopt the egalitarian ideals of community development and Panchayati Raj which in a way went against the hierarchical structure of the traditional society. There was an "ironic dilemma":

> Effective planning and development could not be achieved without the participation of the local centers of power as well as the participation of the villagers who were to adopt the new ways – two classifications that overlapped a good deal – but at the same time, the more these people participated in the planning and administration of development, the more they were able to frustrate changes that the Indian government wanted to make in village life.
>
> (Neale, 1985, p. 686)

Another reason why planning by the elected local bodies failed was that there was in reality very little financial devolution. The district or Block budgets of the development department and many other departmental programmes were voted on by the local governments. They however did not have the power to alter the budgets. For example, in education, they could not decide on the rate of payment of the teachers nor could they change the school building programme. In the case of public works also only about 10% of the budget could be altered by the local bodies. Along with this the Panchayati Raj Acts of the different states gave veto power to the District Magistrates to nullify the acts of the local governments. Although the elected representatives had some informal power of influence, they did not have more powers than the district magistrates and the BDOs. Neale, (1985, p. 685) writes:

> when one considers the long history of the power and prestige of the chief of the chief officer of the district and the reflected power and prestige of his subordinates, there is no cause to be surprised that members of the Samitis and Parishads regarded such battles as lost before they were begun.

By the late 1960s new realities had set in and the Government of India sought to increase agricultural production and tackle the rising population pressure. Community development programmes were directed to drop the "non-essential" aspects of the programme and concentrate on the improvement of agricultural output. This destroyed community development as a joint project of experts and villagers and turned it into a system of administering programmes of rural credit, loans in kind, subsidies, demonstrations etc. The BDO became the person who checked on the conduct of these programmes. The VLW became the conduit of information coming from above rather than processing information from below to above.

Neale's argument in fact was in line with the diagnosis of the Ashok Mehta Committee Report which was published in 1978 (Government of India, 1978). While analysing the problems that plagued the Panchayati Raj system, the report observed:

> The tempo of development administration in seed supplies, fertilisers distribution, promotion of minor irrigation or enforcement of the civil supplies regulations, procurement of food grains, or performance of other welfare functions required such an intensive effort the year round that all the available staff at lower levels had almost to be requisitioned back by the parent department. It is this vastness and growing complexity of development programmes that has sometimes been used as an excuse for bypassing the PRIs in the name of their structural inadequacies without PRIs being entrusted with these challenging tasks.
>
> (Government of India, 1978, p. 5)

In other words, fast-paced development was used as an excuse to keep the Panchayati Raj institutions powerless. The report also pointed out that "bureaucracy had probably its own role in dissociating the PRIs from the development process." They preferred the line hierarchy as an organisational principle.

The officers felt primarily responsible to the respective state governments. The bureaucracy did not want to adjust itself to the reality of working under elected representatives at the local level (Government of India, 1978, p. 6).

Conclusion

The Community Development Block was envisaged by the new nation-state as a radically different form of bureaucracy from the old colonial one. The Block was expected to replicate the Nilokheri experiment and lead the rapid development of rural India with the participation of the rural people as its cornerstone. This experiment was to be led by a new kind of bureaucrat – the BDO. Instead of law and order and revenue collection, the BDO was to be the bridge between the people and the bureaucracy and coordinate the development initiatives of the community development programme. The reality, as this essay has tried to show, turned out to be somewhat different. The BDO experiment suffered from four types of problems – (a) it was not possible to solve the conflict between the BDO on the one hand and the line departments on the other; (b) the BDO and the Block, although envisaged as a radically different bureaucratic structure continued to be under the supervision of the District Magistrate and therefore had to play a traditional role as well as a new developmental role which was sometimes in conflict; (c) there was a conflict between the demands of fast-paced development whose needs were determined from above and the desire for democracy from below as envisaged in the Panchayati Raj system and (d) the social background of the BDOs sometimes ensured that the BDOs had conservative aspirations which did not always suit their modernising role.

This does not however mean that the institution of the Community Development Block or the BDO was done away with by the Government of India. What happened rather was that BDOs continued to play a significant role in the implementation of various flagship programmes including the National Rural Employment Guarantee Scheme, of which the BDO is the programme officer. However, the BDO disappeared from the discursive domain. After the empirical studies of Prasad and Mathur in the seventies, hardly any study on the BDO was done. The space was taken over by new social movements, the rise of the *dalits* and democratic institutions such as the Panchayati Raj. In the post-liberalisation phase the discursive significance of the state and its machinery was reduced although they continued to remain important as implementers of rural development programmes (see e.g. Bhattacharya and Chakraborty, 2008). Hence after more than 40 years of studies by scholars like Prasad and Mathur, there is scope for more systematic studies on the topic.

Note

1 The authors wish to thank the Indian Institute of Management Calcutta for providing support for this study. An earlier version of the chapter was presented at the Commonwealth Research Colloquium and Conference held in Valletta, Malta in November 2017. The authors wish to thank the conference organisers and also the Indian Institute of Management Calcutta for providing support for the dissemination of this chapter.

References

Bhattacharya, M. and Chakraborty, B. (Eds.). (2008). *The governance discourse: A reader*. New Delhi: Oxford University Press.

Dey, S. K. (1962). *Nilokheri*. Bombay: Asia Publishing.

Dey, S. K. (1982). *Destination Man: Towards a New Man*. New Delhi: Vikas.

Dey, S. K. (1986). Panchayati raj in independent India: Some personal reflections. In G. Mathew (Ed.), *Panchayati Raj in Karnataka Today* (pp. 32–46). New Delhi: Institute of Social Sciences and Concept.

Government of India (1952). *Report of the Grow More Food Enquiry Committee*. New Delhi: Government of India.

Government of India (1978). *Report of the Committee on Panchayati Raj Institutions*. New Delhi: Ministry of Agriculture and Irrigation.
Mathur, K. (1972). *Bureaucratic response to development: A study of Block Development Officers in Rajasthan and Uttar Pradesh*. New Delhi: National Publishing House.
Mehta, B. G. (1957a). *Report on the team for the study of community projects and national extension service, Volume I*. New Delhi: Government of India.
Mehta, B. G. (1957b). *Report on the team for the study of community projects and national extension service, Volume II*. New Delhi: Government of India.
Neale, W. C. (1985). India: Community development, Local Government, local planning, and rural policy since 1950. *Economic Development and Cultural Change*, *33*(4), 677–698.
Nehru, J. (1953). *Autobiography*. London: Methuen.
Pant, G. B. (1967). The right approach to the people. *Kurukshetra*, revised edition. cf. Mathur (1972), p. 6.
Planning Commission of India (1951). First Five Year Plan, Chapter 15. New Delhi: Government of India. Retrieved November 19, 2020, from https://niti.gov.in/planningcommission.gov.in/docs/plans/planrel/fiveyr/1st/1planch15.html
Planning Commission of India (1956). *The Second Five Year Plan*, Chapter 11. New Delhi: Government of India. Retrieved November 19, 2020, from https://niti.gov.in/planningcommission.gov.in/docs/plans/planrel/fiveyr/2nd/2planch11.html
Planning Commission of India (1961). *Third Five Year Plan*, Chapter 20. New Delhi: Government of India. Retrieved December 14, 2020, from https://niti.gov.in/planningcommission.gov.in/docs/plans/planrel/fiveyr/2nd/2planch11.html
Prasad, A. (1976). *The Block Development Officer: A portrait of a bureaucracy in India*. Patna: Associated Book Agency.
Singh, R. (2007). S K Dey's paradigm of rural development. *Kurukshetra*, *55*(3), 7–10.
Venkatesan, V. (2002). *Institutionalising Panchayati Raj in India*. New Delhi: Institute of Social Sciences and Concept.

Chapter 3

Urban restructuring, forced evictions and transition of the welfare city into entrepreneurial city

The case study of Bawana resettlement colony, Delhi

Aparajita De and Jeetesh Rai

Development and the promise of the city

Didi, hum saher kyu aaye hain? (Didi, why have we moved to the city?) Answering the rhetoric herself Suneeta, a resident of Bawana resettlement colony in Delhi, explains: "we moved to city to find work, send our children to good schools, and to avail of better facilities be that schools for the children or access to good hospitals and doctors, better jobs and of course better futures for all of us. *Hum ek kadam barne ke liye to aaye hain bhale hum jhuggi jhopri me rehte hain. Humare bhi to sapne hain. Hum bhi to aage barna chahate hain. Aap sab ki tarha hum bhi ek behtar zindagi aur bhavisya chahte hain.* (We also want to move a step ahead despite the fact that we may be living in a *jhuggi jhopri*. We too have dreams. We too want to progress. Like you and everyone else we too want a better life and future.)

Suneeta's narrative brings to the fore how the city has always been an aspirational space in the Indian imagination irrespective of the social location of the people living in it, whether poor or rich, privileged or marginalised (Anjaria and Mcfarlane, 2011). The city represents a space that would eventually help them realise these aspirations for a better life. Urban developmental policies and practices whether neoliberal or actualised through state interventions working within transnational regimes or local governments all reflect, play on and feed these aspirations (Soloman and Raman, 2011). Urban scholars have widely debated on questions of "whose" aspirations do urban developmental polities truly represent (Baviskar, 2012). More often than not, these aspirations particularly that of an urban middle class in the Indian context shape developmental policies and practices (Ghertner, 2012). In the case of Delhi the development rhetoric is replete with imagining Delhi as a world-class city (Dupont, 2012). As recently as 2015 the Delhi Chief Minister, Arvind Kejriwal announced that he would make Delhi a world-class city and one of the best cities of the world[1] and is clearly articulated in the Master Plan for Delhi 2021 with the Delhi Development Authority

DOI: 10.4324/9781003159940-3

stressing that the vision 2021 is to transform Delhi into a "global metropolis and a world class city."[2]

The interesting paradox in the development story of India has been that the State has been predominantly engaged with the development of rural areas rather than the cities at large (Ahluwalia, 2019). Yet cities have by and large remained at the heart of Indian imagination of development and progress as Suneeta confesses that the key to a better life and future like everyone else is to be found in the city. The spectacle of development in the city, many scholars argue, is driven by the consumerist ideology of the middle class and its lifestyle, and attitudes that have created urban projects and landscapes dotted with malls, skyscrapers, rapid transport systems, residential enclaves that prioritises middle-class ways of living on one hand (Fernandes, 2004; Nair, 2005). On the other hand, it has effectively erased any other visions and visualisations of the urban developmental trajectory. Chatterjee (2004, 186) contends that post liberalisation there has been greater assertion of the middle class in articulating their rights to the city by claiming greater access to public spaces and a cleaner, healthier environment. As a result, Chatterjee reasons that government and policymakers have directed their energies to improve infrastructure, pollution-free, cleaner environments, evicting squatters and encroachers, rewriting property and tenancy laws and regenerating old, dilapidated areas of the city to high value commercial and residential districts. Chatterjee raises an important question of whether Indian cities are becoming bourgeois. Baviskar (2007) similarly argues that in Indian cities, and in Delhi particularly there has been a strong presence of bourgeois environmentalism that has shaped restructuring processes of the city aligning it with middle-class notions of aesthetics, leisure, safety and health. In Delhi bourgeois environmentalism has compelled legislatures being proposed by the state assembly in banning the use of plastic bags and the Supreme Court ordering the relocation of polluting and non-conforming industries outside the city to reclaiming of "unclaimed spaces," mainly that of polluted spaces like slums and squatters where the urban poor have lived, for mega redevelopment projects that became a part of the larger beautification project and transforming Delhi into a world-class city. (Gill, 2009; Baviskar, 2007; Follmann, 2016). Ghertner (2011b) emphasises the aesthetic judgement of development pointing to what appears as world class is by default deemed to be developed and planned vis-a-vis what appears to be polluting is declared and sanctioned as unplanned and illegal. When urban restructuring is considered, slums not surprisingly appear as congested, polluting and of becoming a "nuisance" produced discursively through the rhetoric of public health and hygiene and have experienced time and again demolitions, large-scale rebuilding, displacement and relocation (Bhaviskar, 2011; Ghertner, 2011b). However, Batra and Mehra (2008) point out that the marginalising imagery of the slum can be traced back to the colonial era where the slum emerges as a site of "disease, decay, danger, and indiscipline" and that are to be developed and re-developed into perhaps a more "modern, rational, and orderly Other" which seems to persist till date in urban development policies and practices. The shift in development ethos and dominance of bourgeois developmentalism in urban restructuring processes seem to indicate that the poor needs to be invisibilised within the new world-class city and perhaps have no right to exist in them (Baviskar, 2007; Batra and Mehra, 2008; Bhan, 2009; Dupont, 2008, 2012). Our chapter here tries to explore how the poor not only exist but within the new regimes of world-class city negotiate and try to struggle for their own right "in" and "to" the city and thereby to possibilities of development. Uitermark et al. (2012) argue that the city is a site of both contention and control between the various social groups and stakeholders living in the city be that the state, the elite, the middle class or the poor. The city evolves into a generative site and develops new innovative ways in which each engages with the other (Appadurai, 2001; Holston and Appadurai, 1996). It is this engagement of the poor, particularly how the urban poor "invents" spaces of participation to voice their own contentions that the chapter, in particular, focuses on.

Transitioning of the welfare city into entrepreneurial city

The opening up of cities to the global economy in order to attract capital and investment have paved the way for processes of restructuring that have transformed institutions of governance, developmental practices and redefined the relationship between the state and urban citizens (Brenner, 1999; Jessop, 1997; MacLeod and Godwin, 1999a, b). Often, these transformations have been marked by social conflicts across the cities pitching for the right to the city and especially access to "urban space" (Purcell, 2002a, 2006b; Tickell and Peck, 1996; Ward, 2000). City governance, Zérah et al. (2011) argue, have responded by emphasising commercial use over social use; policies that are more focused on competition; and functions that are mainly transferred to the newly created parastatal and quasi-state bodies. These changes many observe have robbed the urban citizens of its voice in controlling the decisions that shaped their lives and the geography of the city (Purcell, 2002, 100). Several contemporary scholars (Brenner et al., 2012[3]; Harvey, 2012[4]; Purcell, 2002[5]; Swyngedouw, 2000[6]) contend that because of this shift local urban institutions are more concerned with the region's economic competitiveness and in making the city capable enough to compete with the global economy (Purcell, 2002, 100) further deepening social conflicts.

Harvey (2010) notes the violence and brutality displayed towards the urban poor, particularly in the acquisition of land and dispossession of the urban poor reveal the failure of urban governance. Harvey (2008) writes:

> Consider the case of Seoul in the 1990s: construction companies and developers hired goon squads of sumo-wrestler types to invade neighborhoods on the city's hillsides. They sledge hammered down not only housing but also all the possessions of those who had built their own homes in the 1950s on what had become premium land. High-rise towers, which show no trace of the brutality that permitted their construction, now cover most of those hillsides. In Mumbai, meanwhile, 6 million people officially are considered as slum dwellers are settled on land without legal title; all maps of the city leave these places blank. With the attempt to turn Mumbai into a global financial center to rival Shanghai, the property-development boom has gathered pace, and the land that squatters occupy appears increasingly valuable. Dharavi, one of the most prominent slums in Mumbai, is estimated to be worth $2 billion. The pressure to clear it—for environmental and social reasons that mask the land grab—is mounting daily. Financial powers backed by the state push for forcible slum clearance, in some cases violently taking possession of terrain occupied for a whole generation. Capital accumulation through real-estate activity booms, since the land is acquired at almost no cost.
>
> (Harvey, 2008, 34–35)

It is this failure of urban governance that makes the slums, largely perceived to be areas where urban poor live, a primary target to produce and meet the increasing demands for urban spaces being labelled more often than not as informal or illegal settlements (Chakravarty and Negi, 2016). At the same time Shin (2014), points out that both local and central states engage in scalar politics backing private-led initiatives that would transform cities into international financial centres or technological hubs[7] (Shin, 2014, 03). Events like Olympics in Beijing or in Rio de Janeiro or for that matter Common Wealth Games (CWG) in Delhi have been used as a platform by the local urban authorities for attracting investment and capital, and a lynchpin for economic development that have often resulted in the loss of livelihoods of the urban poor, displacement and dispossession (Shin, 2014, 05). The rapid scale of restructuring that these mega events entail has often caused the uprooting of slums without any alternative strategies like proper relocation and rehabilitation of the poor reflecting the shift of the "State" from welfare oriented to an entrepreneurial entity in its approach towards development (Bhan et al., 2018). In Delhi such massive scale restructuring has been carried out on multiple instances – during the 1982 Asian Games, the neoliberal reforms (in the 1990s) and recently in 2010 for holding the Common Wealth Games (Bhan, 2016). The case of Delhi is very unique in terms of the large-scale evictions (forced), demolitions, dispossessions, gross violations of human rights, unplanned or arbitrarily uncompensated resettlements and the changed path of development in Delhi from a "welfarist" and people-friendly city to an "entrepreneurial" city.

Demolition, eviction and relocation have been an integral part of the urban restructuring, planning and development of Delhi for decades to "fix" and "properly counter" the problem of slums. As of 2011, the number of *jhuggis* across Delhi was estimated to be 4,18,282 with the highest density being in the old city (North Zone) (Risbud, 2016). In Delhi, since 2000 there have been umpteen instances of demolition where the state began removing the slums as a part of preparation for the CWGs of 2010 (Zerah et al., 2011, 20). For example, in 2000, the Supreme Court[8] called for the removal of slums and squatters on public land, which dispossessed almost around 3.5 million people (Baviskar, 2012, b; Dupont, 2011b, 78; Ghertner, 2010, 2011b, 2015; Zerah et al., 2011). Interestingly, the Court labelled the slum dwellers as illegal encroachers or trespassers who are "pick-pocketing" the taxpayer thereby denouncing the provision of compensation for the poor (Zerah et al., 2011, 20).In one of the Delhi High Court judgements[9] the slum-dwellers are quoted as "seen not just as a threat to the adjoining middle class colonies and the city in general," but also as a threat "to the nation itself" (Zerah et al., 2011, 20). A fact-finding report conducted by a civil society organisation[10] revealed that because of the CWGs many "last-minute-demolitions" were carried out without proper resettlement (HIC-HLRN, 2011; also see Bhan and Shivanand (2013). Bhan (2016) points out to this fascinating dichotomy of the citizen versus the encroachers, where the urban poor living in slums is clearly seen as encroachers, that emerges in the language of state and judiciary emphasises this transitioning of the city governance and development from a welfarist to an entrepreneurial one.

Forced evictions and unplanned development: The case of Bawana resettlement colony

The Bawana resettlement colony represents the classic example of bourgeois environmentalism induced urban restructuring. Post the 1991 reforms many industries were shut down and moved to the periphery as part of making Delhi a world-class city, and so were the urban poor working in these industries (Hazards Centre Report, 2007). In 1996, a total of 2,245 industrial units had been identified as hazardous and polluting that came under the purview of the Supreme Court as a part of Public Interest Litigation (PIL) filed by environmental lawyer M.C. Mehta and were ordered to be sealed (Ibid). In 1999, based on the earlier judgement the closure or relocation of almost 40,000 units that were in non-conforming areas that were not necessarily "polluting" was ordered (Ibid). In 2005, the Supreme Court expressed a view that a rapid influx of migrants to the city was causing a debilitating effect on the city's civic amenities and expressed its concern over the mushrooming commercial activities in residential areas in violation of the Delhi Master Plan 2001 (Bhan, 2016). What followed in 2006 was that the Municipal Corporation of Delhi (MCD) began the sealing operation of about 1,000 commercial properties in four days under the police security (Ibid). In the meantime, the Court directed the municipal authorities to clear roads, footpaths and public streets from unauthorized hawkers and squatters (Ibid). The Court also ordered the constitution of a committee that allowed 19 trading activities to continue in residential localities, provided the shops did not exceed 20 square meters and dealt with the daily needs of residents (Hazards Centre Report, 2007).

Bawana became a prime location, as a result of the judicial verdict that was given by the Supreme Court on 19 April 1996, where industries along with people working in them were relocated (Hazards Centre Report, 2007). Further, during the CWG 2010, majority of the population from various slums were relocated to Bawana. Most of the people who were relocated did not get the 99-year lease on their land/house rather were just given 5 to 10 years of license to live during the resettlement process (Centre for Policy Research Report, 2014; Dupont, 2013; Hazards Centre Report, 2007; Interview[11] with the director of a civil society organization on 15 July 2014). During the course of fieldwork and after discussions with other civil society organisations[12] we found that people from over 20 locations across Delhi were reportedly relocated to Bawana. These being Indira Colony, Yamuna Pushta,[13] Yamuna Pushta[14] (30 cluster), R.K. Puram Sector 2,[15] Sant Ravi Das Camp, KGI, Vikaspuri,[16] Camp No. 1, KG 1, Vikaspuri,[17] Banwal Nagar, Pitampura,[18] Balbir Nagar, Bhatti Mines[19] and Indira Nagar, Bhatti Mines.[20]

Most of these evictions were forced, that too without any prior intimation to the slum dwellers that disrupted not only their livelihoods but also their lives. In most cases access to basic amenities that they were enjoying were not to be found in the resettlement sites. One of our interviewees[21] stated that:

> I was born and brought up in Yamuna Pushta. We had been living there for almost 40 years since my grandfather migrated. We had a two room house, with all facilities like water, electricity, bathrooms .... Now, I am married and my two children are going to the government school nearby. With the evictions we have lost everything we had. We have lost all that we had earned for 40 years in just 10-15 minutes. Now, we are on the road with no livelihood options. The government should intervene and show us the proper path for survival. I don't know what benefit this little space of our houses will bring to all the people ... but all the road, shopping malls which they use tomorrow will be constructed at the cost of our lives and our children's future. Both the government and rich people show their power on poor people like us only. It is better to die rather than living like a poor person, because every day is a

> battle for food and shelter, we don't know who will snatch our food and shelter and at what time. This is a life of insecurity and sadness.
> (Interviewed on 10 August 2015).

A similar narrative emerged from one of our focus group discussion[22] with the addition that some of them have so far been evicted and relocated several times. One of the discussants mentions:

> Our parents have been living in Sawan Park since 1958. Our colony was already uprooted once in 1961 and we were relocated to Wazirpur on a plot of 25 square meter. This time, when we were evicted, no notice was given before demolishing that colony. Neither DDA (Delhi Development authority) nor MCD carried out any survey. On 23rd August 2006 DDA officers arrived along with Police force and attacked us. We were left in chaos as we were not given any prior intimation. The DDA authorities brought down the entire slum within few minutes. During the eviction process police abused us. Our children and women were crying but they did not understand this. We were not even allowed to bring our goods out of the house. We lost important documents and belongings. Those who were working in the nearby areas were not allowed to enter into our houses or slums. The DDA authorities left us with no houses and threatened us to leave for Bawana, where the plots were being allotted to us. When police attacked our slum, most of the male workers were not present at home and DDA gave the receipt to our women. In the entire process only very few people were given the receipts.
> (Interviewed on 6 March 2016)

The experiences of the evictees[23] from Yamuma Pusta were no different some even shared the force and brutality with which the "Sarkar" treated them:

> Police authorities woke up us and tortured us at midnight and threatened us that we have to vacate this land before [the] next day afternoon and put our belongings in a vehicle provided by the government. When we asked the authorities the reason behind this eviction they said: you don't need to know the reason behind this eviction rather you just only need to vacate this land before tomorrow afternoon and if you will not vacate the land within a given time period your shelter will be stripped down by the bulldozers.
> (Interviewed on 22 January 2015)

It is evident from the narratives that the slum dwellers were evicted without any prior notice and in an arbitrary manner from their former settlements to Bawana, where they are cut-off from the city centre. Many of our interviewees shared that initially these sites were just barren land and were completely devoid of any basic amenities such as shelter, sanitation and a proper waste management system, water and access to clean drinking water, electricity, hospital, schools and roads. One of the provisions of the new slum policy made survey a compulsory element so that no person was denied his right to house (Dupont, 2013). The ground reality of surveys, however, was that the surveying authorities (DDA, MCD) contacted only the heads of the colonies, instead of contacting individual households, in turn leaving out many households from the ambit of survey. One of the conditions of the policy was that the plots were to be allotted to those households whose names were listed by DDA or MCD and who had proper documents. Since such surveys involved a lot of corruption and manipulation of data by the authorities and middlemen, the affected people could not reap the benefits of the policy. Many of those affected by the evictions and resettlements have not been able to get a plot even to date.

Finding development and finding one's voice

> Before joining Sajha Manch we had no idea about any kind of rights. It is this *Manch* that made us realize about our rights and made us believe that we could raise our voice against this almighty Sarkar (government)! Yes, we never thought earlier in this way! The *Manch* united us, and together we believed we could even challenge the Sarkar. Now we are fighting for everything that includes tenureship rights, ration card issues, water issues, health and education issues.
>
> (Interviewed on 7 January 2017)

Birendra, a resident of Bawana, in the narrative admits that civil society like Sajha Manch has provided a space for them to remake and renegotiate their lives in Bawana post the evictions. Sajha Manch, a civil society organization created in 1999 is an alliance of over 70 organisations[24] working together on issues of housing, shelter displacement and livelihood that concern the urban poor in the National Capital Region. It acted as a catalyst for the people living in Bawana resettlement colony to raise questions against forced evictions but more importantly made the residents aware of the possibilities of reclaiming the city, their voice and future development.

Residents[25] further added:

> At the time when we initially came here, there were nothing here, no work, no transportation facilities that they could use for traveling to work. We were in the condition of starvation because there was no work for us, so no money. And, without money we could not purchase even the minimum amount of food. For drinking water and water for daily use we were totally dependent on the canal running in the nearby

> area. It was through Sajha Manch that we were able to fight and get "something" for us .... In this case a handpump was installed in this area. It was due to its efforts that the water-tanker also started coming at regular basis.
>
> (Interviewed in November 2017)

The residents also shared that the Manch evolved as a platform that brought the residents together as a collective that not only dealt with the larger issues of housing right, unemployment, lack of transportation facilities and basic amenities but very minor everyday problems:

> It has provided us a platform where we could unite, bring our problems to it, problems related to water, employment and transportation. Not only these problems but also the problems related to our day to day lives, something as small as an issue between the neighbours could be raised, discussed and resolved in the Manch.
>
> (Interviewed in November 2017)

Manoj narrates that every aspect of their lives had to be rebuilt from scratch, not only did they have to look for new job opportunities, get plots of land but struggle for getting water, and ensure the safety of their wives, daughters and children.

> Initially when we arrived here local goons harassed our women and girls, mostly at the time when they went to attend nature's call. At that time open defecation was in practice because we have no toilets at our sites. There was no police chawki or any other government authorities where we could go and register a complain. In such conditions it was only Sajha Manch that came to help us in dealing with this problem. There was another major problem in this area at the time .... In the beginning when we returned from work in the evening we were often looted by the local goons. In some instances the goons snatched everything people possessed, and at others even killed people and threw their bodies in the nearby canal. Along with Sajha Manch we protested against the law and order situation or rather the total lack of it here in Bawana. *Our achievement was that we made the authorities listen to our problems.*
>
> (Interviewed in February, 2016)

Despite the struggle of rebuilding their lives in the resettlement colony of Bawana people have continued to stay on and struggle for better basic amenities and housing rights. One may at this point raise the question as to why do the evictees choose to stay on. All the narratives to a certain extent hint at the potential of achieving redressal of their problems both major and minor. But what underlies this potential of achievement is the political possibilities of resistance and engagement with the state.

The Sajha Manch team[26] acknowledges these potentials and possibilities and stated:

> The current resettlement policy is not in favour of these slums dwellers. No rules were followed during the evictions that were carried out arbitrarily. In the name of "beautifying the city" the land was snatched away from the poor and was sold to private authorities. During the 2010 Commonwealth Games the land was sold to private elements after the eviction. Most of the slums were demolished under the orders of Delhi High Court and Supreme Court. The 2010 Commonwealth Games quickened the pace of the eviction. Poor were made the culprits of the environmental degradation, pollution and were evicted ...
>
> People came to Bawana with a hope of getting a house, but here the ground reality was very different. People evicted from Yamuna Pushta did not get the house even after seven years, and, those evicted from Banuwal Nagar, out of 1,600 families only 1,150 got the plots. People evicted from Sawan Park, Kela Godam, Ashok Vihar and Paschim Vihar did not get any plots at all.
>
> A list was prepared on the basis of [a] survey conducted by us. DDA authorities did not carry out the survey efficiently and this led to many evictees not getting the plots. The list included names of people who were not given plots and we focused on finding the cause for them not getting what was rightfully theirs. We have been working in the slum areas from the very beginning and conducted an in-depth survey in [the] year[s] 2007, 2013 and 2015 and our results revealed that there was no shortage of land in Delhi that made the slum's demolition inevitable. Also, in April 2008 along with these evictees we approached the Lt. Governor with a complaint letter where people revealed about the huge corruption occurring in the distribution of plots.
>
> (Interviewed on 24 December 2016)

Interestingly, the achievements and progress made by Sajha Manch was in turn questioned. Residents of Bawana wanted to explore new ways of claiming space and their voice and many broke their affiliation and association with Sajha Manch to form the Bawana Sangharsh Samiti (BSS) in 2008. The slogan of the BSS through the years has been – "We'll fight, we'll win, we'll see the success in the process" and is indicative of the manner in which people want to engage with the State. Both Birendra and Manoj, acknowledge that people feel more empowered and confident to fight for their rights, and perhaps in a more aggressive manner. Moreover, the residents have raised concerns about the nature of the engagement in itself which is controlled by certain civil society organisations. Some even felt that these civil society organisations have in the long run only facilitated the state and the norms of the state in terms of who could be and could not be a beneficiary. Not surprisingly, many of the residents in our group discussion often referred to the civil society as "agents of the government" and added,

> They provide facilities to those who already have some money and documents; these facilities can be given by the government as well. But what about those who don't have any documents? The real task of NGOs is to help those who can't be helped by the government. But, for us the NGOs did no such thing. Neither did the NGOs supported us against crimes committed by the local goons. What are they but agents of [the] government. They promise but don't work for us

Conclusion

Urban authorities, more often than not, have found restructuring as an apt strategy to meet the growing needs and demands at the cost of the living spaces of the urban poor. Restructuring has largely been a tool to intensify the process of concretisation of cities in an unsustainable manner by labelling and justifying it through "development" whereas it has been largely an anti-poor and exclusionary urban policy. Thus, most of these cases have been economically successful but not ecologically or in humanitarian terms. Restructuring has primarily induced both forced evictions and dispossession of the urban poor on one hand. On the other, it has led to the emergence of the "Entrepreneurial City" delineating the "spatial lines" of the city on the basis of economic class. The economically produced "spatial lines" have created socio-spatial pockets like ghettos of the urban poor on the peripheries and these new urban spatialities have sharpened the social lines of Delhi.

The CWGs in 2010 resulted in the displacement of the urban poor on a large scale in Delhi. Since 2004, at least 350,000 people in Delhi have been forcibly evicted as a result of the CWGs. Evictions from the slums were directly related to the building of roads and parking lots for the Games, stadiums as well as those related to "security," "beautification" and "clean up drives" in the city in preparation for the Games. When the urban poor from the slums were evicted from the city's core to the periphery they not only lost their shelter, access to basic amenities but were also identified as encroachers by the state. They were living at the largesse of the state until the civil societies started emerging. Civil societies like Sajha Manch, Housing and Land Rights Network (HLRN), Hazards centre, Bhalaswa Lok Shakti Manch and Human Rights Law Network (HRLN) etc., were vital in mobilising the urban poor and raising the social awareness among the people about their rights to the city. With the help of civil societies, many could get plots, tenure rights, water and access to other basic amenities. The civil societies one may point out played an intermediary role between the poor and the state.

We tried to demonstrate through the chapter that the processes of restructuring and development bring into light the conflict between the urban poor and the middle class and elites of the city. The urban poor's notion of development seemed to revolve around access to better housing, tenure-ship rights, education and livelihood and basic amenities. Whereas the middle class and urban elites' notion of development have been around an infrastructurally and aesthetically developed city that does not include the urban poor and the slums. The slums are viewed as neither infrastructurally nor aesthetically developed reflection of which can be seen in the urban policies that result in the eviction and displacement of the urban poor. Clearly, there is not only dominance of middle-class notions of development but they are seen as key stakeholders of world-class cities. Thus, the urban poor do not find a space in the entire dialogue of world-class cities and struggle to be included in these spaces of participation and policymaking created by the state. To hold a dialogue with the state would then mean to stake a claim to the world-class city and thereby securing development for the urban poor. Here, the urban poor in practice does invent that space of dialogue with the state through civil society organisations, which Chatterjee (2004) ascertains as bourgeois, and falls within the realm of more formal, legalised codes and procedures. Though Chatterjee (2004) argues that the urban poor are forced to operate within a more paralegal, informal sphere but the urban poor, as in the case of Bawana, may critique civil society organisations as "agents of the Government" and yet manoeuvre themselves within a formal and legal process to find their own voice and stake a claim for their own development.

Notes

1 For details see www.business-standard.com/article/news-ians/delhi-to-be-world-class-city-in-four-years-kejriwal-115060401294_1.html (last accessed on 1 May 2020).
2 For details see www.dda.org.in/planning/docs/001_Introduction.pdf (last accessed on 1 May 2020)
3 They discussed that the local institutions are more interested in fulfilling the demands of global economy and bypassing the needs of the locals.
4 Harvey (2012) discussed the role of capitalist urbanisation and the changing nature of local institutions, under the neoliberal era.
5 He discussed the changing nature of local institutions under neoliberal era and advocates that the people should participate in governance and decision-making that ultimately shapes them.
6 Swyngedouw (2000) discussed "authoritarian governance, power, and the politics of rescaling under the capitalist urbanisation and also focused on the changing nature of institutions."
7 Scalar politics are visible across the world, particularly in Global South. Shin cites the example of development of Guangzhou with the objective of it becoming the "International Regional Center." Similarly, in the Indian context

Mumbai is often envisioned as becoming the "International Financial Center." Bangalore as the "Silicon Valley of India" etc. These discourses are used by the urban authorities to justify state backed private-led interventions in the spatial restructuring of the city and targeting slums to produce these developed, modern spaces.

8 In Almitra H. Patel v. Union of India.

9 Pitampura Sudhar Samiti v. Government of National Capital Territory of Delhi- a Common judgement in 63 different petitions filed by the Middle class community through their respective residents welfare associations

10 Housing and Land Rights Network.

11 He is an internationally acclaimed person and working on urban poverty and governance issues from last four decades. Currently he is associated with Delhi-based civil society organisation, Hazards centre.

12 For example, SajhaManch, Hazards Centre, Bhalaswa Lok Shakti Manch, PRIA etc.

13 Approximately 530 families displaced from here (Source: Hazards Centre Report 2007).

14 Approximately 27000 families displaced from here (Source: Hazards Centre Report 2007).

15 Approximately 500 families displaced from here (Source: Hazards Centre Report 2007).

16 Approximately 700 families displaced from here (Source: Hazards Centre Report 2007).

17 Approximately 400 families displaced from here (Source: Hazards Centre Report 2007).

18 Approximately 1,562 families displaced from here (Source: Hazards Centre Report 2007).

19 Approximately 700 families displaced from here (Source: Hazards Centre Report 2007).

20 Approximately 600 families displaced from here (Source: Hazards Centre Report 2007).

21 He is 54 years old, was evicted from Yamuna Pushta, in 2006. He was migrated from Balangir district of Odisha in 1974. Previously he was involved in rickshaw pulling, then in construction work and now he is unemployed.

22 This group of people consists of 8 members aged between 15 to 60 both male (4) and female (4), were evicted from Sawan Park in 2006. They all migrated from Bihar and Uttar Pradesh. They are involved in informal works such as construction work, labour in industry, rickshaw pulling and women in household work etc.

23 This group of people consists of 8 members aged between 13 to 60 both male (4) and female (4), were evicted from Yamuna Pushta in 2004. They all migrated from Medinipur (West Bengal) and Koraput (Odisha). They are involved in informal works such as construction work, labour in industry, rickshaw pulling and women in household work etc.

24 Major important organisations that worked together with the Sajha Manch are: (1) Hazards centre, (2) Delhi Shramik Sangthan, (3) Delhi Janwadi Adhikari Manch (DJAM) and (4) Nirmana Majdoor Panchayat Sangam (NMPS) – it protested for construction workers in Delhi etc.

25 The residents, consisting of 8 people aged between 25 to 60 both male (4) and female (4), were evicted from Yamuna Pushta, Banuwal Nagar, Kelagodam in 2006. They migrated from Uttar Pradesh in 1994. They are involved in the informal sector as construction work, auto-rickshaw driver and domestic help in case of women.

26 Activists are: Jagmohan ji (36 years), Shyam ji (46 years), Bhanuprakash ji (33 years), Sadare bhai ji (39 years) and Gopal ji (45 years), Ranjan ji (36 years). They are working with Sajha Manch team for the last 10 to 15 years.

Bibliography

Ahluwalia, I. J. (2019). Urban Governance in India. *Journal of Urban Affairs*, *41*(1), 83–102.

Anjaria, J S. and McFarlane, C. (2011). *Urban navigations: Politics, space and the city in South Asia*. Delhi: Routledge.

Appadurai, A. (2001). Deep Democracy: Urban Governmentality and the Horizon of Politics Environment and Urbanisation, 13(2), 23–43.

Batra, L. and Mehra, D. (2008). The Demolition of Slums and the Production of Neoliberal Space in Delhi. In D. Mahadevia (Ed.), *Inside the Transforming Urban Asia. Processes, Policies and Public Action*. Delhi: Concept.

Baviskar, A. (2002). The politics of the city. *Shades of Green: A Symposium on the Changing Contours of Indian Environmentalism*, *516*(August), 40–42.

Baviskar, A. (2003). Between violence and desire: Space power and identity in the making of metropolitan Delhi. *International Social Science Journal*, *55*(175), 89–98.

Baviskar, A. (2006a). Demolishing Delhi: world class city in the making. *Mute Magazine*, September 5, Retrieved from http://www.metamute.org.

Baviskar, A. (2007). Demolishing Delhi: World-class city in the making. In L. Batra (Ed.), *The Urban Poor in Globalising India: Dispossession and Marginalisation* (pp. 39–44). New Delhi: South Asian Dialogues on Ecological Democracy and Vasudhaiva Kutumbakam Publications.

Baviskar, A. (2012). Cows, cars and rickshaws: Bourgeois environmentalist and the battle for Delhi's streets. In A. Baviskar and R. Ray (Eds.), *Elite and Everyman: The Cultural Politics of the Indian Middle-Classes* (pp. 391–418). New Delhi: Routledge.

Baviskar, A. (2011b). What the eye does not see: The Yamuna in the imagination of Delhi. *Economic and Political Weekly*, *46*(50), 45–53.

Bhan, G. (2009). This is no longer the city I once knew: Evictions, the urban poor and the right to the city in millennial Delhi. *Environment and Urbanization*, *21*(1), 127–142.

Bhan, G. (2016). *In the public's interest: Evictions, citizenship and inequality in contemporary Delhi*. Athens: University of Georgia Press and Orient Black Swan.

Bhan, G., and Shivanand, S. (2013). (Un)settling the city. Analysing displacement in Delhi from 1990 to 2007. *Economic and Political Weekly*, *48*(13), 54–61.

Bhan, G., Srinivas, S., and Watson, V. (Eds.). (2018). *The routledge companion to planning in the global south*. London; New York, NY: Routledge .

Brenner, N. (1999). Globalisation as reterritorialization: The re-scaling of urban governance on the European Union. *Urban Studies 36*, 431–451.

Brenner, N., Marcuse, P., and Mayer, M. (2012). *Cities for people, not for profit: Critical urban theory and the right to the city*. New York: Routledge.

Brodie, J. (2000). Imagining democratic urban citizenship. In Isin, E. (Ed.), *Democracy, Citizenship and the Global City* (pp. 110–128). New York: Routledge.

Centre for Policy Research Report. (2014). Report prepared by Banda, S., and Sheikh, S. The case of Sonia Gandhi camp: The process of eviction and demolition in Delhi's Jhuggi Jhopri clusters. New Delhi: Cities of Delhi Working Paper. Retrieved August 16, 2015, from http://citiesofdelhi.cprindia.org/reports/the-process-of-eviction-and-demolition-in-delhis-jhuggi-jhopri-clusters/.

Chakravarty, S and Rohit, N. (Eds.). (2016). *Space, planning and everyday contestations in Delhi*. Exploring urban change in South Asia DOI 10.1007/978-81-322-2154-8. Springer India.

Chatterjee, P. (2004). The politics of the governed: Reflections on popular politics in most of the world. New York: Columbia University Press.

Dupont, V. (2008). Slum demolitions in Delhi since the 1990s: An appraisal. *Economic and Political Weekly*, *43*(28), 89–94.

Dupont, V. (2012). The dream of Delhi as a global city. *International Journal of Urban and Regional Research*, *35*(3), 533–554.

Dupont, V. (2011b). The challenges of slums and forced evictions. In M. H. Zereh, V. Dupont, and S. Tawa Lama-Rewal (Eds.), *Urban Policies and the Rights to the City in India: Rights* (pp. 76–97). Delhi: UNESCO.

Dupont, V. (2013). The challenge of "human" sustainability for Indian mega-cities: squatter settlements, forced evictions and resettlement & rehabilitation policies in Delhi. Paper presented to: *XXVII IUSSP International Population Conference*. Busan, Korea, 26–31 August 2013. Session 282: The sustainability of mega-cities.

Fernandes, L. (2004). The politics of forgetting; class politics, state power and the restructuring of urban space in India. *Urban Studies*, *41*(12), 2415–30.

Follmann, A. (2016). The role of environmental activists in governing riverscapes: The case of the Yamuna in Delhi, India. *South Asia Multidisciplinary Academic Journal, 14*, 1–24.

Gavasker, K. K. (2011). Urban restructuring and change: Planning, development practices and impacts on the urban poor. *Institute of Town Planners, India Journal*, *8*(2), 24–44.

Ghertner, D. A. (2010). Calculating without numbers: Aesthetic governmentality in Delhi's slums. *Economy and Society*, *39*(2), 185–217.

Ghertner, D. A. (2012). Nuisance talk and the propriety of property: Middle class discourses of a slum-free Delhi. *Antipode*, *44*(4), 1161–1187.

Ghertner, D. A. (2011b). Rule by aesthetics: World class city making in Delhi. In A. Ong & A. Roy (Eds.), *Worlding Cities. Asian Experiments and the Art of Being Global* (pp. 279–306). Oxford: Blackwell.

Ghertner, D. A. (2015). *Rule by aesthetics: World-class city making in Delhi*. Oxford: Oxford University Press.

Gill, K. (2009). *Bourgeois environmentalism', the State, the Judiciary, and the 'urban poor': The political mobilization of a scheduled caste market*. London: Oxford University Press.

Harvey, D. (2008). *The right to the city. New Left Review*, *53*, 23–40.

Harvey, D. (2009). Is this really the end of neoliberalism? *Counterpunch*, March 13–15 [online]. Retrieved September 17, 2016, from http://www.counter punch.org/harvey03132009.html

Harvey, D. (2010). *The enigma of capital and the crises of capitalism*. Oxford: Oxford University Press.

Harvey, D. (2012). *Rebel cities: From the right to the city to the urban revolution.* London: Verso.

Hazards Centre Report. (2007). *A fact-finding report on the eviction and resettlement process in Delhi.* Retrieved July 12, 2015, from http://www.hazardscentre.com/hazards_publications/pdf/sustainability_planning/fact_ finding2007.pdf.

HIC-HLRN. (2011). *The 2010 commonwealth games: Whose wealth? whose commons? habitat international coalition.* Retrieved May 16, 2021,from https://www.hic-net.org/document/the-2010-commonwealth-games-whose-wealth-whose-commons/

Holston, J. and Appadurai, A. (1996). Cities and Citizenship. *Public Culture*, *8*, 187–204.

IsinEngin, F. (2000). *Democracy, citizenship, and the global city*. New York: Routledge.

Jayal, G. N. (2013). *Citizenship and Its discontents, an Indian history*. Cambridge: Harvard University Press.

Jessop, B. (1997). A Neo-Gramscian approach to the regulation of urban regimes: Accumulation strategies, hegemonic projects, and governance. In M. Lauria. (Ed.), *Reconstructing Urban Regime Theory: Regulating Urban Politics in a Global Economy* (pp. 51–73). Thousand Oaks: SAGE.

Jou, S-C, Anders Lund, H., and Wu, H-L. (2011). Accumulation by dispossession and neoliberal urban planning: 'Landing' the mega-projects in Taipei. In T. Tasan-Kok and G. Baeten (Eds.), *Contradictions of Neoliberal Planning: Cities, Policies, and Polics* (pp. 151–171). New York: Springer.

Lefebvre, H. (2003 [1970]). *The urban revolution* (Translated by Robert Bononno). Minneapolis: University of Minnesota Press.

Levien, M. (2013). Regimes of dispossession: From steel towns to special economic zones. *Development and Change*, *44*(2), 381–407.

MacLeod, G. and Godwin, M. (1999a). Space, scale and state strategy: Rethinking urban and regional governance. *Progress in Human Geography*, *23*, 503–527.

MacLeod, G. and Godwin, M. (1999b). Reconstructing an urban and regional political economy: On the state, politics, scale, and explanation. *Political Geography*, *18*(6), 697–730.

Marcuse, P. and Madden, D. J. (2016). *Defense of housing—the politics of crisis.* London: Verso Books.

Mawdsley, E. and Truelove, Y. (2011). Discourses of citizenship and criminality in clean, green Delhi. In I. Clark-Deces (Ed.). *A Companion to the Anthropology of India* (pp. 407–425). Oxford: Blackwell Publishing Ltd.

Menon-Sen, K., and Gautam, B. (2008). *Swept off the map: Surviving eviction and resettlement in Delhi.* Delhi: Yoda Press.

Nair, J. (2005). *The promise of the metropolis: Bangalore's twentieth century.* New Delhi: Oxford University Press.

Peck, J. (1998). Geographies of governance: TECs and the neo-liberalization of 'local interests'. *Space and Polity*, 2, 5–31.

Purcell, M.. (2002). Excavating Lefebvre: The right to the city and its urban politics of the inhabitant. *GeoJournal*, *58*, 99–108.

Purcell, M.. (2006). Urban democracy and the local trap. *Urban Studies*, *43*(11), 1921–1941.

Risbud, N. (2016). *Safe and inclusive cities, Delhi: City profile; poverty, inequality and violence in urban india: Towards inclusive planning and policies*. New Delhi: Institute for Human Development.

Ruet, J. and Tawa lama-Rewal, S. (2009). *Governing India's metropolises*. New York: Routledge.

Shin, H. B. (2014). Urban spatial restructuring, event-led development and scalar politics. *Urban Studies*, *51*(14): 2961–2978.

Solomon, J B., and Bhuvaneswari, R. (2011). Claiming land: Rights, contestations and the urban poor in globalized times. In M. H. Zereh, V. Dupont, and S. Tawa Lama-Rewal (Eds.), *Urban Policies and the Rights to the City in India: Rights, Responsibilities and Citizenship*. Delhi: UNESCO.

Stoker, G. (1998). Governance as Theory: Five propositions. *International Social Science Journal*, *55*, 17–28.

Swyngedouw, E. (2000). Authoritarian governance, power, and the politics of rescaling. *Environment and Planning D: Society and Space 18*, 63–76.

Tickell, A. and Peck, J. (1996). The return of the Manchester men: Men's words and men's deeds in the remaking of local state. *Transactions of the Institute of British Geographers*, *21*, 595–616.

The Hindu. (2018). The national daily newspaper, India, 18th June.

'The Wire' (2016). Interview to 'The Wire'- Gautam Bhan on the "Encroacher" Versus the "Citizens". Accessed on 29/07/2016 from https://thewire.in/books/gautam-bhan

Uitermark, J., Nicholls, W. and Loopmans, M. (2012). Cities and Social Movements: Theorizing beyond the Right to the City. *Environmental and Planning A*, *44*, 2546–2554.

UNHRC. (2014). *United Nations Human Rights Commission Report*. Retrieved from :https://www.ohchr.org/en/hrbodies/hrc/coidprk/pages/reportofthecommissionofinquirydprk.aspx

Ward, K. (2000). A critique in search of a corpus: Re-visiting governance and re-interpreting urban politics. *Transactions of the Institute of British Geographers*, *25*, 169–185.

Ward, K. and Imbroscio, D. (2011). Urban politics: An interdisciplinary dialogue. *International Journal of Urban and Regional Research*, *35*(4), 853–871.

Zereh, M. H., Dupont, V and S. Tawa Lama-Rewal (Eds.), (2011). *Urban Policies and the Rights to the City in India: Rights, Responsibilities and Citizenship*. Delhi: UNESCO. Retrieved from http://nesdoc.unesco.org/image/0021/002146/214602E.pdf

Chapter 4

Mapping the development paradigm of Northeast India from ancient past to present in the realm of political history and economy

Anjan Chakrabarti

Introduction

The overall impression of the Northeast is a bit unknown to the people of the rest of India. In general, we, the rest of the Indians hardly venture beyond Assam, or occasionally we do visit as tourists Shillong of Meghalaya or Arunachal Pradesh. Else, we, the ordinary Indians are mostly unaware of their origin and identity. The Northeast does survive in isolation from the rest of India, economically, socially, culturally and politically, especially from the colonial period. It is considered the most conflict-ridden regions of India and South Asia (Chakrabarti & Chaudhuri, 2019).

Similarly, the people of the Northeast who are ethnically distinct and are having a preponderance of the Tibeto-Burman languages look at the rest of India with an eye of suspicion and apprehension. However, the Northeast of India, which today consists of the seven sister states of Assam, Manipur, Nagaland, Tripura, Arunachal Pradesh and Mizoram; and the late entrant "one brother" Sikkim,[1] is geographically isolated from the mainland and strategically important. With the largest concentration of India's tribal population[2] and characterised by extremes of uneven development and consciousness of deprivation, it is, not surprisingly, politically sensitive and contains a range of extremist and separatist movements and parties. Nevertheless, local, state and national elections are held regularly and reinforce and legitimise democratic politics in this region (and thus in India too). Equally, they help to integrate the region with the rest of India (Chaube, 1985). The Northeast at large remains a vague, unknown, mystic category to the rest of the world beyond the "Siliguri-Coochbehar corridor." The Siliguri-Coochbehar corridor symbolises the nebulous zone of "the beginning" as well as "the end" of this territorial demarcation of the "North-East" with the rest of India, especially in the post-independence period. The northeastern region of India has great strategic significance due to its external boundary lines with China, Bhutan, Myanmar and Bangladesh and the rest of the Southeast Asian countries.

DOI: 10.4324/9781003159940-4

However, the ancient period narrates different stories. Two essential shades can be traced. First, during the ancient period, the region acted as a linkage between the Indian subcontinent with east, southeast and inner Asia along the southern Silk Route. Trade, culture, faith, and people moved through this route from Central China and Southeast Asia. The Ganges/Brahmaputra Delta is believed to be the central hub of the southwestern route (Gan Fuxi, 2009). Second, the isolation of this region from mainland India is primarily a colonial construct and politico-historical reality. The post-independence scenario can be segregated into two parts. Having some continuity in policy formulations, a sharp change has been observed after the adoption of the neoliberal policy by the Government of India during the late 1990s and introduction of the Look East/Act East policy to augment trade with East and Southeast Asian countries. There may be a synergy between neoliberal policy and Look East Policy in a changing geopolitical and economic situation, but the moot point is that how is it going to strengthen the economy of northeastern states and can it integrate Northeast with the rest of India and will it become the gateway of Southeast Asia economically, socially, and (or) implicitly culturally? An attempt has been made here to trace the changing trajectories of politico-history and economy of the region from the ancient past to the present and ramifications on the Asian subcontinent.

Pre-colonial period in perspective

History in recent years has been a highly contested field in India. Competing readings of the past shaped major political conflicts and such conflicts abound in Northeast India. Former Governor Lt. General of Assam, S.K. Sinha of Assam lamented that while Indian historians speak of the Indus valley civilisation and the Ganges Valley civilisation, they never speak about the Assam Brahmaputra Valley civilisation.

Two major trade routes, namely the Silk Route or the terrestrial route and the Indian Ocean trade route predominated the economy, culture and polity of the ancient past of the Asian subcontinent. The Silk Route was an extensive network of trade routes connecting East Asia and South East Asia with East Africa, West Asia, and southern Europe. The lucrative trade of silk from the Han dynasty (207BCE–220CE) from China was carried along this road and became famous as the Silk Road (Miho Museum News, 2009). Trade through the Silk Road played a significant role in the development of the civilisation of China, Korea (UNESCO), Japan, the Indian subcontinent, Iran, Persia, Europe, the Horn of Africa and Arabia. The route also opened up the long-distance political and economic relations among the civilisations (ibid). The operation of the Silk Road was routed in four directions. The northern route travelled through the Chinese province. The southern way moved from China through Karakoram Mountain and touched present-day Pakistan. Through northern Pakistan, it crossed the Hind Kush Mountain, reached Afghanistan, and was connected to the northern route near Merv, Turkmenistan. Moving straight, to the west through mountainous northern Iran, Mesopotamia and the northern tip of the Syrian Desert, the Silk Route reached the Levant. From the Levant, gathered ships at the Mediterranean Sea, took the commodities to Italy. While the land route headed to the north through Anatolia or south to North Africa, another division road moved from Herat touching different ports of Mediterranean en route, and from those ports, goods were carried to Rome by ships.

However, from the perspective of Northeast India, the southwestern Silk Route has paramount importance. This route is believed to be the Ganges/Brahmaputra Delta, which was undoubtedly the major international trading centre. Gemstone and other merchandise from Java and Thailand had been traded through this route. Bin Yang (2008), the Chinese archaeological writer, reaffirmed that from the 12th Century, the international trade route Sichuan-Yunnan-Burma-Bangladesh, which was also known as the "Ledo" route was extensively in use. Gold and Silver were mostly traded from Yunan to Bangladesh through northern Burma. The evidence emerging from ancient cities of Bangladesh, especially from the excavation of ruins from Wari-Bateswar, Mahasthangarh, Bhitagarh, Bikrampur, Egarasindhur and Sonargaon proves the existence of international trade centres in this route (Killon, 2006: 66; Yang, 2008).

In addition to the terrestrial Silk Route, the Maritime Silk Route establishes connectivity between China to Southeast Asia, Indonesia, the Indian subcontinent, the Arabian Peninsula, Egypt and Europe. Trade and commerce encompassed the South China Sea, Strait of Malacca, Indian Ocean, Gulf of Bengal, Arabian Sea, Persian Gulf and the Red Sea. Maritime Silk Route got blended with Southeast Asian maritime trade, the spice trade, Indian Ocean trade and, since the 8th century, it got connected with an Arabian naval network (Gommans, 2015: 182).

The Indian Ocean trade route was the most crucial interface between East and West. Exchanges of goods, faith, culture and art were regular features. The Mauryan empire in India, the Han Dynasty in China, the Empire of Persia and the Roman empire were having extensive trade relations through the Indian Ocean. Spices from India, silk and porcelain from China and ivory, gold, sandalwoods and slaves were major trading items. Along with trade, Buddhism, Hinduism, Jainism was reached from India to Southeast Asia (www.indianoceanhistory.org). However, the golden era of the Asian subcontinent started waning out from the 15th century and precisely with the arrival of Vasco Da Gama from Portugal to the southern point of Africa (Gommans, op cit. 184–187). In 1602, the appearance of and manifestation of the Dutch power, the Indian Ocean and finally, in 1680, the intrusion of the East India Company in India's body polity changed the entire historical discourse. Political control over vast parts of Asia, especially India, Indonesia, Malay and much of Southeast Asia and Africa went into the hands of Europeans (Liberman, 2009). The two-thousand-year-old Indian Ocean trade got crippled, and European hegemony was established. The rich ancient past of Eurasia lost its glory permanently, and the politics of subjugation became a reality. India's Northeast has not been spared. The Ganga/Brahmaputra delta as a major trade centre, terrestrial connectivity of Northeast through the Silk Route lost its relevance and became mere historical references.

The era of colonial intervention

The British had initially maintained a policy of non-interference towards the tribal politics in the Northeast. However, it was at the willingness and compulsion of the successive weak rulers of the Ahom Dynasty; the British agreed to adopt a new policy of direct/partial interference which later took the form of the annexation of Assam and eventually the whole of the Northeast region (Singh, 2004). The British drove out the Burmese from Assam in 1826 and steadily consolidated and expanded their presence in the Northeast. They brought the Garo Hills, the Naga Hills and the Jaintia Hills within the Assam province that brought a new group of people and who added linguistic, ethnic and cultural heterogeneity in the region. In annexing these tribal game territories, the British had to face stiff resistance and bloody fights from the natives. As a learning experience, the British during the period 1843–1872 adopted the policy of "gradual abandonment of the policy of non-intervention to one of slow but steady penetration" and avoided any direct tussle or confrontation with these semi-civilised, naked *junglees* of the frontier region. The writings of British officers like Reid (1978), Allen (1979), Woodthorpe (1980), Dunbar (1994), McCall (2003), and others reflect on the dilemmas faced by the colonial administration in the region. The British to maintain their foothold in Northeast India began to devise the policies of appeasements in varying degrees. These protective enclaves were the outcome of the stiff resistance posed by the aborigines to safeguard their homeland and their rights and traditional practices from being swallowed by the "Alien British rule." British rule also weakened communal control of land "through the payment of compensation for land acquisition to 'owners', chiefs and 'rajas'" (Chaube, 1999: 44).

In 1873, the British introduced the inner-line[3] regulation. It empowered the Governor of Assam to ensure that no British subject could cross or go beyond a certain frontier that was drawn along the foothills of the northeastern and southwestern border of the Brahmaputra valley. The areas beyond the inner line were inhabited by the hill tribes where the government did not want to apply complicated civil rules. The inner lines awarded the hill tribes a special status. Most notably, the Inner-Line Regulation did not define the actual boundary of the British possession nor did it indicate the territorial frontiers. Its sole purpose was to prohibit the plains people from entering into the hills without the permission of the government. The inner lines were drawn to protect the hill tribes from any interference from the plains area and to provide a simpler administration for the hill people. The "Line System" was primarily introduced to protect their commercial interest and suit their security concerns in the region. During the British rule, the cross-border trades received momentum with the breakthrough of tea and crude oil. For example, India experienced a 10% cumulative annual rate of growth in tea exports between 1858 and 1901, when Assam contributed 90% of India's export (Dutt, 1990: 391). However, the overall impact was very negligible in the Northeast and the reasons were: (i) "the tea plantation was developed into enclave production without having any linkage with the hinterland" (Barua & Das, 2008); (ii) the wage policy pursued by the planters backed by the colonial authority was such that the wage rates in the tea gardens were much lower than what could be earned when employed by the railways and public works department or in agriculture (Dasgupta, 1986: PE-2); (iii) appropriation of land by the agents of the company without any compensation being paid to the owners of the land; (iv) the railway network passing through jungles connecting the tea plantation to the river/seaport and thereby leading the entire hinterland in the outskirts which prevented internal market formation; (v) lack of technological changes in agriculture and suppression of local entrepreneurship(Barua, 2005). Colonial rule mostly followed this mechanism for India as a whole, and this is the crux of colonial rule or mercantile policy in general.

Post-colonial administration in the Northeast inherited this structure. Though at the outset, it seems to be a strategy aimed at fending off the areas, it also contained the initial kernel of plural legal regimes of land use, property, ownership and control over resources. Indian democracy is fraught with this dilemma. It cuts both ways, on the one hand, it acts as a great unifier among the groups concerned and injects confidence among marginal social groups of their ability to determine their own "selves" and break from the majoritarian encapsulation. On the other, it divides that group from the "larger other" and threatens the larger nation (India) in the making (Chakrabarti & Chakraborty, 2010).

As early as 1874, the British Indian government passed the "Scheduled Districts Act" followed by the Government of India Act 1919 which empowered the Governor-General in the council to declare any territory to be "Backward track," where laws passed by the British Indian government could not apply. The Government of India Act 1935 further elaborated on the Act of 1919 by introducing the "excluded" and "partially excluded areas," which excluded these areas from the operation of laws applicable to the rest of British India.

The "Line System" allowed for limited colonisation of lands by settlers and areas dominated by indigenous groups were marked off as "Out of bounds" for settlement. Modernism/Modernity[4] and the sentiments of nationalism, that is, territorial loyalty seek to substitute primordial loyalties of clan, tribes, castes, race, community and language but in practice end up churning these primordial sentiments even deeper as evident from the Indian experience. The Northeast, in general, has been experiencing this need for re-drawing the boundaries in the northeastern territorial zones and spaces, that is, re-marking the geopolitics and ethnopolitics based on the logic of traditional game land that the people had lost due to the British and other external forces. Post-colonial Northeast India has witnessed numerous ethnic movements culminating in varying degrees of violence due to a plethora of factors acting simultaneously in a multi-layered fashion ranging from the permanent quasi-martial law that envelops the whole of the Northeast; to the vulnerability of its strategic geopolitical location; to the logic of patchwork territories which reflects the spectre of colonial administration. In this sense, we can agree that the "North-East" itself is "a colonial construct or more so a residue of Colonial existence" as argued by scholars like Ranabir Samaddar (2004), Subir Bhaumik (2010), S.K. Chaube (1999) and others.

Also, the near absence of cultural and political assimilation of the tribes of Northeast with mainland India and the limited impact of Indian freedom struggle on tribal-dominated northeastern states had made the situation more complicated (Chandra et al., 2008: 142). The separation of Burma from India in 1937 and the partition of India in 1947 had accentuated the geopolitical and economic isolation of this region. In fact, due to the partition of India, the region lost its water, road and railway connectivity through erstwhile East Pakistan. The Chinese occupancy of Tibet and closure of the border with Burma further crippled the economic and political well-being of the region (Verghese, 2004).

Post-colonial policy and development strategy towards Northeast

The post-colonial administration of the region carried forward the colonial legacy under the new name of "Sixth Schedule" and the continuation of the exclusivist policies, for instance, the "Inner-Line Permit" and the "Autonomous Districts." At least ten autonomous councils under the sixth schedule[5] of the Indian Constitution were created to strengthen the process of independent regional self-governance and socio-economic development. Inner-line permit (introduced by the British government during the colonial era) has still been continuing so that the tribal-dominated region remains insulated from the in-migration of people from outside the region. It justifies the need to protect the backward region and its people from being taken over by the wave of Sanskritisation, dilution of property rights over resources, especially land. It has also kept the labour market insulated or being swamped by the people from the rest of India. However, in actual this colonial hangover[6] led to the mushrooming of politics of "Ethnic Enclaves." The direct repercussions of the "Nehru-Elwin model"[7] (Elwin 1959; Chandra et al. 2008) of "exclusivist-isolationist" administration of tribal region in the Northeast were felt on exchanges between the hills and the plains.

Many writers have assumed that the development of technology, the growth of population and the elaboration of the division of labour would lead to the assimilation of earlier small communities into ever larger, more centralised and rationalised economic and political organisations. All the northeastern states are treated as "special category states"[8]which receive substantial financial and non-financial support from the Central Government. The special category status is decided by the National Development Council (NDC) on the recommendation of the Planning Commission. The Planning Commission has laid down certain criteria[9] for receiving the status of special category state. The Planning Commission further assumes that special category states have a low resource base and are not in a position to mobilise resources for their developmental needs irrespective of their per capita income. As and when new states were created by carving out of Assam, or by giving statehood to erstwhile union territories of India, except Goa all were provided special category status (Bhattacharjee, 2014: 48).

As special category states, all the northeastern states currently receive 90% of their plan assistance as grants and the remaining 10% as loans, while it is 30:70 for non-special category states. The special category states receive preferential treatment in the distribution of normal central assistance from state plans, and they would have been in a disadvantageous position had the Gadgil formula[10] applied to them. The Gadgil formula puts more weight on the population, whereas all the northeastern states have a low population. From the total central assistance available for state plans, funds are earmarked for externally aided projects and special area programmes and special constitutional provisions within the state boundaries (Chakrabarti & Chakraborty, 2010: 547–559).

Also, for the economic and social development of northeastern states, the North-Eastern Council was constituted in 1971 by the act of parliament of India. The North-Eastern Development Finance Corporation Ltd. was established in 1995 and 2001, the Union Government set up the Department of Development of North-Eastern Region and upgraded to a Ministry in 2004 as DoNER or Ministry of Development of North-Eastern Region (www.mdoner.gov.in/). This ministry looks after the development requirement of this region and also advocates its special needs to other ministries of the Government of India as well as to policymakers. The policies of industrial licensing, concessional finance and investment subsidy, growth centres, as well as freight equalisation of some major industrial input, have also been used to promote economic development. The National Committee on the Development of Backward Areas commissioned by the Planning Commission in 1981 has identified three types of fundamental backwardness in the region namely areas of tribal concentration, hill areas and chronically flood-affected areas. The whole of the Northeast has been categorised as an industrially backward zone. To add a fillip to entrepreneurial activities, in 2017, North Eastern Development Finance Corporation Limited (NEDFi) in association with the Ministry of Development of North Eastern Region (M-DoNER) has launched the first dedicated venture capital fund named North East Venture Fund (NEVF)" for the northeastern region with a corpus of Rs. 100 crores. It is decided that investments in start-ups, early and growth-stage companies, investment in new products and technologies, investment in innovative business model with a superior value proposition and potential for high growth in earnings and profitability will be encouraged. The minimum investment size shall be Rs. 25 lakhs and the maximum limit has been set up at Rs. 10 crores. The enterprises related to food processing, tourism, health care, IT and ITES, aggregation of service will receive priorities.

Look East/Act East policy and Northeast

During the liberalisation era (post-1990s), India shunned the policy of "import substitution" and adopted a policy of export-led growth to overcome India's sluggish growth performances and balance of payment crisis. It moved away from protectionist regimes and government control of economic decision-making and embraced market forces in almost all spheres of economic activities. It gave birth to India's "Look East" policy, which is an admixture of foreign and free-trade policy. Internal security concern in northeastern states which has strong international linkages also played a catalytic role to formulate the "Look East" policy. To counter the growing economic, political and military influences of China, India, on the one hand, tries to develop cohesive relationships with East Asian and Southeast Asian countries including Myanmar and on the other, attempts to improve trade balance with these countries. The end of the Cold War and ascendency of the US as superpower made India's policy of non-alignment outmoded. The worldwide growth of regional trade blocks and India's policy compulsion toward export-led growth in the post-1990s scenario also forced to move away from multilateralism towards a policy of strategic alliance with the East and Southeast Asian bloc of countries and economic sub-regionalism, given the failure of South Asian Association for Regional Cooperation (SAARC) as a viable alternative (Issabelle Saint-Mezard, 2003). Though

India had strong historical bonding by way of religion, language, culture and civilisation with East and Southeast Asian countries, it had little political and economic interaction with them (Naidu, 2004).

The tremendous rise of China both as economic and political power also put India on tenterhooks. To forge close ties with East and South Asia thus become both economic and geopolitical compulsion for India (Grare and Mattoo, 2003) and failure of India to manoeuvre SAARC forced India to look at East and South Asian countries to protect, consolidate and expand economic interests (Devare et al., 2014;Bhattacharya, 2011; Chakraborty and Ray, 2014; Haokip, 2015). These efforts led to creating some cooperative economic ventures incorporating Southeast and East Asian countries. India became one of the partners of the Association of Southeast Asian Nations (ASEAN) along with Indonesia, Malaysia, Philippines, Singapore, Thailand, Brunei, Darussalam, Vietnam, Lao, Myanmar and Cambodia in 2002, and a member of East Asian Summit in 2005.[11] Bay of Bengal Initiative for Multi-Sectoral Economic Cooperation (BIMSTEC) comprising Bangladesh, India, Myanmar, Sri Lanka and Thailand and Bangladesh–China–India–Myanmar Forum for Regional Cooperation (BCIM) was launched in 1997 (Srikanth, 2016), the Ganga–Mekong Suvanaphoom Programme, the South Asian Free Trade Area (SAFTA)[12] in 2004 and the South Asian Sub-Region for Economic Cooperation (SASEC) in 2001 (Naidu, op cit.). Given the fact that European countries and the USA have remained dominant trade partners from the pre-independence period, however, there is a decline in percentage change of trade with these two dominant partners. On the contrary, the percentage change is increasing with Asian countries, and the creation of regional trade blocks are certainly paying off (Table 4.1). However, the bilateral relation of India with Asian partners is facing continuous ups and downs, and the growing influence of China on Nepal, Myanmar, Bangladesh and Sri Lanka is becoming a challenging proposition for India to handle.

Northeast has been identified as the ideal buffer zone bridging South East Asia both for internal security purpose and to ensure development in that region. This new development paradigm in a way was the result of the failure of the "old development paradigm" where the major thrust of development policy as articulated by various packages of development under the

Table 4.1 Percentage change in export and import between (2004/05–2007/08) and (2010/11–2013/14)

Percentage change in export and import	*Europe*	*America*	*Africa*	*Asia*
Export (2010/11–2013/14)	18.0	16.8	8.9	50.2
Export (2004/05–2007/08)	23.3	18.9	7.8	48.5
Import (2010/11–2013/14)	18.0	11.0	8.5	60.2
Import (2004/05–2007/08)	21.6	10.3	6.3	48.9

Source: Economic Review 2015–2016, Govt. of India.

aegis of successive prime ministers since Deve Gauda was to pump in as much money as possible for the development of this region (Barua & Das, 2007). It has been implicitly accepted that the dole-development model did have serious limitations. Northeast has been projected as a gateway to East and South-East Asia. Trade has been identified as a panacea to bring an overall economic change to the landlocked northeastern states and the problems of poverty, unemployment and underdevelopment.

It has been mentioned in one of the government reports that "the Northeastern region shares only 2 per cent of the border with the mainland of the country and the balance of 98 per cent is shared with an international border, i.e., Bangladesh, Myanmar, China, and Bhutan. It is considered natural and necessary for the region to look at neighbouring countries for markets. Promotion of border trade is likely to create opportunities for people to earn a livelihood, simultaneously providing greater avenues for private investments in infrastructure" (IIFT, 1995). Also, sub-regional forums comprising East and Southeast Asian countries proposed different economic and connectivity projects. Asian Highways – AH1 and AH2 – were endorsed by the United Nations Economic and Social Commission of Asia and the Pacific (UNSECAP) pass through northeastern states (UNSECAP, 2003). It is opined that increased connectivity will connect the landlocked regions with neighbouring countries and shall enhance business and trade between the countries and the regions through the reduction of time, distance and travel costs (Shepherd et al., 2011; Aggarwal, 2015). A plethora of connectivity projects are either proposed or in the process of execution by China and India and more than often, they are contentious rather than complementary. China is extending financial and technical support to build road and railways in Myanmar, Thailand and Mongolia, which will connect these countries with landlocked backward regions of China. With the help from the Asian Development Bank, China is also pursuing connectivity projects like Asian Highways, One Belt One Road (OBOR) which shall link China with other Asian countries as well as European countries (Holslang, 2010).

India is also following China's footsteps, for geopolitical as well as economic apprehension and compulsion and helped Myanmar to complete 160 km of the Tamu-Kalemyo sector of the proposed Trilateral Highway that supposes to connect India, Myanmar and Thailand. India also pursued the Mekong–India Economic Corridor (MIEC) project that would give access to India to Laos, Cambodia and Vietnam (De and Singh, 2015). A highway linking Kolkata in India and Kunming in Yunnan province of China has also been proposed, and it supposes to link Dhaka and Chittagong in Bangladesh, India's northeastern states of Manipur and Assam and Myanmar's Mandalay and northern provinces. The corridor will also touch Silchar, Imphal and Moreh in the Northeast (Rana and Uberoi, 2012; Juergens, 2014). India and Bangladesh have also agreed upon road and railways which will link northeastern states to Dhaka and from there to Kolkata. Negotiations are on to link seaports of Bangladesh and Northeast and South East Asia (Chatterjee et al., 2015). The moot point is, does post-colonial as well as post-liberalisation era bring changes in the economy of the Northeast?

A brief account of the economy of Northeast

It has been observed that the share from the primary, secondary and tertiary sectors to the Gross State Domestic Products (GSDP) at current prices for the northeastern states changed over time. The share of the primary sector is falling consistently; the share of the secondary sector has remained static while the share of the tertiary sector is increasing and contributing most to the GSDP (Figure 4.1). Consistent fall in the share of agriculture is worrisome because more than 60% of the people derive their livelihood from agriculture. It also implies a fall in per capita income from agriculture and allied activities. It is also hinting towards the marginalisation and casualisation of agricultural workers. This phenomenon is real not only for the northeastern states but it is again happening in the rest of the Indian states. Coming to the secondary sector, the share of manufacturing, the backbone of the secondary sector and indicator for industrialisation is hovering around 5%.

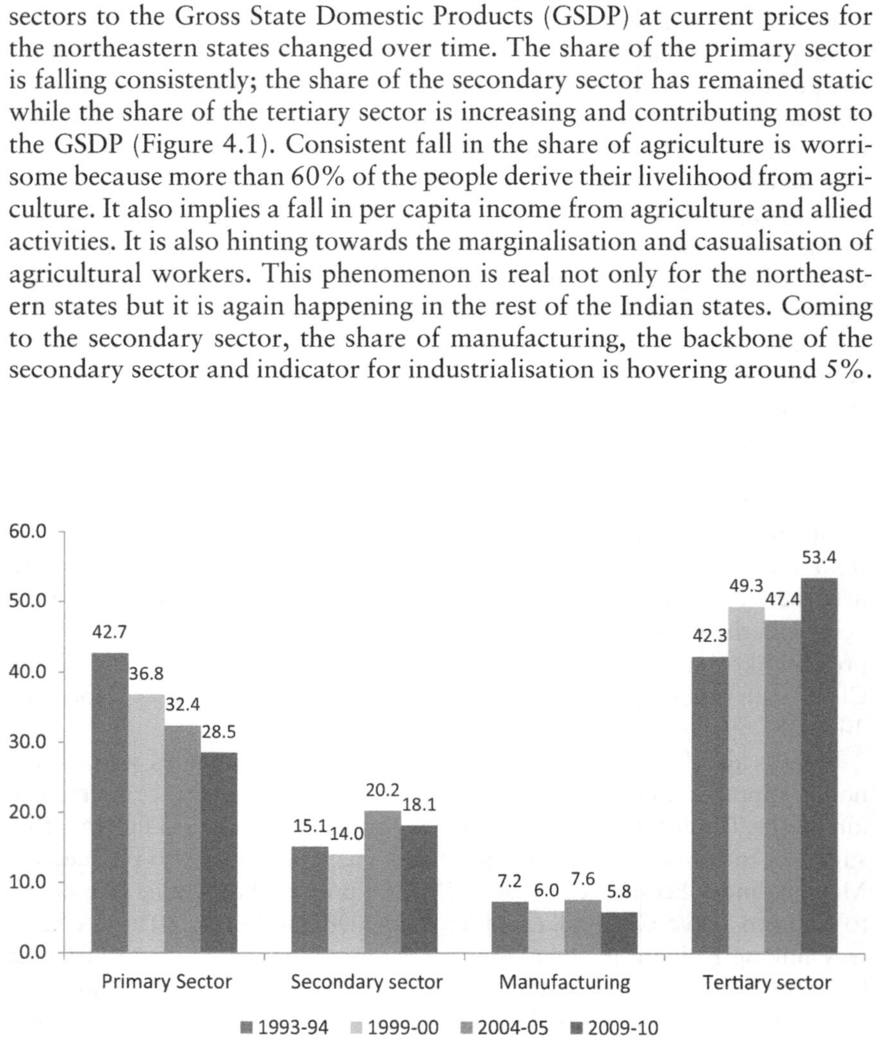

Figure 4.1 Sectoral Share of GSDP (at current prices) of NE Region (1993-94 TO 2011-12)
Source: Calculated from data collected from CSO, and www.mospi.gov.in

Only Assam is the exception because Assam has a certain degree of manufacturing base, and oil and natural gas do generate income for the secondary sector. Unlike other northeastern states, a fair degree of expansion of the private sector has also taken place in Assam. It shows the absence of the private sector in secondary activities and limited development of industrial activities among the northeastern states.

Similarly, for the tertiary sector, 50% to 60% contribution comes from public administration, which broadly covers the services of the state government administration and other services. Again, other services include activities about educational, medical and veterinary, research and scientific, sanitary, recreational, rest of the services, international and extra-territorial bodies and lottery services. Therefore, the bulk of the income generated under "other services" is primarily coming from government and quasi-government employment. It implies that the high share of the tertiary sector to GSDP is also arising out of government employment and more precisely, where the government is playing the direct role. Also, Barring Assam, own tax-revenue collection as a percentage of GSDP is abysmally low (between 7–8%) for the northeastern states.

Therefore, the development process solely depends on Central assistance as grant-in-aid. Any reduction (though it is most unlikely) in central assistance will make the economy of this region more vulnerable. The private sector has not grown, and as a result, all these states have failed to create an economy outside agriculture, and most of these states are still dependent on primitive agricultural methods. The region remains a net importer of goods services from the rest of India (Chakrabarti, 2019: 50–53).

Conclusion

The economic structure and development pattern of the northeastern states of India observed in the last three decades are not only the outcome of post-colonial policies of the Government of India, but also the colonial era and change in political boundaries of India during independence do have a considerable impact on the changing structure of labour market and economy of northeastern states.

Policies followed in the post-independence period have added macroeconomic imbalances to the region. Most available funds are being taken for payment of salaries to burgeoning government employee and little available for investment in development. The absence of manufacturing and large-scale trading activities has made the multiplier inoperative, and India's Northeast continues to be the net importer of goods and services. The outflow of funds also takes place through the low credit-deposit ratios of bank branches (Nathan, 2005: 2488). Poor intra-state, inter-state, and intra-country connectivity have further crippled the mobility of labour, goods, and services and allowed the size of the economy to remain small and has a direct bearing on the labour market and employment. Also, the continuance of "inner-line permit" has restricted the movement of labour to the Northeast, and as a result, labour market is likely to confront inelasticity of supply over time.

It has been perceived by the Government of India that "Look East" policy will reinvigorate economic growth in Northeast and the region will become an entrepreneurial hub. However, this became elusive in reality. The goods and services produced in Northeast is miniscule in volume and lacks comparative advantage to be part of international trade between India and East and Southeast Asian countries (Chakrabarti, 2018). Transportation cost will abnormally escalate if goods have to be traded from India through Northeast India to Southeast Asia because of the distance and uneven topography and it will prove to be economically unviable. As a result, India's entire trade with this region is still depending on maritime transport. Undoubtedly, the "gateway" can never be an efficient entry point for the exporters located in the hinterland.

Ambitious road, railways and sea networks have been conceived, but to become a reality is also a critical proposition. The rural road network is still abysmal in most of the northeastern states, and they are yet to be connected to the major cities within Northeast as well as with the rest of India. Consequently, most of the areas, other than Assam incur high transportation costs for the internal import of goods and services.

Serious law and order deficiency, rampant corruption, insurgency problems, serious ethnic, linguistic, and religious strife among the heterogeneous tribal groups often act as a deterrent to bringing in investment in the Northeast. Alternatively, forging a durable relationship with Bangladesh and bringing a time-bound solution to the immigration problem and water disputes, the road, railways and water transport system through Bangladesh can become much more cost-effective and beneficial for the development of the economy and create employment opportunities for northeastern states vis-à-vis Bangladesh. As a matter of fact, the bulk of the goods and services can be traded from Calcutta along the coast to Chittagong port in Bangladesh, and thereafter, through Bangladesh railroad, the goods can be brought to Akhaura (around 100 km), adjacent to Agartala, and can be transported to various parts of the northeastern states. This shall substantially reduce the cost of intra-country trade with the northeastern region of India. The revival of riverine traffic between Calcutta and Assam through Sundarban and Bangladesh may be another feasible solution to facilitate trade in the Northeast. It will help the entire sub-region to grow. Oranges and pineapples from Meghalaya, ginger, tea, jute and *muga* silk from Assam may be exported to Bangladesh and from there to West Asia and Europe (Banerjee et al., 1999: 2551). This proposition has strong possibilities to enhance trans-regional and trans-national entrepreneurial activities. Therefore, ancient history provided a Northeast

India, which was much closely integrated with East and Southeast Asia. However, the economic, cultural subjugation got prominent during the colonial period, and post-independent India has failed to break the colonial legacy.

Notes

1 Sikkim became an Indian state in 1975 and was put under "special category state". Prior to that Sikkim was under monarchic rule. In 2003, the state of Sikkim became a part of the North-East Council.

2 According to the 2011 Census the percentage of scheduled tribe population stands at 64.2% for Arunachal Pradesh; 85.2% for Meghalaya; 94.5% for Mizoram; 89.1% for Nagaland; 32.3% for Manipur; 31.1% for Tripura; 20.6% for Sikkim and 12.4% for Assam, respectively. The all-India percentage stands at 8.2%.

3 The Inner Line Regulation, 1873 prescribed that "the local government by notification in Calcutta Gazette may prohibit all British subjects, or any class of British subjects, or any person, sending in or passing through, such districts, from going beyond such line without pass under the hand and seal of the executive officer" who "may authorize to grant such pass and the local government from time to time cancel very such prohibition."

4 There is a lack of unanimity on the issues of the concept and term "Modernity." In most cases, it is identified with anything that is contemporary. The tendency to equate modernity with technology and other contemporary attributes including accepting neoliberal policy as sacrosanct is faulty. Modernity has to be equated and reflected through attitudes (towards "Self" and "Others"). For detailed readings see, Dipankar Gupta (2000). *Mistaken Modernity India Between worlds*. New Delhi: Harper Collins/The India Today Group.

5 The Sixth Schedule of the Indian Constitution makes special provisions for the administration of what were then "The Tribal Areas of Assam." In the colonial period, those areas were mostly protected enclaves, where tribal peoples could supposedly pursue their "Customary Practices" including kinship and clan-based rules of land allocation including kinship and clan. They were called "backward tracts," later replaced by the term "Excluded Areas" because they were excluded from the operation of laws applicable in the rest of British controlled India. The Sixth Schedule provides for autonomous regions within those districts with elected councils with powers to regulate customary law, to administer justice in limited cases and to determine the occupation or use of land and the regulation of shifting cultivation.

6 We used the word "hangover" to make our point that the "Isolationist model" had its overwhelming influence on the policies adopted by the Government of India which at that time frame was synonymous with the personality and leadership of Jawaharlal Nehru. Nehru was much enamoured by Elwin's model and sought to trace the official policy of the government in Verrier Elwin's book *A Philosophy for NEFA* (1959), which speaks in volumes about the Isolationist bent of the policies adopted for the region during that time frame in Indian politics. Xaxa argues that "it is rather intriguing that national policy has to be sought in a book rather than an official government document" (For details see, Xaxa, Virginius. (2005). Politics of Language, Religion, and Identity: Tribes in India. *Economic and Political Weekly*. March 26–April 1, pp. 1363–1370.). However, it would be wrong to say that the Isolationist policies alone influenced the attitude of the Government of India. Especially when keeping in consid-

eration the trends that had developed during that time regarding the nature of the government policy towards the region and the resultant birth of different "Schools of thought" each of which were as strong as the other and each as convincing as the other. The emergence of the two schools namely the "Isolationist" led by Elwin and the "Assimilationist" led by Ghurye and the prolonged "thesis-antithesis" between the two resulted in the emergence of the hybrid "Integrationist" (Elwin and Ghurye) model.

7 In Nehru's words, "the essence of our struggle for freedom was the unleashing of a liberating force in India. This force did not even affect the frontier people of in one of the most important tribal areas. Thus they never experienced a sensation of being in a country called India...their chief experience of outsiders was that of British officers and Christian missionaries who generally tried to make them anti-Indian... All this North-East border area deserves our special attention, not only the government's, but of the people of India. Our contacts with them will do us good and will do them good. They add to the strength, variety and cultural richness of India"(Chandra et.al, op cit 143). With this conviction, Nehru with an able assistance from Verrier Elwin had laid down the following guiding principles for governance and development for the North-Eastern states of India (Elwin, 1959):

i) People should develop along the lines of their own genius and any imposition on the tribal people should be avoided. Their own traditional arts and culture should always be encouraged.
ii) Tribal rights over land and forest should be protected.
iii) Efforts have to be taken to train and build up a team of their own people to do the work of administration and development. Some technical personnel from outside will no doubt be needed, especially in the beginning. But the introduction of too many outsiders into tribal territory should be avoided.
iv) These areas should not be administered areas nor should these areas be overwhelmed with a multiplicity of schemes. Rivalry should be discouraged and the local social and cultural institutions need to be taken into account.
v) Results should be judged not by statistics or by the amount of money spent but by the quality of human character that is evolved.

– Jawaharlal Nehru

Extracted from the Foreword to A Philosophy for NEFA, by Verrier Elwin, 2nd Edition, 1959

8 Assam and Nagaland were accorded special category status in 1969, Manipur, Meghalaya and Tripura in 1972 when they were created, Sikkim in 1975 and Arunachal Pradesh and Mizoram in 1987.

9 Note submitted by the adviser, Financial Resource Division, Planning Commission dated 16.11.2006 to the member (AS) and Deputy Chairman of the Commission. Also stated in Rajya Sabha in response to unstarred Question No 1614 dated 03.12.2009. The criteria as laid down are respectively (i) hilly and difficult terrain; (ii) low population density and/or sizeable share of tribal population; (iii) strategic location along borders with neighbouring countries; (iv) economic and infrastructural backwardness and (v) non-viable nature of state-finances.

10 In 1969, D.R. Gadgil, the then Deputy Chairman, Planning Commission developed the formula for the distribution of Central assistance to states wherein 60% of funds will be transferred based on population; 10% on the basis of per

capita income only to the states below the national average; 10% on the basis of tax effort in relation to per capita income; 10% on account of continuing major irrigation and power schemes and rest 10% on consideration of the special problems of the states.

11 Malaysia, Philippines, Singapore, Thailand, Brunei, Vietnam, Laos, Myanmar, Cambodia, China, Japan, South Korea, India, Australia and New Zealand are the members of East Asian Summit.

12 The agreement on the South Asian Free Trade Area (SAFTA) was signed on 6 January 2004 during the 12th SAARC Summit in Islamabad but it came into effect from 1 January 2006

References

Aggarwal, S. (2015), Do Rural Roads Create Pathways Out of Poverty? Evidence from India. Working Paper, March, Hyderabad, Indian School of Business. Retrieved from, http://www.isb.edu/faculty/shilpa_aggarwal/files/shilpa-aggarwal-rural-roads.pdf.

Allen, B. C. (1979), *Gazetteers of Bengal and North East India*, New Delhi: Mittal Publications.

Banerjee, P., Hazarika, S., Hussain, M., and Samaddar, R. (1999), Indo-Bangladesh Cross-Border Migration and Trade. *Economic and Political Weekly*, *34*(36), 2549–2551.

Barua, Alakesh, and Das, S. K. (2007), The Look East Policy and the Northeast: New Challenges for Development. Conference on 'India's Look East Policy-Challenges for Sub-Regional Cooperation.' Indian Council for Research on International Economic Relation and Omeo Kumar Das Institute of Social Change and Development, Guwahati; 7–9 October.

Barua, Alokesh, and Das, K. Santosh (2008), Perspective on Growth and Development in the Northeast: The Look East Policy and Beyond. *Margin: The Journal of Applied Economic Research*, 2(4), 327–350.

Barua, Alokesh (2005), History, Trade and Development: An Exploration of the North-East Economy. In Alokesh Barua (Ed.), *India's North-East: Development Issues in a Historical Perspective*. A Publication of French Research Institute in India, New Delhi: Manohar.

Bhattacharjee, G. (2014), The Reality of Special Category States. *Economic and Political Weekly*, *XLIX* (40), 48–56.

Bhattacharya, Rakhee. (2011), Look East Policy: Twenty Years After. *FPRC Journal*, *8*, 168–172.

Bhaumik, Subir. (2010), *Troubled Periphery: Crisis of India's North East*, New Delhi: SAGE Publication.

Chakrabarti, Anjan, and Chaudhuri, Rimu (2019), Changing Trajectories of Developmental Policies in Northeast India and a Reality Check o Trans-Regional and Trans-National Entrepreneurial Activities. In Sasi Misra, Sunil Shukla and Ganapathi Bhattani (Ed.), 13th Biennial Conference on Entrepreneurship (Conference papers), Vol.II, Entrepreneurship Development Institute of India, Ahmedabad, Bookwell: New Delhi, 817–830.

Chakrabarti, Anjan. (2018), Changing Trajectories of Global Agenda of Development and Ramifications on Economy, Environment, and Society: Reviewing Developed and Developing Regions with Special Emphasis on India. *International Journal of Sustainability and Development (IJDS), Japan*, 7(1), 269–280.

Chakrabarti, Anjan. (2019), Changing Trajectories of Economic Growth and Employment in Northeast India: An Empirical Assessment in Employment. In Virginius Xaxa, Debdulal Saha and Rajdeep Singha (Ed.), *Employment and Labour Market in Northeast India: Interrogating Structural Changes* (pp. 39–72), UK: Taylor Francis Group, Routledge.

Chakrabarti, Anjan, and Seakhar, Anup. (2010), Emergent Development Approach: A Critique of 'Money-bags' Centre Directed Dole Development in North-East India, *Indian Journal of Political Science*, *LXXI*(2), 547–559.

Chakraborty, Gorky, and Ray, Ashok K. (2014), *The Look East Policy and Northeast India*, New Delhi: Akar

Chandra, Bipan, Mukherjee, Mridula, and Mukherjee, Mukherjee (2008), *India since Independence*, New Delhi: Penguin Books.

Chatterji, Rakhahari, Chaudhury, Basu Ray Anusua, and Basu, Pratnashree. (2015), India-Bangladesh Connectivity: Possibilities and Challenges. Kolkata: Observer Research Foundation, Retrieved from, http://www.orfonline.org/research/india-bangladesh-connectivity/.

Chaube, S. K. (1985), *Electoral Politics in Northeast India*, Madras: Universities Press.

Chaube, S. K. (1999), *Hill Politics in Northeast India*, Hyderabad: Orient Longman.

Dasgupta, Ranajit (1986), From Peasants and Tribesmen to Plantation Workers Colonial Capitalism, Reproduction of Labour Power and Proletarianisation in North East India, the 1850s to 1947, *Economic and Political Weekly*, *XXI* (4), PE-2 TO PE-10.

De, Prabir, and Singh, P. K. H. (2015), Look East to Act East: Internal Connectivity Challenges to India's Northeast, paper presented at the seminar on Integrating Northeast in India's Act East Policy, New Delhi: Indian Council of World Affairs, 23 February.

Devare, Sudhir T., Lawle, Shivali, Tiwari, Gauri, and Luhach, Swarnakshi (2014), India's Look East Policy Act East Policy: A Bridge to the Asian Neighbourhood, Symbiosis Institute of International Studies, Symbiosis International University, Pune.

Dunbar, George. (1994), *Frontiers*, New Delhi: Osmos Publication.

Dutt, R. C. (1990), *The Economic History of India*, Vol. 2, New Delhi: Low Price Publications.

Elwin, Verrier (1959), *A philosophy for NEFA*, Shillong: North-East Frontier Agency.

Gan, Fuxi (2009), Silk Road and Ancient Chinese Glass' in 'Ancient Glass Research along Silk Roads', (edited.) Robert H Bill, Shouyun Tian, Singapore: World Scientific, p 41. Retrieved from https://http://en.unesco.org/silkroad/countries-alongside-silkroad-routes/republic-korea.

Grare, Freidric, and Matoo, Amitabh. (2003), Introduction. In Freidric Grare and Amitabh Mattoo (Ed.), *Beyond the Rhetoric: The Economics of India's Look East Policy*, New Delhi: Manohar Publishers.

Haokip, T. (2015), *India's Look East Policy and the Northeast*, New Delhi: SAGE India.

Historical Overview: Continuity and Change in the Indian Ocean. Retrieved from https://www.indianoceanhistory.org/assets/Site_18/files/Era%20Overviews/Historical%20Overview060109.pdf.

Hoslang, J. (2010), China's Roads to Influence. *Asian Survey*, *50*(4), 641–662.

Indian Institute of Foreign Trade (IIFT). (1995). Industrial Development and Export Potential of the North-eastern Region, Vol.1, Report Prepared for the Ministry for Commerce, Government of India

Jos, Gommans (2015), The Construction of a Global World, 1400-1800 CE. In Jerry H. Bentley, Sanjay Subrahmanyam, Merry E. Wiesner-Hanks (Ed.), *The Cambridge World History: Volume 6*, UK: Cambridge University Press.

Juergens, Leonora (2014), BCIM and BIMSTEC: Two Competing Initiatives for Northeast India? India-Articles # 4454, 20 May, New Delhi: Peace and Conflict Studies.

Liberman, Victor (2009), *Strange Parallels: Southeast Asia in Global Context, c. 800–1830*, Cambridge: Cambridge University Press.

McCall, A. G. (2003), *Lushai chrysalis*, Aizwal: Tribal Research Institute, p. 65.

Miho Museum News (Shiga, Japan), Vol 23, March 2009 "Eurasian Winds towards Silla",

Naidu, G. V. C. (2004), India and Southeast Asia: Look East Policy. *World Focus*, *25*(9), 7–10.

Nathan, Dev. (2005), Hill Economies of the North-Eastern Region: Emerging Challenges and Opportunities. *Economic and Political Weekly*, *40*(24), 2486–2488.

Rana, Kishen S. and Uberoi, Patricia (2012), *India's Northeast States, the BCIM Forum and Regional Integration*, monograph, No.1, December, New Delhi: Institute of Chinese Studies.

Reid, A. S. (1978), *Chin-Lushai Land*, Calcutta: Firma KLM, p. 16.

Saint-Mezard, Isabelle (2003), The Look East Policy: An Economic Perspective. In Freidric Grare and Amitabh Mattoo (Eds.), *Beyond the Rhetoric: The Economics of India's Look East Policy*, New Delhi: Manohar Publishers.

Samaddar, Ranabir (ed.) (2004), *The Politics of Dialogue: Living Under the Geopolitical Histories of War and Peace*, Aldershot: Ashgate.

Shepherd, Ben, Rerafica, B. Ramonette, Bay-haqi, Akhmad, and Jing, Hao (2011), The Trade Impact of Enhanced Multimodal Connectivity in the Asia Pacific Region. *Journal of Economic Integration*, *26*(4), 624–650.

Singh, Chandrika. (2004), *North-East India*, New Delhi: Manas Publications, pp. 53–78.

Srikanth, H. (2016), Look East Policy, Subregional Connectivity Projects and North East India. *Economic and Political Weekly*, *L1*(47), 45–51.

Ulric, Killon (2006), *A Modern Chinese Journey to the West Economic Globalisation and Dualism*, USA: Nova Science Publishers, p. 66.

UNESCAP (2003), Asian Highway Handbook, 22 December, United Nations Economic and Social Commission for Asia and the Pacific, New York, Retrieved

December 11, 2017, from http://www.unescap.org/resources/asian-highway-handbook.
Verghese, B. G. (2004), *India's Northeast Resurgent: Ethnicity, Insurgency, Governance, Development*, New Delhi: Konark Publishers.
Woodthorpe, R. G. (1980), *The Lushai Expedition, 1871–1872*, Gauhati: Spectrum Publication, p. 37.
Yang, Bing. (2008), *Between Winds and Clouds: The Making of Yunnan*, New York: Columbia University Press.

Chapter 5

A Multisited ethnography of land management in the context of the development policy in West Bengal

Abhijit Guha[1]

Prologue

Anthropologists still seem to be preoccupied with the endangerment of tribal populations, particularly hunter-gatherers and pastoralists in Asia, Africa and Latin America. Till today, fewer anthropologists have paid attention to the marginalisation of the peasantry by forces unleashed by technology and globalisation. In third world countries, globalisation is also a mocking combination of technological advancement and colonial laws (Guha, 2004, pp. 4620–4623).[2]

In India, the colonial Land Acquisition Act of 1894 used to be employed to acquire private land for the installation of various development projects and this law had provision for monetary compensation only. In West Bengal during the wake of the New Economic Policy adopted by the Central Government, the pro-peasant Left Front Government (LFG), which began its career through the distribution of land to the landless and recording of the rights of the sharecroppers, gradually becamemore interested in acquiring land (including agricultural land) for big industrial projects by the application of the colonial Land Acquisition Act. During this period the LFG did not show much interest to protect small peasants affected by the acquisition by adopting a pro-peasant rehabilitation policy. The typical Leninist slogan "Land to the tillers" was transformed by the Bengal communists to "Agriculture is our foundation and the future lies with industry" (Communist Party of India (Marxist), 2007).

Under this broad background I have constructed my ethnography mainly in a self-reflexive fashion in different sites and that is why I call it a multisite ethnography. I have used the term ethnography not in the usual anthropological sense of the term, as the holistic description of a culture but as a description of my own interaction with land acquisition in a particular state of India in various locations, like affected villages, government offices, assembly archives, committee room of the Parliament house and various public places outside the villages where I conducted the fieldwork over a long period of time. Following recent anthropological orientation this may

DOI: 10.4324/9781003159940-5

be called a multisite ethnography of governmental land grab or acquisition in the nameof development (Marcus, 1995, pp. 95–117; Gellner, 2012, pp. 1–16; Auyero, 2004, pp. 417–441; Burawoy, 2013, pp. 526–536).

Site I: In the university or how I became engaged in studying land grab?

During the mid-1990s three students of the Department of Anthropology at Vidyasagar University[3] was carryingon their fieldwork forM.Sc. dissertations in a village named Paschim Amba, only eight kilometres from the Midnapore railway station. They selected a hamlet inhabited by the Koras[4] and started measuring human bodies and collected data on family, marriage and kinship following the standard anthropological methodology. On one usual afternoon in the department, when we were discussing the colourful Kora marriage ceremony, a student remarked, "The colour and pomp of Kora marriage will soon go away since their lands are being taken over for a big pig iron industry of the Tatas."

The remark of the student had shaken me and on one Sunday morning in 1995, I landed up in Paschim Amba village where I first met a peasant leader named Trilochan Rana(he passed away and had no objection whenever I used his real name in my book and papers) who was then leading a militant movement against the acquisition of agricultural land for private industries by the then LFG.In Trilochan Rana's house I met a good number of peasants hailing from Amba, Mahespur, Kantapal, Gokulpur, Baharapat, Shyamraipur and other villages of the area. Very quickly, they started to narrate quite enthusiastically, the gloomy story of how their lands had been acquired by the governmentfor the industries in the name of development. Trilochan Rana depicted how they were trying to protest against this kind of anti-peasant policy suddenly adopted by the LFG in the wake of liberalisation in India. Ironically, Mr Rana, who was a former Naxalite,[5] took refuge under the Congress party[6] to organise this peasant movement. He asked, "But sir, how coming from a university you can help us in this struggle against land acquisition?" At that moment, I could not give any direct answer to this straightforward and pointed question.

While returning to Medinipur after my first visit in the field, I was thinking of the possible course of my individual action on land acquisition. Should I take up research on this problem?[7]In fact, I had to struggle withthis issue myself for a long time simply because it was not just passing through the railway station in Gokulpur twice a week like the serviceholders commuting from Kolkata to Medinipur did. Anyway, after my maiden visit to the field many events occurred and I went to those villages several times accompanied by the students. During this period, I arrived at two firm decisions. One was to do my PhD dissertation on this problem and the other was to support these dispossessed peasants by writing popular articles on the various adverse effects of land acquisition on the socio-economic life of the enterprising Sadgop cultivators and poor Lodha[8] and Kora families living on both sides of the southeastern railway track between Medinipur and Kharagpur railway stations. Through my participatory fieldwork, gradually, I could develop feedback with the peasants and while collecting data I took an active part in organising a public meeting within Paschim Amba in collaboration with the district unit of a human rights group, the Association for the Protection of Democratic Rights (APDR). This ultimately culminated in a deputation to the District Magistrate on the adverse economic and environmental impacts of land acquisition in this area. But it also became clear that the APDR leaders who were educated Bengali middle-class urbanites were not much interested in championing the rights of the poor sharecroppers and marginalised tribal peasants dispossessed from their major means of production under the New Industrial Policy adopted by the West Bengal Government in 1994.[9]

What I could ultimately sustain was continued research on land acquisition for development projects by combining field and archival materials and dissemination of my research findings in various academic and popular forums. The methodology of my research can hardly be called "purely anthropological" let alone "neutral" since my holistic perspective did not end in the village but moved beyond into the files, notes and gazette notifications at the Land Acquisition Department of the district administration and also to the West Bengal Assembly Proceedings (Guha, 2007a, pp. 58–72).

Site II: Reaching the global

Under the above background, the chief aim of my research was not to engage in a theoretical debate on activist research versus cultural critique as has been done by Charles Hale in one of his articles published in *Cultural Anthropology* (Hale, 2006, pp. 96–120) on the land rights of indigenous peasants in Nicaragua, but to write an ethnography of land expropriation by the state under a pro-peasant communist party-led government in the West Bengal state in India. The point of departure of this ethnographic description however lies in juxtaposing typical anthropological field data with a variety of archival sources and my personal experiences of interaction with the politicians at the highest level of policymaking on the issue of reforming a colonial law, which wasin vogue in India till the enactment of the new law named Right to Fair Compensation and Transparency in Land Acquisition, Rehabilitation and Resettlement Act,2013which was passed on 29 August 2013 in the Lok Sabha and on 4 September 2013 in Rajya Sabha. The Act has provisions to provide fair compensation to those whose land is taken away, brings transparency to the process of acquisition of land to set up factories or buildings, infrastructural projects and assures rehabilitation of those affected for the first time in the history of the country (Ministry of Law and Justice, Government of India, 2013).

Under this context I will now make a brief survey of the global literature on land grab by the governments, which is the second important arena of this multisite ethnography.[10]

Interestingly, in the current literature, the acquisition of farmland by the domestic governments for industries and other non-agricultural uses is not considered under the expression "land grab". Land grab in the literature(including media reports) is used as a blanket phrase to refer to large-scale commercial land transactions between countries involving transnational corporations for the production of food, biofuels and timber (Borras, Jr. and Franco, 2012, pp. 34–59; Murphy, 2013, pp. 3–5). The international funding agencies on the other hand prefer to use the term "compulsory acquisition" (FAO, 2008, pp. 5–17) and "land transfer" (World Bank, 2011, pp. xxv–xlv) in which people are displaced from their major means of production by the state. Without using the term land grab, the UN Special Rapporteur on right to food in his 2009 report, however,emphasised putting in place proper institutional arrangements to ensure land rights, food security, pre-investment impact assessment and transparency for the local populations prior to all kinds of large-scale land acquisitions or land leases by the developing countries which are attracting international business investments under the impact of globalisation (Schutter, 2009, pp. 12–15). An Oxfam discussion paper titled *Sleeping Lions*on international investment treaties and access to food, land and water also used the term "land grab" and pointed out succinctly that in the developing countries natural resources like land and water have "cultural and communitarian significance" that "exceeds their mere use and exchange value"(Oxfam, 2011, p. 5). Apart from the aforementioned macro-level policy-oriented reports, academic attempts to look into the phenomenon of land grab from a global perspective have also started (Schutter, 2011, pp. 249–279).

In a recent introductory article titled "Towards a better understanding of global land grabbing" published in *The Journal of Peasant Studies* (Vol. 38, No. 2 March 2011, pp. 209–216) written by Saturnino M. Borras Jr., et. al., the authors viewed land grab basically as a kind of land deal politics having a global dimension with local and micro-level facets including narratives of peasant resistance, and they did not want to restrict their area of enquiry only to large-scale commercial land transfers between countries (Borras Jr., et. al., 2011, pp. 209–216). In one of the papers presented in an international conference on "Global Land Grabbing" held at the University of Sussex during 6–8 April 2011, an ethnographic description of a Chinese agricultural project in Senegal has been constructed by the author to reveal how the Chinese business investment in using land for agriculture interventions really worked or not-worked in Senegal (Buckley, 2011, pp. 1–36). Under these broader policy and academic orientations, I use the term land grab in this paper to refer to the expropriation of land by the domestic government with the help of the *eminent domain* of the state for the profit-making private companies for non-agricultural uses in the state of West Bengal in India. I now embark on my third site on land grab.

Site III: Facing lawmakers

I was sitting in front of about 20 members of Parliament (MPs) from different parts of the country at the big Parliament Library building, New Delhi, the capital of India on 17 June 2008. I was feeling nervous, although I was invited as an expert to give suggestions towards the reforms to be undertaken on the century-old Land Acquisition Act of India by which the government's power of *eminent domain* is used to be exercised to acquire land for "public purpose" in lieu of monetary compensation given only to the land titleholders. These MPs are all politicians whom I have never studied ethnographically but to whom I addressed recommendations in my articles, and now they were sitting around me to ask difficult questions on the subject. I was facing the very powerful Parliamentary Standing Committee on Rural Development who would prepare a new land acquisition and rehabilitation law for the country. Their draft would be sent to the cabinet of ministers for its placement in the Parliament.

The Deputy Chairman began the discussion by asking me to highlight the major points which I recommended to insert in the proposed bill. I then talked at length trying to convince the MPs about the aspects which were neglected in the bill. I emphasised the recognition of local self-governments while getting the consent of the affected people for land acquisition, protection of food security at the household level and avoidance of agricultural land from the scope of land acquisition for private profit-making industries. The Deputy Chairman with a smiling face reacted by saying that I have raised certain "basic issues and philosophy" behind the Act and there was no dispute on the idea, which Imentioned but the question was, one could not avoid land expropriation since private companies were already purchasing huge chunks of land in the rural areas of the country. Then the Deputy Chairman (politically, he belonged to one of the communist parties of India) tilted his head towards me and asked about my opinion on the role of the government in the whole affair. I smelt the rat. It was clear to me that the standing committee may not be interested in increasing the role of local governments, household-level food security and all other local issues which I had been observing as a field anthropologist in cases of acquisition of huge chunks of fertile farmland in Medinipur villages where the farmers did not agree to sell their land to the big industrialists. In the rest of my discussion with the members of the standing committee, I kept on emphasising putting the people first through local governments, and it appearedthat the point was not viewed seriously by the elected members of the Parliament, although they advised me quite politely to send the suggestionsin writing. There ended my encounter with the policymakers. I will now go back to the story of my engagement with the actual scenario of land grab by the government which I observed and also described ethnographically with active participation in my research and popular articles since 1995. Let me now move on to the villages – my fourth site.

Site IV: Peasant resistance in Medinipur villages: A decade before Singur and Nandigram

The protests launched by the landowning farmers of Gokulpur and Amba (two of my study villages) against land acquisition took many forms, even though these did not last for a long period as it happened recently in Singur in the Hooghly district of West Bengal. (Guha, 2007b) Several peasants took up the statutorily available means/instruments to put up their objections against land acquisition under section 5A of the Land Acquisition Act during December 1995. An unpublished report of the Land Acquisition Department of erstwhile Midnapore district dated 21 June 1996 vividly recorded the objections and described in detail how the latter were overruled by the District Magistrate and Collector.

The objections submitted by 342 land losers contained the following points: (i) The acquisition of agricultural land would affect the farmers seriously by throwing them out of employment, (ii) the land losers will not get compensation at the rate they expect and (iii) the proposed acquisition is against public interest and is beyond the purview of the Act. It is interesting to observe how the concerned officials of the Land Acquisition Department overruled all the objections raised by the farmers. Before rejecting the objections, the officials, however, recognised the severity and magnitude of the acquisition. I quote from the report.

> It is a fact that since large quantum of land is being acquired and the people chiefly subsist on agriculture many people will be seriously affected in earning their livelihood and avocation.
>
> (Departmental Report, 1996, p.1)

But this was the only sentence in the whole report which upheld the interests of the peasants. The rest of the three-page report was devoted to justify the acquisition through the elaboration of some arguments. The arguments of the officials centred around the low agricultural yield of the lands which are monocrop in nature. Moreover, the report also mentioned the merits of the location of the land, which provided important infrastructure facilities for the industry like nearby railway line and the national highway. It is learnt from the report that during the hearing of the objections the petitioners could not “specify their individual difficulty in parting with the land" although the same report said that "most of the objectors submitted that they have no objection if employment is assured to them, in the company in favour of whom acquisition is being done." It is not clear from the report why the authors of the same could not understand the nature of "individual difficulty" in parting with the land which is their main source of livelihood. Three points raised in the report are quite significant and shows the insensitive way of dealing with such an action on the part of the Government which was going to have a severe impact on the subsistence pattern of a group of rural cultivators in a monocrop region. First, at one place the report mentioned: "It is worthwhile to point out that objections have been received only from 342 landowners for the acquisition of 526.71 acre[s] which will affect at least 3000 landowners, if not more." It seems the official position rested on the logic that as the overwhelming majority of farmers would not face any difficulty (at least there was no record of objection under the Land Acquisition Act) so there was no need to record any objection against this acquisition. Second, after citing the locational advantages of the land, the officials overruled objections regarding the question of earning a livelihood by saying that the proposal had been approved both by the screening committee and by the state after considering all aspects. Incidentally, the screening committee for the approval of any project comprises the *Sabhadhipati*(Chairman) of the Panchayat Samiti (the second tier of the statutory local self-government) and the Member of the Legislative Assembly (MLA) of the locality. It was obvious at that time that these people's representatives who were members of political parties of the LFG would not object to a proposal which had already been approved by the cabinet and the concerned ministries of their own government. The temporal order of consultation and approvals appear important. Third, the report dealt with the point "job for land" simply by saying that the Land Acquisition Act does not provide any relief except compensation. But the Government may take up the matter with the company particularly for those farmers who would become landless and would be devoid of any source of earning a livelihood.After having overruled all the objections, the procedure for land acquisition made headway.

Besides, recording objections within the legal framework of the Land Acquisition Act, the farmers of this area also took recourse to extra-legal means to fight against the acquisition of their agricultural land which is narrated below. The information on this part of the peasant protest has been collected from interviews of the leaders and participants of this movement as well as from press reports and the various written memoranda submitted by the villagers to the district and state administration. In the following section the succession of the important events of the peasant resistance has been described.

The vast rural area which lies between Medinipur and Kharagpur townships was dominated by the two left political parties of the state, namely, CPI and CPI (M), which are also the major partners of the LFG. The Congress, which was the then opposition party in the state, had some followers in the area. This party being the major supporter of economic liberalisation did not raise any objection when the news of industrialisation in this area came to be known. In fact, Congress welcomed this decision of the LFG. They only raised doubts about whether the industrialists would at all choose West Bengal as a suitable site for industrialisation. In the study area, Tata Metaliks was established on about 200 acres of agricultural land during 1991–1992. Before the establishment of Tata Metaliks the leaders and cadres of CPI (M) and CPI organised meetings and continued individual level campaigns on the bright possibility of getting jobs by the land losers in the industry. But when the Tata Metaliks started production, the promise for providing jobs was proved to be a false one and the peasants also experienced the lengthy as well as tedious process of getting compensation from the district administration. All of these caused sufficient disillusionment among the peasants who were once hopeful about the positive effects of the establishment of an industrial estate in this region. The decision of the state government to acquire agricultural land in the same area for Century Textiles Industries Ltd (CTIL) was taken under this background. The pessimism created among the peasants owing to the establishment of Tata Metaliks inspired some of the inhabitants of this locality to agitate against the acquisition of land for another pig-iron unit. The movement gained popularity under the leadership of Trilochan Rana [a former CPI (ML) leader] during 1995–1996 who joined the trade union wing of the Congress Party and put considerable pressure on the district administration.

Two interesting incidents may be mentioned in this regard which would throw some light on the reasons behind the popularity of this movement among the farmers. The first incident took place in the month of May 1995 when Trilochan Rana organised a good number of peasants to put a deputation to the Tata Metaliks company authorities demanding some compensation for the damage caused by the movement of trucks carrying goods for the company over unacquired agricultural fields (there was no crop in the fields at that time) of those farmers. The trucks damaged the dykes of the fields (*ails*) and the soil. Under the pressure of the peasants the company had to pay compensation in kind to 75 peasant families in presence of the *pradhan* (elected head of the lowest tier, i.e. Gram Panchayat of the statutory local self-government)Kalaikunda GP. Some amount of fertiliser was given to those peasants whose lands were damaged.

In the second incident Trilochan Rana put a deputation to the district administration about the damage caused to the unacquired agricultural fields of some peasants for putting pillars to demarcate acquired lands for Century Textiles Company in Kantapal, Mollachak and other adjoining villages. Those cement pillars were fixed by digging at about 4 sq.ft. of land to a depth of 3–4 ft. and became permanent structures right on the agricultural fields of the peasants whose lands were not acquired. These pillars served as the boundary of the acquired land for CTIL. About 24–25 such pillars were constructed in early 1996. The peasants argued that the cultivation of fields over a much wider area around those pillars was not possible owing to physical obstruction (Guha, 2007a).

The district administration had to agree with this demand of the peasants and arranged for payment of Rs. 420/- per annum (5.62 US Dollar) as monetary compensation to those families affected by the construction of those pillars. This compensation payment continued for two years but with the decline of the movement the administration discontinued even this paltry compensation.

Both these incidents revealed that under the pressure of an intelligent and organised peasant movement the company authority as well as the Land Acquisition Department had arranged compensation for peasant families having no provision under the existing legal and administrative framework.

The movement reached its peak from the later part of 1995 up to April 1996 during which the farmers even resorted to violent means. In the first week of January 1996 hundreds of farmers in the Kalaikunda area stormed into the tent of the engineer who was conducting soil testing and land survey on behalf of Century Textiles Ltd. A leading national daily reported on 10 January 1996.

> Land Survey and soil testing work in Mathurakismat Mouza in the Kalaikunda gram panchayat area of Kharagpur rural police station undertaken by Century Textiles – a Birla group of Industries – had to be abandoned following stiff resistance from villagers last week … The farmers also blocked Sahachak for nine hours yesterday … They also lodged a complaint with the police against the firm.
>
> (*The Statesman*, 10 January1996, p. 6)

On 22 March 1996, the same national daily reported a mass deputation by a group of peasants of the Kharagpur region before the district administration (*The Statesman* 22 March 1996). In this deputation, the peasants demanded land for land or a job for the members of the land loser families. They also demanded a compensation of 3 lakh rupees per acre of agricultural land. After this deputation, about 100 farmers came to the district headquarters at Midnapore town on 10 April 1996 and submitted a memorandum to the District Magistrate declaring that they would boycott the ensuing parliamentary election to protest against the acquisition of fertile agricultural land for industrial projects. The farmers stated in their letter that this acquisition would disturb the local economy and destabilise the environmental balance of the region and this event was also reported in *The Statesman* on

2 May 1996. It is important to note in this connection that neither the state nor district level Congress leadership, nor any MLA of this party showed any interest in supporting this movement of the peasants in the Kharagpur region. The local CPI(M) leadership and the elected panchayat members of this area not only remained silent about this spontaneous movement of the peasants but they also made every attempt to smoothen this agitation by labelling it as a disturbance created by Congress to stall the progress of industrialisation under LFG.Without getting support from any opposition party and facing stiff resistance from the ruling left parties and lacking a coherent organisation, this localised peasant movement against land acquisition gradually lost its intensity. The land losers also made an attempt to organise themselves by refusing to accept compensation money for a very brief period under the leadership of a few local leaders but this effort too did not last long and the movement finally lost steam in the Kalaikunda region. Now I come to the fifth site.

Site V: In the district land acquisition department

The first systematic attempt towards creating a database on land acquisition for different categories of projects had been made by the Land Acquisition Department of the erstwhile Medinipur district in April 1993. The results of this maiden effort have not yet been published, but a typed copy in the form of a report was made available to me. The report which was titled *Land Acquisition Cases of Midnapore: Present Status, Problems, Future Strategy* (1993) was prepared to fulfil two important objectives, viz. (i) to create a database for all the pending cases of the Land Acquisition Department at Medinipur and (ii) to supervise and monitor the calculation of interests for all the pending cases under Act-II in order to reduce Government liabilities. The findings of this Government report presented an "alarming picture" in terms of pending land acquisition cases as well as the Government's financial burden with regard to the interest incurred due to the delay in the payment of compensation after the acquisition. Under the subsection titled "Present Status," the report mentioned quite emphatically "that 293 cases have not at all progressed after handing over of possession to the requiring body (RB)."The Land Acquisition Department had sent estimates for 80% payment but the RBs did not show any interest in the land after taking possession of the same. No action has yet been taken by the land acquistion office for many years. The report categorically stated:

> Action is being taken to send estimates to R.B. as the Govt. liability is mounting. In certain cases where estimates have been sent, there is no response from the R.B. and they express their inability to place fund as it is not included in their respective budget for that year. With the increase in the value of land the liability of the Govt. is increasing in a

> very alarming manner in addition to the deprivation suffered by land-losers due to non-payment.
>
> (*Land Acquisition Cases of Midnapore: Present Status, Problems, Future Strategy, 1993*, p. 1)

It should be noted in this connection that the compensation money has to be deposited by the RB,that is, the department or company which is in need of the land. It may be a Government department (e.g. irrigation or electricity departments) or a private company (e.g. a private hotel or industry) that shall be responsible for placing the fund with the Land Acquisition Department from which payment of compensation would be made. The case of acquisition of land for various Government departments in Medinipur which were pending at the time of the preparation of the aforementioned report showed a huge financial burden on the Government itself.

The report considered another grave aspect of the problem of land acquisition in Medinipur. Under a section titled "Implications" (pp.3–4) it noted that in case of the pending cases where the RBs did not seem to be interested in their finalisation, most of them had actually constructed a building, road or irrigation channel which made it impossible for the land to be returned to the Project Affected Person (PAPs). It is true that there was a provision for de-requisition of land requisitioned under Act-II, but for all practical purposes this rarely happened. To quote from the report again:

> for most of the requisitioned lands the land character has been changed to suit the objective for which the acquisition was made. A completed irrigation project or an industrial estate or a hospital project on a requisitioned land cannot be de-requisitioned.
>
> (*Land Acquisition Cases of Midnapore: Present Status, Problems, Future Strategy, 1993*, p. 3)

The report further observed that even if it is assumed that all the RBs have placed their respective funds with the Collector for making a compensation payment to the PAPs (in the report however this phrase was never used) by 31 March 1994, then also it would not be possible to make a payment of Rs. 26 crores since Medinipur Land Acquisition Department with its existing strength of skilled and specialised staff, working at the normal rate, could make a yearly payment of Rs. 4 crores only. At this rate, the district Collectorate could complete the pending cases within 5–6 years in an ideal situation.

The version of the district administration on the present status of land acquisition in Medinipur district not only revealed its "alarming" and "severe" condition, but it also acted as an "eye-opener" (a phrase used in the report itself) for those in the administration. The report, however, was lacking in certain important aspects of land acquisition which are mentioned below.

1. It only calculated the burden of the Government in monetary terms for making compensation payments under pending Act-II cases. There are no statistics on the total amount of land acquired so far in Medinipur district for any given period or year. There is also no figure on the amount of land acquired under different categories of projects in the district.
2. The report never made any attempt to estimate the number of persons or families who have been affected by land acquisition under the pending Act-II cases in different areas of the district. Except for mentioning the plight of the owners who turned into landlosers in the pending cases, nowhere in the report was found any estimate or statistics about the number of PAPs in Medinipur.
3. It did not also give any list of pending cases of land acquisition for private companies or joint sector business enterprises in the Medinipur district. It only dealt with cases of land acquisition for various Government Departments.

   The Government report on land acquisition prepared by the Medinipur district Collectorate in 1993 meticulously recorded land acquisition in terms of its constraints and shortcomings. Despite its various lacunae, which have been described above, the report revealed how difficult and complicated it was to acquire land for development projects. It also gave an indication about the fact that there was very little hope to arrange for all the compensation payment within five to six years. Under these circumstances, one can not only imagine the kind of harassment caused to the project affected families who have received compensation for the acquisition of their cultivable land, nor have they been allowed to cultivate the land requisitioned by the Government, but lying unutilised.

Huge chunks of fertile agricultural land were selected by the companies and the Cabinet Committee of the West Bengal Government gave approval to this selection. Even a causal trip through this area from Medinipur towards Kharagpur would reveal the presence of a huge tract of undulating lateritic non-agricultural land on the western side of the southeastern railway track lying on the north bank of the *Kasai* river. The landlosers of this area, during our fieldwork repeatedly pointed out that the Government should have acquired the non-agricultural land for the industries instead of taking their agricultural land. When this point was raised before the officers and employees of the Land Acquisition Department of the District Collectorate they simply stated that it was the decision of the Government which the concerned

Department at the district level had to execute. One very experienced and veteran Assistant Land Acquisition Officer once commented to me:

> Well, the screening committee at the district level may turn down a proposal coming from the Writers' Building in Kolkata. But I have seen through my experience that whenever Calcutta wants acquisition Medinipur simply obeys the order. There is hardly any exception.
>
> (Translation by the authorfrom Bengali)

This comment epitomised the power of the *eminent domain* of the state in the case of land acquisition for development projects in a pro-peasant state like West Bengal.

In the context of land acquisition, the recording of the rights of the *bargadars* is very much important since unrecorded *bargadars* are not entitled to get compensation from the Land Acquisition Department. In our study area, an interesting case of a group of unrecorded *bargadars* has been found whose claim for getting compensation against acquisition of land for CTIL was summarily rejected by the department in the middle of 1996.In the following table (Table 5.1) the particulars of the *bargadars* are presented. The data have been collected from the Land Acquisition Department files referred in the earlier section.

A petition bearing memo no. 737/Ban-O-Bhumi dated 23 May 1996 was made by the then *Savapati* of the Kharagpur I Panchyat Samiti to the Special Land Acquisition Officer of the district. In the letter the *Savapati* requested the special land acquisition officer (LAO) to issue compensation notice to 20 unrecorded *bargadars* and 65 pattaholders who have been affected by land acquisition for CTIL. The *Savapati* also alleged the Block Land and Land Reforms Office, which failed to record the names of the *bargadars*. The petition enclosed the individual applications of the affected *bargadars* along with the details (shown in Table 5.1) forwarded by one Ms. Mallicka Mudi, an elected member of the Kharagpur I Panchayat Samiti. All the individual applicants (most of whom were illiterate persons and gave their thumb impressions) stated in their petitions that since they are poor cultivators they could not register their names as recorded *bargadars* so they are not supposed to get compensation for the acquisition of the land in which they cultivate as sharecroppers. The hapless applicants, therefore, requested their elected Panchayat Samiti *Savapati* to enter their names as recorded *bargadars* after proper enquiry and make arrangements for getting land acquisition compensation. Within seven days of the submission of the said petition, The special LAO wrote a letter (memo no. 730/LA dated 3.6.96) to the *Savapati* of the Panchayat Samiti. In that letter the LAO categorically stated that compensation to unrecorded *bargadars* could not be awarded under the Land Acquisition Act and the Land Acquisition Office has already obtained

Table 5.1 The details of the unrecorded *bargadars* under land acquisition for Century Textiles and Industries Limited

Sl. No.	*Name of the bargadar*	*Name of the landowner*	*Name of the Mouza & J.L. No.*	*Amount of land (in acres)*	*Remarks*
1	Mahendra Nayek	Gouri Sarkar	Niranjanbar(154)	.0055	
2	Sushen Nayek	Do	Chaksonadhar(136)	.0122	
3	Srimat Hembram	Sambhu Ganguly	Sujatpur(139)	.02	*Bargadar* belongs to the Santal Scheduled Tribe
4	Bangu Mandi	Badal Chandra Pramanik	Niranjanbar(154)	.0062	ST, Santal
5	Sukumar Patra	N A	Malancha(131)	.0105	
6	Gostha Paloi	Gouri Sarkar	Sujatpur(139)	.0071	
7	Dukha Nayek	Aloka Sen & three others	Malancha(131)	.01	
8	Mohan Nayek	Rekha Ghosh & 2 others	Rajpura(130)	.015	
9	Parameswar Nayek	Do	Do	.025	
10	Ghontu Nayek	Do	Do	.0085	
11	Bangu Mandi	Raghu Kairi	Kantageri(92)	.0176	Santal, ST
12	Bangu Mandi	Raghu Kairi	Niranjanbar(154)	.0084	
13	Sukhendu Bishal	Asoke Sen & other	Chaksonadhar(136)	0.61 & .0061	
14	Mrigen Rana	Asoke Sen & 2 others	Malancha(131)	.005	
15	Krishna Nayek	Santi Mitra & 2 others	Rajpura(130)	.017	
16	Kalipada Chalak	Santi Mitra & 2 others	Rajpura(138)	.0103	
17	Indra Kotal	Rabindra Chakraborty & Soumen Chakraborty	Malancha(131)	.0084	
18	Mahendra Nayek	Biswanath Bhattacharya	Malancha(131)	.0315	
19	Bhonda Nayek	NA	Rajpura(130)	.023	
20	SrinathMudi Laxman Mudi Chunaram Mudi	Anadi Pal & 5 others	Niranjanbar(154)	.025	*Bargadar* belongs to the Kora tribe which is classed as ST

NA: Not available. Source: Author's own.

a report from the concerned Block Land and Land Reforms Office containing an exhaustive list of *bargadars*. The LAO further stated that under the circumstances, no further claim of compensation in respect of *bargadars* could be legally entertained. So, the matter ended at this stage. Interestingly, when the author of this chapter was shown this letter of the *Savapati* to the LAO and a group of officials in the Land Acquisition Department and raised the issue of the non-payment of compensation to unrecorded *bargadars* one officer instantly commented:

> I agree that the BLRO failed to record the names of those bargadars as alleged by the Savapati. But could the elected Panchayat evade its own responsibility in motivating the bargadars to record their names? What the Panchayat have been doing in that area?

The spontaneous reaction of one LAOepitomised the recent ground realities of the rural areas of West Bengal regarding the declining pace in recording the names of *bargadars*, which has been perceptively observed in Mukarji & Bandopadhyay as well as *West Bengal Human Development Report.*My case study shows the endangerment of the unrecorded *bargadars* in the face of a state-sponsored eviction of *bargadars* under the LFG in West Bengal. But where from this endangerment to land reforms generated? Part of the answer to this question may be found at the sixth site of my ethnographic description.

Site VI: West Bengal assembly proceedings or the cyclic ritual of quarrel

Since independence, besides the colonial Land Acquisition Act of 1894, there existed another State Act titled West Bengal Land (Requisition and Acquisition) Act, 1948. The latter Act is no more applicable in West Bengal since 31 March 1993 by a decision of the West Bengal Legislative Assembly. In fact, when this particular piece of legislation was first enacted in the State Assembly it was stipulated that the Act has to be renewed in the Assembly by a majority decision every five years since this is a very powerful and coercive law. The Government opinion was that the state of West Bengal, which had to receive millions of refugees from erstwhile East Pakistan just after independence, needed a huge amount of land for various developmental purposes. For this reason, the Government was in need of an Act, which was more powerful than the colonial Act in acquiring land from the private owners. By West Bengal Land (Requisition and Acquisition) Act the Government could first requisition a particular piece of land for which the payment of compensation may not be made before acquisition while in the earlier Land Acquisition Act of 1894 the Government could not take possession of any land without payment of compensation.

From the records kept in the Assembly Library it has been found that the Act was placed 17 times in the house and got the assent of the president well within a period of two months. Another important fact in this regard is that voting on the amendment of the Act had taken place only twice – once when the Congress party was in power (on 20 February 1973) and at another time when the left parties were in the Government (on 28 March 1967). On both occasions, the parties which were in power won by a majority vote (West Bengal Assembly Proceedings, (54), 1973 and (44), 1967).

The year 1967

The minister in charge of the Land and Land Revenue Department, Mr. Harekrishna Konar of the CPI(M) placed the West Bengal Land Requisition and Acquisition Amendment Bill for extending its tenure in the 44th session of the Assembly on 28 March 1967. During the debate, Mr. Siddhartha Sankar Roy of the Congress Party who became Chief Minister of West Bengal later strongly opposed the bill on legal grounds by saying that in many cases regarding land acquisition in West Bengal the High Court had passed judgements against this Act. He used a Bengali word in a sentence in English to give an added emphasis. To quote Mr. Roy: "This Act is an oppressive and *jabardast* (Bengali word meaning 'overbearing') piece of legislation." He also pointed out the arbitrary nature of the phrase "public purpose" in the Land Acquisition Act. After the speech of Mr. Roy noise and shouting among the members supporting and opposing the bill started and ultimately voting had to be organised by the Speaker. The bill was passed by a majority vote with 131 members voting in favour of the amendment and 72 members against it (West Bengal Assembly Proceedings, (44), 1967).

The year 1970

The Minister Mr. Harekrishna Konar of the CPI(M) introduced the bill for the extension of Act-II and frankly admitted that he had nothing to say about it. He only stated that this Act is necessary for quicker work. No debate took place and the bill was passed in the 50th session of the State Assembly on 29 January 1970 when the United Front Government dominated by the left political parties was still in power for the second time in West Bengal (West Bengal Assembly Proceedings, (50), 1970).

An exception to the rule

A lengthy question–answer session was found to take place in the Assembly on 21 August 1963 regarding the acquisition of cultivable land for the construction of Haldia port in the erstwhile Medinipur district (admitted question No. 1050). The questions and their replies revealed that about 955 acres of fertile agricultural land had been acquired by Land Acquisition Act, 1894, but it remained unutilised at the time when questions were raised in the Assembly. In course of the questioning by a number of members belonging to the ruling and opposition parties (e.g. Sushil Kumar Dhara of the Congress party and Birendra Narayan Roy (independently supported by CPI), it was revealed that some of the farmers had started to cultivate paddy in their acquired lands and the elected members were trying to elicit some statement from the minister in favour of these farmers. The minister, however, tried to evade making any kind of commitment on this particular issue and passed on the responsibility to the port authority for whom the said land was acquired. He, however, admitted that the Government would not have any objection if the farmers could make an unofficial arrangement with the port authority for the cultivation of acquired land where no construction work had yet been started. The minister finally assured the House by saying that priority would be given to provide jobs to the persons whose lands had been acquired for the port (West Bengal Assembly Proceedings,(36),1963).

The West Bengal assembly proceedings with the golden exception just narrated revealed how clever dialogues by the politicianscontinued over the years in a state which earned its name as one of the most politicallyconscious states of India (Guha, 2015, pp. 15–29).

Site VII: The old man of Kantapal and his bullocks

I started with a description of how the MPs in India looked at the problem of land expropriation and found how in the opinion of policymakers land grab was viewed as inevitable under the market forces. In the rest of my description, I narrated how as an anthropologist I became involved in the ethnography of land grab and the protests and bargains of the peasants around it at Medinipur through my fieldwork in the village and also by delving into the archives of the government. I also noticed that the peasants did not give up their land without protest. They put up viable resistances, made bargains with the state and finally surrendered to the state power. I will end my story with an anecdote from my field, which made a nice contrast with what the MPs at New Delhi implicitly communicated to me.

The event occurred near Kantapal village from where the huge chunk of land acquired for Century Textiles could be seen. The author was engaged in a discussion with the locals about the condition of the small dykes (*ail* in the local parlance) raised by the farmers to demarcate the plots of land possessed by different owners within the acquired area. Since no cultivation could be taken up for three successive seasons in the whole area it had turned into a grazing field and the dykes had started to break down. Two consequences of this situation followed. First, farmers who still had unacquired land in the vicinity of the acquired area were facing difficulties in protecting their agricultural plots from grazing cattle. Earlier there were other farmers who also shared the responsibility of driving out the cattle from the fields during the agricultural season. Driving out the intruding cattle in paddy fields is always a collective affair in rural areas. After the acquisition, the numbers of farmers have decreased in this area. Moreover, cows and buffaloes of the milkmen of the urban areas of Kharagpur town have also ventured to exploit this huge chunk of land.

Second, after the breakdown of dykes the poorer people of the area who used to collect a good quantity of small fishes of various types from those agricultural plots as a common property resource, are not getting any fish in those plots. In the discussion three to four persons including one middle-aged woman and an old man were present. All of them were denouncing the Government for the takeover of the fertile agricultural land for Century Company which had not yet been established. When the question arose that if people of this area had started to dislike the ruling party and the Government, then why did they cast their votes at the panchayat and assembly elections to the same party every year? The reply came from the old man which is reproduced here verbatim.

> Look babu,[11] we poor people always have to ride on some animal almost blindfolded. After the ride for some time we start to realize whether it is a tiger or a bullock. But very often we have to twist its tail in order to keep it in the proper direction.
>
> (Translated by the author from Bengali)

All of us including the old man burst into laughter but soon we realised that the joke symbolised the gap between the aspiration of the helpless local peasants in West Bengal and the *distant* policymakers at New Delhi.

Conclusion

In this chapter, I have made an attempt to construct a multisite ethnography of land acquisition by the government for private profit-making companies in *Paschim* (west) Medinipur district of West Bengal under the pro-peasant leftist government. The text of the article is written in a reflexive personal narrative form in which I travelled in time and space juxtaposing my direct fieldwork experiences and encounters around land acquisition with archival data collected from the land acquisition files in the department and the West Bengal assembly proceedings. The study revealed a clear mismatch in the behaviour pattern between the actual cultivators of land and the policymakers and executers of land acquisition operating under the market forces unleashed by the new economic order. The transition from a land-based rural economy towards an industrial regime was not found to be a smooth journey which was characterised by protest, resistance and bargains by the peasants as well as failures on the part of the government and the company despite official claims of industrial development and employment during the transition(Guha, 2017).

Under this background instead of summing up from the preceding sections, I will rather take asojourn in my multisite ethnographic journey and make an assessment of West Bengal in the light of the latest events around its land acquisition scenario.

West Bengal is an unusual, indeed unique state in India. It is the only one of the states inthe country, which has been ruled continuously (since 1977) by a communist party-led LFG for more than a quarter of a century. This government in turn was motivated by a vision of political, economic and social change that had been different from that observed among most other state governments and central government in the country.

A future political or economic historian of West Bengal looking into the genesis of the fall of the communist party-led LFG in West Bengal may be surprised by the absence of any substantial empirical research on the impacts of land acquisition in the state, let alone from a policy perspectiveunder the regime of the LFG. Our hypothetical historian would be further surprised by the fact that quite a good number of Marxist and non-Marxist historians, political scientists and economists of international repute were doing or had done important researches on subaltern movements and consciousness during the period when the left government was making a somersault by pushing back its programmes on land reform and switching over to land acquisition virtually without any comprehensive rehabilitation and resettlement policy. It was the time when the Leninist slogan "Land to the tillers" was being transformed by the Bengal Marxist leaders to "Agriculture is our foundation and industry is our future," and it was also the time when the subaltern scholars were observing their academic silence on land grab and peasant resistance against expropriation of farmland by the state. By maintaining a crucial distance from the present, the Marxists, subalterns and the non-Marxist scholars during the long rule of the left in West Bengal have left a blank archive for the future historians, which in reality was full of sabotage, clever dialogues at the corridors of policymaking, despondency as well as weakly organised spontaneous peasant movements at the grassroots against the exercise of the power of the *eminent domain* of the state until public dissatisfaction culminated by peasant resistances in Singur and Nandigram against governmental land grab that led to the fall of the left government.

Since I began my research on development caused forced displacement with a special emphasis on land acquisition in a particular locale, I also tried to collect public opinion outside my field area. I talked with people from other places who were not affected by land acquisition. For example, I talked, listened and debated with my colleagues, friends, relatives and strangers on the streets and public transport systems on the justification of land acquisition. The people with whom I talked were mostly middle class educated women and men of Bengal. I found most of them had very little idea about the adverse consequences of land acquisition, let alone the intricacies and delay towards the payment of compensation to the land losers. Moreover, whenever land acquisition for industrialisation took place most of the urban and educated women and men were found to hold the view that industrialisation, after all, was the sign of progress that would create employment for the staggering number of unemployed youth of Bengal. For many people, Bengal's declining economic growth was due to the lack of industrialisation. I found very few people who also praised the success of Bengal in agricultural production. Even when somebody showed hopes for agriculture they talked in terms of high yielding varieties of seeds and chemical fertilisers. The educated middle-class Bengali mind was preoccupied with an image of high technology and growth-oriented development whether it was industrial or agricultural. For the typical ordinary educated urban middle-class citizens, West Bengal needed large industries and since industries could not be established without acquiring land, the impact of industrialisation in terms of displacement was not viewed as a major problem.[12]

The scenario, however, changed after the massive resistance of the peasants against land acquisition in Singur and Nandigram during 2006–2007. During this short period a large number of articles, interviews, opinions, debates and news items were published (and it continued) in the newspapers and journals on the development that caused forced displacement in West Bengal. Economists (including the Noble Laureate Amartya Sen), journalists, social activists (like MedhaPatkar) and politicians began to write and talk vociferously on the justification of land takeoverfor private industries in West Bengal.

With Singur and Nandigram, development caused forced displacement and resettlement in thecommunist-ruled West Bengal state of India that became a national and international agenda for debate and discussion. Here, in line with the major objective of this book, I have made an attemptto situate the case of a local land grab by the West Bengal government within a wider national and global context.Vertical ethnographic description from the local field-level scenario up through the several sites (administrative departments, West Bengal assemblyproceedings and Parliamentary Standing Committee) helped me to understand the mechanisms of the failures of a leftist government, which finally led to a stalemate in the path towards capitalist transition at least a decade before the Singur episode. The detailed description of how the governmental bureaucracy functioned to acquire land for the industrialists with a strong policy back-up on the one hand and the daily events around the visceral resistance put up by the land-losing peasants who did not want to become "willing sellers" on the other, revealed the contradictions towards the capitalist path of development and here lay the real value of this ethnographic journey.Multisite ethnography not only helped me to describe land acquisition in some villages of erstwhile Medinipur district but it also became a tool for me to situate local events in the wider context. The outcome of the aforementioned contradiction was asdevastating as a natural disaster since it not only pauperised the peasants without employment either in the industry or rehabilitation in agriculture but also distanced the policymakers from the peasants. The failure of the land acquisition could neither generate a labour force freed from agriculture, (an industrial proletariat) nor created enthusiasm and hope for the capitalist investors. The Bengal leftist government's neo-Marxist theory of riding on the shoulders of land reform to achieve a successful capital-intensive industrialisation finally proved to be a self-defeating exercise since the *praxis* sabotaged both past land reform and future industrialisation. Generating capital and employment either through legal means or by the play of market forces seemed to be mere political rhetoric of the left political parties for contesting election battles in West Bengal. This is the macro-theoretical lesson I learnt from this multisite ethnographic account of land acquisition for development under globalliberalisation.

Notes

1 Acknowledgements: I owe my debts to the sufferers of land acquisition who helped me all through my encounters in the villagers in Paschim Medinipur. I am also grateful to the district administration of erstwhile Medinipur and the library staff at the West Bengal Assembly, Kolkata for providing me the documents, files, letters, notices and proceedings which formed the archival source of my ethnography. I am grateful to the members of the Parliamentary Standing Committee and the secretarial staff of the Lok Sabha for their kind invitation and patient hearing of my arguments during the meeting on the proposed bills on land acquisition in 2007. I express my sincerest thanks to Dr. Ratna Dhar,my Ph.D. student and then head of office and her staff at the Central Regional Office of the Anthropological Survey of India, Nagpur for the invitation and travel support for me to present a shorter version of this paper in the Diamond Jubilee Seminar on *Agrarian Situation in India. Issues and Prospects* organised by the Anthropological Survey of India, Central Regional Centre, Nagpur held during 22November–24 November 2016. I owe my debts to my students at Vidyasagar University for inspiring me to undertake this challenging research on land acquisition in West Bengal.I remain indebted to Suman Nath and Debraj Bhattacharya, the editors of this book for inviting me to write this chapter and also for the critical observations and comments on my initial submission. Last but not the least, I owe my debts to my wife and sons for their moral support to spend my time on land acquisition.

2 Since the independence of India, besides the colonial Land Acquisition Act of 1894, there existed another Act in West Bengal titled West Bengal Land (Requisition and Acquisition) Act, 1948. In the land acquisition department of the government this law was known as Act-II, while the colonial law was termed as Act-I. The former Act is no longer applicable in West Bengal since 31 March 1993 by a decision of the West Bengal Legislative Assembly. In fact, when this particular piece of legislation was first enacted in the State Assembly, it was stipulated that the Act had to be renewed in the Assembly by a majority decision every five years since this was a very powerful and coercive law. The

government opinion was that the State of West Bengal, which had to receive millions of refugees from erstwhile East Pakistan just after independence, needed a huge amount of land for various developmental purposes. By the West Bengal Land (Requisition and Acquisition) Act the Government could first requisition a particular piece of land for which the payment of compensation may not be made before the land takeover, while in the earlier Land Acquisition Act of 1894 the government could not take possession of any land without payment of compensation. In terms of political composition, both Congress and Left-ruled Governments, who were in power, continuously renewed the Requisition and Acquisition Act of 1948 in the State Assembly and applied it to acquire land for "public purposes" not only for the rehabilitation of refugees coming to West Bengal but also for other purposes, like the establishment of industries owned by private companies (Guha, 2011, pp. 79–98).

3 Vidyasagar University is one of the small rural universities of West Bengal state of India which was established in the early 80s with the mission of conducting interdisciplinary research which would cater to the needs of the underprivileged people of the rural areas, particularly of the district of erstwhile Midnapore where it was located.

4 Kora is small tribal community in West Bengal who are found to be engaged in agricultural occupations in the rural areas of the state. (Mitra, 1951).

5 Naxalite movement was a peasant uprising against the oppression of big landlords which arose in West Bengal in the late sixties. The Naxalites believed in the ideology of Mao-tse-Tung and the Chinese Communist Party.

6 The largest anti-communist and centrist political party of India which is now in opposition.

7 When I was planning to embark on my research on land acquisition one senior anthropologist gave me a friendly warning regarding the risks of undertaking such a study on land acquisition.

8 Lodha is a small and socio-economically marginalised tribal community of West Bengal, Jharkhand and Orissa states of India. In some places they are also known as *Sabars* (Mitra, 1951).

9 The LFG of West Bengal published its New Industrial Policy in a book titled *Policy Statement on Industrial Development* which was published on September 23, 1994. In this book the first official statement on the relation between land reforms and industrialisation was made. Under a subhead "Approach of the Left Front Government" it was argued that owing to successful implementation of land reforms and other pro-peasant policies agricultural production in the state had increased along with a corresponding increase in the"purchasing power of the vast majority of common people in the rural areas"(pp. 3–4). The policy paper further stated,"This has created a new market for consumption of industrial products in West Bengal" (p.4) (Govt.of West Bengal, 1994).

10 In a recent paper, I have extended this multisite ethnography in the domain of public opinion around land acquisition (Guha, 2014, pp. 205–228).

11 The word "Babu" or "Baboo" in Bengali is used to address a male person as a gentleman. Its closest English equivalent is Mr.

12 One of the leading academicians of the LFG in West Bengal, Late Professor Biplab Dasgupta (1938–2005) who was the former Vice-Chairman of the Comprehensive Area Development Programme of the Govt. of West Bengal and also a Member of the Parliament(Rajya Sabha) from CPI(M) in an exchange with the author of this article commented: "Problems arising out of the displacement of the tribal population for industrial activities are still quite minor and unimportant taking the state as a whole, and comparing West Bengal with other states, and they affect both tribals and non-tribal equally" (Dasgupta,

2000). The West Bengal Human Development Report which was published in 2004 by the Development and Planning Department of the Government of West Bengal does not contain any chapter or even a section on development caused displacement in West Bengal. Only in chapter I on "Environmental Issues" it has been mentioned: "There has been an appreciable decline in barren and uncultivable land by 41 per cent, which can be explained mainly by the increase of 20 per cent in the area under non-agricultural uses, essentially a transfer of land in favour of urbanisation industrialisation, mining, infrastructural growth (WBHDR, 2004).

References

Auyero, J. (2004). When everyday life, routine politics, and protest meet. *Theory and Society*, *33*(3–4), 417–441.

Borras, Jr.,M.S., and Franco, J.C. (2012). Global land grabbing and trajectories of agrarian change: a preliminary analysis. *Journal of Agrarian Change*, *12*(1), 34–59.

Borras, Jr.,M.S., Hall, Ruth, Scoones, Ian, White, Ben, and Wolford, Wendy (2011). Towards a better understanding of global land grabbing. *Journal of Peasant Studies*, *38*(2), 209–216.

Buckley, L. (2011). Eating bitter to taste sweet: an ethnographic sketch of a Chinese agriculture project in Senegal. Paper presented at the International Conference on 'Global Land Grabbing' organized by the Land Deals Politics Initiative (LDPI) in collaboration with The Journal of Peasant Studies at the Institute of Development Studies, University of Sussex held during 6–8 April 2011.Retrieved from http://citeseerx.ist.psu.edu/viewdoc/download?doi=10.1.1.644.568&rep=rep1&type=pdf.

Burawoy, M. (2013). Ethnographic fallacies: reflections on labour studies in the era of market fundamentalism. *Work, Employment and Society*, *27*(3), 526–536.

Communist Party of India (2007). Thirty years of West Bengal left front govt. Retrieved from http://cpim.org/content/thirty-years-west-bengal-left-front-govt/.

Dasgupta, B.2000. Reply to Abhijit Guha's comment on Biplab Dasgupta's article India's tribal population. *Journal of the Indian Anthropological Society*, *35*(1), 90–92.

Departmental Report. Unpaginated (1996). *Report of the District Land Acquisition Department*. (Unpublished) Midnapore.

Food and Agriculture Organization (FAO) (2008). *Compulsory acquisition of land and compensation. (FAO Land Tenure Series 10)*. Rome: Food and Agriculture Organization of the United Nations.

Gellner, D.N. (2012). Uncomfortable antinomies: Going beyond methodological nationalism in social and cultural anthropology. AAS working papers in social anthropology, 24, 1–16. Austrian Academy of Sciences.

Government of West Bengal (1994). *Policy Statement on Industrial Development*. Calcutta: Government of West Bengal.

Guha, A. (2004). Land acquisition in a West Bengal district. *Economic and Political Weekly*, *39*(42), 4620–4623.

Guha, A. (2007a). *Land, Law and the Left: The Saga of Disempowerment of the Peasantry in the Era of Globalization*. New Delhi: Concept Publishing Company.

Guha, A. (2007b). Peasant resistance in West Bengal: A decade before Singur and Nandigram. *Economic and Political Weekly*, *42*(37), 3706–3711.

Guha, A. (2011). Challenges to corporate social responsibility: a case study from Kharagpur, West Bengal. *Sociological Bulletin*, *60*(1), 79–98.

Guha, A. (2014). Generating public consciousness around land acquisition for private industries. *Social Change*, *44*(2), 205–228. DOI: 10.1177/0049085714525499.

Guha, A. (2015). Acting cleverly in the comfort zone of power and visceral resistance: A case of land acquisition in West Bengal, India. *Indian Anthropologist*, *45*(1), 15–29.

Guha, A. (2017). An ethnographer's journey through land grab for the capitalists in West Bengal by the left front government. In P. D'Costa and Achin Chakraborty (Eds.), *The Land Question in India: State, Dispossession, and Capitalist Transition*. London: Oxford.

Hale, C.R. (2006). Activist research v. cultural critique: indigenous land right and the contradictions of politically engaged anthropology. *Cultural Anthropology*, *21*(1), 96–120.

Marcus, G.E. (1995). Ethnography in/of the world system: The emergence of multisited ethnography. *Annual Review of Anthropology*, *24*, 95–117.

Ministry of Law and Justice, Government of India (2013). *Right to Fair Compensation and Transparency in Land Acquisition, Rehabilitation and Resettlement Act, 2013*. New Delhi: Government of India.

Mitra, A. (1951). *The Tribes and Castes of West Bengal, Census 1951*. Govt. of West Bengal.

Murphy, S. (2013). Land grabs and fragile food systems: The role of globalization. Institute for Agriculture and Trade Policy. Minnesota. Retrieved from https://www.iatp.org/documents/land-grabs-and-fragile-food-systems.

Perez, J., Gistelinek, M., and Karbala, D. (2011). *Sleeping Lions: International Investment Treaties, State-Investor Disputes and Access to Food, Land and Water*. Discussion paper, Oxfam. Retrieved from http://www.oxfam.org

Schutter De, O. (2009). Large scale land acquisitions and leases: A set of core principles and measures to address the human rights challenge. *United Nations Special Rapporteur's Report on right to food*. Geneva. Retrieved from https://www.oecd.org/site/swacmali2010/44031283.pdf

Schutter De, O. (2011). How not to think of land-grabbing: Three critiques of large-scale investments in farmland. *Journal of Peasant Studies*, *38*(2), 249–279.

WBHDR (2004). *West Bengal Human Development Report*. Calcutta: Government of West Bengal: Development and Planning Department.

West Bengal Legislative Assembly Proceedings (1963). Vol. 36. Calcutta: Government of West Bengal.

West Bengal Legislative Assembly Proceedings (1967). Vol. 44.Calcutta: Government of West Bengal.

West Bengal Legislative Assembly Proceedings (1973). Vol. 54. Calcutta: Government of West Bengal.

The World Bank (2011). *Rising Global Interest in Farmland: Can It Yield Sustainable and Equitable Benefits?*Washington, DC: World Bank. Retrieved from https://openknowledge.worldbank.org/handle/10986/2263

Chapter 6

Revisiting Wittfogel

"Hydraulic society" in colonial India and its post-colonial legacies in hydropower management

Arnab Roy Chowdhury and Late Sanjay Kumar Rajhans

Introduction

Karl Wittfogel[1] proffers the theory of "hydraulic society" in his 1957 book *Oriental Despotism* and connects political power to hydraulic systems in ancient civilisations (Wilkinson and Rayne, 2010). Drawing mainly upon the experience in China and Sri Lanka, Wittfogel says that agriculture in the early riverine states of Asia was based on large-scale and centralised water control and transfer. This form of agriculture required expansive hydraulic projects, which needed large workforces derived from "forced labour" and massive managerial organisations for their supervision, which in turn led to the growth of a centralised state power and bureaucracy in these societies. The state became more powerful than society, and "oriental despotism" emerged (Spate, 1959). Oriental despots enjoyed absolute political power and were absolutely corrupt. The state purposefully crushed any initiative led by the affluent class and kept them subservient to its interests. In these societies, power in all forms lay in the hands of the agro-managerial bureaucracy who controlled these hydraulic states, and there was no notion of private land. This explains the stasis of these societies.

In his analysis, Wittfogel (1957) evidently refers to one of the stages of the "historical materialism" proposed by Marx, that is, the "Asiatic Mode of Production"[2] (AMP). Wittfogel says Asian societies were marked by the "exceptionalism" of the AMP, in which state power was based on irrigation and an agro-managerial bureaucracy, but also that the formation of "hydraulic societies" was contingent upon various subsidiary factors. The presence of too little water or too much did not necessarily lead to the "state control" of water, which did not lead to despotic statecraft either – it became possible for a "hydraulic society" to emerge only when the economy was

1. above the level of extractive subsistence;
2. beyond the level of influence of strong centres of rainfall-based agriculture; and
3. below the level of property-based industrial civilisation (Wittfogel, 1957).

DOI: 10.4324/9781003159940-6

The archaeology and anthropology of ancient water management draw heavily from Wittfogel's study, but engagements with Wittfogel's theory have been simplistic (Wilkinson and Rayne, 2010). For the past few decades, social scientists have largely criticised and rejected Wittfogel's theory. China was the epitome of a hydraulic society, according to Wittfogel (1957), but that view has also been contested (Masubichi, 1966). Though to some extent northern Vietnam can be considered an example of a hydraulic society, Wittfogel's view is particularly insightful for civilisations like ancient Egypt, Indus Valley, and Mesopotamia. Various critics have pointed out that an elaborate structure and network of hydraulic works was not necessary for the establishment of a centralised, powerful, bureaucratic and totalitarian state; different historical antecedents led to such a state in Sri Lanka (Leach, 1961) and Bali (Lansing, 1991). There is no shortage of states in the Asian region with moderate hydraulic achievements (Wijeyewardene, 1971); however, the argument for a hydraulic society in Asia and its link with the notion of "oriental despotism" has been unconvincing. Scholars have tried to establish a link between irrigation and state formation in Java (Christie, 1995), Burma (Stargardt, 1986) and Southern Thailand (Stargardt, 1992) – and between the Khmer empire and the irrigation of Angkor (the "hydraulic city") (Groslier, 1979) – though, increasingly, these strong Wittfogelian type of arguments have been seen as untenable (Stott, 1992; de Bernon, 1997) but a relation between irrigation and state formation can definitely be argued.

The agro-hydraulic kingdoms usually supported high population density, centralised economy, and large-scale infrastructures as in India, China and northern Vietnam. However, there were exceptions, too, such as the Kingdom of Majapahit in 14th century Java. It had small-scale infrastructure, despite being a hydraulic society, and it was also largely depopulated, like many other parts of Southeast Asia (Maurer, 1990). Leach (1959) upholds the concept of "hydraulic society" in Ceylon; he states that it was rich in water resources and its despotic rulers harnessed these resources. But that did not give rise to a "hydraulic society" in the Wittfogelian sense; rather, Ceylon was a "sort of feudal society."Many of its grand hydraulic structures took centuries to build; so, obviously, these were the accomplishments of different kings, and not of a single despotic monarch. And such works needed not centralised labour power but groups of temporary labourers who were forced to work (Leach, 1959). Buddhist monasteries provided specialised engineers and professionals whose expertise and help was critical to the design of such structures in Ceylon; hence, no strong bureaucratic state power emerged.

Wittfogel suggests that the modes and relations of production in hydraulic societies were poles apart from feudalism. Leach proposes, on the contrary, that they could have coexisted, and were mutually compatible. "The Indian and Ceylonese type of hydraulic society were decentralised, feudal, and cellular" and based on charismatic and personal leadership, unlike Chinese bureaucratic patrilineal authority. Leach (1959) hypothesises that "[i]n a wide variety of circumstances, [a] hydraulic society possibly lends itself very easily to the development of specialised labour [on] a non-monetary basis" (p. 24).

Kosambi (1957) says that the term "hydraulic society" is a misnomer and that the concept does not fit well in the Indian context because much of the agriculture here is "monsoon based." The crux of Wittfogel's argument is that the right to private property in those societies was prohibited which explains the absence of capitalism and bourgeois social formations. The caste hierarchy also made water use and management even more complex (Shabad, 1959).

However, we do not apply Wittfogel's theory to the Indian context mechanistically or as a master theory; instead, we try to use it as a stimulating and heuristic instrument (Graber, 2001) and understand (or *apply*) it in a tendentious and "possibilistic sense" rather than a "deterministic sense" (Radkau, 2013). We deploy the concept as a heuristic device and base the arguments of this chapter on a historical-sociological reading of extant historiography. We draw examples of various places in the colonial Indian subcontinent (and South Asian region), a massive part of which later became post-colonial India. This wide variety of examples might reflect a patchy history, but it has been done purposefully to elicit a conceptual argument. Also when we refer to colonial "India" (which is historically wrong), we essentially mean it as a geographical location situated in that part of the South Asian region and the Indian subcontinent, which eventually became post-colonial India.

Formation of hydraulic society in colonial India

India was under the rule of the East India Company and "indirect rule" of the British Empire from 1765 to 1858 when conditions akin to a "hydraulic society" developed slowly[3]. The Permanent Settlement Act of 1793 introduced the concept of private property in land (though counter-intuitive to the concept of hydraulic society), altered the agrarian landscape and social relations of power, and had great implications for the agrarian sector and the components of its production system, such as water, as water is the most important input in agricultural production.

Scholars argue that the East India Company's interventions focused primarily on revenue. However, the British tax system was so alien to the land, water and agrarian relations and that the revenue system broke the economy and produced the famines in the first place. These are crucial issues for state formation under colonial rule (Bernard Cohn, 1971).[4]

While explaining the socio-technical context of surface irrigation, Shah (2011) describes the pre-colonial system as "adaptive irrigation" and the colonial transition in irrigation scenario as "constructive imperialism."

There was unprecedented growth in that direction in the second period, under the Direct Rule of the Crown from 1858, when almost the entire major "hydraulic interventions" were made. The private and mercantile British East India Company wanted to control the agrarian sector in India, a satellite colony in their capitalist "world system" (Wallerstein, 1974), and ensure a steady supply of raw material for the Industrial Revolution underway in Great Britain then. In doing so, they transformed the Indian agrarian sector.

A high degree of extraction needs technological inputs to aggregate all the factors necessary to optimise output. The first task was to control the monsoon-dependent Indian agrarian sector by insulating it from the recurrent floods, droughts and famines and making it a relatively "risk-free" and "stable" domain of production (Dyson, 1991). In India, there were water-abundant regions, such as the Bengal Province, and water-scarce regions, such as the Rajputana and the Central Provinces (Baker, 1993). The droughts were meteorological (Grove, 1998); hence, the affected areas did have some "moisture agglomeration" (Wittfogel, 1957). Water is the most important agricultural input; to make water supply reliable, the British initially reconstructed some of the canal systems constructed by Muslim *nawabs* and emperors. Thus, the gravity flow irrigation of the canal system continued to be central to Indian social history in both the pre-colonial and colonial periods (Shah, 2011).

The British wanted to stabilise the agricultural sector and produce particular patterns of crop cultivation for developing industry and extracting high rent. They wanted to cultivate luxuriant, good quality and expensive cash crops that could generate huge economic profit in the world market. Doing so successfully requires maintaining the "conditions of production" in an orderly manner. In turn, it is necessary to control the caprices of nature to ensure a steady production of fine crops, which would ensure the steady economic growth of the colonial "metropole" at the expense of the colonial "periphery" (Alavi, 1975).

Between 1800 and the 1850s, hydraulic interventions in colonial India came mainly in the form of renovating old hydraulic structures in the first phase, when the British profited considerably. The colonial government constructed large canal systems from the 1850s to 1900 and, with the help of private capital, dams and hydroelectric projects from 1890 onwards. In colonial India, canal systems were constructed and renovated in (1) the Madras Canal System; (2) the United Provinces; (3) the Bombay Sind and (4) the Punjab Canal System (Whitcombe, 1995). Floods, droughts, famines and scarcity played an overarching role in the construction of various hydraulic structures – mainly canals and dams. The canals constructed by the Mughal and various other Sultanates in different parts of India degenerated around 40–50 years prior to the East India Company's arrival in 1801–1803 (Whitcombe, 1983). The Western Jamuna Canal, built by Feroz Shah

Tughlak in East Punjab and renovated during Akbar's reign, was extended up to Delhi on the advice of Shah Jahan's engineer Ali Murdan Khan. The *doab* canal, built in the early 18th century and later known as the Eastern Jamuna Canal, was restored by the Rohilla chiefs in 1784. The Bari Doab Canal, preceded by the Hasli canal from Ravi to Lahore (Stone, 1984), was still functional when Punjab was annexed in 1849 (Ali, 1989). Before the British, the Amirs of Sind, the Sikhs, and the Nawabs of Bahawalpur were already using inundation[5] canals for irrigation. It may very well have been that the British started with repairing the existing canals, but quickly they seem to have moved to "bigger plans," that is a desire to extend the irrigated area, needing to lift the water above the flood plain, requiring diversion weirs and/or diverting water further upstream. The British, in that sense, abandoned the original canal design logic. This eventual "learning process" is the early phase of British colonialism. One of the main works of restoration in colonial South India, the Madras Canal System, was built under the auspices of Sir Arthur Cotton, who revived the Cauvery (Mishra, 1997), Coleroon and Krishna-Godavari deltas, and engineered the Madras irrigation system (1820–1846) (Reddy, 1990). It had enormous agricultural and developmental effects for the delta region: the extension of two cropping seasons triggered the intensive (capitalist) agricultural development of the second half of the 19th century. Droughts were mitigated by these restorations and renovation works, from which the colonial government profited financially.

Flood, famine and hydraulic society

Initially, the British considered investing in building new canals but decided against it because of a fiscal shortage. Severe famines in the following decades, however, in the United Provinces of the Ganga-Yamuna *doab* region in Northern India and, especially, the 1837–1838 famine influenced the colonial policy of making large-scale irrigation systems in India (Sharma, 2001). Their experience of famine-affected landscapes shaped their policies in terms of, avoiding political instability, philanthropy and public works. The state constructed networks of roads and railways *sarais* (inns), apart from irrigation canals and dams, to control famines. The huge, famine-affected migrant population was used as "free labour" (or corvée labour) to construct these civil engineering projects, which interestingly matches Wittfogel's theory and Leach's hypothesis of a "hydraulic society." Through these projects, the idea of philanthropy (part of the British "civilising" mission) was moulded into the idea of "public works" (Sharma, 2001). The first purely British canal work, between 1836 and 1857, was a response to severe famines in Central India and the United Provinces. Sir Proby Thomas Cautley was the architect of the Ganges Canal, constructed to supply water to the whole of the *doab* in light of the severe famine that had ravaged the region in

1837–1838. Initially, Cautley found the undulating topography and low-lying valley between the Ganges and the upland plain forbidding, but the 1837–1838 famine made the canal imperative. The Ganga Canal was inaugurated in 1854 and made operational in 1857 (Sharma, 2001).

An increasingly complex and differentiating bureaucracy of public works management was simultaneously developing in colonial India. Until 1854, the engineering department of the army or the military board in each of the three presidencies – Madras, Bombay, and Bengal – controlled public works. Lord Dalhousie abolished the military board and created instead an elaborate bureaucratic framework: a chief engineer in each local government and a central public works secretariat would supervise such works. That developed a basic framework for public works and its system of finance. Dalhousie proposed that these kinds of work be financed by loan capital or borrowed money (Stone, 1984).

The private Madras Irrigation Canal Company and the East India Irrigation and Canal Company in Orissa were formed in 1859 under the leadership of Sir Arthur Cotton and existed until 1866. After spending considerably on renovating the Godavari, Krishna, Pennar and Cauvery, the Madras government had few resources left for further work on canals. In Madras, the government assessed irrigation revenue based on irrigated land and not on the volume of water because technologically sound modules necessary to gauge water use were not available (Mollinga, 2003). This is another example of an emerging hydro-bureaucracy. Revenue was collected by a sophisticated water bureaucracy at different levels, from the village to the province. In many places, the water tax was based on the type of crop sown and irrigated. This practice promoted cash crop cultivation, as it yielded more profit than food crops (Whitcombe, 1983).

In 1861, the East India Irrigation and Canal Company, functioning under the leadership of Cotton in Orissa, planned a canal on the deltaic region of Mahanadi and Brahmani River from Cuttack to Calcutta to improve coastal communications, alleviate droughts and mitigate floods. Stone (1984) claims the scheme was successful in controlling floods in Orissa, although it failed to generate any fiscal profit, but D'Souza (2002) claims that the embankments built on the Mahanadi actually worsened the flood control situation and transformed the landscape of Orissa from a "flood-dependent" agrarian regime to a "flood-vulnerable" landscape. The traditional irrigation system of tanks, wells and ponds was selectively destroyed to make the canal system profitable, and the huge sum of money allocated to the Madras Canal Company was mismanaged and did not return any revenue.

Protective vs productive irrigation

Understanding protective and productive irrigation is crucial to analyse the various aspects of state formation and hydraulic society in colonial India.

The productive irrigation was for revenue and surplus generation mainly through the construction of canals; protective irrigation played a dual function of protecting colonial subjects and the agricultural produce from flood and famine through embankments and reservoirs. These strategies played significant roles in profit making and creating political legitimacy. The making of the hydraulic society is associated with political legitimacy and hegemony, as well as financial profit for the establishment of a strong state. In the Indian colony, which was largely agrarian in nature, controlling and harnessing water (and a balance between two) was necessary to create the presence of a strong colonial state. The colonial administration was however divided in opinion and policy on how to strike a balance, as floods and famines occurred regularly, and managing these contingencies shaped the colonial hydraulic policy significantly.

The colonial government divided "public works"[6] into "state works" – basic infrastructure such as schools and barracks – and "works of internal improvement," such as irrigation. Improvements were both "productive" (remunerative state works to enhance productivity in highly cultivated regions) and "protective" ("non-remunerative" public works to protect valley regions against famines and floods) (Whitcombe, 1983). The notion of protective irrigation[7] evolved in response to these recurrent famines; however, the dominant strategy of colonial irrigation was a mix of protective irrigation in semi-arid regions for preventing famines in drought years, flood control in deltas and diversion of rivers and streams in high-monsoon regions to ensure good harvest and revenue collection.

The dialectical tension and ambivalence of the empire was visible in the balance between protective irrigation and productive irrigation. On the one hand, revenue had to be ensured from the cultivation of rubber, tea and sugar cane. On the other hand, extensive, "thin" protective irrigation had to be supplied to protect the "moral economy" of famine-prone regions and ensure social stability and peace. Protective irrigation systems were based on "scarcity by design": water was spread thinly over an extensive agricultural tract (Jurriens and Mollinga, 1996). Irrigation in the Indo-Gangetic plain is an apt example. Protective irrigation itself did not meet the water requirements of the whole command area; it was a supply-based irrigation system – which had a minimum of control structures and maintained a continuous flow – that maximised return on scarce water rather than on land.

Until the early 1860s, major irrigation works were meant primarily for earning revenue, and were classified as "productive works" that had to pass the "productivity test." That, however, does not imply that due consideration was not given to the "protective" function of these works. In 1867, the colonial government determined to incorporate certain safety measures and designs to mark it as a "protective work" in the north Indian canal schemes as by then the irrigation commission had come to believe that the distinction between "protective" and "productive" was spurious because a "productive work" aims to protect, too (Stone, 1984). Thus the mixture of goals (protective vs productive) in state provision of irrigation and other public works was guided by political, as well as "moral and material" and incentives (Pringle, 1978).

Protective works, through the demonstration of calculated philanthropy, were legitimising tools of colonial governance.

As far as irrigation alone was concerned, on a policy level it was simultaneously linked with famine prevention, revenue stability, settling of unruly tribes, expansion of cultivation, expanded cultivation of cash crops, enhanced taxable capacity, improved cultivation practices and political stability (Stone, 1984).

The report of the Indian Famine Commission (1880) recommended that two canals be built; Sarada Canal was one. But the *Talukdars* of Oudh vehemently opposed the idea of making it, citing the already prevalent well irrigation, groundwater availability, and the lack of evidence of scarcity, drought, or famine in Oudh. They argued that the Sarada Canal would deteriorate the soil condition; cause waterlogging and a diseased terrain, as the Jamuna and Ganges canals had done; and would not be remunerative for the colonial government. It trivialised and neglected all these concerns, and opened the first section in 1928. Later, the canal produced degenerated, waterlogged, fallow lands and malaria in the region[8] (Whitcombe, 1995).

Apart from causing malaria, these mega-hydraulic projects also replaced the traditional water management system (as discussed earlier in the case of Orissa). Sir Proby Thomas Cautley designed the canal system in the *doab* region in the United Provinces, which displaced the well irrigation in low-lying lands (*khadir*). Canal irrigation was a problem for high-lying lands (*bhangar*) also because special lift devices were needed to transfer water from canals to fields, but it did indeed convert the region, into one, producing sugarcane in surplus. In post-colonial India, western Uttar Pradesh became more developed than the eastern part because of these canals (Stone, 1984).

Wallach (1985) argues that the British initially planned it as a protective irrigation scheme on the river against drought and famine. It was built on the faulty assumption that even in normal years, farmers would use canal waters for "irrigated dry crops" like sorghum and cotton; instead, they used the water for irrigating cash crops like sugarcane and paddy. The farmers who owned land at the "head end" of the canal started cultivating cash crops and diverting most of the canal water, and choking supply to the "tail end" (Wallach, 1985).

Some additional problems also cropped up. To irrigate large areas of the Gangetic plains, their perennial rivers need minor diversions. In the Deccan, however, the topography is difficult, and rivers are seasonal and have less water; therefore, they needed expensive dams and storage. Visvesvaraya notes that "account of the great cost of storage, water-supply is three to six times more expensive" in the Deccan (IIC, 1902). Understandably, this water had to be used for revenue generation and, naturally, the block system cultivation of sugarcane became a viable choice for creating regular demand for water (Bolding et al., 1995). After this system proved successful, the new Neera Left Bank canal was opened; between 1900 and 1938, canal irrigation increased sevenfold (Attwood, 1992). Under this block irrigation system, canals made a substantial contribution to stabilising crop production in the Deccan (Attwood, 1987, 1992).

Undivided Punjab in every way was an epitome of "hydraulic intervention," where "deep colonialism" brought about massive rural agrarian transformation (Bhattacharya, 2018). After it was annexed in 1849, "canal colonies" were brought into being in the Indus basin interfluves. In the social milieu of a burgeoning national movement, the British anxiously claimed to be the legitimate ruler and asserted that they enjoyed the support of the Indian peasantry. Beginning in 1885, the British chose to settle in the canal colonies certain groups of people: yeomen (*Sufedpcsh*) and peasants (*Abadkar)* from Punjab mainly of Jat, Arain, Kamboh, and Saini caste of cultivators. Lands were given in grant to the Punjabis working in the colonial military and the ex-servicemen as a sign of their obeisance and loyalty, which was done to politically pacify the anti-colonial movements in Punjab (Ali, 1989). The social structures of village society were kept intact in the allotment of land in these colonies. Generally, lands were assigned only to a single caste to make them the "dominant caste" of the village (Srinivas, 1959).

The peculiarities and patterns of colonial water control can be studied through the conceptual notion of "colonial hydrology," practised as a distinct paradigm of hydraulic intervention (D' Souza, 2006). The British conceived of "native" communities as parts of the natural environment, which was meant to be controlled, and tried to "mathematically model nature" and "naturalise the communities" into a single hydraulic environment of the Indus basin (Gilmartin, 1994). It also set in the procedure of converting nature into a separate "object" and "domain" of the "knowable." One way of doing that was to destroy the traditional irrigation system and converting water into a "commodity." Weil (2006) argues that the rise of the engineering paradigm and the concomitant ascendancy in the respectability of "techno-chauvinism" and "technological optimism" within the culture of the Imperial Civil Services led to the highly reductionist, technocratic approach of engineers replacing traditional ways of water management with a pseudo efficient system which has little understanding of hydraulic geography.

The continued culture of mega projects in post-colonial India

Investment in irrigation was not financially successful until the 1890s, but the following years of ghastly droughts and scarcity ensured a return of net revenue of 7% by 1900. From 1900 onwards, more and more assets were driven towards the development of canals in the Deccan, Punjab and other parts of India. The first hydroelectric power project in India was designed on a small scale in Darjeeling in 1897. It was a tiny 400 kW enterprise financed by the municipality primarily to illuminate the town. Until 1907, hydroelectricity projects were installed in a few places only, such as Mussourie, Shimla, Nainital, and Amritsar (Whitcombe, 1983). Initially, hydroelectricity projects were considered an impediment in the irrigation process but got an impetus through private capital when the Sivasamudram Project was built in 1902. The process was greatly enlarged by 1933.

Due to the colonial legacy of irrigation developed in India, most irrigation projects are also hydropower projects, and these dams are both large in size and height, which has caused a great deal of displacement of people. The first of these dams was the Mulshi dam, built by the British in 1921 in Maharashtra; it is both an irrigation and hydropower dam. The Tata Hydro Electric Project Company was established in Bombay for urban electrification in the 1920s that built the first large hydropower project in Mulshi that was protested against by the farmers. This was the first instance of nascent indigenous capital investing in hydropower projects in later colonial India.

The greater emphasis on river valleys, basins and catchments came from the new engineering notion of the "hydrological unity" of a river basin that was used as the unit of development of water resources. During this phase, the colonial government invested large amounts of capital in harnessing rivers through building big dams which could be used for both irrigation and hydropower (Gulhati, 1972). After independence, US dam engineering had a profound effect on dam building in India, and the Tennessee Valley project inspired Indian engineers to build dams that could serve multiple purposes, that is, flood mitigation, irrigation and hydropower (Klingensmith, 2007). The policy of focusing on multipurpose river valley projects (MPRVPs) adopted in the 1940s was for the "holistic development" of the catchments and submerged areas of dams encompassing electricity power generation, irrigation, flood protection and various kinds of supplementary employment and livelihood generation. The Damodar River Valley project was the first multipurpose river valley project built in India in 1948 (D'Souza, 2003).

All these projects were built to provide cheap electricity to light up towns and big cities and not for irrigation (Whitcombe, 1983).[9] "Protection" as a technical concept survived independence and was linked to the building of large "multi-purpose" (for protection, production and electricity) hydropower projects in India (Roy Chowdhury, 2014a). Construction of "multipurpose" hydropower projects was one of the central planks around which the post-colonial Indian state and its controlled industries took their flight for national development from the 1950s onward. It also gave rise to a hydro-bureaucracy massively immersed in corruption and clearly bore the colonial legacy (for the case of Southern India see: Wade, 1982).

In the case of irrigation in the Deccan, where water was supplied from the Krishna valley basin covering the Bombay Presidency, that gave impetus to cash crops such as sugar cultivation in Krishna valley and the making of a large number of dams in Maharashtra. With large drought-affected agricultural tracts that the state of Maharashtra has, it is not surprising that this state also has the largest number of large dams in India, that is, 1,529 out of 4,291 (GOM, 2006). The state has accomplished about 25 projects on an average per year from 1951to 1994. This is a colonial legacy.

Traditionally the social response to periodic water scarcity in Maharashtra was to construct irrigation wells along the rivers and streams for drought mitigation. However, during the colonial period, there was a major shift away in traditional irrigation systems, favouring centralised large dams with large-scale, canal-based structures. These were constructed to support the production of export crops, such as sugarcane, indigo, cotton and wheat (Gulhati, 1972). Colonial administration also developed water infrastructure mainly for protection against floods, droughts and famines but thiswater was largely diverted for sugarcane cultivation, which is an extremely water-intensive crop. Despite this, the government in the pre-independence period of the 1930s gave leverage to industrial sugarcane development with the construction of the Deccan canal and the establishment of the first sugarcane factory in Krishna valley in 1932 (Wallach, 1985; Bolding, Mollinga and Van Straaten, 1995).

In the post-independence period, the irrigation department of Maharashtra has continued to invest heavily in water for sugarcane development through the construction of dams, such as Koyna, Dom and Ujani. From 1951, through 1970s green revolution to the 1980s more and more land has gone to cane cultivation which has neglected the local millet subsistence production such as *Jowar* and *Bajra* (Phadke R., 2002). From the 1970s onwards there have been multiple kinds of conflicts that emerged around the division of waters. The same colonial legacy of dam building continued in Punjab. The Bhakra Dam on River Sutlej in Himachal Pradesh and Nangal Dam in its downstream in Punjab, jointly called the Bhakra-Nangal multipurpose river valley projects was constructed in 1963. It was famously proclaimed as "the new temple of resurgent India" by Prime Minister Jawaharlal Nehru. It is accorded the sole credit for rescuing India from hunger and famine; help regain self-respect and pride after accepting rotten grain as food aid under the PL 480 programme. It is said to have been the harbinger of the green revolution in India in the 1960s and 70s, and Punjab started producing surplus food crops by bringing more areas under irrigation, using High Yielding Variety seeds and fertilisers. But as Dharmadhikary's (2005) study shows that it later gave rise to the problem of salinity and waterlogging, and led to agricultural crises.

These colonial and post-colonial legacies of mega-hydraulic power projects gave rise to multiple kinds of conflicts, such as interstate water disputes

(Roy Chowdhury, 2013), social movements of the drought-affected people and the dam-affected people throughout India. The most famous of these was Narmada Bachao Andolan (Save Narmada Movement) that emerged in the 1980s against the building of the massive Sardar Sarovar Dam in Gujarat that caused the submergence of land in Maharashtra and Madhya Pradesh that was led by famous activist Medha Patker, whose famous "anti-dam" stance raised the important issue whether mega-dams (and such mega projects) are useful and desirable at all. This movement mobilised the farmers, peasants, Bhil and Bhilala tribes of Madhya Pradesh as well as garnered huge support from the middle class and national as well as international civil society organisations (Roy Chowdhury, 2014a).

In Maharashtra, a number of movements emerged against the building of these large dams and many of these farmers' resistance demanded the building of smaller dams that are built by the local communities, so that it reduces submergence of lands (Roy Chowdhury, 2014b).The Shramik Mukti Dal and its leaders Bharat Patankar and Gail Omvedt started questioning the developmental role of the state in making large dams and started demanding, equal rights to water for dam- and drought-affected people, as well as rehabilitation of the people to be done before the dam is constructed. These demands ultimately led to the formation of rehabilitation law in Maharashtra in the year 1976, the first in India (Roy Chowdhury, 2018). In Independent India, such kinds of movements emerged continuously throughout India even at the margins such as northeastern India raising issues of submergence of land and livelihood, and destruction of cultural landscapes (Roy Chowdhury and Kipgen, 2013).

Conclusion

We apply the concept of hydraulic society as a heuristic device, to understand the water management in colonial India and map its post-colonial legacies briefly. In Karl Wittfogel's conceptualisation of a "hydraulic society," rulers base their design of state power on the centrality of water control and irrigation. In colonial India, the British centralised and institutionalised water management regulations and infrastructure; and their endeavour to establish something akin to Wittfogel's hydraulic society on a pan-Indian scale achieved partial success and played an important role, if not the central role, in statecraft. It is novel to argue that colonial intervention created something similar to a hydraulic society. But this argument is limited in that the direct financial dependence of the colonial state on these projects, as a percentage of the total state revenue, was not very high, despite its considerable political dependence on irrigation projects.[10] What emerged from this was a "negotiated" hydraulic society in colonial India, as the plan and programme of establishing centralised water governance emerged through various negotiated, contingent, structural, conjunctural and contextual factors such as floods and famines.

The centralisation of water happened somewhat inadvertently – through contingencies and in an experiential manner – as the reconstruction of the hydraulic landscape was largely disaster induced (Bhargava, 2007) . To protect imperial subjects from the recurrent floods and famines that affected the Indian landscape, and to enable the agrarian sector to function smoothly and generate revenue and a surplus, the colonial masters endeavoured to set up a "protective" and "productive" irrigation system. Later, during the Second World War, hydropower projects were constructed to produce electricity, and power generation became a lucrative business.

In post-colonial India, these legacies of water management institutions, discourses and practices continued, particularly through the construction of multipurpose hydropower projects that aimed mainly at flood management, irrigation and electricity production.

A "theory" that promoted centralisation of water management based on ideas of high modernity during colonial times, had unfaltering confidence in science and technology and techno-managerial hubris got translated into policies. These policies were derived from principles of modernisation, and were never localised according to historical and socio-spatial contexts. The total dependence on colonial expertise of scientist, engineer, bureaucrats and the negligence of existing local and traditional knowledge of managing water made these policies top-down, and there was no participatory dimension in it. However, the translation of these policies into practice under the colonial government in India was strictly supervised to some extent, even though there was some corruption at the higher level.

As these colonial legacies of water management continued under the new post-colonial state, further gaps emerged between the policies and the practice. Existing social hierarchy, stratification and power differences within and between communities with overlapping problems of corrupt practices of the elites, gave decisive power in their hand, and that excluded the majority non-elite citizens from making any choice, decision or participation in the formulation or implementation process, which passively or actively dispossessed them from their rights over resources like water in the name of "national development," neglecting once again regional and local concerns.

In post-colonial India, the British dam-building model assimilated ideas from the American Tennessee river valley project and created a discourse of mega hydropower projects. Encouraging cash crop-based agriculture, and the green revolution for rural and agricultural development, led to saturation, and problems and conflicts. The colonial legacy of centralised irrigation planning for protective and productive purpose transformed into multipurpose projects in post-colonial times imbibing global ideas, but the overall notion of mega-hydraulic projects and dams created several problems and resistance from affected communities. Movements such as Narmada Bachao Andolan and Shramik Mukti Dal emerged as local bottom-up initiatives and paved the way for "alternatives" to emerge against large grand narratives of water governance by proposing smaller, peasant-built dams. These participatory models of management and development eventually challenged the paradigmatic position of water governance and infrastructural development that was state-centric, unilateral and monolithic.

Notes

1 Karl August Wittfogel (1896–1988) went to the USA after 1933 as a German (Jewish) refugee. Originally, an ardent supporter of communism, Wittfogel thought that a hydraulic society would bypass capitalism and lead directly to communism. However, when he was put to draining moors in a Nazi concentration camp in 1933, he experienced firsthand the despotic and murderous potential of hydraulic engineering, which led him to theorise that artificial irrigation was the offspring of totalitarian rule (Radkau, 2013, pp. 334–335). However, David Blackbourn (2006) – and not Wittfogel – applied this theory to Nazi Germany (and Worster (1977) applied this theory to the water centralization in the arid western region of the USA), and, suggested that Nazi rule in its material core was indeed an example of hydraulic despotism (Radkau, 2013).

2 Marx and Engels identified the development of an Asiatic society in a different course than western societies based on its irrigation-based economic and political power (Price, 1994). The AMP was characterised by ownership of common property, absence of private property in land, centralised state control, and the growth of a powerful bureaucracy. A bourgeois land-owning class did not control the power cores of those societies; the people owned the means of production. These societies, as Marx notes, were in stasis and stand out as being ossified in the stages of historical materialism. Consequently, Marx thought colonialism was a necessary stage for these societies as it introduced into them the dynamicity of capitalism (albeit exogenous) and brought about consequential changes in them through modernisation and development. According to Marx, India was an example of a typical Asiatic society, whereas China was atypical because there was development of private property in land. Tsarist Russia was "semi-Asiatic"despite the absence of an irrigation base. Later, in Russia, Stalin's rule was too similar to the conception of "oriental despotism"; the term "Asiatic Mode of Production" became unpopular for good reasons perhaps – the orientalism inherent in it for instance; and that category was dropped from the schema of historical materialism (Leach, 1959).

3 This, incidentally, is not so different from the time when Egypt, one of Wittfogel's poster children, became a hydraulic society under the British rule (Willcocks, 1913).

4 The transition from Company to Crown rule was a big leap in terms of state formation and for water projects, and there were significant differences in directly and indirectly ruled states. The interventions in water projects were largely in the directly ruled.

5 Known as *Sailab*, this type of irrigation used the excess floodwater in the Indus valley region (Rangachari, 2006), was also practised in Orissa (D'Souza, 2002) and Bihar (Mishra, 1997). British engineers in India did not understand the usefulness of these inundation canals in the agricultural cycle and thought it

harmful and an impediment to agriculture. They perceived the excess water as a "flood" that needed to be controlled by embankments and dams and channelised through canals (Hardiman, 2002).

6 The Department of Public Works was set up in the 1850s. Until then, the Department of Military Affairs and the Military Board were responsible for public works (Whitecomb, 1983).

7 The notion of protection evolved over time and took different shapes in North, West and South India, each with specificities. Combining findings and facts from different regions in one argument does not work very well, so we discuss each region separately to give a very cursory overview. In North India, in relation to protective irrigation, wheat, which is a cash and food crop that consumes little water, makes a lot of difference in comparison to rice in South India, where it is the staple food crop.

8 However, malaria and waterlogging was a bigger problem in North India than in South or West India.

9 World markets collapsed in the Great Depression of the 1930s, and led to the diversification of the canal system and the construction of one major hydroelectric project in the Ganges canal. By the 1940s, though, the situation reverted to the old ways of remunerative irrigation in agriculture (Whitcombe, 1983).

10 However, we lack primary source data for this argument.

References

Alavi, H. (1975). India and the colonial mode of production. *Economic and Political Weekly*. *10*(33/35), 1235–1262.

Ali, I. (1989). *The Punjab under Imperialism, 1885–1947*. Delhi: Oxford University Press.

Attwood, D.W. (1987). Irrigation and imperialism: The causes and consequences of a shift from subsistence to cash cropping. *Journal of Development Studies*, *23*(3), 341–366. DOI: 10.1080/00220388708422037

Attwood, D.W. (1992). *Raising Cane: The Political Economy of Sugar in Western India*. Boulder, CO & Oxford: West View Press.

Baker, D.E.U. (1993). *Colonialism in an Indian Hinterland*. Delhi; New York: Oxford University Press.

Bhargava, M. (2007). Changing river courses in North India: Calamities, bounties, strategies sixteenth to early nineteenth centuries. *The Medieval History Journal*, *10*(1 & 2), 183–204.DOI: 10.1177/097194580701000207

Bhattacharya, N. (2018). *The Great Agrarian Conquest: The Colonial Reshaping of a Rural World*. Bangalore: Orient Blackswan.

Blackbourn, D. (2006). *The Conquest of Nature: Water, Landscape and the Making of Modern Germany*. New York: Norton.

Bolding, A., Mollinga, P.P. and Van Straaten, K. (1995). Modules for modernization: Colonial irrigation in India and technological dimension for Agrarian change. *Journal of Development Studies*, *31*(6): 805–844. DOI: 10.1080/00220389508422392

Christie, J.W. (1995). State formation in early maritime Southeast Asia. *Journal of the Humanities and Social Sciences of Southeast Asia*, *151*(2), 235–288.

Cohn, B. (1971). *India: The Social Anthropology of a Civilization*. New Delhi: Oxford University Press.

Dharmadhikary, S. (2005). *Unravelling Bhakra*. Badwani, Madhya Pradesh, India: Manthan Adhyayan Kendra Publication.

D'Souza, R. (2002). Colonialism, capitalism and nature: Debating the origins of Mahanadi Delta's hydraulic crisis (1803–1928). *Economic and Political Weekly, 37*(13), 1261–1272.

D'Souza, R. (2003). Damming the Mahanadi River: The emergence of multi-purpose river valley development in India (1943–46). *Indian Economic and Social History Review, 40*(1), 81–105. DOI: 10.1177/001946460304000104

D'Souza, R. (2006). Water in British India: The making of a 'Colonial Hydrology'. *History Compass, 4*(4), 621–628. DOI : 10.1111/j.1478-0542.2006.00336.x

De Bernon, O. (1997). Note Sur l'hydraulique théocratique angkorienne. *Bulletin de l'Ecole Française d'Extrème Orient (BEFEO), 84*, 340–348.

Dyson, T. (1991). On the demography of South Asian famines: Part I. *Population Studies, 45*(1), 5–25.

Government of Maharashtra (GOM) (2006). *Maharashtra State Irrigation Commission Report*. Retrieved from Yashada Libraray Pune.

Gilmartin, D. (1994). Scientific empire and imperial science: Colonialism and irrigation technology in Indus Basin. *The Journal of Asian Studies, 53*(4), 1127–1149. DOI: 10.2307/2059236

Graber, F. (2001). Review of Nature and Macht: Eine weltgeschichte der umwelt. *Annales. Histoire, Sciences Sociales, 66*, 247–248.

Groslier, B.P. (1979). La Cité hydraulique angkorienne: Exploitation ou surexploitation du sol?*BEFEO, 66*, 161–202.

Grove, R. (1998). The, East India Company, the Raj and El Nino: The critical role played by colonial scientists in establishing the mechanism of global climate teleconnections. In R.Grove (Ed), *Nature and the Orient: The Environmental History of South and South East Asia* (pp. 301–323). Delhi: Oxford University Press.

Gulhati, N.D (1972). *Development of Inter-State Rivers: Law and Practice in India*. Mumbai: Allied Publishers.

Hardiman, D. (2002). The politics of water in Colonial India. *South Asia: Journal of South Asian Studies, 25*(2), 111–20.DOI: 10.1080/00856400208723477

Indian Irrigation Committee(ICC). 1902. *Report of the Indian Irrigation Commission, 1901–3. Part 4 – Evidence from Punjab, Bombay, Madras*. Calcutta:Office of the Superintended of Government Printing.

Jurriens, R. and Mollinga, P. (1996). Scarcity by design. *ICID Bulletin, 45*(2),31–53.

Klingensmith, Daniel (2007). *One Valley and a Thousand: Dam, Nationalism, Development*. Oxford: Oxford University.

Kosambi, D.D. (1957). The basis of despotism: review of Karl Wittfoge's book. *Economic Weekly, 2*, 1417–1419.

Lansing, J.S. (1991). *Priests and Programmers: Technologies of Power in the Engineered Landscape of Bali*. Princeton, NJ: Princeton University Press.

Leach, E.R. (1959). Hydraulic society in Ceylon, *Past & Present, 15*, 2–26.

Leach, E.R. (1961). *Pul Eliya, a Village in Ceylon: A Study of Land Tenure and Kinship*. Cambridge: Cambridge University Press.

Maurer, J.-L. (1990). Irrigation, riziculture et gestion de l'eau en Indonésie: la modernisation des traditions agrohydrauliques à Java et Bali. *Revue de Géographie de Lyon, 65*(1), 27–37.

Masubichi, T. (1966). Wittfogel's theory of oriental society (or Hydraulic Society) and the development of studies of Chinese social and economic history in Japan. *The Developing Economies*, *4*(3), 316–326.

Mishra, D.K. (1997). The Bihar flood story. *Economic and Political Weekly*, *32*(35), 2206–2217.

Mollinga, P. (2003). *On the Waterfront: Water Distribution, Technology, and Agrarian Change in a South Indian Canal Irrigation System. Volume 5 of Wageningen University Water Resources Series*. Netherlands: Orient Longman.

Phadke, R. (2002). Assessing water scarcity and watershed development in Maharashtra, India. *Science, Technology and Human Values*, *27*(2), 236–261. DOI: 10.1177/016224390202700203

Price, D.H. (1994). Wittfogel's neglected hydraulic/hydroagricultural distinction. *Journal of Anthropological Research*, *50*(2), 87–204.

Pringle, G. (1978). The early development of cost-benefit analysis. *Journal of Agricultural Economics*, *29*(1), 63–71. DOI: 10.1111/j.1477-9552.1978.tb02399.x

Radkau, J. (2013). Nature and power: An intimate ambiguous connection. *Social Science History*, *37*(3), 325–345. DOI: 10.1017/S0145553200014243

Rangachari, R. (2006). *Bhakra Nangal Project: Socio Economic and Environmental Impact*. New Delhi: Oxford University Press.

Reddy, M.A. (1990). Travails of an irrigation canal company in South India, 1857–1882. *Economic and Political Weekly*, *25*(12),619–628.

Report of the Indian Famine Commission (1880). London, Her Majesty's Stationery Office, printed by G.E. Eyre and W. Spottiswoode. Retrieved from https://catalog.hathitrust.org/Record/012155316.

Roy Chowdhury, A. (2013). Decommissioning Large Dams in India: A Comparative Assessment of Mullaperiyar and other Cases. *Development in Practice*, *23* (2), 292–298. DOI: 10.1080/09614524.2013.772563

Roy Chowdhury, A. (2014a). *Subalternity, State-Formation and Movements against Hydropower Projects in India, 1920–2004*. PhD Thesis, Department of Sociology, National University of Singapore.

Roy Chowdhury, A. (2014b). 'Repertoires of Contention' in Movements Against Hydropower Projects in India. *Social Movement Studies*, *13*(3): 399–405. DOI: 10.1080/14742837.2013.830564

Roy Chowdhury, A. (2018). State-formation from below: Social movement of the dam-evictees and legal transformation of the local state in India, 1960–1976. *South Asia: Journal of South Asian Studies*, *41*(1), 194–211. DOI: 10.1080/00856401.2018.1406445

Roy Chowdhury, A. and Kipgen, N. (2013). Deluge amidst conflict: Hydropower, development and displacement in north-east region of India. *Progress in Development Studies*, *13*(8), 195–208. DOI: 10.1177/1464993413486545.

Shabad, T. (1959). Non-western views of the 'Hydraulic Society'[Part 1]. *Annals of the Association of American Geographers*, *49*(3), 324–325. DOI: 10.1111/j.1467-8306.1959.tb01617.x

Shah, T. (2011). Past, present and future of canal irrigation in India, Chapter 6, India Infrastructure Report (pp. 69–89), Mumbai: IDFC. Retrieved from http://www.idfc.com/pdf/report/2011/Chp-6-Past-Present-and-the-Future-of-Canal-Irrigation.pdf

Sharma, S. (2001). *Famine, Philanthropy and the Colonial State: North India in the Early Nineteenth Century*. Delhi: Oxford University Press.
Spate, O.H.K. (1959). The hydraulic society (Book Review). *Annals of the Association of American Geographers*, *49*(1), 90–95.
Srinivas, M.N. (1959). The dominant caste in Rampura. *American Anthropologist*, *16*(1), 1–16. DOI: 10.1525/aa.1959.61.1.02a00030
Stone, I. (1984). *Canal Irrigation in British India: Perspectives on Technological Change in a Peasant Economy*. Cambridge: Cambridge University Press.
Stargardt, J. (1986). Hydraulic works and Southeast Asia polities. In D.G.Marr and A.C.Milner, (Eds), *Southeast Asia in the 9th and 14th Centuries* (pp. 23–39). Singapore: Institute of Southeast Asian Studies.
Stargardt, J. (1992). Le cosmos, les ancêtres et le riz; l'eau dans l'espace urbain des Pyus en Birmanie. In G.Condominas (Ed.), *Disciplines croisées, hommage à Bernard-Philippe Groslier* (pp. 311–35). Paris: Ecole des Hautes Etudes en Sciences Sociales.
Stott, P. (1992). Angkor: Shifting the hydraulic paradigm. In J.Rigg(Ed.), *The Gift of Water: Water Management, Cosmology and the State in Southeast Asia* (pp. 47–58). London: School of Oriental and African Studies.
Wade, R. (1982). The system of administrative and political corruption: Canal irrigation in South India. *Journal of Development Studies*, *18*(3), 287–328. DOI: 10.1080/00220388208421833
Wallerstein, I. (1974). *The Modern World-System*. New York: Academic Press.
Wallach, B. (1985). British irrigation works in India's Krishna Basin. *Journal of Historical Geography*, *11*(2), 155–173. DOI: 10.1016/S0305-7488(85)80062-1
Weil, B. (2006). The rivers come: Colonial flood control and knowledge systems in the Indus Basin, 1840s-1930. *Environment and History*, *12*(1), 3–29. DOI: 10.3197/096734006776026818
Whitecomb, E. (1983). Irrigation. In D.Kumar (Ed.), *Cambridge Economic History of India Vol. II* (pp. 677–737). Cambridge: Cambridge University Press.
Whitecomb, E. (1995). The environmental cost of water logging, Salinity and Malaria. In D.Arnold and R.Guha (Eds.), *Nature, Culture, Imperialism: Essays on the Environmental History of South Asia* (pp. 237–259). Delhi: Oxford University Press.
Wijeyewardene, G. (1971). *Hydraulic Society in Contemporary Thailand?*Canberra: Australian National University Press.
Willcocks, W. (1913). *Egyptian Irrigation*. London. E. & F. N. Spon, ltd.
Wilkinson, T. J., and Rayne, L. (2010). Hydraulic landscapes and imperial power in the near east. *Water History*, *2*(2), 115–144. DOI: 10.1007/s12685-010-0024-1
Wittfogel, K. (1957). *Oriental Despotism: A Comparative Study of Total Power*. New Haven: Yale University Press.
Worster, D. (1977). *Rivers of Empire: Water, Aridity and Growth of the American West*. New York: Pantheon.

Chapter 7

Re-contextualising microcredit

From reinventing development to the financialisation of everyday life

Sarasij Majumder and Debarati Sen[1]

Introduction

Globalisation has been a hotly debated term and concept. Some questioned its newness and others, its naturalness. Historian Fredrick Cooper (2001) characterised "globalisation" as "Banker's Boast" – a euphemism for post–Cold War finance capitalist empire building (p. 192). Nonetheless, the term evoked the transnational character of our everyday and the intimate spheres. The term captured the widening locus of interventions and redressals, beyond the nation-state. It spoke to the expectations, desires and protest subjectivities that transcended national borders. Even anti-globalisation activists at the turn of the century (in Seattle and Washington D.C.) imagined a world without borders that echoed the imaginaries of finance capitalists. The transnational imagery transformed globalisation simultaneously into a metaphor for mainstream development and also for an alternative vision for myriad connections across continents to uplift the poor.

Microcredit and/or microfinance seized the transnational imagination of both the policymakers with liberal visions of globalisation of the free market and state austerity and the grassroots activists in the early 1980s. Touted as the alternative route to transnational connections that bypass the nation-state, the corporations, and connect the local with the global like never before, microfinance seemed to overturn the post-war structures, institutions and tenets of development. Seeing poor rural women as worthy of loans and their peer-group pressure as collateral not only disrupted the top-down vertical vision of development intervention, it also questioned the modernisation narrative that could hardly envision agency of rural women of the global south, who were imagined to be mired in tradition and engulfed in collectivism.

The globalisation and transnational project did not see Westernisation as the necessary first step for development. Rather cultural differences and local particularities were seen as unique and necessary endowments or capabilities that could be monetised and traded to fetch an income and profit for the community-based enterprise. The liberal capitalist vision dovetailed

DOI: 10.4324/9781003159940-7

with academic critiques of development and modernity. The latter saw development as a discursive formation constituting knowledge, institutions and practices reiterating the power and domination of erstwhile colonial powers over territories that they once controlled and moulded after themselves erasing or devaluing their particularities and differences.

Mindful of the trenchant critiques of the World Bank, the president of the World Bank had sought to reinvent the Bank in the late 1990s and early 2000s. James Wolfensohn sided with protestors in Seattle and Washington D.C. He agreed with protestors and defended the World Bank claiming that he is "ahead of the protestors" (*International Herald Tribune, 2009*, 2000, p. 19). The Bank, Wolfensohn emphasised, is empowering the poor to sell goods in the market place through microlending instead of funding large projects.

Wolfensohn's desire to beat the protestors in their own game with microloans is a telling example of the development establishment's attempt to tame its critique – how anti-development can be turned into basic tenets of new development policies. This became evident, anthropologist Julia Elyachar (2005) notes, in training programmes linked to microlending schemes funded by the World Bank and other development agencies (p. 496). Training programmes that Elyachar (2002) attended in Cairo taught community and NGO leaders to respect the hidden entrepreneurial qualities of the third world poor, particularly women. The celebration of the entrepreneurial spirit of the poor came with a focus on the informal or the micro-enterprise. The informal economy, that is, the realm beyond the reach of state interference and sanctions, replaced the formal economy as the main target of intervention. Such a shift accorded well with the neoliberal ideology that advocated contraction of the state from the economy.

However, a concrete and governable scale emerged in the world of development that was variously called the local, community, or the people. The rhetoric was one of the devolution of power from the state and the elites to the people. Empowering the people and the communities directly based on what they understand as their needs bypassing the state became the solution to the ills of top-down development that reeked of socialism or cold war optics. Market triumphalism of dry economic theory found in people, the informal economy and in their so-called spontaneity its concrete content in the development sector. "In the same buildings where neoliberal economic agendas were worked out as development programs," Elyachar (2002) writes, "the people and the community were embraced in the guise of the informal economy" (p. 497). In the non-governmental organisations (NGOs) circuit, where funding proposals circulated and dollar donations registered, "the people" acquired an "economic tint" (Elyachar, 2002, p. 497).

"People," here, were not the nation-state or the nation but communities or individuals who live together. NGOs emerged as representatives of the people bypassing the existing democratic structures affiliated to the state with deeper histories of political struggles, institutional memories and economic hardships. NGOs became synonymous with civil society and distributed loans farmed out by international organisations, such as the World Bank or USAID and development agencies. Often NGOs tapped into large grants and turn the money into microloans. Some banks turned themselves into NGOs and started practising microlending at the market rate. Thus, NGOs and the civil society sector embodied a mechanism that lowered institutional cost credit recovery through its reliance on social networks and mutual trust in the community.

Microlending and NGOs became a surreptitious conduit for the entry of global capital in various forms and guises into the villages, households and localities that were once thought to be distant and contained within the nation-state. This was jarringly demonstrated when the Grameen Bank of Bangladesh, the originator of the microlending phenomenon, signed a contract with the multinational agricultural firm Monsanto (which has been at the centre of debates about genetically engineered foods). Monsanto used the microloan credit networks of Grameen Bank in Bangladesh to distribute its seeds, collect payments and monitor farmers who tried to store their seeds for reproduction rather than buying Monsanto's genetically engineered, self-destructing variety. NGOs and their microlending networks based on community trust, thus, could become private police that enforce financial discipline for the reproduction of corporate capital in the name of empowering people (RAFI, 1998).

Hence, scholars studying microfinance have described microfinance either as poverty capital (Roy, 2010) or as empowerment debt. Julia Elyachar (2005) argues microfinance prepares a populace conducive to neoliberal market rule that emphasises entrepreneurship and seeing economic values in social networks. Ananya Roy (2010) sees microfinance as poverty capital which discovers the poor as a good investment because it can generate steady, regular and long-term returns on investment. Others, such as Lamia Karim (2011) argue microcredit empowers the NGOs instead of the people. NGOs' power over the micro-debtors increases so much that they emerge as a parallel state wedded in a transnational network of money and credit flows. While Elyachar (2005) and Roy (2010) focus on the global power of finance, Karim (2011) highlights the messiness inherent in the working microfinance on the ground defying the expectations of free-market relations presumed in the economic models.

Thus, the effectiveness of microfinance is not the issue because microfinance's ability to alleviate poverty is at best minimal (see Duflo et al., 2013, also discussed later in this chapter). The more important area of both academic and development concern is how does microfinance affect and transform relations among and between villagers, genders, citizens and the state and the NGOs? What kind of political and gendered subjects does microfinance create? And what role does the state play in this new kind of management of poverty that seeks to bypass its structures? In other words, studying microfinance is looking at relationships, practices and cultures that this practice of extending microcredit loans spawns. Rather than taking a total view that sees the life-world of the poor colonised entirely by the microfinance discourse disseminated by the NGOs, we see strategies, tactics and practices that have implications far broader than simply contesting capitalism or its hegemonic discourse.

In the rest of the chapter, we are going to briefly talk about the history of microcredit, microcredit and social capital, aspects of empowerment that relate to microcredit, and gender relations, and state-citizen relations.

The emergence of microcredit

Seeing the emergence of microcredit critically is an important first step in understanding microcredit's role in restructuring the management of poverty and the poor's understanding of themselves amidst global policy trends. Any critique of microcredit should begin by contesting the usual telling of microcredit's history that sees Mohammed Yunus as the inventor of microcredit. While societies, economies and NGOs in India and Bangladesh had a part to play, a conjunctural perspective to ascertain the emergence of the form that microcredit eventually took explains a lot about its spread.

Some British colonial officials often promoted cooperative credit societies to shield the villagers from moneylenders. The trajectory of these credit societies was chequered (Turnell, 2005). Turnell (2005) observes that cooperative credit societies were introduced in the whole of India and Burma in the first three decades of the 20th century. The societies were state funded but promoted free market and proclaimed freedom from state interference. The number of credit cooperatives operating in different parts of South Asia reached approximately 100,000 by the 1930s and enrolled roughly 1 million members. However, the paucity of funding, local politics and increasing clout of the money lenders within these cooperatives led to the decline of these credit cooperatives. Nonetheless, the significance of cooperative credit societies in rural development was acknowledged by activists and academics. Anthropologist Clifford Geertz (1962) identified rotating credit societies as key stepping stones for communities to transform themselves from agrarian peasant societies to one in which trade became central (p. 262).

In the post-independence period, banking increased in rural India but the informal operation of cooperative credit societies continued. In 1972 lawyer and labour organiser Ela Bhatt organised women into cooperatives and offered them banking and social services. However, the development policies pursued by the respective states in many of the South Asian countries sought to industrialise the countries and eventually absorb a surplus population from the agricultural sector or the villages. This so-called subsumption of the informal sector into a formal sector always remained a pipedream. It created a vast pool of informal sector workers who were waiting for resources to trickle down.

Consequently, the post-colonial developments came under three kinds of critiques. One line of argument affirmed that the capitalist development that the states pursued made them dependent on the erstwhile colonial powers, and is responsible for the poverty and the proliferation of the informal sector in their respective countries (Gunder Frank, 1966). Another line of critique saw capitalist development and modernisation as a process that rarely tolerates differences and diversities of livelihoods and lifeways in the so-called non-capitalistic or the informal sector (Escobar, 1994). Third, the state with its huge investments in infrastructure and the public sector came to be seen as an inefficient behemoth inimical to capitalist development and profit maximisation (see Harvey, 2005).

Development, therefore, adopted new rhetoric that would address the first line of Marxist critique, incorporate the second one and address the demands of the third, which came mostly from internal lending organisations such as the International Monetary Fund or IMF and the emergent neoliberal think tanks emboldened by the Washington Consensus.

Bangladesh, among other nations, was at a juncture that offered favourable context for the emergence of microcredit. Bangladesh was newly independent and did not have a large state sector as India. Politically, too, Bangladesh was unstable and dependent on foreign aid and external capital for developing large projects. Under these circumstances, the NGO sector flourished and worked towards capacity building, enhancing awareness and group sensitisation. Development in these circumstances became focused on people and communities rather than big infrastructural developments and manufacturing that India invested in. Microcredit in this scenario made perfect sense because it served and justified the international aids, it required small intervention at the locale scale without upsetting the powerful pressure groups in Bangladesh and it was not dependent on the state. The only sector that it had to confront was the group of local money lenders.

In this emergence of microcredit as a development tool, histories, cooperatives and credit collectives were erased, probably because microcredit initiatives from the very beginning sought to follow market principles, that is, charging market-based interest rates. The subsidies that were part of the earlier credit or cooperative movement were undermined. This charging of high market-based interest from the poor and claiming that as development or redistributive tool is the mark of the wider rise of neoliberal orthodoxy which saw credit expansion as an alternative to increased wages. While Bangladesh and other developing countries were not on the classical trajectory of capitalism (Sanyal, 2009), these countries would soon join the global commodity chain as sites of production or outsourced factories.

Broadly, therefore microcredit transpired at the juncture of several shifts in power and thinking about the economy and its relationships with the state. First, the failure of teleological thinking than the expected surplus population would be absorbed from the informal to the formal sector. The population within the informal sector had to be managed or governed (see Sanyal, 2009). Second, the withdrawal of the state sector from large-scale investment in health and education and other infrastructural opened up spaces in which NGOs could bridge the gaps and needs. Third, poverty alleviation came to be seen through the lens of financialisation that is, rather than transferring resources or money to the poor, they were seen as opportunities for expansion of credit.

In practice, microcredit projects unfolded in diverse ways. We turn to such case studies next and try to address the questions that we posed earlier.

Microcredit and social capital

Many decades after the adoption of microcredit as a development and poverty alleviation strategy researchers and policymakers alike focus on what strategies make it work. The measure of success is capitalocentric, which is directly correlated with loan repayment or replenishment of the money or capital invested with interest. A certain segment of scholars wanted to better understand what types of networks existed among the poor and which ones facilitated loan use and recovery. Here scholars turn to a branch of institutional economics inspired by the work of Elinor Ostorm (1994) who noted that social capital has been left out of discussions on economic models. Ostrom (1994) argued that social capital can be used to attain what would normally be unattainable. In her discussion on social capital, Ostrom (1994) explores the aspect of institutionalised rules in allocating resources and establishing rights and duties. Rights and duties then protect groups from free riders or people who take more than their fair share. This notion of free riders is also explored by Knoke (1988). He argues that when collective planning occurs, measures can be adapted to deter the unfair consumption of public goods. Linking this to social capital and group lending, when the collective group goals are placed above individual interests, then free ridership is less likely to occur, as was tested by Muller and Opp (1986). Microlending, structured around groups, sets up the dynamic of collective group goals by making the success or failure of one impact the others. In this context, the strengthening of locally institutionalised group norms would be critical for success.

Recognition of the role of social relationships in influencing economic processes has been increasing among economists. Anthony (1997) argues that while sociologists recognised how social processes influence the economic world, a branch of social sciences, economic sociology, studies how social processes impact economic institutions. Returning to Ostrom's (1994) emphasis on institutionalised social capital, the connection between social capital and microlending becomes even clearer, with her argument that rules are developed by self-governing communities that enable individuals to solve various problems in the community. As microlending is increasingly geared towards the empowerment of socially isolated women living in poverty-stricken environments, microlending institutions based on collective action can complement efforts to empower individuals and communities.

Social capital while important is hard to wrap one's head around since it had multiple determinants and may be culturally specific. Postelnicu and Hermes (2018) further emphasise the difficulties in quantifying social capital because of its different facets. They draw on the work of Nahapiet and Ghoshal (1998) to summarise these different facets of social capital into three broad categories:

> *structural social capital* (the presence or absence of relationships between individuals, the configuration of their networks, the characteristics of interpersonal connections, such as network connectivity, density), *relational social capital* (the type of relationship developed through past social interactions, like respect, trust, acceptance, friendship, sociability), and *cognitive social capital* (shared norms and languages, shared narratives).
>
> (p. 45)

They point to a lack of attention to social capital in determining the success of microfinance institutions and call for a closer look at social contexts from which emanate different forms of social capital impacting financial behaviour. Building on Nahapiet and Ghoshal (1998),

> they argue that social capital formation is facilitated by social determinants such as trust (i.e., relational social capital) or shared cultural aspects (i.e., cognitive social capital) and hypothesize that social capital-based lending contracts are likely to be more successful in societies where fewer hurdles are encountered in the process of social capital accumulation.
>
> (pp 45)

We will eventually come to a discussion of what kinds of social capital lead to success but here for now we need to look at a few other conceptualisations of social capital.

Sociologist Paromita Sanyal (2009) offers a general definition of social capital as the information, trust and establishment of norms within social relationships. Social capital is the result of shared information, mutual trust and shared norms in a loose network of cooperation. She continued by remarking that the institutionalised norms and informal behavioural expectations that are a part of the group dynamic of microfinance can spill over into other aspects of women's lives and therefore, the women's participation in group meetings (as would occur in group-based microfinance schemes) indeed fosters social capital.

Another way of viewing social capital and how it relates to microlending is by examining the typology of social capital and how it interacts with various economic transactions. Portes and Sensenbrenner (1993) look at what aspects of social capital impact the economic goals of the community members. They identified four specific areas: value introjection, reciprocity transactions, bounded solidarity and enforceable trust. By value introjections, Portes and Sensenbrenner (1993) are talking about an underlying morality that moves people beyond greed. The second aspect has to do with the social interactions between people that add value such as favours, information and overall good deeds that are then reciprocated. They term these interactions social intangibles. The third aspect relates to collective sentiment in the market where individual self-interest merges and forms something greater. The final aspect has to do with the benefits associated with membership in the collective. When taken together, these four aspects determine how networks are formed and add to the microcosm of informal market exchanges. Though these elements influence the economic welfare of the members within the immigrant communities in America (the population they were interested in), it did not always work to benefit them, especially if restrictions were placed on membership within the community, too few had too much power or influence, and the pressure on those who choose to exit the community and find success as an individual.

The cost/benefit risks of social capital for the individual involved has been well studied within the United States. Woolcock (2001) gains insights from a study that confirmed the findings of Portes and Sensenbrenner (1993). However, despite the risks to individual success, Woolcock (2001) has asserted that social capital is a way of using social relationships as collateral in microfinance programmes. Therefore, the underlying assumption is that group may advance farther than individuals and that how they socialise plays into their ability to gain access to microfinance. For the advancement of the group to be more beneficial for the individuals Woolcock (2001) suggests the social capital would have to, "(1) nurture vibrant communities; (2) facilitate progressive incorporation of the poor into the formal economy; (3) produce coherent, competent, and credible institutions; and (4) ensure that dynamic, complementary relationships are forged and maintained between communities and development organizations" (p. 197).

Interestingly absent in these discussions are considerations of the double-edgedness of social capital as an asset. One can say that in many communities in which loan taking was confined to traditional borrowing from money lenders, the type of social capital that existed was predatory. Even if it was not the case, existing moralities that uphold social reproduction at the community level become assets for loan-giving companies. This is amply shown in Lamia Karim's (2008) study of Bangladesh. She shows how neo-liberal logics and Islamic morality come together to make the moral code of gendered existence (women's honour and shame) the collateral which ensures loan return while further financialising women's lives. In the economic environment of state austerity, these loans fill the financial gap of meeting food and survival needs.

The financialisation of life enters through these gendered moral relations at the community level. This is seen in the experiences of loan officers and borrowers of private microfinance initiatives like DENA [a pseudonym Sohini Kar (2018) uses in her book]. The precarity of the loan officers is a notable feature of Kar's (2018) ethnography and enables her to make a distinct contribution to the growing body of ethnographic work on microfinance. The loan officers enjoy the "respect" they earn from borrowers and can also wield power by categorising borrowers as "high-risk" (Kar, 2018, p. 100). Here existing forms of structural inequities play into the labelling of a "high-risk" borrower and eventually loans denied. The complexity of the everyday practices of a loan officer belies the standard negative image of moneylenders in Indian society. Kar (2018) writes that

> loan officers have to struggle against their stigmatization as debt collectors while ensuring they complete their work. To emphasize their difference, they use powerful and coercive affective pressures such as embarrassment and shame rather than violence to make sure borrowers pay.
>
> (Kar, 2018, p. 5)

Kar's (2018) findings of loan officers in Kolkata corroborate Lamia Karim's (2008) findings in Bangladesh where honour and shame are also used as collaterals.

The potential friction between borrowers and these ground-level executives is mitigated by both parties navigating existing socialities on which social capital stands. Kar's (2018) findings are similar to our ethnographic work on microcredit practices in rural Darjeeling where sociality is key to loan disbursal and loan return and is a key component of risk management (Sen and Majumder, 2015). Kar's (2018) ethnography demystifies the much thrown around the idea of social capital seen as the anchor through which privatised microfinance companies potentially ensure a 90% return on loans. Instead, Kar (2018) upholds the complex layers of relationships and moralities around finance that emerge in the loan return process. In her research the emerging moralities around money stood out in the Bengali phrase *taka ta khachchina* [translated by Kar (2018) as "we don't eat the money" (pp. 193)] that women borrowers used to mark responsible use and re-investment of loans to ensure return. Financialisation of lives is rampant where the poor use private company loans to fill in for the lack of state services. Kar (2018) demonstrates how successive political parties at the helm of affairs have promoted microcredit as a way out of poverty and/or a step to empower women. Kar (2018) makes a distinction between financial inclusion, popularised by lending companies, and enfolding, which "marks how financialization captures everyday life" (p. 17).

Social capital has also been used by the World Bank to shift the onus of development from the state to the civil society, as mentioned earlier. The shift meant that microlending/microcredit was used to provide what economists define as "public goods," such as water and sanitation. In some societies such provisions are usually provided and maintained by the government or the state because either these goods or provisions cannot be divided or consumed privately or any idea of doing so defeats the whole purpose and utility of such provisions, and morally and legally all citizens should have access to such goods. Thus, the idea of using microfinance as a market-based mechanism for generating demand for public goods and services represents a radical extension of the idea of the entrepreneur. The entrepreneur and his/her attitudes, networks and predilections for bearing costs and risks, and earning a profit, it is thought, can be harnessed for the social and collective benefits and ends. The underlying assumption is that microfinance, entrepreneurship and debt obligations can also set the ball rolling for cooperative behaviour or actions which do not have immediate material value or ensure people pay for the provisions that they consume (i.e. prevent them from being free rider). Here microfinance is not simply reliant on existing or emerging social capital in communities but it seeks to foster it.

The most outlandish extension of such logic has been to use microfinance as a tool to create peace and order. A Melon-MIT-funded research on microcredit and conflict mitigation in Cameroon refuted its hypothesis that microloans caused community members to interact with members with whom they have tensions, differences or enmity (Heen, 2004). Nonetheless, funding and interest in such projects continued.

Regarding water and sanitation, studies show that the attempts to push households to buy those provisions through microfinance loans encountered problems on many fronts (Mader, 2015). First, many targeted families refused to take loans to buy water or sanitation connections because the NGOs could not justify how that will have an immediate impact on their earnings. The households that opted for such loans did so based on attitudes and values that were not rooted in the financial cost-benefit calculation but in desire for certain kinds of lifestyles or some were coerced. Second, there was a lack of funding for the overheads or infrastructures, i.e. main pipes for sanitation or delivery of sufficient water. This shows that without microfinancing and government involvement in bearing long-term costs, it is difficult to sustain supplies of such provisions. Third, poorer or disadvantaged households got excluded or dropped out of the scheme because of the general disadvantages that they encountered in the society which are inimical to earning a steady livelihood.

Questions of empowerment

The foregoing discussion on social capital shows that the networks and affinities through which the success of microcredit comes about in certain communities entrench structural power and inequities including entrenching state power through financial debt. Honour, shame, kith and kin ties become collaterals for loan returns. In this context how is women's empowerment to be worked out? We present a range of possibilities, but our general findings based on our ethnographic research are that microcredit complicates women's position in their communities and the path to empowerment is difficult.

Some scholars equate the empowerment potential of microcredit with poverty alleviation. Dr. Mohammad Yunus, the founder of the Grameen Bank, recognised that women were often the poorest in Bangladeshi society and received only 1% of all credit (Ahmed, 2008). Therefore, he reprioritised the involvement of women in poverty alleviation as women would be more likely to spend the money on the welfare of the household (Ahmed, 2008). For instance, in a study concerning the lending institutions within Bangladesh, Goetz and Gupta (1994) begin by questioning whether portrayals of the success of microcredit in Bangladesh are accurate in terms of the extent of control women have over their loans. They conducted a study based on 275 loans from four organisations in villages throughout Bangladesh, where they used the purposive selection to find a variety of participants who have participated for a variety of time and loan amounts. Of the four organisations, Goetz and Gupta (1994) found that Grameen Bank had the best record in terms of how much control women had over their loans. On the other side, banks also need to ensure control over their money. Sharma and Zeller (1997) looked at the loan delinquency rates of nationalised commercial banks versus group-based credit institutions. Their study used data from the International Food Policy Research Institute that looked at 868 loan transactions from 41 villages that were examined from the differing lending agencies in Bangladesh, Association for Social Advancement (ASA, BRAC and Rangpur Dinajpur Rural Service (RDRS)). Sharma and Zeller (1997) found that especially in remote areas, group lending had significantly higher repayment rates than at nationalised commercial banks.

Ferdoushi Ahmed along with Siwar and Idris (2011a, b, c, d) have coauthored several studies based on the impact of microcredit credit in Bangladesh on rural women. In their article on women's participation, Ahmed, Siwar, and Idris (2011d) explore how microcredit is a tool that lifts women out of poverty and encourages their participation in the Grameen Bank, Bangladesh Rural Advancement Committee (BRAC), ASA, and

Proshika Manobik Unnayan Kendra (Proshika Centre for human development, Proshika). Overall, they argue that the Grameen Bank model, which has had overwhelming success in their eyes (97% of borrowers are women, 97% loan recovery rate, and most impressive, recent reports state that 68% of borrowers have crossed the poverty threshold line. The authors (2011d) argued that this model, which is a variety of lending and savings plans has been a success in other countries as well, such as the Philippines, Kenya and Malaysia.

In another study, centred on how microcredit improves family income Ahmed, Siwar and Idris (2011a) continued their assessment of the successes of the Grameen Bank. Their study consisted of two groups of respondents, "with credit," comprised of Grameen Bank members, and "without credit." Both groups were from the Panchagarh District. They used face-to-face interviews randomly selected from their sample. Their findings indicate that women with credit contribute more to their overall household incomes, and those incomes are substantially higher than those without credit. Their study implied that microcredit positively contributed to income and inspired women to actively engage in income-generating activities (Ahmed, Siwar and Idris, 2011a). Pitt and Khandker (1998) also examine how the gender of the participant mattered in terms of groups-based microcredit's impacts on poor households in Bangladesh. They specifically examined participants in programmes by the Grameen Bank, BRAC, and Bangladesh Rural Development Board's (BRDB) Rural Development RD-12 programme. There were 87 villages in their household survey sample, 40 with credit programmes, 15 without, and 22 with female-only groups and 10 with male-only groups. They surveyed 1991–1992.

In yet another study, Ahmed, Siwar and Idris (2011b) explore the relationship between women's well-being and microcredit in Bangladesh. In this study, the authors again used face-to-face interviews to collect data from 200 rural women in the Pachagarh Districts. They were specifically studying the effects of microcredit on well-being vis-à-vis the women's empowerment to leave the home and seek outside employment. Typically, poor women in Bangladesh are not allowed to participate in activities outside the home that may help them contribute to their family's economic situation. Their findings support the role of microcredit in helping both alleviate poverty and sustain their livelihoods. Moreover, by participating in microcredit programmes, women were more empowered to act independently, such as going to the market alone. In their concluding remarks, the authors have suggested that participation in the Grameen Bank leads to greater gender equality in Bangladesh (Ahmed, Siwar, and Idris, 2011b).

Rankin (2001) notes that many view microcredit as the way to eliminate global poverty and women are targeted as agents of change. However, while Rankin (2001) acknowledges there is great potential for women to benefit from microcredit, the process of microcredit is derived from a neoliberal agenda that has impacted gender and development thinking. This forces the needs of women to be recognised within the neoliberal framework and uses their participation as a way of strengthening financial markets. Thus Rankin (2001) argues that the government should have better regulating neoliberal agendas as a way of balancing the reinforcement of social hierarchies.

Microlending is not the only intervention for poverty reduction and should not be counted in as such, according to MacIsaac (1997). He argues that microcredit has the potential to be a part of poverty alleviation; however, the poorest of the poor rarely benefit from microcredit, perhaps in part because it is not the right form of intervention. MacIsaac (1997) agrees with Hilson and Ackah-Baidoo (2011), arguing that structural issues at the heart of poverty are not addressed through microcredit. He goes even further, stating that microcredit is a minimalist approach that may neglect the social mobilisation necessary to address poverty. Still, he argues that microcredit, when limited to just one of many intervention types may indeed have some positive impacts on women by addressing immediate poverty.

Mayoux (1998) also recognises how microfinance is increasingly targeting women as fundamental participants in poverty reduction as well as benefitting women's status in society. However, she contends that claims of the success of microfinance in this capacity must come with a caveat; gender considerations must be taken seriously. In a later study Mayoux (2002) found that microfinance programmes must be designed in such a way that the components of social credit must work to empower the poorest of women. Building on social capital can increase poverty alleviation. She argues that microfinance groups could be an entry point for women to begin to build their business networks; however, those groups should not restrict horizontal networking outside of the group. The group should provide training and workshops to help them create a strategy concerning their economic growth and to mitigate the constraints they are up against. Mayoux (1998) also argues for the need to incorporate men into these processes as this would provide an avenue to address gender issues within the household. Since household hostilities over loan return and women's increased exposure to public life has been an issue this gender-inclusive approach was thought to be important. This finding corroborates Sen and Majumder's (2015) observations: that household-level resource struggles get acute when compounded by strict gender ideologies at the community level which augment the social risk for women.

Microlending has long been an established practice to help small, usually family-run businesses to expand or get started. For a myriad of reasons, especially the global focus on the development and empowerment of women, microlending agencies have targeted women entrepreneurs specifically. Sanyal (2009) observes that microfinance programmes aimed at targeting poverty are almost exclusively focused on women and groups. The purpose of this focus has been to empower women by giving them a chance to be economically independent. Sanyal (2009) raises the important question of how this empowerment has impacted women's social relationships with each other. Sanyal (2009) defines women's empowerment as their ability to become self-reliant, make their own choices and have control over both the material and non-material aspects of their lives. However, she explained that many women do not experience this form of empowerment, especially in South Asia.

The way that group microlending impacts the social relationships of women can be twofold, impacting both women as a group as well as individuals. According to Anthony (1997), norms emerge within the group in what she calls group-mediated social control. At the same time, the group's access to loans can be contingent on one member's standing, thus the whole of the group is impacted by the credit of one. Then there is the impact on the individual. Women learn from and teach each other. They can pursue new business opportunities collectively. Social capital is increased through the women's participation in group lending programmes, which will then contribute to the development of the community and open the community's access to outside resources.

Noted scholars of microcredit caution against taking a homogenising approach when assessing the empowerment effects of microcredit. They emphasise looking at the gendered subject formation that has resulted from women's development in general comparing it to specific effects of microcredit on subjectivity. Economist Naila Kabeer (2001) also focuses on the methodology of seeking results and its impact on the findings. Kabeer (2001) takes a comparative approach and explores the methodologies and conclusions of six studies on the question of microcredit as a tool to empower women. She then provides her own study. She finds there are three that find negative results and some going so far as to disempower women (even increasing domestic violence). The other three studies find that microcredit may positively impact women's empowerment. Kabeer's (2001) study showed that girls benefitted from loans as their mothers used the money to promote their education. She also found that society, not just individual men, had more to do with disempowering women and that in some cases, certain loans helped women achieve greater parity in household decision-making. The differences between the various results found were traced to the types of questions the researchers asked, according to Kabeer (2001). Where she focused on both surveys and testimonials, she tried to view each woman as an individual rather than a group of homogeneous subjects.

To avoid homogeneity in study results, Karim (2008) takes a more intersectional approach and found that certain groups benefitted more than others. In her study of the Grameen Bank, she found that rural middle-class women benefitted the most from the lending programmes. These women or their husbands have pre-existing skills that enable them to best make use of the lending programme. Karim (2008) differs from Kabeer (2001) in that she sees the lending programme as a way for NGOs, who manipulate their reports in ways to secure more funding from Western donors, to profit. This critique is a far cry from the empowerment potential others see though Karim (2008) is not alone in her opinion. Elyachar (2005) also sees that the role of NGOs in promoting microlending schemes is suspect. She examines how Cairo's workshops are changing, in one part due to the emergence of young entrepreneurs who promote and benefit from microlending which is promoted by NGOs. The NGOs along with the young entrepreneurs are not successful in transforming the undercurrent of workshop culture in Cairo, but instead compete with it; thus demonstrating that microlending programmes may not be successful at addressing what Karim (2008) sees as societal structures that disempower women.

Women's different expectations reveal themselves in grounded case studies from Rajasthan (Moodie, 2008) and Uttar Pradesh (Sharma, 2008) and mark the emergence of new socialities where women get to discuss other problems they are facing with finances and more. They stay involved to gain from these forms of social relationships. In other places in India, like Darjeeling (West Bengal) Sen and Majumder (2015) have shown that women develop a differential understanding of the risk based on the social stigma they face and their constant efforts to navigate such. Thus they use the faulty iteration of the English word for risk – riks – to underscore their many contributions to the health of family and village life through the successful navigation of men's ire and shaming. They put forward that these risks are as dangerous as the financial risk that loan officers always want them to mitigate. Women also used the savings from microcredit to practice inter-lending to reduce interaction with outsider men which irked their family members who questioned these types of male–female interactions.

Ahmed, Chowdhury and Bhuiya (2001) have also conducted studies on the emotional well-being of microcredit recipients in Matlab, a rural area in Bangladesh. They utilised secondary, cross-sectional data from the BRAC-ICDDR, B Joint Research Project. Using this data, they test to see the effect of microcredit on rural women's emotional well-being. Their findings differ from the study conducted by Ahmed, Siwar and Idris (2011b) in that they suggest that there is some anxiety associated with microcredit programmes, and as a result, women who perceived themselves as household contributors reported more emotional stress. The authors note that BRAC was not in Matlab for an extended period and thus the findings should be treated with caution, though a later study confirms the findings of the study at hand.

Additional studies centred on Bangladesh include Pitt, Khandker and Cartwright's (2006) study concerning women's empowerment through microcredit by examining the impact of microcredit on men and women in households (as only one member of a household can receive a loan). The study was based on a large-scale household survey distributed throughout rural Bangladesh. The households were randomly selected in 87 villages and represented three programmes, the Grameen Bank, BRAC and BRDB RD 12. A total of 1,798 surveys were sent out. This survey was conducted in the late 1990s and built off a similar effort in the early 1990s. The survey was divided into nine thematic groups ranging from purchasing power to household economic decision-making to fertility. These themes were then accounted for in the overall sense of empowerment. The authors (2016) found that, in general, women were empowered by microcredit, and when the microcredit was taken out by women, it tended to benefit the household welfare more overall than when it was taken out by men.

Similar to Bangladesh, many scholars have explored microlending in India, and specifically how microlending is designed to specifically empower women. Garikipati (2008) explored the question of women's empowerment as a result of microcredit in India. Garikipati (2008) conducted detailed surveys of 117 married couples who were involved in microcredit programmes in India, and 174 who were eligible, but chose not to participate in the years 2001–2002. She concludes that lending is beneficial to women and households, especially when the women manage the money, and that microcredit alone may not be sufficient for addressing all the needs associated with poverty in India. Holvoet (2005) also explores the concept of empowerment of women through microfinance in India. She used household surveys as well credit from both Tamil Nadu Women's Development Programme (TNWDP) and Integrated Rural Development Program (IRDP) and also selected women involved in IRDP but who lived in villages without groups. They also limited their area to the Morappur Block of the Dharmapuri District. Holvoet (2005) concludes that while women may get more say in how to use the loan, increased decision-making does not translate into other spheres of household management, although participation in group programmes does yield a shift in bargaining levels within the household between married couples. Groups, coupled with peer pressure, tended to keep families on track for using the loans as intended as well.

Rai and Ravi (2011) question the likelihood of borrowing partners versus nonborrowing partners making insurance claims when part of the microlending programme has compulsory insurance. Their sample consisted of 802,998 individuals in India whose coverage began after 1 May 2006. Rai and Ravi (2011) suggest that borrowers are better informed than their spouses, and male borrowers may not share insurance information with their spouses. When the borrower is female, she is more likely to share insurance information. There also may be a gap of financial literacy within the village that prevents people from understanding how insurance works. Finally, they have noted that borrowers have higher opportunity costs from being sick and thus may seek medical attention sooner as their position as a borrower requires them to be active.

Lahiri-Dutt and Samanta (2006) looked at how lending groups in India promoted social capital. They raised the question of whether, due to the small group microcredit success, all groups and networks should be viewed in a positive light. They explore the collapse of self-help groups run by the Development of Women and Children in Rural Areas (DWCRA), which ran a microfinancing programme in India. They used secondary data, interviews of officials, statistics and census data from Burdwan state in West Bengal. They also interviewed women who had participated in successful and failed groups. They discovered that part of group failure was related to the overestimation of programme coordinators on interest in group participation in Burdwan among women, as well as religious differences that limited some women's participation. Finally, the networking and freedom that was achieved within the group did not translate to other areas of participation for women.

Other cases that have been studied are in many countries, mainly concentrating on Nigeria. Igzubara (2004) examined empowerment in Nigeria. Igzubara (2004) looks at two programmes in Abia state, Genderlift Foundation Project (GFP), and the Rural Women's Economic Aid (RUWEAP). With the help of a research team, data was collected through interviews of groups and individuals. Of the 117 individuals interviewed, the majority were female participants in microcredit groups, some staff members of the two programmes, and some husbands of the borrowers. Igzubara (2004) found that participation in microcredit somewhat benefits women in terms of their economic independence and the condition of their livelihood. However, it was noteworthy that many of the women interviewed did not strive for equality with their husbands, and rather, were able to put their children through school, and overall, they reported an increased say in household decisions. However, Igzubara (2004) has argued that the benefits of microcredit remain concentrated on their income and do not shift overall patterns of male dominance. Omorodion (2007) also looked into microcredit programmes in Nigeria, focusing on the Better Life Programme (modelled after the Grameen Bank) in Benin City in Edo state. She interviewed 20 Esan women in microcredit groups. In keeping with Igzubara's (2004) findings that gender role dynamics were unchanged by the microcredit programmes, Omorodion (2007) found that microcredit programmes increased women's anxiety as their husbands often took the loan money and prevented the women from paying back the loan. Part of the weakness of the programme is that it took a top-down approach according to Omorodion (2007) and did not factor in cultural norms and pre-existing social structures within the society, thus the women were not empowered.

While some scholars continue to note some positive impacts on microcredit, the overwhelming evidence from grounded community-based qualitative studies that pay attention to gender relationships and its interweaving with resource struggles are most circumspect of the agenda. Smitha Radhakrishnan's (2018) research perhaps best summarises what such studies conclude. She writes about financial inclusion:

> Including" poor women in the global financial system involves loans, as we might expect, but it also involves a set of "soft" ideas that aim to expand women's identities in a way that integrates paid work into the unpaid work of mothering. Consequently, the expansion of the global financial system, rather than unfolding as a linear progression toward financial inclusion, maybe a contested, uneven process that requires cooperation from working-class women on both material and ideological fronts.
>
> (p. 84)

Radhakrishnan (2018) and Stephen Young (2010)) (working in Andhra Pradesh) both underscore the interpellation of housewives as "entrepreneurial mothers" remains a central trope in enabling loan seeking. Like Sen and Majumder (2015) we see through Radhakrishnan's study that women try to maintain their sense of self, their subjective references, and increasingly reject loans when the terms are turned against them.

Conclusion

Microcredit or microfinance in its current form is a governance mechanism. But it operates differently from the way governance conventionally works with its direct and indirect ties to the government agencies, or the state. Microcredit has unleashed decentralised governance of people in the informal economy eking out livelihoods precariously through debt. Through debt, people are tied to NGOs, financial institutions, and also the state. Through the training and disciplining practices, people are also drawn to ideologies and ways of being. But neither the state nor its coercive power is the main mode of governance. Debt or credit, for the most part, regulates individuals, communities and relationships through self-regulation. Borrowers discipline themselves through notions of shame, guilt, desire, achievement, self-reliance and entrepreneurship. These notions do not always work according to the scripts imagined by the organisations that extend loans but have their own social lives based on particular histories and social relationships. These histories and relationships, however, tend to become stained by the spectres of financial obligations.

Microcredit as a development or poverty alleviation tool is an outcome of financialised capitalism. It tapped into a necessity and desire to be self-reliant, and the aspirations for liberation from a centralised authority that had existed in communities for a long time. Yet in these desires to be different and autonomous lay the seeds for a financialised global society. In spite of their multiple trajectories, each site affected by microlending is a testament to the failure of financialised capitalism. One can only hope that a global solidarity of communities and individuals' question and contest the financial institutions and their lending practices and not just the state.

Note

1 The names of the authors appear in alphabetical order.

Bibliography

Ahmed, F. E. (2008). Microcredit, men, and masculinity. *National Women's Studies Association Journal*, *20*(2), 122–155.

Ahmed, F., Siwar, C., & Idris, N. A. H. (2011a). Contribution of microcredit for improving family income of the rural women in Panchagarh district of Bangladesh. *Australian Journal of Basic & Applied Sciences*, *5*(5), 360–366.

Ahmed, F., Siwar, C., & Idris, N. A. H. (2011b). Improving well-being of rural women through participation in microcredit programme: Evidence from Bangladesh. *Australian Journal of Basic & Applied Sciences*, *5*(8), 857–862.

Ahmed, F., Siwar, C., & Idris, N. A. H. (2011c). Sustainable livelihood amongst rural women through microcredit programme in Bangladesh. *Australian Journal of Basic & Applied Sciences*, *5*(7), 116–120.

Ahmed, F., Siwar, C., & Idris, N. A. H. (2011d). Women's participation in microcredit programme: Some evidence in Bangladesh. *Australian Journal of Basic & Applied Sciences*, *5*(7), 106–115.

Ahmed, S. M., Chowdhury, M., & Bhuiya, A. (2001). Micro-credit and emotional well-being: Experience of poor rural women from Matlab, Bangladesh. *World Development*, *29*(11), 1957–1966.

Anthony, D. (1997). Micro-lending institutions: Using social networks to create productive capabilities. *International Journal of Sociology and Social Policy*, *17*, 156–178.

Axelrod, R. (1986). An evolutionary approach to norms. *American Political Science Review*, *80*(4), 1095–1111.

Campbell, M. L., & Teghtsoonian, K. (2010). Aid effectiveness and women's empowerment: Practices of governance in the funding of international development. *Signs: Journal of Women in Culture & Society*, *36*(1), 177–201.

Cooper, F. (2001). What is the concept of globalization good for? An African historian's perspective. *African Affairs*, *100*(399), 189–213.

Drolet, J. (2011). Women, micro credit and empowerment in Cairo, Egypt. *International Social Work*, *54*(5), 629–645.

Duflo, E., Banerjee, A., Glennerster, R., & Kinnan, C. (2013). The miracle of microfinance? Evidence from a randomized evaluation. Working Paper 13-09, MIT Department of Economics Working Paper Series.

Elyachar, J. (2002). Empowerment money: The World Bank, non-governmental organizations, and the value of culture in Egypt. *Public Culture*, *14*(3), 493–513.

Elyachar, J. (2005). *Markets of Dispossession*. Durham, NC: Duke University Press.

Escobar, A. (1994). *Encountering Development: The Making and Unmaking of the Third World*. Princeton: Princeton University Press.

Garikipati, S. (2008). The impact of lending to women on household vulnerability and women's empowerment: Evidence from India. *World Development*, *36*(12), 2620–2642.

Geertz, C. (1962). The rotating credit association: A "Middle Rung" in development. *Economic Development and Cultural Change*, *10*(3), 241–263. doi:10.1086/449960

Goetz, A. M., & Sen, G. R. (1994). Who takes the credit? gender, power and control over loan use in rural credit programmes in Bangladesh. *World Development*, *24*(1), 45–63.

Gunder Frank, Andre. 1970 (1966). The Development of Underdevelopment. In Rhodes, Robert (Ed.), *Imperialism and Underdevelopment* (pp. 4–17). New York: Monthly Review Press.

Hashemi, S. M., & Schuler, S. R. (1996). Rural credit programs and women's empowerment in Bangladesh. *World Development*, *24*(4), 635–653.

Harvey, D. (2019). *A Brief History of Neoliberalism*. London: Oxford University Press.

Heen, Stacy (2004). The role of Microcredit in conflict and displacement mitigation: A case study in Cameroon. *PRAXIS The Fletcher Journal of International Development*, *XIX*, 31–51.

Hilson, G., & Ackah-Baidoo, A. (2011). Can microcredit services alleviate hardship in African small-scale mining communities? *World Development*, *39*(7), 1191–1203.

Holvoet, N. (2005). The impact of microfinance on decision-making agency: Evidence from south India. *Development and Change*, *36*(1), 75–102.

Hoque, M., & Itohara, Y. (2009). Women empowerment through participation in micro-credit programme: A case study from Bangladesh. *Journal of Social Sciences*, *5*(3), 244–250.

Izugbara, O. C. (2004). Gendered micro-lending schemes and sustainable women's empowerment in Nigeria. *Community Development Journal*, *39*(1), 72–84.

Kabeer, N. (2001). Conflicts over credit: Re-evaluating the empowerment potential of loans to women in rural Bangladesh. *World Development*, *29*(1), 63–84.

Kar, Sohini. (2018). *Financializing Poverty: Labor and Risk in Indian Microfinance*. Palo Alto: Stanford University Press.

Karim, L. (2008). Demystifying micro-credit: The Grameen bank, NGOs, and neoliberalism in Bangladesh. *Cultural Dynamics*, *20*(1), 5–29.

Karim, L. (2011). *Microfinance and Its Discontents: Women in Debt in Bangladesh*. University of Minnesota Press.

Keating, C., Rasmussen, C., & Rishi, P. (2010). The rationality of empowerment: Microcredit, accumulation by dispossession, and the gendered economy. *Signs: Journal of Women in Culture & Society*, *36*(1), 153–176.

Kim, J. C., Watts, C. H., Hargreaves, J. R., Ndhlovu, L. X., Phetla, G., Morison, L. A., ... Pronyk, P. (2007). Understanding the impact of a microfinance-based intervention on women's empowerment and the reduction of intimate partner violence in South Africa. *American Journal of Public Health*, *97*(10), 1794–1802. doi:10.2105/AJPH.2006.095521

Knoke, D. (1988). Incentives in collective action organizations. *American Sociological Review*, *53*(3), 311–329.

Lahiri-Dutt, K., & Samanta, G. (2006). Constructing social capital: Self-help groups and rural women's development in India. *Geographical Research*, *44*(3), 285–295.

Mader, P. (2011). Making the poor pay for public goods via microfinance: Economic and political pitfalls in the case of water and sanitation. *Max-Planck-Institute for the Study of Societies* Discussion Paper 11/14

Mader, P. (2015). *The Political Economy of Microfinance: Financializing Poverty*. New York: Palgrave Macmillan.

Mayoux, L. (1998). Tackling the down side: Social capital, women's empowerment and micro-finance in Cameroon. *Development and Change*, *32*(3), 435–464.

Mayoux, L. (2002). Women's Empowerment or Feminisation of Debt? Report Based on One-World Action Conference, One World Action. London.

Moodie, Megan. (2008). Enter microcredit: A new culture of women's empowerment in Rajasthan? *American Ethnologist*, *35*(5), 454–465.

Muller, E. N., & Opp, K. (1986). Rational choice and rebellious collective action. *American Political Science Review*, *80*(2), 471–488.

Nahapiet, J., & Ghoshal, S. (1998). Social capital, intellectual capital, and the organizational advantage. *Academy of Management Review*, *23*(2), 242–266.

Omorodion, F. I. (2007). Rural women's experiences of micro-credit schemes in Nigeria. *Journal of Asian & African Studies*, *42*(6), 479–494.

Ostrom, E. (1994). Constituting social capital and collective action. *Journal of Theoretical Politics*, *6*(4), 527–562.

Portes, A., & Sensenbrenner, J. (1993). Embeddedness and immigration: Notes on the social determinants of economic action. *American Journal of Sociology*, *98*(6), 1320–1350.

Postelnicu, L., & Hermes, N. (2018). Microfinance performance and social capital: A cross-country analysis. *Journal of Business Ethics*, *153*, 427–445.

Pitt, M., & Khandker, S. R. (1998). The impact of group-based credit programs on poor households in Bangladesh: Does the gender of participants matter?. *Journal of Political Economy*, *106*(5), 958–996.

Pitt, M., Khandker, S. R., & Cartwight, J. (2006). Empowering women with microfinance: Evidence from Bangladesh. *Economic Development and Cultural Change*, *54*(4), 791–831.

Radhakrishnan, S. (2018). Empowerment, declined: Paradoxes of microfinance and gendered subjectivity in urban India. *Signs*, *44*(1), 83–105.

Rahman, A. (1999). Micro-credit initiatives for equitable and sustainable development: Who pays? *World Development*, *27*(1), 67–82.

Rai, A., & Ravi, S. (2011). Do spouses make claims? Empowerment and microfinance in India. *World Development*, *39*(6), 913–921.

Rankin, K. N. (2001). Governing development: Neoliberalism, microcredit, and rational economic woman. *Economy & Society*, *30*(1), 18–37.

Roy, A .(2010). *Poverty capital: Microfinance and the making of development*. London: Routledge.

Rural Advancement Foundation (RAFI) Press Release (1998) Grameen Turns Mean? From Poverty Fighter to Peasants' Pinkerton. July 7 https://www.etcgroup.org/sites/www.etcgroup.org/files/publication/406/01/nrgrameenturns98.pdf accessed on June 2, 2021.

Sanyal, P. (2009). Credit to collective action: The role of microfinance in promoting women's social capital and normative influence. *American Sociological Review*, *74*(4), 529–550.

Schuler, S. R., Hashemi, S. M., & Badal, S. H. (1998). Men's violence against women in rural Bangladesh: Undermined or exacerbated by microcredit programmes? *Development in Practice*, *8*(2), 148–157.

Sen, D., & Majumder, S. (2015). Narratives of risk and poor rural women's (dis)-engagements with microcredit-based development in eastern India. *Critique of Anthropology*, *35*(2), 121.

Sharma, A. (2008). *Logics of Empowerment*. Twin Cities: University of Minnesota Press.

Sharma, M., & Zeller, M. (1997). Repayment performance in group-based credit programs in Bangladesh: An empirical analysis. *World Development*, *25*(10), 1731–1742.

Turnell, S. (2005). The rise and fall of cooperative credit in colonial Burma. Macquarie University, Department of Economics Research Papers 0509. Retrieved from http://ideas.repec.org/p/mac/wpaper/0509.html.

Woolcock, M. (2001). Microenterprise and social capital: A framework for theory, research, and policy. *Journal of Socio-Economics*, *30*, 193–198.

Young, S. (2010). Gender, mobility and the financialisation of development. *Geopolitics*, 15, 606–627.

Chapter 8

The making of a neglected tropical disease

Discourse on snakebite and its medical management in India

Rahul Bhaumik[1]

Introduction

The protection and promotion of health and welfare in the Global South are considered to be one of the most important functions of international health system during the late 20th and early 21st centuries. However, the ways in which present health promotion campaigns and prevention measures target marginal and less empowered social groups of the developing countries and try to police their health, sickness and well-being, somehow inform us how global health has closely entangled itself with "the art of governing" (Foucault, 1991). The practitioners of critical medical humanities no longer consider the pragmatic concern for public health and its social determinants in low- and middle-income countries as an apolitical effort of biomedical rationalism. The identification, classification and prevention of disease, as well as the regulation of public health, in these regions are largely manoeuvred by the political economy of health – one which essentially determines illness and medical condition in terms of social, economic and cultural factors. Relying upon this understanding, this chapter seeks to address venomous snakebite in tropical countries like India, as a specific site for understanding the politics of identifying, defining and categorising an extrinsic injury as a "neglected tropical disease" (NTD). In doing so, it tries to present a critical reading of the World Health Organization (WHO)-led biomedical discourse, its relation to the larger discourse on tropical poverty and inadequate funding in socio-medical infrastructure – discourses that specifically seek to document the particularity of tropical condition within which "peculiar" diseases like snakebite can easily prevail and spread. While recognising the politics of "Otherisation" of snakebite as a disease predominantly affecting the tropical poor and disenfranchised, this chapter also intends to discuss the ways in which the local health professionals and stakeholders deferentially engage themselves with the traditional system of

DOI: 10.4324/9781003159940-8

snakebite cure and thereby dispense with the sinister techniques of Othering. Thus, this chapter makes an effort to foreground the local practices which indicate that the realities on the ground as tackled by the medical practitioners, health workers and members of the non-governmental organisations (NGO) are far more complicated and multifaceted than one can think of. In other words, this chapter tries to historically trace the complex and layered story of negotiation between the global and the local, that is often missing in the development studies research on public health in general and epidemiology of snakebites in India in particular.

The tropicalisation of snakebite

During the late 18th century, the systematic scientific study of snakes and their bites was first introduced in India. The snakebite envenomation research that followed under the aegis of colonial scientific and medical institutions variously aided the colonial government to sustain and strengthen its command over India – partly by reducing the risk of mortality that might involve in the colonial project and most significantly by asserting European racial and cultural superiority over a "wild," "dangerous" and "snake-ridden" tropical country (Bhaumik, 2017). Thus, from the outset, the colonial scientific study of Indian snakes and their venoms turned out to be a part of British Orientalist engagement with tropical nature and fauna. In his landmark study, David Arnold (1998) has used the lingering issue of "tropicality" to stress an especially potent and prevalent form of Othering. He draws on the work of Edward Said and points out that the tropics need to be understood "as a conceptual, not merely physical, space" (p. 2). "By looking at the tropics as a social construction rather than as material reality," Arnold says, "we can see something of the complex processes that informed the production of colonial knowledge" (p. 2). Based on this premise, it can be said that the British medical engagement with venomous Indian snakes and the consequential health measures were often laced with a sub-terrainial discourse of colonial difference. For example, Indian snakes formed a significant part of the British imagination of tropical wilderness, a cruel, chaotic and disease-laden condition posing a threat to the life and health of the colonisers. In order to interpret and manage Indian snakes and the consequence of their bites, the European medical practitioners constructed their own imaginative geography and accordingly conceptualised snakebite envenomation as a disease of a warm or hot climate. They emphatically and repeatedly claimed that the rapid progress of several symptoms of this disease peculiarly occurred in a tropical environment. They also proclaimed that if the victim was situated in the tropics, the cure would be more difficult. Thus, the symbiotic relationship between the "evil" of snakebite envenomation and the tropical condition was exclusively fashioned during the colonial period. The idea of the tropics provided the European physicians an opportunity to construct a fundamental difference between Europe and India, intending that the temperate European landscapes, climate and constitutions were superior to those of snake-infested tropical India. This construction of a non-European Otherness immensely helped to ensure European intellectual mastery over the tropics as well as furthered the colonial presence in India (Bhaumik, 2017).

Seven decades have passed since India became independent. But the venomous Indian snakes and the disease caused by their bites are still being essentially associated with the concepts of sylvan, savage and degraded tropics. Indeed, during the past few decades, an overwhelming tendency to map snakebite within the topography of tropical condition is sorely evident in global medical academia. For example, while claiming an integral relationship between the perilous condition of the tropics and the degree of destructibility of snakebite, a group of scientists remarks in the *PLoS Medicine*:

> Venomous snakes are found throughout most of the world (including many oceans), except for a few islands, frozen environments, and high altitudes. Envenomings and deaths resulting from snakebites, however, are a particularly important public health problem in the rural tropics. Populations in these regions experience high morbidity and mortality because of poor access to health services, which are often suboptimal, and, in some instances, a scarcity of antivenom, which is the only specific treatment.
>
> (Kasturiratne et al., 2008, p. e218)

Similarly, while highlighting the role of idiosyncratic circumstances in making tropical people "particularly" prone to snakebite, some medical practitioners of Liverpool School of Tropical Medicine infer that "snakebite victims typically live in impoverished, remote subsistence farming communities" (Harrison et al., 2019, p. 834). Jean-Philippe Chippaux (2017), a renowned French physician and toxicologist, more lucidly calculates the disease burden posed by tropical snakebite. In a letter to the editor of the *Journal of Venomous Animals and Toxins Including Tropical Disease*, he writes: "Of course, it also occurs in industrialized countries and even outside the tropics, but more than 95% of cases do take place in tropical and/or developing countries" (p. 38). He continues: "Snakebites disproportionately involve the poorest of the poor, mostly in rural areas" (p. 38). Thus, it becomes a shared practice among the international medical practitioners, policymakers and stakeholders to characterise the problem of snakebite as a marker of an environment that is essentially an Other, unfamiliar in terms of its medical condition, economic order and social structure. Of course, this perceived Otherness has nothing to do with the mechanism of disease biology; rather, it closely informs the discourse of tropicality which essentialises the prevalence of some particular diseases like snakebite in the tropics.

The present-day scientific attempts to establish a relationship between the impoverished condition of the tropics and the huge disease burden created by snakebite accidents certainly remind us of the colonial Orientalist engagement with snakebite envenomation. Although the tradition of tropicalising snakebites goes back centuries, there have been some fundamental changes in recent perceptions. Unlike the colonial medical-zoological literature, snakebite in contemporary scientific texts is regarded as a significant public health problem which deserves special attention, quick mobilisation of funds and comprehensive infrastructural roadmap for tackling the emergency (Anon, 2019, pp. x–xiii). The lack of essential socio-economic infrastructures, necessary medical facilities, requisite financial assistances and proper environmental education in most of the tropical countries are specifically thought to be the main causes aiding the rapid progress of this medical disorder. Thus, the very process of tropicalisation is now associated with some systematic issues, those which did not attract much attention during the colonial era. While engaging with these new issues, the contemporary medical discourse inevitably embraces the question of raising and investing a huge amount of money for proper management of snakebites in the tropics. That is why some of the scholars enthusiastically realise: "There is an urgent need to ... garner substantive global investment in a number of actions at every stage in the snakebite victims' route to recovery" (Harrison et al., 2019, p. 836).

NTD and the politics of difference

The tendency to promote snakebite as essentially "a disease of poverty" (Harrison et al., 2009, p. e569), is now a part of a much larger discourse, a global one specifically directed by the mandates of the WHO. There have been many changes in the field of international health since the establishment of the WHO as a specialised agency of the United Nations in 1948. As "the global guardian of health," this agency has been playing a commendable role in seeking and gathering voluntary financial contributions, creating a global network of scientists, physicians and health policymakers, collaborating with various actors across the health system, furnishing worldwide technical health assistance, managing efforts to eradicate epidemic, endemic and other diseases and promoting health in low- and middle-income countries. But, as this leading health agency largely presumes that diseases are caused and sustained socially and economically (Cueto, Brown and Fee, 2019, p. 2), its mechanism of identifying, categorising and controlling a particular disease in a particular region is often coupled with the politics of difference. For example, since the beginning of the new millennium, the ways in which the WHO-led global academia began to classify some diseases as the NTDs – mainly affecting indigent and nonurban people living in some of the most underdeveloped communities in sub-Saharan Africa, Asia, Latin America and Oceania – surely reinforce the representation of the vast and diverse area, between the Tropic of Cancer and the Tropic of Capricorn, as the poverty-stricken, disease-laden and uninhabited Other. Thereby the landscape comes to be known as utterly distinct from the affluent, salubrious and comfortable temperate zone.

Aided by the advocacy of modern medical practitioners and laboratory scientists, the term NTD is officially introduced for those ailments which are strongly associated with poverty, flourished in impoverished environments and thrived best in tropical areas. According to a recent report by Margaret Chan (2017), a Chinese-Canadian physician and the Director-General of the WHO:

> Once widely prevalent, many of these diseases gradually disappeared from large parts of the world as economies developed and living conditions and hygiene improved. Today, the neglected tropical diseases have their hotbeds in the places left furthest behind by socioeconomic progress, where substandard housing, lack of access to safe water and sanitation, chronic hunger, filthy environments, and abundant insects and other vectors contribute to their efficient transmission.
>
> (p. 74)

What is evident from the above definition is that an NTD is socially, economically and culturally determined – one that is designed to preview the peculiar condition within which a disease can prevail easily and make itself difficult to prevent. In this regard, Arianne Shahvisi (2019) argues:

> NTDs are not really tropical, since that would imply environmental determinism; they are not really neglected, since that would imply some accidental omission rather than systematic marginalisation. Rather, NTDs affect Global South people whose limited access to health systems and other determinants of good health is influenced not by the environment, but by histories of exploitation and marginalisation directed by the interests of the Global North, interests that are now inscribed within the global economic system. Those affected by NTDs are those who have been cast off. Their health status is overlooked because they defy the logic of profitability, and empathy is limited because they are constructed as Other in such a way as to curtail identification.
>
> (p. 232)

However, what is important to bear in mind is that it is the WHO, the foremost international health agency, which hegemonically retains the exclusive ability to decide which disease is an NTD and which is not. Inclusion of any disease in its list of NTD depends on two hypothetical orientations: (a) the essentialist assumption that the particular disease is "neglected" in the sense of funding, research and treatment and (b) the supposition that this particular disease is concentrated only in the sylvan and unwholesome "tropical" regions. Thus, there is no scientific basis in such disease classification by the WHO, regardless of their so-called logical claims. Instead of "natural kinds" all NTDs are therefore "social kinds" (Shahvisi, 2019, p. 225).

Perhaps, Shahvisi (2019) most lucidly exposes and interrogates the ways in which the notion of "tropicality" influences the collective understanding of the determinants of a disease. She writes:

> After all, "tropical" does not just describe a climate or a geography, it describes a historical project and carries a set of value-laden associations. It might be objected that, unlike the Orient, the tropics *do* constitute a natural kind in terms of climate and physical geography, and that these factors unavoidably influence the character of the regions, especially with respect to disease type and prevalence.
>
> (p. 227)

Indeed, the discourse of tropicality predominantly exalts the temperate world over its tropical (often developing) counterpart and subtly demonstrates the cultural superiority of the earlier and the backwardness of the latter in regard to healthcare expenditures, facilities and infrastructures. It is in this cultural process, the idea of the impecunious, troublesome tropics provides an opportunity to construct a fundamental difference between the disease burden of snakebite of the tropical regions and that of the temperate zones. As a result, in biomedical cosmology, the tropics bear a resemblance to the snakebite-laden landscape which "is largely devoid of safe, effective and affordable treatments for something that is eminently treatable" (Williams, 2015, p. h5378). Such exotic and unhealthy landscape definitely needs to be controlled in order to ensure better protection to the victims, those who even lack minimum "political voice" due to their poor and rural subsistence (Bhaumik, 2013, p. f628; Williams et al., 2019, p. e0007059).

It is also important to mention here that the conceptualisation of an abysmal tropical geography as a grave causative agent is meticulously facilitated and promulgated by hegemonic literary-cultural enterprises of global biomedical establishments. For example, a growing body of scientific writings portrays steadfastly the inhabitants of low- and middle-income countries as extremely helpless before the jaws of snakebite death; as if, being the underprivileged tropical subjects, they are destined to be bitten, injured and deceased. It goes without saying that the appropriate biomedical intervention is thought to be the only way to bring these impuissant, voiceless victims of the tropics into a secure social and environmental order. To arrive at a solution, what seem to be the key steps are specifying the aetiology of the disease, locating its bio-distribution and accordingly categorising, naming and dealing with it.

The making of snakebite as an NTD

Over the past few decades, a series of articles, lectures, communications and reports have begun to express a common concern that, despite the high degree of its pernicious effect on the agrestic, underprivileged communities, issues related to snakebite have not received the attention they deserve from biomedicine and its cultural authorities. For example, David A. Warrell, emeritus professor of tropical medicine at the University of Oxford and one of the investigators involved in the Million Death Study, laments:

> Worldwide, snakebite has been neglected and forgotten and its victims abandoned by medical science and public health systems ... This neglect is particularly surprising in India, which has long been regarded as the country that suffers the worst snakebite problem in the world but whose doctors have the greatest experience and skill in dealing with this ancient scourge of mankind.
>
> (Quoted in Bhaumik, 2013, p. f628)

In the same way, a review article in the *Toxicon* claims:

> Snakebite envenoming is a global public health problem of such size and complexity that it deserves far more attention from national and regional health authorities than it has been given up until now. This environmental and occupational disease affects mainly agricultural workers and their children in some of the most impoverished rural communities of developing countries in Africa, Asia, Latin America and Oceania. It therefore fulfils the criteria of a "neglected tropical disease" as it affects, almost exclusively, poor and politically un-empowered people living in rural parts of generally low-income, tropical countries.
>
> (Gutiérrez et al., 2009, p. 1224)

What is specifically crucial to notice here is that the way in which the feature of being "neglected" is imposed on the disease of tropical snakebite. This culturally attentive capacity empowers the biomedical authority to further characterise the disease as "the most neglected of all neglected tropical diseases" (Williams et al., 2011, p. 1735). No doubt this is a unique approach to deal with the so-called "cruel anachronism," an approach that deserves more explanation.

Unlike the identification of other neglected ailments of the Global South, the categorisation of snakebite as an NTD has an interesting history. As it is commonly assumed that snakebite instigates a severe yet largely neglected threat to communities living at subsistence level in tropical and subtropical countries, over the past few decades an earnest attempt has been made to include it in the list of NTD. Given the high propagation of the extent of the burden due to snakebite in the rural parts of the world, the WHO included this disease in the list of NTD in 2009. "What this implies is that snakebite is in a group of diseases that prevail in tropical and subtropical conditions in 149 countries affecting more than a billion people, costing developing economies billions of dollars of loss every year" (Menon, Joseph and Whitaker, 2017, p. 78). Thus, after the prolonged period of underrating, snakebite envenomation was recognised by a leading international health organisation with the socio-geographical criteria, based on which a disease can be identified as NTD. However, mere recognition as an NTD did little to provide an incentive for the development of a multifaceted scheme to address the neglected problem of tropical snakebite. Apart from drawing academic attention to this "world scourge" through some publications (Kasturiratne et al., 2008, p. e218) and developing a standard guideline for the production, regulation and control of anti-snake venom immunoglobulins (Anon, 2010), the WHO, initially, did not make any provision to seek global funding to alleviate the burden of this devastating disease. Although calculated figures have testified that cases of people getting killed by snakebites could be six times higher than instances of people dying from other tropical diseases (Williams et al., 2010, p. 89), the lack of effective advocacy campaigns and policy initiatives precluded this disease from attaining priority in major global health programmes. As a consequence, the WHO, without giving any trustworthy explanation, removed snakebite from the list of NTD in 2013 and termed it simply as a "neglected condition," and then dropped it altogether from the list in 2015 (Bagcchi, 2015, p. h5313). This drastic decision immediately hampered efforts to engage the attention and support of medical authorities, pharmaceutical companies and research funding agencies. The situation grew worse when the problem of shortage of antivenom was aroused in different tropical countries.

All these, apparently indicate that global health is a highly power-ridden matrix where a particular disease such as snakebite might get importance or ignorance on the basis of the publicity of its severity, magnitude and social implications. This is why, continuous advocacy interventions are particularly needed in order to gain the support and investment of global health agencies, governments and research funders. To meet this goal, several international medical charities and NGOs such as the Global Snakebite Initiative, the Health Action International, the Médecins Sans Frontières and others began to actively engage with key public health agencies, academics, national governments, industries and civil society stakeholders in formulating a "new" approach to global snakebite reduction. Facing the ground-level realities, they stepped out with more effective efforts so that snakebite regains its NTD status and gets considered as a top-priority tropical disease. It was the networks, capabilities and exertions of the numerous clinicians, herpetologists, epidemiologists, medical institutions, humanitarian foundations and leading international NGOs that required the WHO to categorise snakebite envenomation as an A-list NTD on 9 June 2017, giving it a high priority for large scale action and research.

The relegation of traditional medicine

After the final incorporation in the list of NTD, snakebite now accretes the attention it deserves from the international health community. Undoubtedly, a new momentum is generated which considerably informs the national governments, antivenom manufacturers and grassroots healthcare professionals about the need for "improvement." The international snakebite experts have now begun to claim that there are four main impediments that ought to be overcome in order to eradicate or reduce the magnitude and social implications of the snakebite problem in tropical regions, like India (Chippaux, 2017, p. 38). The first challenge is to organise the collection of epidemiological data so that the actual requirement for antivenoms at an operational, local level can be properly gauged. The second challenge is to educate the endangered poor people of rural areas and encourage them to evade traditional healings and go to their nearest health centres if a medical emergency occurs. The third challenge is to resolve the enduring issue of antivenom shortage. "The fourth and final challenge is training of health personnel, including physicians, nurses and public health professionals" (Chippaux, 2017, p. 38). Although these approaches to intuit snakebite envenoming apparently purport to be purpose-driven and apolitical, in the true sense, they are far from even being peripheral to the exercise of cultural politics of Othering. The recent medical initiative aiming to study snakebites in India has two layers of hegemonic disposition. At one level, it is an indication of the self-conscious claim of biomedical establishment that it can solely manage the problem of snakebite-induced mortality, sequelae and social suffering in regions which are highly affected. At another level, it serves as an ideological weapon to demonstrate the superiority of biomedicine over traditional therapeutics. It enhances the concerned physicians' status as knowledgeable persons who only can produce "scientific" knowledge about the aetiology, pathophysiology, diagnosis and therapy of the disease. Thus, the emerging field of global health privileges the biomedical practitioners to take a "civilising" role – one that enables them to inferiorise and discard all other alternative methods to manage snakebite. It is in this context, poverty, ignorance and trust in traditional faith healers are continuously being charged for the high disease burden of snakebite in India. Moreover, the traditional treatments of snakebite in India become subjected to intense scrutiny, and the containment of these evil practices becomes almost a mission for the growing biomedical sectors in India.

According to the epidemiological surveys undertaken across India, snakebite envenomation is an occupational disease that mainly affects poor farmers, herders, fishermen, hunters, plantation workers, labourers on development sites and other manual labourers including working children. As one article of the *Journal of Forensic and Legal Medicine* observes:

> These are the people who work in the field and in the rainy season are the most susceptible victims of snake bite. The sociological impact of such incidence is immense as these groups of people are the earning members and form the work force of the family. Hence death of these individuals affects the total family as they are economically dependent on them.
>
> (Chattopadhyay and Sukul, 2011, p. 19)

Rural and semi-urban people who live in poorly constructed houses under insanitary condition, sleeping on the floor or working barefoot in fields during sowing and harvesting seasons seem to be extremely vulnerable to the risk of venomous snakebites (Bawaskar and Bawaskar, 2002, pp. 81–82). Moreover, as the surveys unequivocally show, these communities are often located far from an effective healthcare system and lack access to adequate transportation facilities and communication services. "The closest clinic/ health centres rarely possess the resources to effectively treat snakebite. Victims therefore often need to travel long, costly distances for several distressing hours before locating a hospital with the requisite clinical capacity. This delay increases the severity of envenoming and likelihood of death" (Harrison et al., 2019, p. 836). Thus, it is a common observation that the large number of snakebite incidents and consequential deaths in India are mostly among the communities that are not well equipped with simple facilities. These facilities can reduce their confrontation with venomous snakes and improve their subsistence levels.

There is no paradox that all these suboptimal symptoms greatly intensify the prevalence of snakebite in India. But what appears to be most awful is that a number of victims instead of using formal healthcare services regularly consult traditional healers. This tendency of evading hospital-based medical treatment has presumably worsened the snakebite scenario of India. On the one hand, such practices are thought to pose a major impediment in finding out the true incidences of snakebites, their impacts and characteristics. On the other hand, they hamper the process of eradicating the problem with proper biomedical interventions. It is in this context, the traditional modes of healing snakebite are considered as the social anathema to the emerging biomedical ascendency in the tropics. One well-known international biochemist and molecular biologist notices:

> The lack of regional medical care in many rural parts of the developing world results in local biases, whereby the majority of developing world snakebite victims will first seek out traditional healers rather than modern clinical care. When modern medical care is finally sought after a delay due to traditional healers being first sought out, the elapsed time has worsened symptoms and thus increasing the likelihood of a poor outcome, and it is often modern medicine that is blamed rather than the fault rightfully directed at the delay and the practices of traditional healers which in many cases actually contribute to the poor outcomes. Traditional medicine is thus a major problem and cultural intransience makes engagement with traditional healers a particularly challenging sociological problem to deal with.
>
> (Fry, 2018, p. 170)

So, leaving traditional medicine out of biomedical control might prove socially injurious, because traditional medicine, being the means of anomaly and aberration, has the potential to challenge the established order of biomedicine. This, as expected, creates a strong sense of anxiety among the clinicians, instigates an animosity towards the irrational and time killing "quack treatments" (Chattopadhyay and Sukul, 2011, p. 20).

As the WHO-led global biomedical establishment and its local collaborators robustly claim a monopoly over "scientific" knowledge about snakebite, they never fritter any single opportunity to condemn all the age-old traditional healing systems as "irrational," "unscientific" and "superstitious" practices. For example, while drastically discarding the efficacy of the indigenous method of snakebite cure, one of the leading international authorities of clinical medicine states in the *Lancet*:

> In most tropical developing countries, traditional healers undertake the immediate treatment of snake bite, using topical and ingested herbs, incisions, snake stones, ligatures, and other injurious techniques. Traditional treatment delays presentation, distorts the clinical picture, and can cause bleeding, infection, gangrene, and other complications. Modern methods of health promotion should be applied to educate affected communities. Swift transport to hospital or dispensary should be encouraged, and ineffective and harmful traditional treatments should be discouraged.
>
> (Warrell, 2010, p. 77)

Such grave dissatisfaction against the delay in hospitalisation due to the use of folk healers is also very common among the local physicians responsible for treating victims of snakebites in healthcare centres in the remote parts of India (Ralph et al., 2019, p. k5317). The consensus is that the traditional treatments of snakebite, whatever may be their modalities, have repeatedly failed to prove themselves as beneficial. Therefore, it is important to make the population of India understand through mass education. "Delay in hospital admission should be discouraged in any way" (Ghosh, 2018, p. 696). Goaded by such persuasion, a number of Indian scientists and wildlife activists even demand strict police action against the "witch doctors" pretending to cure snakebite victims by using herbs and mantras (Bawaskar and Bawaska, 2019, p. e1178; Lorea, 2018, p. 263).

Actually, in the realm of biomedicine, there is no place for "ineffective" and "harmful" therapeutic procedures of *Ojha* (witch doctor), *Gunin* (medical man), *Janguru* (medical magician), *Vishvaidya* (Ayurvedic physician) and other traditional snakebite curers – the ones who are experts in healing snakebite in their own ways and continue their practices among the rural communities despite the triumphant march of modern health system. It is the hegemonic project of bringing the whole snakebite-laden landscape under the complete control of biomedicine that enormously nullifies these medicine men, relentlessly rejects any possible existence of rationale behind their medical practices. The traditional snakebite curers have been specifically proved to be "non-scientific" and "dangerous," as the "scientific" study of snakebite is considered to be an exclusive part of clinical toxinology – a laboratory-based discipline that "deals with the effects of natural toxins of microbial, animal and plant origin on human beings and domestic animals, particularly their prevention, diagnosis, treatment, epidemiology and pathophysiology" (Warrell, 2010, p. 77). It seems quite axiomatic that indigenous healers are not competent enough to engage with such sophisticated medical knowledge. Thus, a strong sense of cultural superiority prevails among the practitioners of biomedicine and thereby enabling them to attain a position of mentors, possessing authentic knowledge of snakebite envenoming – a sense that makes them competent to judge the traditional snakebite curers and their ignorant patients (Bhattacharya, 2015, pp. 68–74).

The incorporation of indigenous knowledge

However, if one tries to presume, on the basis of the kind of evidence presented above, that whatever the traditional healers know and do have always been characterised as improbable and vague, that would be a mistake. There are some local-level studies which meticulously engage with traditional management of snakebite and, to some extent, find relevance in indigenous therapeutic beliefs and practices. Some civil society groups also advocate the need of using the on-field knowledge of local practitioners of folk medicine (who are still the immediate authorities that the less affluent patients consult) in order to propagate awareness on snakes and their venomous bites among the communities in jeopardy. Such initiatives taken by numerous local groups and agencies surely discard the simple interpretation of worldwide triumph of biomedical knowledge, practice and technique.

For example, despite the frequent reiteration of utter inefficaciousness of faith healing, there are some recent researches which accentuate the fruitful role of folk medicine in curing snakebite envenomation. Yogendra Kumar Gupta and Sharda Shah Peshin (2014), two toxicologists associated with the All India Institute of Medical Sciences, New Delhi, provide an interesting account of some important plants which have long been used in folk medicine for treating snakebites. Although to some extent, they are sceptical about the therapeutic effectiveness of some medicinal herbs, they do not discard all the potentialities of indigenous remedies as antidotes. In an article published in the *Journal of Clinical Toxicology*, they argue:

> Due to inadequate health care facilities especially in rural areas of India, people largely depend on alternative treatment by traditional healers who have knowledge based on ancient culture, ethnic practices and herbal antidotes. The plant kingdom provides an inexhaustible source of various herbal compounds with pharmacological potential which hold the key to antivenin activity. A plethora of medicinal plants, available locally, are used widely by traditional healers. Numerous traditional and folk medicines in the form of plant sap, pastes, decoctions, powders and pills are used by traditional healers for treating snake envenomations ... However ambivalence in approach is observed when compared with present day medical science. Though the modalities are debatable, yet they could be useful in remote areas.
>
> (p. 1000182)

Gupta and Peshin are no exceptions, in believing that folk medicine is often based upon observation, clinical trials and experiments and can play an effective role in cases of venomous snakebites. Over a period of time, plenty of scholars equally found relevance in snakebite-cure-related folklores of different tribal communities living in far-flung areas. While doing ethnobotanical research among the tribal and local people of the Rayalaseema region of Andhra Pradesh, a group of scientists unswervingly appreciate: "the traditional medicinal mode is very efficient, supportive and successful in the treatment of snake bite" (Padma et al., 2016, p. 55). These attitudes towards traditional snakebite cure testify to a sharp deviation from the WHO mandated guidelines and directives to "improve" the situation. They rather attest to the different ways of looking at the pragmatic knowledge that indigenous people have about species and ecologies.

In several other ways traditional knowledge is considered to be beneficial. Specialised snake charmers-cum-folk healers, mainly of low-caste and tribal origins, are often regarded as barefoot educators and therefore deployed by some national and regional NGOs to provide educational awareness to local risk groups. Possessing a unique ability to handle and tame venomous snakes with a tremendous knowledge of different species and their behaviours, these specialists are often proved to be more acceptable to the rural folks rather than any other educated personnel. That is why, the Chennai Snake Park Trust, Madras Crocodile Bank Trust, Snakebite Healing and Education Society and Friends of Snakes Society, some widely known voluntary organisations working across the country, regularly conduct outreach and education programmes where people of different ages are taught about snakes and their ecological values through lecture demonstrations by these traditional experts. As a special report of the Snakebite Healing and Education Society says:

> Faith healers enjoy tremendous followings and we have found that any awareness raised through them (and with the help of local political leaders, opinion builders and bureaucrats) has been always well received by local communities. While this can be difficult and time consuming to accomplish, it can also be rewarding.
>
> (Kadam et al., 2019, p. 17)

Indeed, modern scientists often interact with indigenous healers and exchange their experiences with these so-called non-scientists without portraying them as incapable of receiving and providing advanced knowledge about snakes and venoms. Romulus Whitaker, a renowned herpetologist and wildlife conservationist, who had been working with the Irula tribe of Tamil Nadu for nearly 50 years, had used their dexterity in capturing and milking venomous snakes in order to supply venoms for the production of antivenom in India. In 1978, he established the Irula Co-operative Venom Centre under licence from Tamil Nadu Forest Department with an objective to provide these aboriginal people an opportunity to maintain their "traditional skills and lifestyle through the sustained yield use of wildlife" (Whitaker and Andrews, 1995, p. 129). Currently, all the works of this registered society are "handled and mostly managed by the tribal people themselves – from the skilled and dangerous job of capturing snakes and extracting their venom to the operation of the lyophilizer (freeze drier), which processes the venom" (Whitaker and Andrews, 1995, p. 129). Whitaker and his "tribal" colleagues are now "modernising venom production, so it meets the WHO standards in collaboration with Dr David Williams, Australian Venom Research Unit, University of Melbourne and CEO, Global Snakebite Initiative" (Whitaker et al., 2019, p. 22). Thus, the need for incorporating tribal and local knowledge into biomedical practices has been coherently perceived and acknowledged. This undoubtedly serves as a strong evidence of respectful dialogue between two differently professed practitioners of snakebite medicine. All these sufficiently indicate that even within the modern biomedical sphere a wide indigenous stratum consisting of various local professionals can always engage itself in the process of translating and transmitting "scientific" knowledge.

Conclusion

From the above discussion, it is increasingly evident that the "scientific" engagement with venomous Indian snakes and the management of their bites is closely associated with the global politics of Othering – an underlying cultural process stirred up by the WHO's instructions to project snakebite as a disease of poverty prevailing chiefly in tropical countries like India, where appropriate measures to detect, prevent and control the disease are utterly limited or neglected. This chapter has shown how this hegemonic procedure, by identifying, categorising and terming snakebite as an NTD, intends to encourage biomedical ascendency over the tropics and its denizens who seem to be struck down by poverty-stricken and disease-laden conditions of their own country. In relation to this, this chapter has also foregrounded the ways in which the various professionals and stakeholders in the remote field of healthcare in India negotiate with, abide by or depart from the strategies of the WHO to get better results. It has revealed how non-biomedical practices of local and tribal experts receive enormous recognition in various parts of this country. Therefore, despite the pervasive deprecation and denouncement by global academia, indigenous experts have managed to continue their contribution in the making of biomedical science concerning snakes and snakebites. This reappraisal, derived from the local entanglements, will be a useful correction to the previously uniform approbation of the biomedical treatment of snakebite and disapprobation of the traditional system of snakebite cure in international circles. However, the perceived underlying division between the two is actually quite problematic.

Note

1 I am grateful to Debarati Bagchi for going through earlier draft of this chapter and for suggesting several useful modifications.

References

Anon (2010). *WHO guidelines for the production control and regulation of snake antivenom immunoglobulins*. Geneva: World Health Organization.

Anon (2019). *Snakebite envenoming: A strategy for prevention and control*. Geneva: World Health Organization.

Arnold, D. (1998). India's place in the tropical world, 1770–1930. *The Journal of Imperial and Commonwealth History* *26*(1), 1–21.

Bagcchi, S. (2015). Experts call for snakebite to be re-established as a neglected tropical disease. *British Medical Journal* *351*, h5313.

Bawaskar, H. S. and Bawaskar, P. H. (2002). Profile of snakebite envenoming in Western Maharashtra, India. *Transactions of the Royal Society of Tropical Medicine and Hygiene* *96*(1), 79–84.

Bawaskar, H. S. and Bawaska, P. H. (2019). Snake bite: Prevention and management in rural Indian settings. *The Lancet Global Health 7*(9), e1178.

Bhattacharya, B. (2015). Snakes and snakebites: A survey. In B. Mukhapadhyay and D. K. Som (Ed.), *Snakes, snakebites and treatments: An extensive and painstaking survey of South 24 Parganas, 2008–2012* (pp. 27–123). Canning: Juktibadi Sanaskritik Sanstha.

Bhaumik, S. (2013). Snakebite: A forgotten problem. *British Medical Journal 345*, f628.

Bhaumik, R. (2017). Snakes, snakebites and British medical-zoological engagement in early colonial India: Health, medicine and ideology. *Romanian Journal of Sociological Studies New Series 1*, 49–67.

Chan, M. (2017). *Ten years in public health, 2007–2017*. Geneva: World Health Organisation.

Chattopadhyay, S. and Sukul, B. (2011). A profile of fatal snake bite cases in the Bankura district of West Bengal. *Journal of Forensic and Legal Medicine 18*(1), 18–20.

Chippaux, J. (2017). Snakebite envenomation turns again into a neglected tropical disease! *Journal of Venomous Animals and Toxins Including Tropical Diseases 23*, 38.

Cueto, M., Brown, T. M. and Fee, E. (2019). *The World Health Organization: A history*. Cambridge: Cambridge University Press.

Foucault, M. (1991). Governmentality. In G. Burchell, C. Gordon and P. Miller (Ed), *The Foucault effect: Studies in governmentality* (pp. 87–104). Chicago: University of Chicago Press.

Fry, B. G. (2018). Snakebite: When the human touch becomes a bad touch. *Toxins 10*(4), 170.

Ghosh, S. (2018). Management of snake bite – An update. *Medicine Update 18*, 691–96.

Gupta, Y. K. and Peshin, S. S. (2014). Snake bite in India: Current scenario of an old problem. *Journal of Clinical Toxicology 4*(1), 1000182.

Gutiérrez, J. M., Williams, D., Fan, H. W. and Warrell, D. A. (2009). Snakebite envenoming from a global perspective: Towards an integrated approach. *Toxicon 56*, 1223–35.

Harrison, R. A., Hargreaves, A., Wagstaff, S. C., Faragher, B. and Lalloo, D. G. (2009). Snake envenoming: A disease of poverty. *PLoS Neglected Tropical Diseases 3*(12), e569.

Harrison, R. A., Casewell, N. R., Ainsworth, S. A. and Lalloo, D. G. (2019). The time is now: A call for action to translate recent momentum on tackling tropical snakebite into sustained benefit for victims. *Transactions of the Royal Society of Tropical Medicine and Hygiene 113*(12), 835–37.

Kadam, P., Majumdar, D. B., Menon, J. C., Raut, S., Sirur, F. and Santra, V. (2019). Snakebite Healing and Education Society (SHE India). In David J. Williams and Robert A. Harrison (Ed.), *RSTMH special report on snakebite* (pp. 14–17). London: Royal Society of Tropical Medicine and Hygiene.

Kasturiratne, A., Wickremasinghe, A. R., de Silva, N., Gunawardena, N. K., Pathmeswaran, A., Premaratna, R., Savioli, L., Lalloo, D. G. and de Silva, H. J. (2008). The global burden of snakebite: A literature analysis and modelling

based on regional estimates of envenoming and deaths. *PLoS Medicine 5*(11), e218.
Lorea, C. E. (2018). Snake charmers on parade: A performance-centered study of the crisis of the Ojhā healers. *Asian Medicine 13*(1–2), 247–75.
Menon, J. C., Joseph, J. K. and Whitaker. R. E. (2017). Venomous snake bite in India-why do 50,000 Indians die every year? *Journal of the Association of Physicians of India 65*, 78–81.
Padma, Y., Sarojinidevi, N., Ratnam, K. V., Reddy, G. T. and Raju, R. R. V. (2016). Herbal/folk remedies used for snake bites by tribals/rural people of Rayalaseema region, Andhra Pradesh, India. *Journal of Medicinal Plants Studies 4*(2), 52–56.
Ralph, R., Sharma, S. K., Faiz, M. A., Ribeiro, I., Rijal, S., Chappuis, F. and Kuch, U. (2019). The timing is right to end snakebite deaths in South Asia. *British Medical Journal 364*, k5317.
Shahvisi, A. (2019). Tropicality and abjection: What do we really mean by 'neglected tropical diseases'? *Developing World Bioethics 19*(4), 224–34.
Warrell, D. A. (2010). Snake Bite. *Lancet 375*, 77–88.
Whitaker, R., and Andrews, H. V. (1995). The Irula Co-operative Venom Centre, India. *Oryx 29*(2), 129–135.
Whitaker, R., Jesudasan, A., Kartik, A. and Ch, G. (2019). Madras crocodile bank trust. In David J. Williams and Robert A. Harrison (Ed.), *RSTMH special report on snakebite* (pp. 18–23). London: Royal Society of Tropical Medicine and Hygiene.
Williams, D., Gutiérrez, J. M., Harrison, R., Warrell, D. A., White, J., Winkel, K. D. and Gopalakrishnakone, P. (2010). The global snake bite initiative: An antidote for snake bite. *The Lancet 375*, 89–91.
Williams, D. J. (2015). Snake bite: A global failure to act costs thousands of lives each year. *British Medical Journal 351*, h5378.
Williams, D. J., Gutiérrez, J., Calvete, J. J., Wüster, W., Ratanabanangkoon, K., Paiva, O., Brown, N. I., Casewell, N. R., Harrison, R. A., Rowley, P. D., O'Shea, M., Jensen, S. D., Winkel, K. D. and Warrell, D. A. (2011). Ending the drought: New strategies for improving the flow of affordable, effective antivenoms in Asia and Africa. *Journal of Proteomics 74*(9), 1735–67.
Williams, D. J., Faiz, M. A., Abela-Ridder, B., Ainsworth, S., Bulfone, T. C., Nickerson, A. D., Habib, A. G., Junghanss, T., Fan, H. W., Turner, M., Harrison, R. A. and Warrell, D. A. (2019). Strategy for a globally coordinated response to a priority neglected tropical disease: Snakebite envenoming. *PLoS Neglected Tropical Diseases 13*(2), e0007059.

Chapter 9

Negotiation by the waste pickers

In the context of socioeconomic and cultural marginalisation

Nandini Sen

Introduction

Waste picking communities face "multiple deprivation and destitution" (Auyero, 2011). Yet, through their efficient negotiation and engagements with different stakeholders (NGOs, families, community members, waste retailers, club leaders, club members, mainstream housing complexes, corporate firms and charity organisations and local corporation) the waste pickers can lead to a better understanding and explanation of marginalisation which have converged in both fruitful and failed negotiation themes. This can be understood in clearer terms if we can look at Kala, the waste picker who was relaxing at his Park Circus squatter, who explained to the researcher how the waste pickers divide their illegitimate work areas (Sen, 2018). They allocate few streets for specific waste pickers and the Dhapa Dumping Ground is the common general area. They consider these streets and the Dhapa dumping ground their cheque and their skills of segregation of waste into organic and recyclable wastes their pen to write and sign the cheque. This is their first step of negotiation (Sen, 2018). It is ironical that though there are few state developmental schemes for migrant workers, this community is not even allowed to take advantage of the bare minimum citizens' rights and civic facilities. The community is considered as the surplus workforce by the other stakeholders (Sen, 2018).

Partha Chatterjee (2004) has argued that the norms of mainstream society were extended only to the urban elite, who appropriate elements of the state and other public wealth (Chatterjee, 1993); the marginalised population of the waste pickers is regulated through policies that exclude, rather than extensively share, the national resources with them. One of the most explicit attempts of the chapter is to explain the negotiation of the waste pickers with other stakeholders (waste retailers, civic society, state and NGOs) and to look at the problem through the concept of "development." While the term "development" has multiple meanings, Cooper, and Packard (1997: 2) accept a " development orthodoxy" as referring to foreign aid and investment on favourable terms from which the discussed community is miles

DOI: 10.4324/9781003159940-9

apart. The chapter will demonstrate how the transfer of different capitals of human, sociocultural and religious will happen (Bourdieu, 1986) will happen where a community is almost severed from the different policies and governmental practices and promotion of health and education, and when socioeconomic planning has miserably failed them from both ends of the waste pickers and the other stakeholders. This would give birth to underground market economies which will affect the community's overall growth and different levels of negotiations

The negotiations of the waste pickers involve a kind of perception from either the marginalised community or the mainstream/elite/state's sociocultural, economic and religious and ritualistic participation, with an impact on the marginalised community's obligations and exchanges. For marginalised people like the waste pickers, exchanges with, and obligations to the state and the mainstream/elite society are rare. Waste pickers are reluctant to share any common practices with their " opposition," as all parties see their own positions as distant from the others – here the other is the community of waste pickers. Spatial segregation leads to the phenomenon whereby the state and the waste pickers who are remote from each other in sociocultural spaces tend to find themselves by choice or necessity distant from one another in geographic space as well. Nevertheless, while waste pickers and the state are very distant in social space, they can " encounter one another and interact briefly and intermittently in physical space" (Accpeted) (Bourdieu, 1989: 16). This will affect how plans are put into practice and how people and places are conceived by policymakers (Legg, 2006). The chapter will examine how policymakers and other stakeholders like the NGO personnel can link the marginalised community to individual and community-based rights, needs and desires.

Although the waste pickers can create new rules and tacit resistance to evade state control quite successfully, their vulnerability cannot be denied. They are under a constant physical threat of deportation or being forced to leave the city. The state exploits the illegal status of these marginal non-citizens, who, in consequence, are paid very little. The waste pickers work for the urban population, clearing garbage from public spaces, which the state cannot do efficiently, but in return they are not offered membership of the mainstream society. In retaliation, they discover new and diverse forms of illegality and non-formalities. This unstable juxtaposition of legal opposition and illegal marginalised people weaving a network of multiplicity as regards the law shakes the state justice system and its framework of uniform law. Thus, a body of overlapping, heterogeneous, non-uniform and private membership emerges in support of the non-citizens (Appadurai and Holston, 1996).

The state and the mainstream/elite society also get support from other authorities (like police and jurisdiction) through " privatisation of security and extra-legalisation of justice," which harshly andbrutally controls the marginal (Appadurai, 1996b). " Justice" via private security and enforcers alongside the state's extra-legal police strength, is used to try to take full control of these illegal waste pickers, who are thus exploited in the name of protection of the elite civic society and the state. This kind of violence has a deep effect on their constitutional justice and the entire process of democracy with its highly esteemed concept of citizenship (Holston, 2009; Appadurai, 2002).

The state is overwhelmed by the concept that it is all powerful, beyond any question. It can ignore, exclude or sometimes include powerless/dominated people within its framework but the state ignores the fact that it, too, can be ignored by the powerless waste pickers and they can survive independently of the state in terms of the economic, sociocultural and religious aspects of their lives. (Bourdieu, 1989) The marginalised waste pickers, on the other hand, feel completely ignored, excluded and deprived of their basic rights by the state; it is at this stage that they create their alternative position. They steal garbage; they earn money without paying taxes; they hook electricity illegally; they occupy state land (the so-called no-man's land). The state is either egalitarian or, to withhold a share of rights and resources from them, the state excludes the community from any mainstream activities. This suggests both the state is uninterested in making marginalised people part of this public consumption/civil services and that the state is not neutral in its distribution and redistribution of basic amenities, which fall under the category of public consumption. The whole system for distribution and redistribution of citizens' tax money for education, health, shelter, sanitation, food rationing and banking is bureaucratic and biased against marginal people like the waste pickers in Calcutta (ethnography: 2011– 2013; Sen, 2018).

Background of the negotiations

Marginalised people are not sufficiently socially connected to procure "legally recognised jobs, valuable information and investment opportunities" (Bourdieu, 1989: 278), they cannot sustain these social and cultural connections, as they are not allowed to conduct the " exchange of both material and symbolic goods, for example, gifts and mutual recognition" with members of the elite/mainstream society (Bourdieu, 1989: 278). This chapter argues that when the waste pickers cannot build up a social network then they are inevitably excluded from mainstream " material and symbolic resource centre" (Bourdieu, 1989: 278). It is clear from the ethnography (Sen, 2018) that this is exactly what has happened in this waste picker community

As such, emerging mainstream society and accompanying elites fundamentally drive this process of marginalisation to promote their own advancement in socioeconomic terms (Kelly, 1991; Arnold, 1993, 1995a, b). The waste pickers' marginalisation revolves around elite/mainstream society strategies to develop control over power and other resources, creating resource imbalances and altering the subsistence potentials of populations like theirs. Such social differentiation through non-stratified and non-formal processes is related to power and politics that are dependent on human agency (Arnold, 1995a). In essence, state and policymakers will tacitly accept the work carried out by the waste pickers because it suits them: nobody in mainstream society wants to be involved in waste collection and recycling but it has to be done, so "allowing" a willing marginalised group to do it solves the problem (Sen, 2018). Certainly, I have found that some consultation and negotiation will be required between the waste pickers and the mainstream society (NGOs, corporate sector, and Government Conservancy section) and state but this communication is, in any case, an essential part of the success of mainstream society/elite in the emergence of social hierarchy (Binford, 1983; Paynter, 1985; Brumfiel, 1992). Relations between the mainstream majority and the marginalised minority (waste pickers) are not categorically ones of exploitation of one group by the other, but rather are based on individual " patron–subordinate" relations (Amborn, 1990: 398). This need for not only economic but also social, cultural and religious exclusion between the mainstream and marginalised societies generates a continuous structured interaction, which may negate the image of total exclusion and segregation of the marginalised people (Pankhurst, 2003).

There can be other opposing points of view which put the community in critical conditions where they may have some individual choices and freedom to enjoy their own cultural and sexual activities, but at the same time they never can share formal civic rights with other citizens irrespective of religion, race, language or culture. Due to their occupation related to waste they further go through a sociocultural identity crisis "which calls for differential treatment of a particular group" depending on their "vulnerability or historical injustice" (Chatterjee, 2004: 4–5), lack of sociocultural and political capitals (Bourdieu, 1986, 1989). Although the waste pickers do not belong to the structured formal economy as it is evident from the fact they cannot access the real market prices, wages and markets and so on (Chatterjee, 2004; Sen, 2018) however, through their negotiation, non-participation and their expertise on their business of waste they could create their own underground market and economy. Despite all its vulnerabilities due to their minority position, migrant and occupational position (related to waste) the community also can adjust their own perspectives, establish and recreate their territories and survive the strong mainstream sociocultural environment (Sen, 2018).

The process of negotiation involves garbage as the main medium connecting waste pickers to their immediate and rural families, waste retailers, club, co-waste-pickers, male bonding, NGOs, mainstream/elites, state, and waste pickers' strategies building up control over their labour, culture, politics, resources and information (Arnold, 1995a, 1993; Brumfiel, 1992), which in turn creates dependencies, obligations and loan-debts among the waste pickers. The ability of aspiring elites/mainstream, waste retailers to negotiate with the waste pickers in terms of their labour, transportation, crafts/ occupation, information and resources gives a clue to the pickers' negotiation success giving birth to mutual dependencies of the waste pickers and the other stakeholders despite the fact that the secondary stakeholders never acknowledge the waste pickers' contribution. The chapter will reiterate that the waste pickers of Calcutta, living in an urban fringe area, are clear examples of mostly failed negotiations in an urban context of a developing country. They are homeless, invariably to have migrated, and to have queer neighbourhoods. They construct their own shelters on the peripheries with precarious materials and illegitimate conditions, which are widely known as squatter settlements. They represent sites of insurgence as they introduce new identities and practices into the city that disturb established histories. Analysing their circumstances encourages the research to explore the shared "spaces" in urban areas, touching upon different social imaginations and the nature of the negotiations. These insurgent, or fringe, shared spaces may be described as the places where the negotiations happen. This insurgency may lead to new forms of social structures, which are absorbed into the old and indicate uncertain alternative futures of the waste pickers.

By virtue of their institutional invisibility and the small scale of their activities, the pickers are not usually noticed and rarely accorded any social significance (Scott, 2009). And, nowadays, more conscious of their rights and of state schemes, concealing their contempt is essential for their survival. It is then, deliberate, that the waste picking community, hides its rage in front of both the waste retailers and the outside world, even when they are underpaid. For example, the waste pickers will join feasts given by the retailers and NGOs even when they are very angry about their exclusion from their right-based schemes.

Silent defiance and subtle negotiation

The waste picker community, face " multiple deprivation and destitution" (Auyero, 2011). Yet, through their efficient negotiation and engagements with different stakeholders (NGOs, retailers, club members, mainstream housing complexes, corporate firms and charity organisations), the waste pickers in the research ethnography do create a better understanding of ideological marginalisation – which converges in both fruitful and failed negotiation themes. The chapter will address " points ofexchange" between the various faculties and deconstruct the clash between the non- formal and formal markets as well as patron–client relationships and marginalisation. The chapter touched up the way the waste pickers subvert mainstream notions. After being uprooted from their agricultural bases, the waste pickers struggle through the job of segregating recyclables as best they can. They are happy to work as waste pickers – even given the unfair wages, the low financial value of waste, and unjust price negotiation, none of which satisfy them mentally or physically. Mainstream society, generally represented by the state and police, shows little concern towards them; keeping their ego intact at the expense of the waste pickers, means they thrust continuous misery onto them. Their houses are under siege as police shamelessly demand bribes and plunder them under the guise of obeying the law. Yet, the state never feels it has failed these waste pickers in terms of social welfare, it simply questions how the community can continue to bear the fabric of marginalisation.

Waste pickers share the same qualities and powers and they have the same interest in making merry after work. Their tacit agreement is that each keeps to his own side of the squatter settlement and they meet in a common space where they gamble, play cards and plan evening visits to sex workers and ways to feed their addictions. Female waste pickers never join in this merrymaking; they have families to care for, household chores and television as their leisure activities. Women pickers like Nazma, Hamida, Ayesha Bibi passively share the brutal indifference of their male counterparts. They are isolated, occasionally attending the focus group discussions and meetings called by the NGOs regarding their businesses and health or educational issues relating to their children and families. The women sacrifice themselves as much as the men are self-seeking. As a result, the project coordinator and the health supervisor of the NGO Tiljala Society for Human and Educational Development (also locally referred to as T-Shed) observes that the atmosphere of the waste pickers' community is not cohesive and that they suffer from isolation.

Certainly, the waste pickers, especially the women and the children, confided in the researcher their misery and endurance of " social warfare" (the waste picker's voice) whenever they attend to receive treatment or give birth at a state health care centre, or when they wish to enrol in minimal formal schools like corporation schools. The battle continues when they go to fetch water from nearby slums. Despite this, it is quite clear to the researcher, through interviews with the state and NGO representatives, that the authorities always stick to their indifference and hard egotism. The women and the children are afraid to speak out or to participate in the programmes offered to them by the NGOs or any state project. The men, if more vocal, are not heard. Waste pickers like Nazma, Hamida and Sohail explain how they are forced to lead a life of panic. However well they defend and regulate their "space" (shelter, leisure area, markets and transport pathways), they run the constant risk of being raided and/or evicted; their shelters, their materials and their businesses destroyed. In addition, this space is inherently vulnerable. When a fire gutted 450 shelters within an hour on one April day in 2014, the entire existence of the community was in jeopardy.

It underlined the community's need to set their space within wider relations of unequal power, resources and representations. They had to seek help and support from the outside world – state, neighbouring international hotels and NGOs.

To be responsive and to survive in a competitive market like waste recycling, these waste pickers must coordinate with big retailers who have a strong network of suppliers from local grocery markets, retail chains and restaurants. Quite often the retailers are unhappy with the waste pickers as they can only supply a small collection, hampering bigger profits. These waste picker-cum-retailers believe they are the real players in the whole chain of non-formal recycling. Johra, a retailer says, "We are highly organised, apparently we may seem to be illegal professionals. We convince our employee waste pickers that this work seems to be the real hard work, but it has its charm and it is sexy as in the end the waste materials are like gold." Johra takes pride in their easy loans to the waste pickers so that they can gain the upper hand over them. However, she and her husband Hannan never display deep displeasure with their waste picking employees and they are preferred by the waste pickers.

The solidarity of the waste pickers is built up through their gossip, character assassinations of other stakeholders, and public shunning of the retailers. In order to avoid drawing scorn upon themselves, they sometimes take up work even with reduced wages. Such short-term gains made by their constant adjustment may add to the anger of their fellow waste pickers and could be referred to as the acceptable limits of self-seeking (Scott, 1985). " You can't cut your friends" is a unity dreaded by the retailers. The waste picker who crosses this limit is no longer respected by his waste picker friends and neighbours. Loyalty to a retailer is not so highly prized. Husna, Kausar Mallik and Ayesha Bibi, Sabra Begum and Arjina Bibi, all complain to the researcher that although they try to stick to one retailer for a long time, they are forced to move to another " when the retailer cheats regularly and does not keep promises made during the bargaining process." Ayesha Bibi was shocked when she found out that her retailer was hard and stern and refused even an extra penny for her well-being. Arjina left for another retailer to receive a fairer deal, and more opportunities, in order to achieve her dream of a better shelter. Ayesha comments that the retailers certainly take advantage of their weaker position. She affirms, " We are here to gulp double-edged threats and exploitation from the Calcutta Municipal Corporation (CMC), the police and the retailers." The police, she adds, beat up people like her and burn their waste.

The making of urban peripheries

The waste pickers are typical of marginal people who almost never use violence to claim their spaces; they always occupy the public spaces of modern cities that have been abandoned. They can never touch " the residential enclaves, the division of corporate luxury zones" (Sen, 2018). At most, theyappropriate spaces that are " forbidden sectors of illegally constructed shanties, with its endless neighbourhoods of unemployed youth" (Appadurai and Holston, 1998). Cities like Calcutta, therefore, experience the most significant crisis of state membership and the civic authorities understand that state and civil society must rethink the concept of citizenship. It has been claimed that the extraordinary urbanisation of the 20th century has produced urban peripheries of devastating poverty and proportionate inequality in cities worldwide (Holston, 2009). All people, like the waste pickers, who live in these urban peripheries struggle to obtain basic resources for daily life and shelter. These struggles, in turn, give rise to insurgent citizenship which tries to acquire rights within cities, which are very weak and full of dichotomies. Holston (2009: 245) marks this phenomenon as " new kinds of citizen power and social justice." The " insurgent urban citizenships" contain both inequality and new forms of destabilisation and violence. The waste pickers build up fragile shelters in urban fringes, which are illegal and irregular in nature. In these situations, they confront extreme inequality and segregation from urban institutions in terms of religion, culture, health care, shelter, food and education. It is certainly my experience that not all peripheries/ fringe areas produce insurgence, but they produce some form of collision and conflict (Sen, 2018). In the long run, the waste pickers – these "marginalised citizens and non-citizens" – contest their volatile conditions and the regular exclusions they face. Thus, they disrupt the established norms of " urban democratic citizenship" (Holston, 2009: 245). This disruption is clearly the projection of their peripheries/marginal positions.

The mainstream/elite civic society strategically segregates public life so that "the urban poor in the peripheries" are pushed to a bare life of servility (Scott, 2009: 246). "The structures of inequality incite these hinterland residents to demand a life worthy of citizens" (Holston, 2009: 246). The chapter debates how far these "non-citizens" of waste pickers can articulate their demands with force and " originality." Rather their struggle forms to cope with their daily, domestic life in the remote urban peripheries. In spite of daily struggles for housing, sanitation and security they do not even receive the dignity of " bare citizens." Further, they are sequestered in areas away from the elite centre, creating a different order of citizenship and exclusion. These uprooted and dispossessed marginalised people in the context of the 20th- and 21st -century urbanisation have helped to develop urban peripheries as their own place in the city by their signature irregular, illegal types of shelter and ways of life. They appropriate this soil of the city and demand the right to inhabit it. They also pronounce their " right to reside with dignity, security and mobility."

The chapter contests the point that these marginal-/non-citizens even have an appropriate awarenessabout their rights, dignity, security and mobility

(Sen, 2018). I agree that these marginalised people with "horrific urban conditions" (Holston, 2009: 249), are left with very little room for dignity and vitality. The waste pickers are autonomous in nature. They have been denied political rights, excluded from property ownership, estranged from law, incorporated into non-formal labour market as servile workers and forced into segregated and illegal conditions of residence in a remote, no-man's land that is devoid of any infrastructure. The situation is paradoxical in the sense that marginalised communities can keep their freedom, as they are completely cut off from the centre/state and are situated in the interior-remoteness, but for this freedom they must exchange their dignity and basic state welfare schemes.

If we take up Bourdieu's (1989) deduced theory which says that if the state is X which successfully claims a monopoly of the legitimate use of physical and symbolic (p. 56, B, Rethinking) power over a definite territory and majority of the population, then the waste pickers are subverting the whole scheme (Sen, 2018). Their exclusion and non-participation break the notion of interdependency between citizens and the state (Bourdieu, 1989). The extreme non-participation and exclusion of marginalised people in state/NGO programmes can be explained as subversion and as the breaking down of the power structure through which the state and the elite/main-stream society operates (Sen, 2018). The different dimensions of this process (state) – armed forces, taxation, law, etc. – are interdependent (Bourdieu, 1989), but the chapter will show later that the waste picker community is outside this interdependency.

Everyday negotiations in their life , their food , health hazards and hygiene

To recap, then, daily, the waste picker's life is one of facing coercion from the retailers, insulting and disrespectful attitudes from the police, and life-threatening events like evictions and destructive fires. And yet, at the grassroots level, this is not the worst aspect; that is reserved for the daily challenges of their waste picking routine. The waste pickers even negotiate with their bodies through exposure to dirt and infection, to bites from insects, rats, snakes, scorpions and dogs.

Johra's employees and other waste pickers in the community regard the couple as true entrepreneurs, and almost all the waste pickers the researcher met during the ethnography do at least some business with Johra and Hannan. Some waste pickers, like Husna and Ayesha Bibi, even refuse to go into business or save with the NGO association for waste pickers as they feel more obliged to do business with the couple. Johra and Hannan have not only become big retailers, but they represent the zenith of the dream in the world of waste. Johra explains how the retailers, along with the waste pickers, mix some other materials with their plastic bottles for larger profits.

The domestic life of the waste pickers of Calcutta deserves further exploration because, despite inappropriate behaviours and endemic vices, it would be wrong to suggest that family life does not exist, but it is complex and erratic. In a comfortless, ill-furnished and filthy house, often neither rain-tight nor warm, with a foul odour filling overcrowded rooms, domestic comfort is impossible. The male waste picker works the whole day through, as do the wife and elder children; they meet in the night and morning only, the males apparently only doing so to receive home-cooked food. In the evenings, the male waste pickers meet up because of the perpetual temptation to drink. What family life is possible under such conditions? Yet the waste picking community cannot escape from the family and must live in the family.

The consequence is a succession of family troubles and domestic quarrels, which are demoralising for parents and children alike. Male neglect of all domestic duties, and of the children especially, is only too common among the waste picking people. And yet the children growing up in this way, amidst these demoralising influences, are expected to turn out to be good and moral.

During all festivals, the younger generation of men hire videotapes and stereos to enjoy dancing. The males constantly consume alcohol or feed other addictions, which hampers the development of the community. On the other hand, women waste pickers like Nazma, Hamida, Husna, Sabjan and Johra (once upon a time also a waste picker) have all invested their money in their villages, by buying land for agriculture and building homes, to enhance and develop their economic and social capital. Few male waste pickers invest so much in the future, those such as Hannan and Kala are exceptions. Regarding waste picker children, the NGO management regrets that the parents are largely irresponsible with regards to their children's well-being. Nowadays, as they have easy money, the waste picker community participates in every main festival, following the calendar of the slum people, retailers and wholesalers.

Despite all of this, the club secretary insists that the club's own relationship with the waste pickers is positive, based on exchange and sharing. He and his club colleagues deny any harassment of the waste picking community. They claim that mainstream society " likes the waste picking community and does not look at them as outsiders but as friends." The club is Hindu, and as such, the secretary says, they invite the waste pickers to attend the Hindu festivals and, in turn, the waste pickers return the invitation whenever they throw parties, mainly during the Eid festivals. The club members say there is no discrimination during the holy occasions; everyone sits together to share the same food and have the same fun. According to the club members their help is never sought in relation to police harassment against the waste pickers. But whenever the community members are in trouble for stealing or anti-social behaviour, they come to. Mr Sahu (the club leader), who says that the waste pickers sometimes steal household items – inexpensive, good quality plastic – and others are heavy drinkers and consume drugs. Whenever these pastimes create trouble with friends and neighbours, the waste pickers run to the club members for advice and to pacify the situation.

In terms of work, the club secretary maintains a strong opinion on the relationship between waste pickers and retailers: it is generally a good one, assisted by club members' negotiation when required. Every day, he says, the waste gatherers and retailers must exchange money and waste in the waste recycling units, so neither party will ever harm the other, and neither do the recycling unit's owners ever insult the waste picker community. If they did, the waste pickers would boycott that specific owner. They argue that the waste pickers have a very successful market and are therefore never afraid of the retailers. However, the club members do identify a possible "treachery" on the part of the waste pickers. Sometimes thewaste pickers take advances from the retailers and then, with the loan in hand, go to other owners to sell their items – so they need not repay the loan money. At this point the owners *do* use abusive language to criticise the waste pickers. This insult works: the waste picker feels ashamed and returns to the previous retailer. The waste picker says, " Sorry, elder brother. I am wrong. Please forgive me. I will never do this. Please cut my interest from the lower range."

Significantly, the club secretary is highlighting another area of important negotiation between the waste pickers and the waste retailers. The relationship between the community and their retailers(and, indeed, the club) can be fair but is always fundamentally unequal. Although the waste pickers and the retailers live in similar condition and environment, the retailers never consider waste pickers for kinship or arrange marriages with the waste pickers' families. The reason for this formality is because the retailers consider the waste pickers to have a lower status, socially and economically – and they are the ones who give easy loans to the waste pickers whenever they need money. Waste pickers like Nazma, Hamida and Husna are aware that the retailers will never consider them equal and marriageable, but their relationship with the retailers still carries a bond, which has positive ramifications for their profession and earnings. The pickers may sometimes visit the retailers' houses for feasts, festivals and rituals, but the retailers never reciprocate by visiting the waste pickers' shelters. Before the pickers had a television in their houses, they were welcome to go to a retailer's house to watch TV, but this is a kind of investment; it ensures that the picker's children continue the same business arrangement as their parents. Hannan, the retailer, practised this, and during a festival like Fateha-Dwazzam, Hannan still prepares biriyani and invites all his picker clients to share the food.

Hannan is a Bihari Muslim from Canning; his wife, Johra Bibi, is a member of the women's organisation of the ruling party (previously CPI(M) and now Trinamool Congress). They both nurture a strong connection with the police, so they never worry about extortion. Hannan sustains his long-term business with the same waste pickers due to his patience, permanency and inclusive, empathetic attitude towards the community. This couple helps the waste pickers during their marriages, funerals and crisis collections, they even offer jobs to children who lose their parents at an early age and support other retailers in conflict situations, including domestic ones. Recently Kauser, another retailer, was arrested after his wife complained at the police station. But Johra and other field women helped to get him released. Hannan's sense of justice and tremendous capacity for hard work have made him the preferred retailer in the locality. Other waste retailers, such as Kadbanu, cannot maintain this level of constancy – sometimes succumbing to criminal extortion – but all of them try to give the standard rates to the waste pickers. At the same time, though, they do not have any faith in each other. They cannot build up a saving group or self-help group, whereas other communities are more successful in this regard. An unfortunate feature of their mistrust is that they never help other waste pickers if an attack comes from the outside. When the slum dwellers attack one of their members, they never come out of their shelter to defend their neighbours.

Hasi Bibi, Chymoon Bibi, Litun Sheikh, Aynoor Seikh, Amirun Bibi, Asura Bibi and Aftoon Bewa spoke about a conference of waste pickers at Pune (a city in Maharashtra) in early 2012, which identified several areas in which the waste pickers of Calcutta fell behind their counterparts in Pune . First was the needfor identity cards. With such documentation from the NGO they could go directly to the mainstream households and collect the recyclable waste – as is done in Pune – and they would be harassed, beaten up or arrested by the police for being without ID. Countering this, though, the NGO is sure that the waste pickers do have identity cards, or at least their voter's card, because they go back to their villages during election times. That aside, the waste pickers also discovered that those in Pune receive money, gloves, shoes and even transportation and replacement from the Maharashtra State Government. If the Maharashtra State delays the provision of these essentials, then the waste pickers stop working and the state comes under pressure to resume provision. Third , they noted that in Maharashtra the women waste pickers were self-sufficient and never depended on the male waste pickers, and finally, the Maharashtra State Government has even provided the waste pickers there with medical insurance. This would be unthinkable in Calcutta, West Bengal.

As a result of this discussion, the few Calcutta waste pickers who joined that day's meeting resolved to form some kind of unity to procure their rights from the state. This arises from the fact that waste pickers nowadays can see through the empty promises of the NGOs and the state. Both previously promised to secure community identity cards, some uniforms and recognition of their occupation via information about various state schemes for employment and insurance. Farzana, Monowara and Yasmin told me that nothing has been done by another Focus Group Discussion (FGD) meeting on 10 June 2012. This time, the discussion mentioned a programme about unskilled labour that had been held on 10 and 11 May 2012, encouraging a movement against the abuses faced by the waste pickers. But only five of the community had attended.

On a separate occasion, the NGO workers tried to explain to Raju, Soleman, Sabra, Monoara, Chhad Banu and Putul the importance and utility of redeveloping the Waste Pickers' Association and saving schemes. The community could have a working, viable association, but it is dysfunctional not least because male waste pickers like Raju, Soleman and Kauser slide too easily into gambling, alcohol and other entertainments. The NGO workers, they say, try to inspire the waste pickers to address these alcohol-related problems, but without success ... After hearing this, it was the NGOs failures that concerned most of the subsequent FGD. The NGOs previously promised fair prices in waste deals with the community, good saving schemes, vocational trainings and advocacy for the betterment of the community none of which – again – they did, but neither did the waste picker community – again – take any initiative. The NGO says it has tried to create micro insurance and saving schemes with the waste pickers, but as they (say they) have no identity cards and fall within the migratory category they cannot be linked with the proper banking facilities.

Human Rights Day was on 10 December 2012, and at the specially planned FGD, the NGO workers explained the significance of human rights to the community people. The organisers then asked Arjina Bibi and others why they had not turned up at the councillor's office to discuss their water scarcity. They blankly answered that he has repeatedly rejected their appeals and they were sure that the councillor would never listen to them. The NGO workers tried to convince Hasi Bibi, Monoara Bibi and Soleman Bibi that as Association members they would have opportunities to demand legal addresses, welfare schemes for unemployed youths and elderly people, and birth certificates. The NGO worker said, " We will guide you to take the right path. You can follow this right path and can succeed if your community is unified. You must demand your own respect. We know you have no basic amenities like toilets, sanitation, water and no legal documents. You can sort out all these through this association." This whole situation seemed ironic, as waste pickers like Raju, Anwar, Husna and Monoara are aware that joining any Association will not solve their problems, nor (from experience) will the NGO workers ever fully stand beside them – it is not possible for this feeble NGO (Tiljala SHED/T-Shed) to organise the community to demand their identity and food ration cards – so they do not have time to pursue such mirages. However, in these meetings, the waste pickers do behave differently. They are extremely dignified and Raju, Husna and Monoara's speech is emphatic, clear and not repetitive.

As this chapter has expanded, several voices of the NGO management and staff, the club leader and club members, waste pickers and the retailers have emerged. It is very clear, that while all have valid wishes and opinions, there is little cohesion, a lot of argument – and even more inertia. The NGO management tries to establish that they are doing their best to achieve the betterment of the waste pickers, but the waste pickers rarely respond appropriately to the facilities and education provided by the NGO. The NGO staff blame the waste pickers for their negligence and lack of motivation. In another Focus Group Discussion meeting, on 7 January 2013, the waste pickers explained that the police station never accepts their complaints about harassment – they are always called the thieves. No one in the mainstream/elite society even considers the waste pickers as proper human beings. Sheik Munna, Saira and others admit that they lack the unity and discipline to fight against such inhuman attitudes. The NGO workers tried to create leadership among them, but none of the above waste pickers was ready to be the leader. They would not agree to visit the police station to talk to the officer in charge about procuring water and sanitation. However, Korimon, Sheik Munna, Ajmeri and Saira are certain that the police officer in charge or the councillor would refuse them flatly and that their old spaces and basic amenity crisis would continue.

However, it is revealed that although the patron–client relation has ultimately failed in terms of NGO activities, patron–client relations between the retailers and the waste pickers still function. The retailers are clever enough to understand the intricate policies of control over resources. They can attract the waste pickers and establish a long-term relationship with them through their sense of constancy, integrity and networking with mainstream politics and state apparatus, such as the police. The retailers help the waste pickers by intervening when there are problems like police harassment. These retailers are the only stakeholders, apart from the NGO, able to negotiate successfully with the waste pickers and create a position for them in the non-formal market of recycling. The NGOs utilise them to collect the recyclable waste from the mainstream/elite housing complexes and corporate firms for income-generating programmes. To gain recognition for the waste pickers, the NGO tries to find a practical solution and says it does give them informal identity cards for temporary periods. Thus, the waste pickers find themselves less socioculturally marginalised when they go to collect waste from housing complexes and corporate firms. According to the waste pickers, despite this and their ability to segregate waste positioning them in the non-formal market, their recognition is often suppressed by the dominant state and other elite/mainstream sectors.

The corporate stakeholders are all part of a formal market. They are liberal in their views about the position of the waste pickers, but at times they are insensitive regarding the non-formal market system to which the waste pickers belong. The corporate stakeholders are judging, theoretically, the lives of the waste pickers and taking a benevolent stance towards them. However, their experience is derived from the formal market and does not allow them to encode the mechanism of the non-formal markets of the marginal people. Instead, they are prompted to regard the waste pickers as subordinates and dependents from the peripheral regions. It is obvious from corporate people's language that they can appreciate the waste pickers' economic marginalisation. The state protects those who have formal and legal status at the expense of marginalised people to maintain the status quo. In return, the corporate stakeholders keep up their minimum responsibilities, which involve paying taxes or participating in the pacification of the marginalised people by donating their recyclable wastes through the NGO. In summary, these liberal corporate people think that they own a set of rights as legal citizens and they acknowledge the corresponding duties – in this case, the donation of wastes to the marginalised people.

Conclusion

The chapter supports the notion that consultation and negotiation with those "who are being marginalised is an essential part of elite/mainstream society's success in the emergence of social hierarchy" (Brumfiel, 1992: 89). While the process of marginalisation does increase power inequalities as the elites/mainstream society take charge of the contexts in which they will work, the waste pickers can also participate by resisting the hegemony. Focusing on the perspectives of the waste pickers, they seek to understand ways " in which the marginalised, while excluded from certain activities, could simultaneously be included as significant actors in the social and cultural reproduction of society" (Sen, 2018). Negative terms like "depressed," "submerged" and "pariah" (outcast) and the image of complete ostracism portray a complex reality of simultaneous integration and exclusion of marginalised people (Amborn, 1990: 409). To put it explicitly, from the mainstream point of view, waste pickers are a necessary evil – and as such, they are not entirely powerless; the evidence lies in the fact they do survive as a community, and with the specific lifestyle discussed earlier. However, such marginalisation partially (at least) arises from a passive process: when the population increases many more are unfortunately forced to take up certain occupations and thus fall to a lower echelon (Arnold (1995a: 94). This has little to do with direct mainstream/elite manipulation, meaning that on some level, the marginalised waste pickers are simply victims. From this perspective, the rise of social differentiation is unrelated to " ambition, power, or politics; there is no role for human agency, socioeconomic negotiation, factional competition" (Arnold, 1995a: 94).

Waste pickers are the flashpoint for a series of uncertainties that mediate between everyday life and its fast-shifting global backdrop. This community creates uncertainties about national self and citizenship. Their legal status is quite ambiguous, which can destabilise the meanings of consumption and legal system; their movements challenge the policing system; their monetary transactions almost never come under national economies and usually stand between legal and criminal transactions; their mixed and unsophisticated languages question national cultural coherence (Sen, 2018). Spending time within the waste picker community, the researcher has experienced first-hand how their lifestyles constitute an easy way to create tensions in urban setups, their lives being multi-focal and a source of anxiety to the security of the state. When some of them manage to create wealth, they become a sore point for elite economics, and when they are poor, they become convenient symbols of failure in the chain of development and welfare. This is the reality for the waste pickers. From this point of view, " marginality began where sovereignty and tax ended" (Scott, 2009: 31). Thus, waste picking people " are best understood as runaway, fugitive, marooned communities – fleeing the oppressions of the state-making projects of slavery, conscription, taxes, forced labour, epidemics, and warfare" (Scott, 2009: IX). The characteristics that stigmatise the waste pickers are their very location at the margins, their physical migration, their occupation and diet, their flexible social and kinship structures, their religious heterodoxy, their egalitarianism, and their non-literate oral culture. These features of their economic, social and cultural life are better adapted to survival if they remain passive in the political environment of states rather than themselves making states. Hence, they have invented their own culture and heterodox religion to evade hierarchical, codified " state capture and state formation" (Scott, 2009: 9). The researcher can symbolically evaluate the self-governing (marginalised) people and the state-governed (mainstream) people respectively –"without history and with history" which provide many possibilities for " comparative triangulation" (Scott, 2009: 3).

Like Homi Bhaba (1994) the researcher too does not want to glorify margins and peripheries. However, Bhaba (1994) clarifies that the communities which have "to survive, to produce, to labor and to create, within a world-system whose major economic impulses and cultural investments are pointed in a direction away from them" (Bhaba, 1994: xi) can face severe negative, "oppressive and exclusionary" hurdles which may instigate them to resist such toxic and prejudiced environments (Bhaba, 1994: xi) in their own way of non-participation in projects structured for them (Sen, 2018) . In fact, Sen (2018) suggests that any new agenda of any state should include all emerging sources of citizenship and the issue of their repression. Multiple causes are deemed responsible for the insurgence of marginalised people, which include huge migration to the important cities of the world, unemployment, de-industrialisation, sexual revolution, and democratisation (Holston, 1998, 2008). The re-territorialisation of this huge new marginalised community within the city – with its own histories, cultures and demands disrupting the assumed categories of existing urban life – has resulted in new spaces of insurgent citizenship – the waste pickers – that execute a special kind of diverse and everyday resistance. The nature of their resistance is pervasive, passive and virtually unbeatable because it does not openly challenge the basic structure of domination, or contest the hierarchy, and it never escalates into any major open conflict with the opposition. Depending on the circumstances, the waste pickers change their level of resistance, " oscillating from rare organised acts to general silent and anonymous acts" (Scott, 1995: 300) – whether it is against police harassment, a state oblivious to their welfare system, mainstream society's denial of their rights or biased price negotiations and resource sharing with the retailers. It generally lacks organisation and coordination and is not linked with outside political and ideological movements; there are no " elements of riots, demonstration, arson and open violence" (Scott, 1985). Part of the reason for this is the sprawling geographical nature of the waste picker community. Scattered across the different fringe areas of the city and formed from a diverse collection of lower classes from various economically poor regions, there is often a lack of discipline and leadership amongst the people. Even if the whole community is involved in resistance, it rarely takes the shape of a conventional social movement.

Furthermore, my ethnographic evidence suggests such avoidance of confrontation by the waste pickers, is a self-conscious strategy: resistance with no formal organisation, no formal leaders, no manifestos, no dues, no name and no banner may well work in these people's favour. By virtue of their institutional invisibility and the small scale of their activities, they are not usually noticed at all and rarely accorded any social significance (Scott, 2009). And, nowadays, more conscious of their rights and of state schemes, there is a second explanation for why, even in the face of continuous discrimination and prejudice from the state and mainstream society, the waste picker community never breaks out into a major riot. Put simply, marginalised people accept discrimination as their destiny. Their social defamation, indignity and cultural degradation influence them to take negative recourses into demoralisation and dysfunctionality. Instead of revolt, they avenge their anger by dissociating themselves from their neighbours, restricting their networks (even with NGOs) and retreating from joint activities and building any movements. " This social withdrawal and symbolic misidentification, in turn, undermine their local cohesion, hamper collective mobilisation and help to generate the very atomism that the dominant discourse on zones of urban dispossession claims is one of their inherent features" (Wacquant, 2010b). The rich retailers and mainstream society/elites repackage the huge economic disparity between them and the marginalised people as status, prestige and social control by using acts of generosity and charity. These acts are gentle, hidden forms of exploitation and are well sustained by the opposition, who must design their social authority link after link by means of strategic gifts, charity, loans, sociability, feasts and other concrete and symbolic services.

Here, the researcher will conclude by saying that the process of exclusion from the regular institutions and economy of the mainstream society influences the waste pickers of Calcutta to be outside the total aim of development, policies and state and mainstream practices (Sen, 2018) and to distrust the mainstream organisations and institutions. Such exclusion prohibits a collective movement for the community's rights and adopts instead an "individualistic ideology of achievement" (Wacquant, 2008: 180). The perennial non-participation in the NGO-arranged education, health care system, saving schemes, self-help groups and other training programmes reflects the waste pickers' absence of community feeling, and they refuse to recognise the collective nature of their problem (Sen, 2018). The waste picking community from the " symbolically spoiled zones" (Wacquant, 2008: 197) experiences sociocultural ostracisation from mainstream society on the one hand, and on the other, it negotiates with the stakeholders as far as possible for freedom from economic marginalisation. These negotiations give rise to a patron–client relationship indicating the failure of the state in mitigating any solution for the community through planning and policymaking.

Imagine the city of Calcutta getting choked by garbage. What can be the reason behind this choking? The waste pickers are not talking to mainstream society. They have stopped communicating and negotiating with other stakeholders. They have the power to suffocate civic society. If the pickers are once at least aware of their value as Green entrepreneurs (by segregating organic and recyclables materials) they can really plan and prepare for the suffocation by complete non-participation and non-negotiation. They can justly deny all the unscrupulous adjectives about them as they rarely break ground rules of the mutual negotiation process with the other stakeholders. If they want, they can proceed towards closures by not collecting and segregating wastes. The research chapter would rather question the bargaining power of the waste pickers as the retailers, elites and state pose as if they are in full control of the implementation of the business and waste conservation without acknowledging the key roles of the waste pickers as environmentalists and entrepreneurs. The chapter will further like to work on the passivity and the invisibility of the waste pickers which may enable the policymakers to mitigate justice and include the community for mutual benefit and prosperity.

References

Amborn, H. (1990). *Differenzierung und Integration. Vergleichende Untersuchungen Zu Spezialisten und Handwerkern in Sudauthiopischen Agrargesellschaften*. Munich: Trickster.

Appadurai, A. (1996). Sovereignty without Territoriality: Notes for a Postnational Geography. In Yaegar, P. (Ed.), *The Geography of Identity* (pp. 40–58). Ann Arbor, MI: University of Michigan Press.

Appadurai, A. (2002). Deep Democracy: Urban Governmentality and the Horizon of Politics. *Public Culture*, *14*(1), 21–47.
Arnold, J.E. (1993). Labor and the Rise of Complex Hunter-Gatherers. *Journal of Anthropological Archaeology*, *12*, 75–119.
Arnold, J.E. (1995a). Social Inequality, Marginalization, and Economic Process. In Price, T. and Feiman, G. (Eds.), *Foundations of Social Inequality* (pp. 87–103). New York: Plenum Press.
Arnold, J.E. (1995b). Transportation Innovation and Social Complexity Among Maritime Hunter-Gatherer Societies. *American Anthropologist*, *97*(4), 733–747.
Auyero, J. (2011). Researching the Urban Margins: What Can the United States Learn from Latin America and Vice and Versa? *City and Community*, *10*(4), 431–436.
Bhaba, H. (1994). *The Location of Culture*. London: Routledge.
Binford, L.R. (1983). *In Pursuit of The Past*. New York: Thames and Hudson.
Bourdieu, P. (1986). The Forms of Capital. In Richardson, J. (Ed.), *Handbook of Theory and Research for the Sociology of Education* (pp. 241–258). New York: Greenwood.
Bourdieu, P. (1989). Space and Symbolic Power. *Sociological Theory*, *7*(1), 14–25.
Brumfiel, E.M. (1992). Breaking and Entering the Ecosystem – Gender, Class and Faction Steal the Show. *American Anthropologist*, *94*, 551–567.
Chatterjee, P. (1993). *The Nation and Its Fragments: Colonial and Post-Colonial Histories, Princeton Studies in Culture, Power, History*, Volume 4. Princeton University Press.
Chatterjee, P. (2004). *The Politics of the Governed; Reflections on Popular Politics in Most of the World*. New York: Columbia University Press.
Cooper, F. and Packard, R. (1997). *International Development and the Social Sciences: Essays on the History and Politics of Knowledge*. Berkeley, Los Angeles: University of California Press.
Holston, J. (1998). Spaces of Insurgent Citizenship. In Sandercoch, L. (Ed.), *Making the Invisible the Visible: A Multicultural Planning History* (pp. 37–57). London: University of California Press.
Holston, J. (2008). *Insurgent Citizenship: Disjunction of Democracy and Modernity in Brazil*. Princeton: Princeton University Press.
Holston, J. (2009). Insurgent Citizenship in an Era of Global Urban Peripheries. *Cities and Society*, *21*(2), 245–267.
Holston, J. and Appadurai, A. (1996). Cities and Citizenship. *Public Culture*, *8*(2), 187–204.
Kelly, R. (1991). Sedentism, Socio-Political Inequality, and Resource Fluctuations. In Gregg, S.A. (Ed.), *Between Bands and States* (pp. 135–158). Southern Illinois University Center for Archaeological Investigations, Occasional Papers No. 9, Carbondale: Southern Illinois University Press.
Legg, S. (2006). Post-Colonial Developmentalities, from the Delhi Improvement Trust to the Delhi Development Authority. In Raju, S., Kumar, M.S. and Corbridge, S. (Eds.), *Colonial and Postcolonial Indian Geographies* (pp. 182–204). London: SAGE.
Pankhurst A. (2003). Chapter 1. Introduction: Dimensions and Conceptions of Marginalisation. In Freeman, D. and Pankhurst, A. (Eds.), *Peripheral People: The Excluded Minorities of Ethiopia* (pp. 1–26). Lawrenceville, NJ: Red Sea Press.

Paynter, R. (1985). Surplus Flow between Frontiers and Homelands. In Green, S. and Perfman, S.M. (Eds.), *The Archeology of Frontiers and Boundaries* (pp. 163–211). Orlando: Academic Press.

Scott, J.C. (1985). *Weapons of the Weak: Everyday Forms of Resistance*. New Haven, CT: Yale University Press.

Scott, J.C. (2009). *The Art of Not Being Governed*. New Haven, CT: Yale University Press.

Sen, N. (2018). *Urban Marginalisation in South Asia: Waste Pickers in Calcutta*. Routledge/Edinburgh South Asian Studies Series. London: Routledge .

Wacquant, L. (2008). The Militarization of Urban Marginalization: Lessons from the Brazilian Metropolis. *International Political Sociology*, 2, 56–74.

Wacquant, L. (2010b). Crafting the Neoliberal State: Workfare, Prisonfare, and Social Insecurity. *Sociological Forum*, 25(2), 197–220.

Chapter 10

Dominant party rule, development and the rise of Hindu nationalism in West Bengal

Subhasish Ray

The Bharatiya Janata Party's (BJP) spectacular growth in India's electoral space since 2014, at both the national and sub-national levels, is widely perceived as a harbinger of a new "common sense" in Indian politics. According to a scholarly articulation of this perspective, Narendra Modi has forged a new social consensus around Hindutva, the party's ideological core, by conflating it with two ideas that have hegemonic sway in Indian political discourse, nationalism and development (Palshikar, 2017). Challenging this characterisation, an alternative view suggests that Hindutva, even in this new avatar, will be stopped at the border of strong regional party systems (Chiriyankandath, 2018). In light of the latter thesis, West Bengal offers an interesting case study. Due to three and a half decades of dominant party rule under the Left Front (LF), which continues with few modifications under the successor Trinamool Congress (TMC) regime, a very distinct secular authoritarian political culture has evolved in the state, wherein allegiance to the "party" supersedes allegiance to all other social institutions, including religious institutions (Bhattacharyya, 2009, p. 60). Yet, as the BJP's unprecedented surge in the 2019 Lok Sabha election indicates, Hindu nationalism seems to be emerging as a popular alternative to authoritarian secularism (Traub, 2018).

Due to its large population, a history of dominant party rule, and the status of being one of the major Indian states, West Bengal has been the subject of a long line of research that has examined its distinctive political history to illuminate contemporary debates about democracy and development. This chapter seeks to contribute to an emergent body of research in this tradition that has sought to examine the rise of the BJP in the state (Kanungo, 2015; Nath & Chowdhury, 2019a, b; Purakayastha, 2018). According to Purakayasthya (2018, pp. 13–14), the BJP's current stream of Hindutva politics poses a serious challenge to the "pre-existing structures of party society and political society consolidated and catered to by the left and by the present ruling regime in West Bengal," which have neglected the "religion question," in their bid to "gain electoral absolutism." On the same lines, Nath and Chowdhury (2019b) conclude their ethnographic study

DOI: 10.4324/9781003159940-10

of four recent cases of communal conflict in the state thus: "West Bengal is experiencing an increasingly organised form of identity based political mobilisations which is both ontologically and epistemologically different from LF promoted party society." A key assumption that underlies these arguments is that the BJP being an upper caste-dominated party cannot connect to West Bengal's agrarian poor through party society-like linkages. Yet, as noted by Thachil (2011), the BJP has found electoral success among subaltern voters elsewhere in India by politicising social service provision by affiliates of the Sangh Parivar in areas underserved by state institutions. Given that the Rashtriya Swayamsevak Sangh (RSS) and its front organisations have considerably expanded their footprint in West Bengal since the 2014 Lok Sabha election (Kanungo, 2015), and the well-documented inefficiencies of the bureaucracy-mediated structure of public service delivery under the TMC (Ray, 2020; Ray & Dutta, 2018), it is plausible that, far from a rollback of party society, what the state may be experiencing is a recalibration of the same.

To what extent does the BJP's dramatic electoral success in West Bengal in the 2019 Lok Sabha election indicate a fundamental rupture of party society? This chapter offers, what is to the best of this author's knowledge, the first systematic exploration of this question. More specifically, the chapter asks: What are the individual-level correlates of taking up membership in the various Sangh Parivar affiliate organisations in West Bengal and what do they tell us about motivations for joining these organisations? Is the motivation purely ideological? Or do these groups simply provide an organisational receptacle for expressing secular dissatisfaction with the TMC because of the sudden political and electoral decimation of the LF? More importantly, is there significant overlap between the correlates of membership and the correlates of voting for the BJP?

The chapter examines this question in the empirical context of the state's Junglemahal belt, covering the tribal-dominated districts of Purulia, Bankura and Paschim Medinipur. Junglemahal went from LF dominance to TMC dominance in the backdrop of a Maoist insurgency that lasted from 2005 to 2011. The BJP made major gains in the region in the 2018 Gram Panchayat election (Das, 2018), and subsequently, carried that performance forward in the Lok Sabha election. Indeed, a post-election study observed that the BJP's surge in vote share in West Bengal in the Lok Sabha election relative to the 2016 Vidhan Sabha election was highest in Junglemahal (Basu & Das, 2019). It is also instructive to note that RSS expansion in the state has been most prominent in scheduled caste (SC), scheduled tribe (ST) and other backward class (OBC)-dominated areas, including Junglemahal (Kanungo, 2015). Other than the RSS, the second most prominent Sangh Parivar affiliate active in the region is Seva Bharati, the Parivar's social service wing, and its various feeder organisations, such as Sishu Mandirs and Ekal Vidyalayas (Daniyal, 2018).

My analysis is based on original survey data collected in Junglemahal in the run-up to the 2019 election. The survey covered 1,140 respondents in 38 villages with a legacy of Maoism-related violence. Using questions embedded in the survey on membership in cultural organisations and inclination to vote for the BJP, I show that the growth of Hindu nationalism in the region is clearly predicated on an embedded mobilisation strategy on the lines identified by Thachil (2011) in Central India. While the data reveals a statistically significant correlation between affinity towards Hindutva policies and propensity to vote for the BJP, such affinity plays no role in the decision to join the RSS or the Seva Bharati, which is primarily driven by secular dissatisfaction with the TMC's governance failures.

The rest of this chapter is structured as follows. The second section discusses the state and regional context of the 2019 Lok Sabha vote in Junglemahal. The next section discusses the data and methods used in the study. The fourth section presents the core findings, and the last section concludes.

The political context of the BJP's ascendance in Junglemahal

The case of West Bengal offers an intriguing context. Despite the traditional unfriendliness of the state to the BJP brand of politics, the party has turned itself into an ascendant political force in recent years.

To assess how the BJP has emerged as the largest opposition party in a state where leftism is politically institutionalised – albeit less so under the TMC compared to the LF – it is important to briefly revisit political developments in the state since 1977, when the LF was swept to power by a popular movement. At the risk of overgeneralisation, it is possible to classify these developments into four phases.

The first phase, roughly covering the period 1977–1990, saw the LF adopting a programmatic approach to policy making,[1] which produced two major policy innovations that catapulted West Bengal to pole position among Indian states in terms of pro-poor policies. The first of these innovations, the much-studied land redistribution program, involved the registration of *bargadars* (sharecroppers) and the redistribution of ceiling-surplus land, both extraordinary developments in the context of an agrarian society. The second innovation was the use of elections for choosing the non-bureaucratic staff of Gram Panchayats, a practice that has subsequently become a norm across India.

The second phase, lasting from 1990 to 2011, began as the gains from the reforms of the first phase started petering out, and the state's agrarian sector entered a prolonged period of stagnation. The hallmark of this new phase was the LF's increasing reliance on patron-client networks for retaining power, albeit with the key difference that these networks were far more robust than similar entities elsewhere in India (Corbridge, Williams, Srivastava, & Veron, 2012). Indeed, according to Bhattacharya (2009, p. 60), the deep embeddedness of these networks in rural life gave clientelism in West Bengal the specific form of "party society" that is, a political space in which the "party" was expected to mediate in each and every aspect of social relations.

The phase of Left hegemony without economic growth came to an end with the TMC's historical victory in the 2011 Vidhan Sabha election. The conditions for the TMC's rise had taken hold after the 2006 Vidhan Sabha election when the LF, inspired by the East Asian growth model (Kohli, 2006), tried to push through pro-big business policies to revive the state's economy. The move backfired as mass protests broke out against the government's drive to acquire land for large industrialisation projects, initially in Singur and Nandigram, two small townships in the outskirts of Kolkata, the state's capital, and subsequently in Junglemahal. The TMC, and its leader, Mamata Banerjee, quickly became the face of these protests.

The period 2011–2016, which coincides with the TMC's first term in power, marks the third phase in West Bengal's post-1977 political trajectory. Interestingly, contrary to popular expectations, the TMC's rise made no dent on the grip of party society over rural West Bengal, with the organisation simply taking over the mantle of the "party" from the LF (Nath, 2018). There was one key difference, however, in that the TMC was able to make significant improvements in public service flows that had almost ground to a halt in the last years of LF rule. Indeed, popular schemes such as *Sabuj Saathi* (Green Friend) – under the scheme, all students enrolled in higher education in public schools across the state receive bicycles free of cost – and *Kanyashree Prakalpa* (Scheme for Daughters) – under the scheme, unmarried girls receive conditional cash transfers for pursuing higher education – propelled the party to a second term in power, when it was re-elected in 2016.

The 2016 Vidhan Sabha election also ushered in the fourth and most recent phase of West Bengal's contemporary political development because it marked the beginning of the erosion of TMC dominance and the parallel rise of the BJP as a key player in the state's politics. Though the party failed to make significant gains in terms of seat share, it made rapid gains in terms of vote share, emerging as the third-largest political force, behind the TMC and the LF. Incidentally, the RSS had always maintained a rudimentary presence in the state even during the period of LF and TMC dominance. However, the BJP's strong showing in the 2016 election, and in the 2014 Lok Sabha election, gave a new fillip to the organisation as it considerably ratcheted up its activities. Much of this expansion took place in the state's SC, ST, and OBC-dominated areas of North and South 24 Parganas, Nadia, Murshidabad, rural Howrah, East Midnapore, and the Junglemahal belt. Here, the Sangh's ideological rhetoric focused on politicising issues such as the inclusion of Muslims in the OBC reservations category, but no less significant was the organisational outreach into these communities, with community members being promoted into important leadership positions (Kanungo, 2015).

In the event, the 2019 election saw the BJP wresting an unprecedented 18 seats and a staggering 40% of votes cast (the incumbent TMC won 22 seats and 43% of the votes cast). As noted earlier, it was in Junglemahal that the party had its strongest showing. In the 2018 Gram Panchayat election, the party had captured 33% of the panchayat seats in Purulia and nearly 40% of the seats in the Jhargram sub-division of Paschim Medinipur (Das, 2018). In the Lok Sabha election, the party won in all the parliamentary constituencies in the region, barring Ghatal (see Figure 10.1). Table 10.1 illustrates the BJP's spectacular electoral growth in the six parliamentary constituencies nested in Junglemahal, with the party replacing the CPI(M) as the main competitor of the TMC within the space of a decade.

It is instructive to note that Junglemahal had been one of the major epicentres of Maoist violence in the country from 2005 to 2011. In 2010, out of the total number of 1,180 Maoist-related fatalities that year, 425 were recorded in Junglemahal alone (South Asia Terrorism Portal, 2015). The proximate reason for the onset of Maoist violence was the militarisation of a peaceful protest by the region's tribal population against the LF

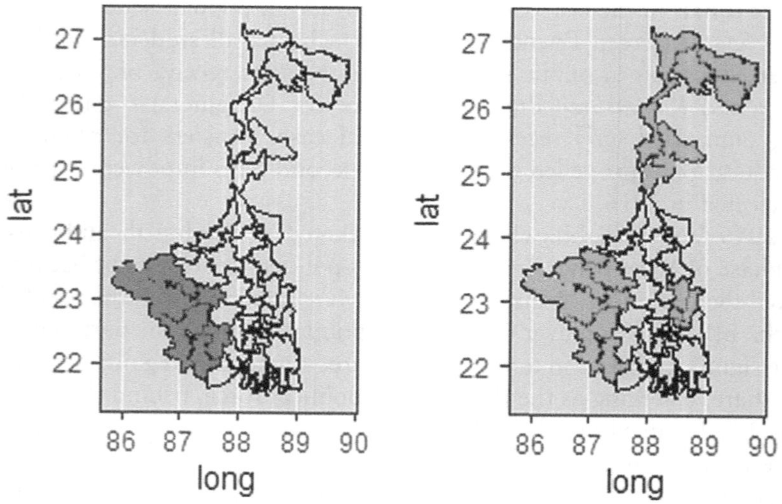

Figure 10.1 Parliamentary constituencies in Junglemahal (red) and parliamentary constituencies won by the BJP in West Bengal (orange). Note: Statewise Parliamentary Constituency Map shapefiles are provided by Data Community Maps Projects, made available under the Creative Commons Attribution 2.5 India).

Table 10.1 Vote share of major political parties in Junglemahal Lok Sabha constituencies[1]

	2009			*2014*			*2019*		
Constituency/party	*TMC (%)*	*LF (%)*	*BJP (%)*	*TMC (%)*	*LF (%)*	*BJP (%)*	*TMC (%)*	*LF (%)*	*BJP (%)*
Ghatal	40.92	53.50	2.99	50.14	31.06	6.93	48.20	6.51	40.95
Jhargram[2]		56.89	4.74	53.63	25.97	9.74	43.68	5.37	44.52
Medinipur	42.62	47.29	4.99	45.95	31.30	14.26	42.29	4.41	48.60
Purulia[3]		44.13	2.38	38.81	26.06	7.15	34.17	5.04	49.27
Bankura[4]		47.66	4.33	39.10	31.13	20.31	36.49	7.30	49.19
Bishnupur	33.26	43.71	3.98	45.51	33.74	14.11	40.73	7.22	46.23

Source: Election Commission of India; [2,3,4] TMC did not contest in Jhargram, Purulia, and Bankura parliamentary constituencies in 2009.
Note: [1] Percentage of votes secured over total votes polled in the constituency.

government's decision to give the go-ahead to a large-scale steel plant project in the Salboni area. When Mamata Banerjee came to power in the historic 2011 assembly election, riding a groundswell of popular support, she took up post-conflict reconstruction in the region with a gusto. This came in the form of a "Chief Minister's special package for Junglemahal," which included a wide range of developmental initiatives, from providing rice at rupees two per kilo for below poverty line households to the construction of sports facilities (Banerjee & Ghosh, 2016). In a major break from pre-conflict practice, however, the responsibility for delivering these public services was completely divested from elected local officials and entrusted with state bureaucrats, who, in turn, were made directly answerable to the Chief Minister's Office.

In a study on the post-conflict public service delivery regime in Junglemahal, Ray and Dutta (2018) document how the massive flow of developmental resources into the region coexisted with a deep sense of ambivalence among the region's residents about these developmental initiatives. For example, it was not uncommon to find households where each family member had been enrolled in a government-subsidised health insurance scheme, but no one in the family had actually availed of the benefits of the scheme. When asked why they had not used their health insurance card, the common refrain was that no one from the panchayat had explained how to use the card. Indeed, "distance" from the panchayat was a recurrent theme in these interviews. Probing this theme further, the study argues that the disjuncture between output and outcomes was directly related to the public service delivery model that Ms Banerjee had adopted, relying exclusively on the bureaucracy to deliver those services. This form of securitised development, the study noted, was a major departure from Bengal's cultural hardware since long years of Left rule had entrenched social expectations for political parties to mediate in the delivery of public services.

Fast forward to the present, although few studies have systematically assessed the BJP's ascendance in Junglemahal, the available evidence clearly points to the massive growth in the region of outreach activities by social service organisations allied with the Sangh Parivar. Jhargram Town in Paschim Medinipur is a hub of these activities, hosting a Vanavasi Kalyan Ashram, with feeder networks of Sishu Mandirs and Ekal Vidyalayas (Daniyal, 2018). It is also worth noting that almost all the top-level leaders of the BJP in Junglemahal have close connections with the RSS and are actively involved in building these institutions, including Dr. Kunar Hembram, who was the party's (successful) candidate for the Jhargram parliamentary constituency.

Data and methods

The pre-election survey in the Jungle Mahal parliamentary constituencies was conducted between February and March 2019. The survey is part of an ongoing research project on post-conflict politics. The survey respondents were selected using the multi-stage random sampling method. Specifically, using data on the incidence of Maoist violence in West Bengal from the South Asia Terrorism Portal and other sources, I identified 38 villages in these constituencies that had experienced at least one incident of Maoist violence from 2005 to 2014. Within these villages, every *n*-th household was selected – with *n* varying by village – yielding a total of 1,140 respondents. The survey instruments were designed in collaboration with the India Election Studies team, which has implemented similar surveys in other electoral contexts in India (Neyazi, Kumar, & Semetko, 2016). The survey was administered by Quest Sankalpa, a Kolkata-based market research firm, and conducted in the local *lingua franca*, Bengali.

Dependent variables

To assess membership in BJP-affiliated organisations, I exploit the following survey item: Are you a member of any social, cultural or religious organisations? If yes, could you please tell me the name of the organisation you are most involved with? Figure 10.2 plots the distribution of the responses to this item. As the figure illustrates, the majority of respondents in my sample were not involved in any cultural or religious organisation. Among those who were involved, the organisations that attracted the maximum number of members were the RSS and the Seva Bharati. It is plausible to assume that this division of members also captures different levels of involvement with the Sangh Parivar. While RSS membership clearly involves restrictions on political attitudes and behaviour, membership in a service organisation such as Seva Bharati comes with fewer strings attached. Accordingly, I coded two binary variables measuring involvement in the Sangh Parivar from this survey item. The first measure, denoted as

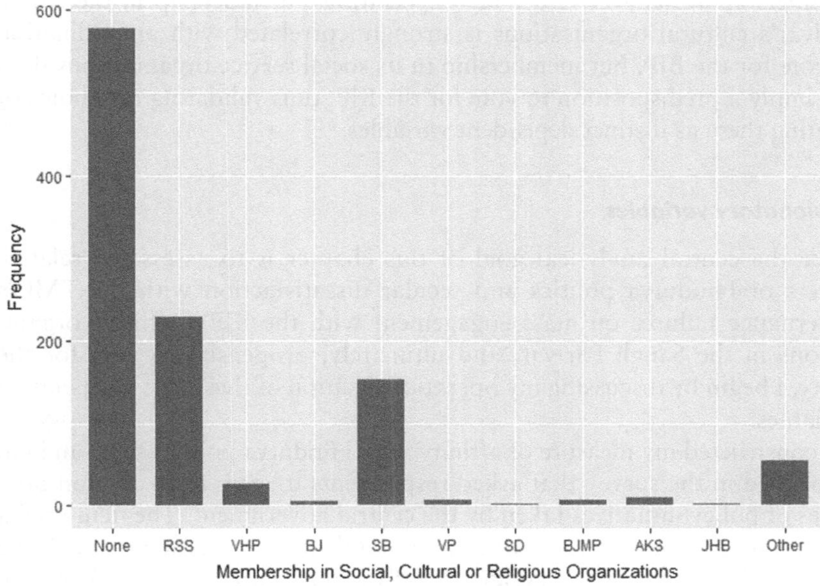

Figure 10.2 Distribution of membership in Social, cultural or religious organisations in Junglemahal. Note: RSS = Rashtriya Swayamsevak Sangh; VHP = Vishwa Hindu Parishad; BJ = Bajrang Dal; SB = Seva Bharati; VP = Vanbandhu Parishad; SD = Seva Dal; BJMP = Bharat Jakat Majhi Pargana; AKS = Adivasi Kurmi Samaj; JHB = Jai Hind Bahini.

Table 10.2 Cross-tabulation of latent support for BJP by membership in social service vs cultural organisations

	Inclined to vote for BJP	*Not inclined to vote for BJP*
Member of Seva Bharati/Vanbandhu Parishad	12	146
Member of RSS/VHP/BJ	185	73

member of social service wing, takes a value 1 when a respondent reported being a member of the Sangh Parivar's social service wings, Seva Bharati or Vanbandhu Parishad, and is 0 otherwise. The second measure, denoted as *member of cultural wing*, takes a value 1 when a respondent reported being a member of the RSS or the Vishwa Hindu Parishad or Bajrang Dal, and is 0 otherwise.

To assess latent support for the BJP, I coded the binary variable *bjpvot19*, which takes the value 1 if a respondent reported that she was most inclined to vote for the BJP in the Lok Sabha election, and is 0 otherwise. Table 10.2

reports a simple cross-tabulation of latent support for the BJP against the membership variables. As per my expectations, membership in the Sangh Parivar's cultural organisations is strongly correlated with an inclination to vote for the BJP, but membership in its social service organisations does not imply a predisposition to vote for the BJP, thus validating my choice of treating these as distinct dependent variables.

Explanatory variables

Since the central analytical goal of this chapter is to assess the relative effects of Hindutva politics and secular dissatisfaction with the TMC's governance failures on mass engagement with the BJP's affiliate organisations in the Sangh Parivar, and ultimately, propensity to vote for the party, I begin by discussing my operationalisation of these key independent variables.

I constructed my measure of affinity with Hindutva politics from an item embedded in the survey that asked respondents to state their opinion on a series of policy initiatives taken by the central government. The item used a five-point scale, where 1 denotes the respondent totally disagreed with the policy and 5 denotes the respondent totally agreed with the policy. Although it is a moot question whether a policy initiative can be classified unambiguously as "social" – for example, is demonetisation an economic policy or an attempt at social engineering? – I take the view, following Boulding (1967, p. 7), that "one common thread that unites all aspects of social policy and distinguishes them from merely economic policy" is that "[B]y and large it is an objective of social policy to build the identity of a person around some community with which he is associated." Hence, I code a policy initiative as "social" only when it is solely designed for the purposes of social integration. Accordingly, I focus on responses to the following policy initiatives: 10% reservations for extremely backward communities, National Register of Citizens, and the government's handling of inter-communal relations. Once policies were classified in this way, I conducted a simple correlation analysis, which revealed a high degree of clustering in responses to each type of policy. Accordingly, to simplify the analysis, I created an index for social policy by adding up the respondent's responses to each policy initiative. I denote this measure as *social policy index*.

To capture secular dissatisfaction with the TMC, I focused on two factors that were repeatedly flagged in political discourse surrounding the Lok Sabha election as the party's Achilles heel: corruption in panchayats and the threat of violence against opposition party members. I coded attitude towards local government using an item in the survey that asked respondents to assess how much they trusted the local panchayat on a scale of 1–5, where 1 denoted that they did not trust the institution at all and 5 denoted that they trusted the institution completely. I denote this variable here as *trust in local government.* To measure attitude towards insecurity, I use an item in the survey that asked respondents about the degree to which they were worried about becoming a victim of crime in the near future on a scale of 1–5, where 1 denoted that they were not concerned at all and 5 denoted that they were very concerned. I denote this variable here as *threat of crime.*

The remainder of the variables included in the analysis were selected carefully to control for potential sources of omitted variable bias. These can be classified into four categories of variables measuring: (i) past voting record; (ii) demographic characteristics of respondents; (iii) perceptions of leaders and (iv) effect of campaigns.

To assess the effect of past voting record on the propensity to vote for the BJP, I utilise a survey item that asked respondents about the party they had voted for in the 2016 Vidhan Sabha election. Accordingly, I coded a binary variable indicating whether the respondent voted for the BJP in 2016, denoted as *bjpvot2016.*

To capture the effect of the demographic characteristics of respondents on the propensity to engage with the Sangh Parivar, I focus on the following attributes on which data was available for the largest number of observations: religion, caste, class, gender, age and education. My measure of religious identity is a binary variable, *muslim*, indicating whether the respondent self-identified as a Muslim. I operationalise caste coding the binary variables *sc*, *st* and *obc*, which indicate whether the respondent belonged to either of those communities. My measure of class is based on a survey item that asks respondents the number of status assets they owned out of a list of 16 assets, denoted as *class.* My measure of gender identity is a binary variable indicating whether a respondent was *male.* I capture the so-called "demographic dividend" enjoyed by Narendra Modi using self-reported *age* (Basu & Mishra, 2014). Finally, my measure of *education* is coded on an eight-point scale, where 1 denotes that the respondent is illiterate and 8 denotes university education.

Moving forward, the next control variable models the effect of party leaders on party choice. I construct this variable from an item in the survey that asks respondents to rate the performance of party leaders on a five-point scale, where 1 denotes very poor and 5 denotes very good. Focusing on the BJP, I code a measure of leader approval for Narendra Modi, denoted as *approval for modi.* Here, I expect to find evidence in favour of the so-called "Modi wave," i.e. the effect of Narendra Modi's personal popularity on the inclination to vote for the BJP cutting across demographic and regional barriers (Chari, 2019).

The BJP's asymmetric success in using social media to reach new voters has been extensively documented (Sardesai, 2014). To capture this effect, I code a binary variable, *social media contact*, indicating whether the respondent was contacted by the party via social media channels, such as Whatsapp, Twitter, Facebook etc. I also code the respondent's level of engagement in the election campaign on a four-point scale, where 1 denotes no interest at all and 4 denotes very interested. I denote this variable as *campaign interest*.

Table 10.3 provides the descriptive statistics for all the variables used in the empirical analysis that follows. As we would expect, the data shows a clear trend of support for the BJP growing over time. While 18.4% of the respondents reported voting for the party in 2016, more than twice that number, roughly 38%, indicated they were inclined to vote for the party in 2019. The data also shows a fairly high level of engagement with Sangh Parivar affiliates. Among those who responded to the question about membership in social/religious/cultural organisations, roughly one in every four respondents indicated being a member of a Sangh Parivar cultural organisation whereas roughly one in seven indicated being a member of a service organisation. In other words, close to 40% of those who responded belonged to one or the other type of organisation, which is again in conformity with our expectations. Moving on to our core independent variables, the average respondent in my sample revealed strong approval for the central government's handling of at least two of the three social issues counted in the social policy index, showing a substantively important affinity with Hindutva politics. By contrast, she was more neutral in her assessment of local government performance and the threat of violence.

My basic estimation strategy involves running logistic regression models with membership in the various Sangh Parivar affiliates and propensity to vote for the BJP as the core dependent variables. Among the independent

Table 10.3 Descriptive statistics

Junglemahal

Variables	*Observations*	*Mean*	*Std. dev.*	*Min*	*Max*
bjpvot19	1140	0.377	0.484	0	1
bjpvot16	1140	0.184	0.387	0	1
member of cultural wing	1066	0.242	0.428	0	1
member of social service wing	1066	0.148	0.355	0	1
sc	1140	0.376	0.484	0	1
st	1140	0.299	0.485	0	1
obc	1140	0.243	0.429	0	1
muslim	1140	0.084	0.277	0	1
male	1140	0.776	0.416	0	1
education	1125	2.198	1.500	1	8
class	1138	3.010	2.175	0	16
age	936	44.35	13.082	18	92
approval for modi	1135	3.130	1.209	1	5
social policy index	1132	9.981	3.333	3	15
trust in local government	1139	3.056	1.233	1	5
threat of crime	1139	2.837	1.265	1	5
campaign interest	1130	2.512	0.947	1	4
social media contact	1128	0.328	0.470	0	1

variables, past voting record, social media contact and campaign interest are only used to predict support for the BJP. While these variables may be correlated with membership in Sangh Parivar affiliates, they are obviously more relevant for electoral rather than membership choice.

Results

Table 10.4 presents my main empirical findings. The reported figures are logit coefficients with standard errors clustered at the village level included in parentheses.

Table 10.4 Logit models of engagement with Sangh Parivar

Independent variables	*Model 1 dep. variable membership in social service wing*	*Model 2 dep. variable membership in cultural wing*	*Model 3 dep. variable bjpvot19*
bjpvot16			3.239***
			(0.415)
sc	0.603	0.680	-0.481
	(0.694)	(0.539)	(0.431)
st	0.917	-0.455	-1.302**
	(0.702)	(0.448)	(-0.414)
obc	1.257*	0.388	-0.971*
	(0.687)	(0.553)	(0.404)
muslim	0.954†	-3.117**	-2.323***
	(0.523)	(1.043)	(0.660)
male	0.887**	0.452	-0.014
	(0.327)	(0.294)	(0.304)
education	-0.078	-0.122	-0.038
	(0.092)	(0.122)	(0.075)
class	0.168*	0.162*	-0.201***
	(0.078)	(0.082)	(0.055)
age	0.003	0.004	-0.012†
	(0.008)	(0.007)	(0.007)
approval for modi	-0.314**	-0.300**	0.689***
	(0.115)	(0.109)	(0.137)
social policy index	-0.019	-0.002	0.086†
	(0.061)	(0.048)	(0.051)
trust in local government	-0.170	-0.304**	-0.328**
	(0.171)	(0.112)	(0.120)
threat of crime	-0.016	0.169	0.421***
	(0.137)	(0.116)	(0.119)
campaign interest			-0.153
			(0.134)
social media contact			0.160
			(0.246)
constant	-2.347†	-0.832	-1.805
	(1.216)	(0.993)	(0.732)
Observations	847	847	897
Pseudo R2	0.091	0.135	0.331

Note: †$p < 0.10$; *$p < 0.05$; **$p < 0.01$; ***$p < 0.001$

Comparing the predictors of various types of engagement with the Sangh Parivar, what stands out in sharp relief is the disparate effect of ideological affinity on membership in the Parivar's social and cultural organisations, on the one hand, and propensity to vote for the BJP, on the other. We see from Models 1 and 2 that ideological closeness to the Parivar, as proxied by strong approval for the central government's social engineering policies, does not lead to greater chances of membership in either its social service or cultural organisations. By contrast, the same measure is positively correlated with the propensity to vote for the BJP and the effect is statistically and substantively significant. To see this, note, the coefficient of the social policy measure in Model 3 implies that a one unit increase in the social policy index is associated with a roughly 1.3 %-point increase in the propensity to vote for the BJP and this effect is statistically significant at the 0.10 level. Interestingly, we observe a similar pattern in the effect of Narendra Modi's leadership: a one unit increase in approval for Modi is associated with a nearly 10%-point increase in the average propensity to vote for the BJP and this effect is statistically significant at the 0.001 level. However, this relationship is reversed when the dependent variable is membership in the Sangh Parivar affiliates. Respondents who gave a positive rating to Modi's leadership were significantly less likely to be members of either the Seva Bharati or RSS than respondents who gave a negative rating.

If ideological affinity with the Sangh Parivar or even support for Modi is uncorrelated or negatively correlated with membership in its social service or cultural organisations, what are the factors that contribute to membership in these organisations? Focusing on Model 1 in Table 10.4, we see that being a male, Muslim, a member of the OBC community, and having a higher class status are significant predictors of membership in the Parivar's social service organisations. Although the disproportionate presence of Muslims in the Sangh Parivar's social service wings would appear to be perplexing at first glance, this simply attests to the apolitical image that is painstakingly promoted by these organisations in the poor communities that they serve. This point is validated by looking at Model 2, which probes the correlates of membership in the Sangh Parivar's cultural organisations, which are more obviously political in their outlook. Here, as we would expect, being a Muslim is negatively associated with membership choice, and the effect is statistically significant at conventional levels.

Model 2 also draws our attention to the most salient factor shaping membership choice, namely, dissatisfaction with local government performance. We see that the higher the level of trust in local government the lower the propensity for joining the RSS. Conversely, the lower the level of trust in local government the higher the propensity for joining the RSS. Moreover, the effect of this variable is highly statistically significant. To see this, note, the coefficient of the trust variable in Model 2 implies that a one unit increase in trust is associated with a roughly 5%-point decrease in the average propensity for joining the Sangh Parivar's cultural wing and this effect is statistically significant at the 0.01 level.

To summarise, analysing Models 1 and 2 yields two key insights. First, those among our respondents who joined the Sangh Parivar's social service or cultural organisations showed little affinity for its ideological positions. Second, and relatedly, the most salient factor driving membership choice is dissatisfaction with local government performance.

Moving forward to Model 3, it was noted earlier that ideological affinity with the Sangh Parivar does have a determinative effect on a higher propensity to vote for the BJP, as does strong approval for Narendra Modi's leadership. Next, we assess the other significant predictors of this variable. We see from the model that as in the case of membership in the RSS, being a Muslim is associated with a significantly lower chance of voting for the BJP. The effect of trust in local government is also carried forward. The higher the level of trust in local government the lower the propensity of voting for the BJP, and conversely, the lower the level of trust the higher the propensity of voting for the BJP. The model also reveals a significant effect of the threat of crime, which is absent from the membership models. Specifically, the estimated coefficient of the variable implies that a one unit increase in concern about crime is associated with a roughly 6%-point increase in the propensity to vote for the BJP, and the effect is statistically significant at the 0.001 level.

Another striking result from Model 3 is the effect of the class variable. Here, we see that propensity to vote for the BJP is lower the higher a respondent's class standing. Conversely, the lower a respondent's class standing the higher the propensity of voting for the BJP. Moreover, this effect is substantively and statistically significant. Specifically, an additional unit of class status is associated with a roughly 3%-point lower chance of voting for the BJP, and the effect is statistically significant at the 0.001 level. Combined with the result that respondents from the region's backward communities – whether SC, ST or OBC – were less inclined to vote for the BJP than respondents from the upper castes, what this result reveals is a strong class dimension in the propensity to vote for the BJP, namely, the less well-off among these communities had a stronger inclination to vote for the party than their more well-off brethren.

Before stepping back to discuss these findings in the aggregate, it is worth mentioning two results that did not conform with my initial expectations. Specifically, I find no effect of education and of the election campaign variables. These results are, however, easily explicable when one considers the distribution of educational attainments in Junglemahal. As Table 10.3 shows, the average respondent in the sample had only completed primary school education, which obviously has spillover effects on the campaign variables, with only 32% of the sample reporting a social media contact by the BJP. It is unsurprising therefore that with little variation on these factors across the sample, their effects turn out to be negligible.

What then does the preceding discussion tell us about the core analytical question that motivated this study? Does the BJP's emergence in West Bengal mean the dissolution of party society? Or is the Sangh Parivar operating in ways that suggest that it is simply adapting itself to the demands of party society? Taken in their totality, my findings clearly reveal that the Sangh Parivar is working through rather than against or outside the structures of party society in line with an embedded mobilisation strategy. Specifically, they indicate that the Parivar's core activists are individuals with higher class standing who are attracted to it because of strong dissatisfaction with the performance of local government institutions. These well-heeled activists then fan out into the local community to promote the Parivar's political and ideological agenda by mobilising the less well-off members of the community, either through social service provision or by the demonstration effect of their very presence in the Parivar despite their secular orientation.

In addition to the models reported above, I also ran analyses to assess the extent to which my findings are sensitive to issues of model misspecification, alternative operationalisations of the main variables etc.[2] These included models incorporating village fixed effects, models replacing affinity for the central government's social policies with a direct measure of inter-communal trust, and models replacing the generalised trust and fear variables with more specific measures, such as, for example, the fear of the return of Maoist violence. Aside from these models, I also did sub-sample comparisons of outcomes between BJP and TMC-dominated Gram Panchayats and between individuals carefully matched on relevant covariates using propensity matching methods. My findings remain robust across all these specifications.

Conclusion

The spectacular emergence of the BJP as a serious contender for power in West Bengal, a state with a history of institutionalised leftism, poses intriguing questions about contemporary party politics in India. This chapter contributes to a growing body of research that has sought to explain this puzzle. To date, this literature has focused on the growing appeal of the BJP's ideology among the state's electorate, which has then been used as a springboard to argue that its emergence marks a fundamental break from business-as-usual. This chapter complicates this narrative by exploring a hitherto underexamined aspect of the party's rise in West Bengal, namely, its organisational basis. Using original survey data collected from the state's Maoist-affected Junglemahal belt prior to the 2019 Lok Sabha election, including measures of membership in the Sangh Parivar's social service and cultural organisations and inclination to vote for the BJP, I show that far from challenging the contours of the political society established in the region under

LF and TMC dominance, the party and its affiliates have been reworking and recalibrating it to their own advantage. More specifically, I show that ideological alignment with Hindutva and positive assessments of Modi were significant in explaining propensity to vote for the BJP, but had surprisingly little salience in predicting membership in the Sangh's service and cultural organisations, the conduits through which mass ideological preferences are shaped. Instead, the most salient factor in shaping the decision to become a Sangh activist was dissatisfaction with local government institutions.

This observation has interesting implications for the evolving development theory-policy-practice interface in West Bengal. Most crucially, it underscores the continuing relevance of "party society" as a theoretical frame for assessing the politics of development in the state. The TMC's failure to stem the BJP's rise is ultimately rooted in the party's absence from the everyday spaces of citizen-local government interactions. As noted by Ray and Dutta (2018) in their study of public perceptions of service delivery in Junglemahal, the region's residents revealed a strong preference for the involvement of elected party officials in the administration of these services. Yet, the modus operandi of the TMC regime has been precisely the opposite, namely to rely on the unelected arms of the local government for delivering services. While this strategy was ostensibly adopted to re-establish public services at short notice after the conflict interregnum, Mamata Banerjee's populist proclivities, and related to this, her reluctance to institutionalise the party organisation, further entrenched the bureaucracy in its service provision role at the expense of elected officials (Ray, 2020). Here, the public's culturally grounded imperative of party society came into conflict with the TMC government's politically motivated use of the bureaucracy, a tension that the BJP, given its strong organisational presence in the region, was uniquely positioned to exploit.

The analysis presented in this study is not without limitations. Most obviously, it is restricted to a single region. Future research should explore the possibility of implementing a similar survey elsewhere in West Bengal, particularly in non-SC-ST-OBC-dominated areas. Second, the analysis is less precise about the mechanisms through which the Sangh Parivar is expanding its footprint in West Bengal. The charged circumstances under which the 2019 election was held meant that it was not plausible to embed questions in the survey about the specific benefits that respondents may have received from the Sangh Parivar affiliates. This issue should be easier to address in future surveys as the BJP sheds its "upstart" tag in West Bengal's politics and assumes the mantle of a regular claimant to power. Going forward, these and other lines of inquiry can be the basis of a very productive research agenda exploring the developmental politics of religious nationalism in the context of an ex-communist state.

Notes

1 The concept of "programmatic strategy" used in this chapter is in line with Stokes et al's (2013) usage of the term as signifying a strategy of linking to voters, which involves: (a) proclaiming prior to elections that the party will unconditionally implement a political program if it is voted to power and (b) specifying criteria by which voters can judge whether the party has implemented the program.

2 The results of these analyses are available from the author upon request.

References

Banerjee, A. & Ghosh, A. (2016). Traversing Jungle Mahal: Field notes on democracy and development in the Santhal regions of Bihar and West Bengal. In V. Mudgal (Ed.), *Claiming India from below: Activism and democratic transformation* (pp. 54–73). Abingdon: Routledge.

Basu, D. & Das, D. (2019, May 27). Three factors that led to the BJP's impressive gains in West Bengal. *Wire*. Retrieved from https://thewire.in/politics/election-results-2019-bjp-west-bengal?fbclid=IwAR0izF96ZQam-ASlVCgz8ljYHKCs_lGoRO7MAltdGJyWO4Al4Yp0DZpdjhU

Basu, D. & Mishra, K. (2014). BJP's demographic dividend in the 2014 General Elections: An empirical analysis. Retrieved from https://scholarworks.umass.edu/cgi/viewcontent.cgi?referer=https://www.google.com.sg/&https://redir=1&article=1172&context=econ_workingpaper

Bhattacharyya, D. (2009). Of control and factions: The changing 'party society' in rural West Bengal. *Economic & Political Weekly*, *XLIV*(9), 59–69.

Boulding, K. E. (1967). The boundaries of social policy. *Social Work*, *12*(1), 3–11.

Chari, M. (2019, May 28). What is a Modi wave? Political scientists are looking for answers. *Scroll.in*. Retrieved from https://scroll.in/article/924872/what-is-a-modi-wave-political-scientists-are-looking-for-answers

Chiriyankandath, J. (2018). 'Yes but not in the South': The BJP, Congress and regional parties in South India. In M. Rehman (Ed.), *Rise of saffron power: Reflections of Indian politics* (pp. 44–61). London: Routledge.

Corbridge, S., Williams, G., Srivastava, M. & Veron, R. (2012). Politics of middlemen and political society. In A. Gudavarthy (Ed.), *Re-framing democracy and agency in India: Interrogating political society* (pp. 171–200). London: Anthem Press.

Daniyal, S. (2018, July 16). How the BJP is gaining in West Bengal's one-time Maoist stronghold, Jungle Mahal. *Scroll.in*. Retrieved from https://scroll.in/article/886576/ground-report-how-the-bjp-is-gaining-in-west-bengals-one-time-maoist-stronghold-jungle-mahal

Das, S. (2018, December 25). Year of clashes, BJP rise in Bengal. *Deccan Herald*. Retrieved from https://www.deccanherald.com/national/year-violent-land-agitation-709850.html

Kanungo, P. (2015). The rise of the Bharatiya Janata Party in West Bengal. *Studies in Indian Politics*, *3*(1), 50–68.

Kohli, A. (2006). Politics of economic growth in India, 1980–2005 Part II: The 1990s and beyond. *Economic & Political Weekly*, *41*(14), 1361–1370.

Nath, S. (2018). 'Cultural misrecognition' and the sustenance of Trinamool Congress in West Bengal. *Economic & Political Weekly*, *LIII*(28), 92–99.

Nath, S. & Chowdhury, S. R. (2019a). Manufacturing polarisation in contemporary India: The case of identity politics in Post-Left Bengal. *International Journal of Conflict and Violence*, *13*, 1–9.

Nath, S. & Chowdhury, S. R. (2019b). Mapping polarisation: Four ethnographic cases from West Bengal. *Journal of the Indian Anthropological Society*, *54*, 51–64.

Neyazi, T. A., Kumar, A. & Semetko, H. A. (2016). Campaigns, digital media, and mobilization in India. *The International Journal of Press/Politics*, *21*(3), 398–416.

Palshikar, S. (2017). India's second dominant party system. *Economic & Political Weekly*, *52*(11), 12–15.

Purakayastha, A. S. (2018). Communalisation of politics in West Bengal: Religion and the public sphere. *Economic & Political Weekly*, *53*(16), 12–15.

Ray, S. (2020). Bureaucracy unbound? The end of dominant party rule and the politics-administration interface in West Bengal. *India Review*, *19*(1), 1–32.

Ray, S. & Dutta, M. J. (2018). Insecure peace: Understanding citizen-local government relations in a Maoist-affected region in India. *Critical Asian Studies*, *50*(1), 37–57.

Sardesai, R. (2014). *2014: The elections that changed India*. New Delhi: Viking.

South Asia Terrorism Portal. (2015, April 24). *Fatalities in left-wing extremism 2005–2015*. Retrieved from http://www.satp.org/satporgtp/countries/india/maoist/data_sheets/fatalitiesnaxal05-11.htm#

Stokes, S., Dunning, T., Nazareno, M. & Brusco, V. (2013). *Brokers, voters and clientelism: The puzzle of distributive politics*. Cambridge: Cambridge University Press.

Thachil, T. (2011). Embedded mobilization: Nonstate service provision as electoral strategy in India. *World Politics*, *63*(3), 434–469.

Traub, A. (2018, July 10). India's secularists have an authoritarianism problem. *Foreign Policy*. Retrieved from https://foreignpolicy.com/2018/07/10/indias-secularists-have-an-authoritarianism-problem/

Chapter 11

Harnessing the digital revolution for development

The Indian experience

Anit N. Mukherjee

Introduction

Across the world, digital technologies are transforming the way in which citizens interact with states. Previous systems, especially in developing countries, had a significant role for community or local decision-making, with a high degree of personal interactions between the government, their agents and the people (Sen & Dreze, 1995). These are being superseded by new, more remote, delivery mechanisms as digital technology, in particular, for identification and payments, is engaged to reform public service delivery.

The costly, and sometimes difficult, changes in administrative processes and delivery mechanisms are motivated by the ultimate objective of making governments more inclusive, efficient and accountable. The success of the reform process, therefore, depends critically on whether the delivery of public goods and services have, or have not, improved along these three dimensions. It also depends on whether citizens perceive the changes as being beneficial, or whether they impose additional challenges to exercise their claims on the state (Gelb & Mukherjee, 2019; Gelb, Mukherjee & Navis, 2018; Gelb & Diofasi Metz, 2018).

Governments face complex challenges as they expand the use of digital technology to improve public services in particular and better development outcomes in general. In terms of the narrow goal of efficiency, they have to address issues of identification, targeting of beneficiaries and delivery mechanisms in a coherent way. Previously disparate data systems, sometimes with conflicting information, must be integrated, while the inevitable date entry errors will need to be resolved. Even with the best communications efforts, many people will have a limited understanding of the new systems. Some will not be able to use them effectively, requiring protocols for managing exceptions and speedy dispute resolution. All these challenges, and many others, make it even more important that the new systems, once bedded down, perform better than the old ones. This, in turn, makes it even more important to be clear on the problems – how serious are they, and how will digitisation solve them?

DOI: 10.4324/9781003159940-11

This leads to the question of whether technology in general, and information and communication technology (ICT, henceforth digital technology) in particular, can help countries like India break the cycle of poverty and inequality, and accelerate the process of development broadly defined. Technology can be transformational for development through its positive impact on inclusion, efficiency and innovation. However, a review of the evidence suggests that the effect of technology on global productivity, expansion of opportunity for the poor and the middle class, and the spread of accountable governance has so far been less than expected (World Bank, 2016). The spread of digital tools such as the internet and mobile phones have had a beneficial impact but has also given rise to concerns about the power and influence of social media and mass messaging platforms to undermine confidence in governance processes, which is ultimately detrimental for better development outcomes (Freedom House, 2017).

Understanding the complexity of the digital revolution and its impact on development poses a significant challenge for both researchers and practitioners. While there is a large and growing body of literature, inferences, lessons and recommendations are highly context specific, as are the tools of analysis across disciplines. In this chapter, I do not attempt to undertake a comprehensive survey of all the available evidence. The focus is much narrower: I use India as a case of a developing country in the throes of a digital revolution and examine how digital tools are being applied to address key developmental challenges – improving the delivery of public services, subsidies and transfers; addressing gender inequalities embedded in social norms; and improving accountability, choice and voice of citizens as they interact with the state. We end by reflecting on the existing and emerging challenges posed by the digital revolution, synthesising what we have learnt through the experiences of undertaking policy reforms in India and elsewhere.

India's digital transformation – an overview

Digital governance reform in India rests on three pillars popularly known as the "JAM trinity." This includes (i) the Jan Dhan programme, the government's financial inclusion mission to increase access to bank accounts, (ii) the biometric ID Aadhaar and (iii) mobile phones. From mid-2015, the financial inclusion programme known as Jan Dhan Yojana (JDY) has opened nearly 311 million bank accounts, helping India achieve 80% coverage of those older than 15 years in 2017 compared to only 53% in 2014 (Demirgüç-Kunt et al., 2018). Following a nationwide rollout in 2011, the Aadhaar programme has registered nearly 1.25 billion individuals on its biometric database, achieving almost universal coverage in just over five years (Dalberg, 2019). Finally, mobile phone subscriptions increased from 17 per 100 inhabitants in 2007 to 87 in 2018, achieving almost universal access within a decade (ITU, 2020). The relatively low cost of data-enabled value-added services is providing an opportunity to integrate mobile services into the overall digital governance framework, especially for government-to-people (G2P) payments and subsidies.

Building on these three different, though related, platforms, both federal and state governments have undertaken large-scale restructuring of the subsidies and transfers under their jurisdiction. In social pensions and other cash-based programmes, payments to beneficiaries in over 400 programmes are now sent directly to their Aadhaar linked bank accounts through the Direct Benefit Transfer (DBT) mechanism. For LPG cooking gas, rather than mandate low prices for cylinders sold to households, the government now delivers the subsidy component directly to bank accounts of eligible consumers who pay the market price for the cylinder which is effectively a voucher-type system. Finally, for food rations through the public distribution system (PDS), the federal government encouraged the use of biometric authentication at Fair Price Shops (FPS), the point of distribution, with the objective of reducing leakage and diversion that was reputed to be endemic in the previous system. Digital technology is therefore being used in different ways across a spectrum of delivery mechanisms – cash, voucher and in kind.

These changes have been implemented in a relatively short period of time. In PDS for example, under the old system, families were entitled to receive subsidised food grains if they possessed a "ration card" which contained details of its individual members. Similarly, households received subsidised cooking gas cylinders if they were duly registered with state-owned oil marketing companies. The transactions were recorded in physical booklets that were issued to the beneficiaries of individual schemes. Beneficiary lists were maintained in databases managed by implementing departments and agencies of both the federal and state governments. These lists were widely believed to contain duplicate entries or non-existent beneficiaries, leading to widespread corruption and leakage in the distribution of government subsidies (Overback, 2016; Khera, 2011).

In an attempt to remove the anomalies in the delivery of public subsidies, the new system has progressively incorporated digital technology for the identification of beneficiaries and keeping a record of the transactions. For the distribution of PDS food grains, households in Rajasthan were mandated to re-register their ration cards in a digital format during the Bhamashah registration process. In addition, they also had to provide Aadhaar numbers of all the individual members which enabled them to biometrically authenticate at the FPS and collect their food rations. The list of subscribers of LPG cooking gas was initially deduplicated by matching names and addresses, and genuine subscribers were assigned a unique beneficiary number or LPG ID. Aadhaar was made mandatory for new cooking gas connections while existing consumers were encouraged to link their LPG ID with Aadhaar (Mittal et al., 2017). All DBT programmes, including social pensions, required beneficiaries to provide an active bank account and a mobile number, items that many of them did not have before. The digital transformation therefore is not only in government systems and processes but also for people to adapt to this new digital governance architecture (Alston, 2019).

The reforms have been quite controversial and a subject of much debate in academic and policy circles, not only in India but globally. In addition to concerns over privacy and data protection, questions have been raised over the utility and efficacy of implementing Aadhaar authentication in large government programmes (Khera, 2017). There has also been a continuing debate on the fiscal savings from Aadhaar-enabled programmes, with the government offering substantial estimates and others disputing them. Several issues remain unresolved, not least due to the unavailability of systematic data on the impact of the reforms on actual beneficiaries of the programme.

Leaving aside the question of fiscal savings, the challenge is to improve the quality of delivery of services through digital reforms without excluding legitimate beneficiaries. While one common rationale for the use of digital tools in programme implementation is the potential to remove duplicate, non-existent or inactive entries from the list of beneficiaries across programmes, there were also specific issues that the new digital infrastructure intended to address. In PDS and PAHAL for example, diversion of subsidised rations and cylinders and variability in the timing of their distribution was believed to be pervasive in the old system. Pension delivery through the postal system was said to be unreliable, and it was asserted that delivery agents sometimes charged "fees" for their service. On the other hand, it is also possible that the new systems could be exclusionary or cause inconvenience to beneficiaries, due to problems in biometric authentication for PDS rations, or connectivity failures. For PAHAL or pensions, where benefits are transferred directly to bank accounts, limited access to banks and the time-cost of withdrawing money could cause additional hardship under the new digital system.

These tradeoffs are not unexpected, but they do have a bearing on the impact of digital technologies on programme efficiency and equity, and therefore on development outcomes more broadly. More importantly, it is important to understand whether the changes are beneficial or not from the perspective of the beneficiaries themselves. Below, we report the results from a field survey conducted in Rajasthan that examine the design and implementation of digital reforms at the state level. We end the chapter with some key lessons drawn from India and elsewhere that can help use the opportunity provided by the digital revolution to achieve better development outcomes.

Creating a digital social registry for public service delivery: Examining Rajasthan's Bhamashah programme[1]

Bhamashah is one of the first nuclear-family-level identity systems in India. Started in 2014, it seeks to create a digital platform for the delivery of public services for all residents of the state who receive benefits financed by the state government. As in a number of other digital reforms, implementation preceded legislation. The Rajasthan government gave legal backing to the Bhamashah programme through The Rajasthan Bhamashah (Direct Transfer of Public Welfare Benefits and Delivery of Services) Act of 2017. Following the passage of the legislation, the Bhamashah family identification number has been made mandatory for beneficiaries to avail their entitlements from over 150 schemes that are wholly or partially funded by the Government of Rajasthan.[2] Families who do not receive any public benefit are not required to register in the programme. However, with more services being included under the ambit of the Bhamashah programme, the proportion of households registered is likely to increase over time.

Programme design and use of technology

The Bhamashah scheme registers each family with a unique family ID number and issues a family card that lists individual members along with their Aadhaar numbers. It also captures other socioeconomic and demographic characteristics during the registration process, thereby creating a comprehensive database for residents of Rajasthan following the principle of "one family, one identity."

Residents apply for the Bhamashah card at a registration camp or electronically through "E-Mitra", agents who facilitate the process. Each member is registered with biographic details and their Aadhaar number. The data is digitised and uploaded to a central server for processing. Under the scheme, a centralised data warehouse called the Bhamashah Resident Data Hub (BRDH) maintains the family level information, determines eligibility for public benefits and keeps a digital record of delivery of entitlements for both individuals and families. After a final check, the BRDH clears the issuance of the Bhamashah card bearing a unique household identifier, which provides them access to benefits, both cash and in kind.[3]

From its inception, more than 64 million people in 17.4 million households (83% of estimated total households) had been enrolled under the Bhamashah scheme by December 2017. The remaining households may have chosen not to, or migrants who were left out during the (location-specific) registration process. Since 2014, nearly 860 million transactions had been routed through the Bhamashah platform transferring nearly $4.5 billion in government payments for public subsidies and social assistance directly to beneficiaries.

The design of the Bhamashah programme is based on a "whole of government approach" platform approach incorporating schemes from almost all administrative departments of the state government. On the implementation side, it brings together the three technology platforms – ID (Aadhaar), banking and the mobile system. Each member of the household is listed on the family card with their respective Aadhaar numbers. The bank account of the designated head of household is registered on the family card and all cash transfers are delivered into this account. Finally, the family card is linked with one active mobile number, thereby bringing all the three platforms together in an integrated fashion.

Moreover, against the backdrop of a strongly patriarchal society, the programme mandates that the designated head of household be a woman. It thus aims to promote women's empowerment by making them the primary recipient of all transfers from the government, both cash and in kind. This is seen as an especially important spillover from the move towards digital governance in the state. While it cannot realistically be expected to revolutionise gender norms immediately, it is hoped that its impact on these and on women's agency, will be visible in the years to come.

Rajasthan's digital governance reform represents both an opportunity and a challenge for efforts to understand the perceived impact of digital service delivery. Most existing studies consider the impact of digital reforms in the context of a particular scheme or sector, such as the LPG programme or the PDS (Mittal et al., 2017; Dreze et al., 2017). In contrast, Bhamashah provides an opportunity to look at an effort to reorganise and consolidate a number of disparate programmes around the theme of a nuclear family.[4] Such a step could be the precursor, for example, to more extensive consolidation, even to the point of a family-based universal benefit programme. But Bhamashah is not itself a major benefit programme in the sense of pensions or the PDS. The only two benefits specifically related to it are an upfront registration payment of Rs. 2,000 to below poverty line (BPL) families, and premium support for the Bhamashah Swashta Bima Yojana (BSBY) health insurance programme. Both are discussed in detail in a separate report[5] but are not the main benefit programmes considered in this chapter.

The challenge arises because the experience of consolidation into Bhamashah – at the same time as the PDS, pension and other programmes were being digitised and reformed – will inevitably influence people's views of the reforms as a whole and, by extension, views on the digitisation of the major individual programmes. Those not eligible for benefits had no reason to enrol, although the programme is now being extended as a requirement for other services, such as state driving licenses. The motivation for families to enrol varied. The most important reason was the threat of denial of benefits, along with the demonstration effect of mass enrolment drives conducted by the state government. Nearly 70% of the survey respondents cited these as the main reason for Bhamashah registration. In addition, nearly 60% reported that the monetary incentive of Rs.2,000 influenced their decision to enrol in the programme – even though only 40% of eligible beneficiaries reported having received the amount (own survey – see details below).

However, the processes of digitisation and restructuring benefits into the Bhamashah programme were not smooth. They created uncertainty and inconvenience for many people and may also have led to some exclusion of legitimate beneficiaries.[6] While the government made a significant effort to include as many families as possible through local registration camps and enrolment agents (known as E-Mitra-s), it is possible that some categories were not fully covered, especially migrants or those who could not prove residency as required to access state programmes. Since our survey is designed to capture the experience and perception of beneficiaries who have enrolled in Bhamashah, we are not able to fully understand the possible extent of exclusion, or how it does, or does not, relate to the digitisation process.

Survey design and methodology

As described in the previous section, the delivery of public services in India is undergoing rapid change with the implementation of the JAM framework – Jan Dhan (financial inclusion), Aadhaar and mobile. Different programmes have designed the reforms in various ways, depending on their objectives and intended outcomes. Delivery system reforms fall broadly into three categories: (i) biometrically authenticated physical uptake, or BAPU, as seen in PDS and subsidised fertiliser delivery; (ii) cash transfers on proof-of-purchase as in the reform of cooking gas subsidies (a voucher-like mechanism) and (iii) DBT of social pensions and scholarships and other monetary payments from the government into beneficiary bank accounts. The two main goals of these reforms have been fiscal savings (which we do not consider in this chapter) and improved delivery of transfers and subsidies to ultimate beneficiaries.

States have further innovated these platforms and shaped programme design and delivery mechanisms taking into account the situation on the ground. In addition to improving service delivery, the reforms in Rajasthan aimed for two further cross-cutting objectives: greater financial inclusion and the empowerment of women. With a focus on three major programmes, this provides a framework of five major objectives to be investigated through the survey.

The field survey of beneficiaries of government programmes was carried out between May and July 2017. The sample included a total of 633 households spread across all seven administrative divisions of the state. We selected a representative district from in each division, two blocks (one each urban and rural) in each district and, within these, randomly selected villages and wards for enumeration, dividing the total sample for the district in proportion to its rural-urban population ratio. The geographical distribution of the survey is summarised in Figure 11.1. The survey design and full questionnaire available from the link below.[7]

A detailed questionnaire, administered to the selected families, gathered information on the socioeconomic status of the family, their experience

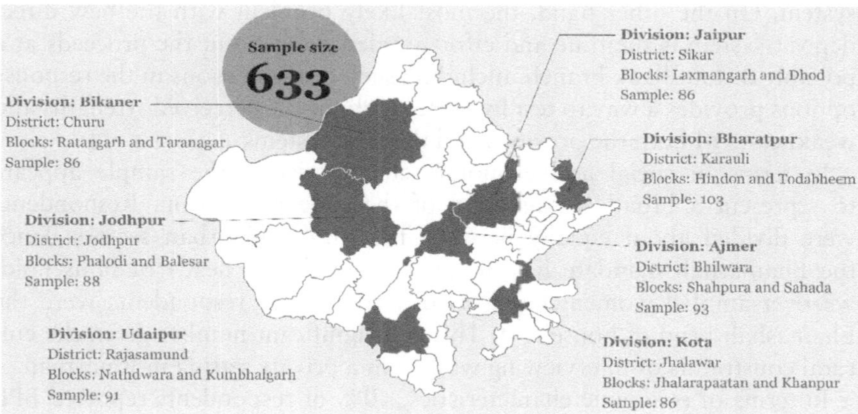

Figure 11.1 District, block and sample for Rajasthan survey. Source: Gelb, Mukherjee and Navis (2018).

with the Bhamashah enrolment process and their perception of the changes in the modes of programme delivery. It was emphasised at the outset that this was an independent survey without any involvement of the government (no officials accompanied the survey or monitored results) and respondents were encouraged to provide their honest assessment without the threat of any repercussions for their expressed opinions. The questionnaire was structured to gather scheme-wise information from beneficiaries with the objective of distinguishing between the various delivery mechanisms and modes of technology usage, including authentication, bank transfers and mobile phones. In addition, we included questions on the use of banking services and mobile technology, with special attention to the role of women. This allows us to analyse the data from the lens of women's economic empowerment through the design of the programmes on one hand and the extent of digital empowerment through the use of mobile phones on the other, as well as financial inclusion.

The structure of the questionnaire followed some simple principles. First, we tried to be neutral in the construction of questions – asking for a view on whether the quality of service delivery through the new systems was seen to be better, the same, or worse than that of the previous arrangements. Since the changes are relatively recent, the possibility of recall bias is low. Second, respondents were invited to provide the reasons for their opinions. The response options for these questions included choices related to several of the hypotheses about the workings of the old and the new systems noted previously. For example, it is sometimes argued that shifting from pensions hand delivered by postal officials to direct pension deposits into a bank account will improve the regularity or completeness of payment, but improvement is only possible if these had been problematic in the previous system. On the other hand, the most likely problem with the new direct deposit system is the time and effort needed to cash out the proceeds at a possibly distant bank branch. Including such considerations in the response options provides a way to test hypotheses about the perceived strengths and weaknesses of both the previous and the new systems.

In terms of social and economic characteristics, the sample appears to represent a broad cross-section of the state population. Respondents were divided about equally between the rural and urban sectors. Since the Bhamashah mandate has designated females as heads of household, we oversampled women; nearly two-thirds of our respondents were the Bhamashah head of household. This is a significant number given the cultural constraints of interviewing women in a private setting in Rajasthan.

In terms of economic characteristics, 40% of respondents reported BPL status. Just over 40% of all households surveyed (including urban) did not own any agricultural land. Another 30% reported having less than half an acre of land and other secondary occupations to fulfil their economic requirement. In terms of reported income, nearly 10% of households reported receiving less than Rs.2,000 per month ($30 at the exchange rate at the time of writing); these we termed "destitute" to distinguish them from the broader BPL group. Just over 80% of households in our sample earned between Rs.2,000 and Rs.10,000 a month ($150) while around 7% were above this threshold. This distribution of income appears to reflect the reality on the ground, where there are still many very poor families and few high earners. There is a reasonable degree of correlation between these various measures of social and economic status, as well as between them and other indicators, such as possession of a mobile phone.

In terms of income-related indicators and above poverty line (APL)/BPL status, there is no overwhelming difference between urban and rural respondents. However, the districts from which the sample was drawn show a fair amount of heterogeneity. The income per head in Bhilwara, the richest district sampled, is roughly twice as high as in Churu, the poorest district. The sectoral composition of economic activity also differs across districts, with industry and commerce more dominant in the richer ones and agriculture more pronounced in the poorer.

In order to assess the experience and perception of changes in the mode of delivery of public services, these need to be received by a fair number of households. Out of 633 households, 535 received PDS (85%), 413 received the PAHAL cooking gas subsidy (65%) and 126 received old-age pensions (20%). Almost all households surveyed received at least one technology-enabled benefit and some received several.

Other notable features of the sample are the degree of Aadhaar coverage and financial inclusion. Aadhaar was universal, as might have been expected since these were programme beneficiaries. Every household had at least one

Table 11.1 Selective summary of the sample

		Frequency	*Per cent*
Location	Urban	310	49.0
	Rural	323	51.0
Cardholder's Gender	Male	226	35.7
	Female	407	64.3
Household land ownership	Landless	262	41.4
	Less than 0.4 acre	199	31.4
	More than 0.4 acre	172	27.2
Monthly household income	< INR 2000	63	10.0
	INR 2,000–INR 5,000	261	41.2
	INR 5,000–INR 10,000	263	41.6
	INR 10,000 and over	46	7.3
BPL status	Yes	256	40.4
	No	377	59.6
Does the household have at least one mobile phone?	Yes	594	93.8
	No	39	6.2
How many bank accounts does the household have?	0	1	0.2
	1	94	14.9
	2	333	52.6
	3	126	19.9
	4 or more	79	12.4

bank account and nearly 95% of households owned at least one mobile phone (Table 11.1). As explained below, this degree of financial inclusion had not prevailed prior to the reforms – it points to the considerable success of the rollout of both biometric ID and financial inclusion initiatives within a short period of time. As bank and mobile linkage with Aadhaar become universal, the government will be in a position to use this framework for other schemes, such as fertiliser and rural credit. Our survey results are a pointer to whether the existing mechanisms are working as expected and what can be done to make them better from both the system and beneficiary standpoint.

Summary of results

In each of the three different classes of programmes that we investigated, namely, in kind distribution (PDS), vouchers (PAHAL) and cash transfers (social pensions), between 40 and 60% of beneficiaries had an unambiguously positive perception of the reforms (Figure 11.2). Twelve percent of PDS beneficiaries, and only a few percent of cooking gas subsidy voucher (PAHAL) and social pensions reported that the new system was worse than the previous one. We consider the case of PDS, the largest programme in our sample, in more detail below.[8]

- Process of digitisation

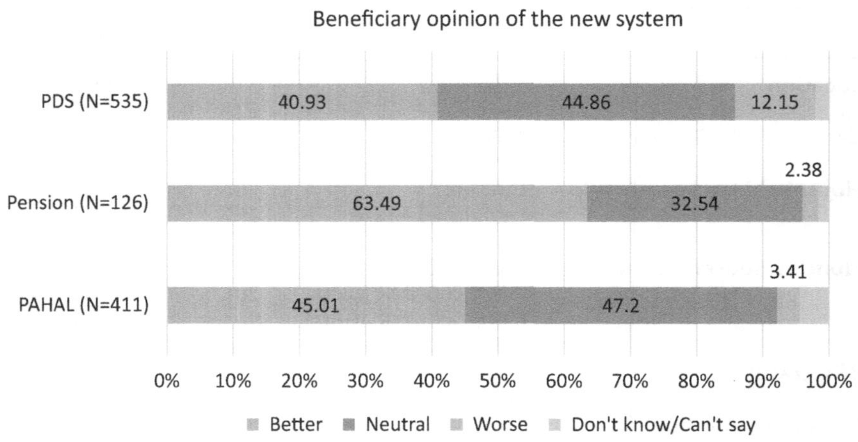

Figure 11.2 Beneficiary perception of technology-enabled delivery of services. *PDS – Direct biometric authentication for in kind delivery*

In the recent past Rajasthan's PDS system has undergone several significant changes to its delivery mechanism. In 2012, the government mandated the digitisation of ration cards to weed out false and duplicate beneficiaries. By all accounts, however, the process did not go as planned, with complaints of mishandling of data and erroneous entries creating significant inconvenience for the beneficiaries. Following the passage of the National Food Security Act (NFSA) in 2013, there was a further effort to reclassify families based on BPL or APL status in accordance with the new financing formula announced by the federal government. Our qualitative focus group discussions captured a sense of frustration on the part of the beneficiaries with the frequency of administrative directives and a lack of transparency in the revision of the eligibility list for PDS.

Bhamashah registration – including linking ration cards to Aadhaar, bank account and mobile numbers – was yet another process that the beneficiaries needed to go through to obtain their PDS quota. In contrast to previous attempts to reform the PDS, the new system requires beneficiaries to biometrically authenticate themselves at the FPS and directly interact with the new technology-enabled framework. At the same time, dealer margins were increased several-fold from their previously very low levels, to compensate for the smaller degree of diversion expected from the new system. Margins were increased to roughly 5% of the market prices of the products. We understood that without this increase many dealers would have ceased business.

- **Beneficiary perception of digitisation**

As noted, our survey finds that just over 40% of PDS beneficiaries prefer the new system better than the old one while 12% find it worse. Why do they express these views? Almost all of those who preferred the new system cited increased control over one's benefits, that under the new system no-one was able to take their rations on their behalf (Figure 11.3). This does not, of course, prove that rations were actually diverted under the old system (we did not actually measure how much they received), but it indicates substantial concern that they were not reaching the entitled beneficiaries. The second most frequent reason cited was satisfaction with using new technology. Despite frustrations with the new system (as further discussed below) this suggests a good deal of support for digital governance more broadly.

Interviews with PDS dealers provide some anecdotal support to the proposition that diversion had been reduced. When faced with the question of whether the digitisation of the system, combined with higher margins, had changed the social or economic position of dealers, one responded: "Before, in the old system, I was considered a thief when I stole, and also when I did not steal. Under the new system, I am considered more as a businessman."

What about the 65 respondents who say the new system is worse than the previous one? Most of their problems appear to relate to the biometric authentication process. Responses suggest that barely a quarter of the beneficiaries are authenticated at the first attempt although 96% said that they were usually authenticated in four attempts or less (Table 11.2). Only 6 respondents out of 535 stated that fingerprint authentication "never works."

- **Beneficiary experience of digitisation**

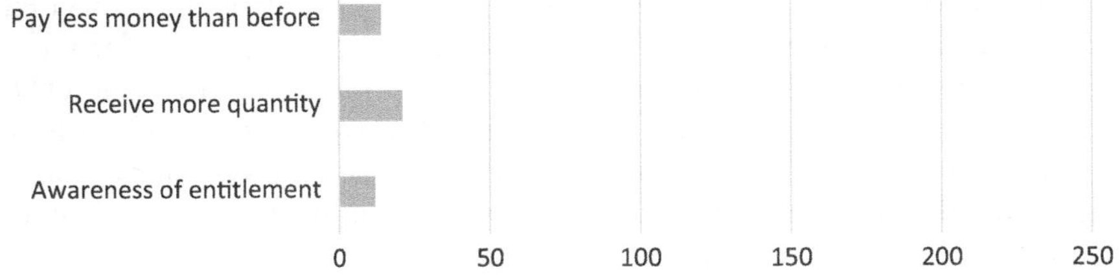

Figure 11.3 Reasons for better perception of new PDS system.

Table 11.2 Distribution of the number of attempts required for fingerprint authentication

On average, how many attempts does it take for fingerprint authentication?	*Number*	*Percentage of total*	*Attempt success rate*	*Cumulative percentage*
Once	127	23.74	23.74%	23.74
Twice	253	47.29	62.01%	71.03
3 or 4 times	133	24.86	85.81%	95.89
5 or more times	16	2.99	72.73%	98.88
Never works	6	1.12	----	100
Total	535	100		

Ease of authentication is a significant predictor of satisfaction. Ordered logit regressions show that people who report the need for three to four attempts to authenticate are 17% more likely to say the new system is worse than those who report succeeding in only one or two attempts.[9]

What would happen if fingerprint authentication failed to work? A majority (42) out of 82 responded to the question by saying that they would be "denied rations." As discussed further below, this does not always appear to mean that they would actually fail to receive rations, but at the least it points to considerable frustration over the time and effort required to get them. The other major reason for negative perceptions was the need to make multiple visits to the FPS due to connectivity problems. Both authentication and connectivity failures are credible concerns that need to be addressed if the new system is not to inconvenience, or even exclude, genuine beneficiaries (Dreze et al., 2017).

Further insight comes from a more detailed look into responses to the question (Table 11.3). Column 1 shows the responses from those who only reported having been "denied ration." The remaining columns show whether the person "denied ration" had recourse to any corrective action, including under an exception-management protocol. Respondents were provided with multiple options, including returning another day or bringing someone else from the family to the FPS. Another possible choice was the use of an alternative authentication protocol, such as an OTP sent to a linked mobile number.

The results suggest that perceptions of "worse" are strongly associated with onerous processes that require extra time and effort, particularly the need for repeated visits to obtain rations. The option to use a mobile OTP does not seem to have been used frequently. However, not one of the four respondents who cited the use of the OTP rated the new system as worse, suggesting the need for rapid exception-management protocols to be implemented when biometric authentication does not work.

Whether the new systems cause eligible families to be denied rations due to authentication failures is a topic of much debate in India (Khera, 2017).

Table 11.3 Authentication failures and perception of reforms

Authentication failure experience	Perception of Aadhaar authentication for PDS (number of respondents/% of Row Total)				
	Better	*Neutral*	*Worse*	*Don't know*	*Row Total**
Could not take ration at all	5 (11.9)	18 (42.8)	18 (42.8)	1 (2.5)	42 (51.2)
Could not take ration, so another family member comes to take ration	-	5 (83.3)	1 (16.7)	-	6 (7.3)
Could not take ration initially, then used mobile and OTP authentication	-	2 (100)	-	-	2 (2.4)
Could not take ration, needed to visit again	1 (5.3)	5 (26.3)	13 (68.4)	-	19 (23.3)
Could not take ration, need to visit again with another family member	4 (40)	4 (40)	2 (20)	-	10 (12.2)
Could not take ration, needed to visit again with another family member and then used his/her mobile and OTP to authenticate	1 (33.3)	2 (66.6)	-	-	3 (3.6)

Note: Row total percentages are out of total responses (N = 82).

Unfortunately, the framing of our question limits the information we can obtain from the answers. From Table 11.3, in response to the question of what happens if authentication fails, 82 out of 535 respondents stated that they would be "denied rations." However, there is no relationship between "denied" and the number of fingerprint authentications needed; many answer "denied" even when they say authentication works after one or two attempts.

- **Impact of digitisation across socioeconomic groups**

Have the reforms impacted differently on different social or economic groups? We had expected to find fingerprint authentication more difficult for the elderly, farmers and the poor, and also expected some systematic relationships between social and economic variables and views on service delivery. But there are not as many strong and consistent patterns as we had anticipated in our econometric analysis of the survey data.

Authentication is reported as more difficult by rural respondents, especially those we classified as destitute, but BPL respondents as a whole are more likely to say that authentication is easy than APL respondents. Landowners, especially marginal ones with less than one acre, are less likely to say that the new system is better than those without land, but this result does not carry through to larger landowners. We find that authentication is harder for families without mobile phones, hinting at unfamiliarity with technology as one possible reason for less favourable perceptions. Indeed, Bhamashah heads of household who read messages and make mobile calls are more likely to like the new system better (Figure 11.4).

This suggests a link between digital literacy and perception of the digital reforms, a noteworthy result also from a gender perspective. "Early adopters" who had enrolled in Aadhaar before it began to be used for PAHAL were less likely to cite a preference for new technology as a factor motivating their preference for the new PDS system. Moreover, counter to expectation, these early adopters were actually more likely to report difficulties with authentication. However, only some 20% of the total number of responses could be cross-classified in this way.

Our inference from the data is that experience is important in shaping attitudes to the reform and that there is considerable variation in experience that cuts across status and personal characteristics. This could reflect heterogeneity in experience across the different sampled communities, for example, a more or less skilled PDS fingerprint operator, although the limited size of our data set precludes statistical assessment of differences between sites. It could also be that the reference point for the reforms – experience under the old system – differs systematically across groups and individuals so that greater reported difficulties in navigating the new system do not necessarily translate into an assessment that the new system is worse than the old one.

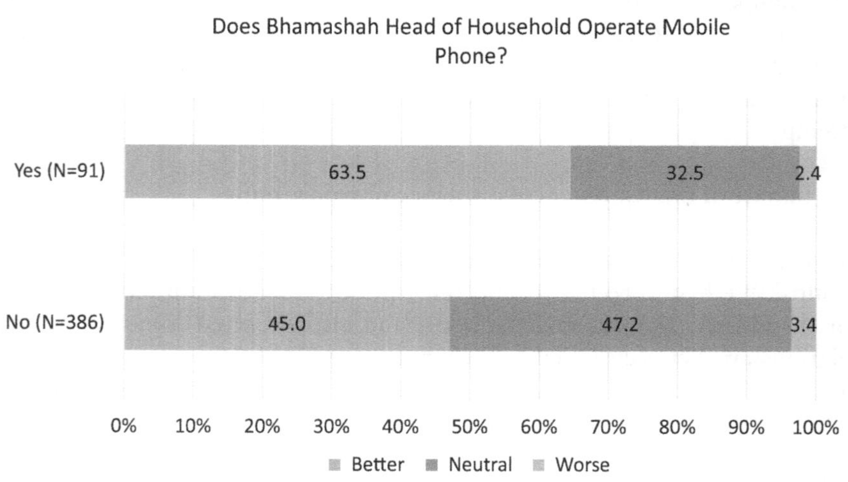

Figure 11.4 Opinion of the new PDS system by Bhamashah head of household mobile literacy.

Financial inclusion and women's empowerment: Have reforms had any impact?

India has made remarkable strides in financial inclusion over the last decade. Data from the Global FINDEX Survey indicates that bank account ownership for persons aged 15 and above has increased from 35% to a remarkable 80% between 2011 and 2017. Seventy-seven percent of women in this age group had a bank account in 2017 compared to only 26% in 2011. Indeed, the gender gap in financial access (as measured by ownership of an account) has also closed rapidly from 20% in 2014 to only 6% in 2017. In contrast to some other countries like Kenya, Tanzania and Bangladesh, where increases in financial inclusion have paralleled growth in the use of mobile money, almost all of the increase in India has been through formal banking institutions, following the launch of the JDY in mid-2014. As the report notes, "this policy benefited traditionally excluded groups and helped ensure inclusive growth in account ownership" (Demirgüç-Kunt et al., 2018, pp. 19).

Data on financial inclusion from our survey in Rajasthan strongly corroborate these national-level findings. Our analysis indicates that bank account ownership at the household level is now universal for the sample. A significant majority of households have more than one bank account and the number of households with multiple accounts is greater for rural compared to urban areas of the state (Figure 11.5).

Both financial inclusion and women's empowerment are objectives of the Bhamashah programme. As noted above, the approach to digital governance

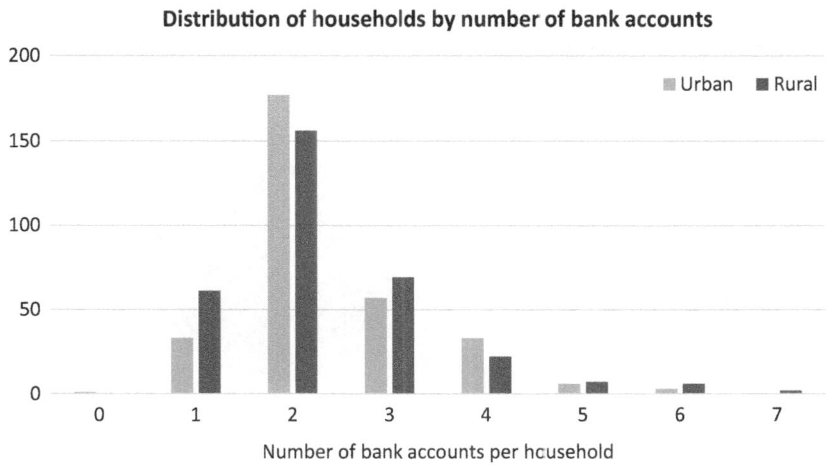

Figure 11.5 Number of bank accounts per household – urban and rural.

in Rajasthan has mirrored the overall JAM framework, with an additional layer of unique ID assigned to each family registered under the programme. Bhamashah also mandates that a woman has to be designated as the head of the family and the database has to include her bank account and Aadhaar number. This provides the architecture of transferring benefits directly to her Aadhaar linked bank account and provides the option of linking the mobile number of any family member in the database to receive information on service delivery and payments.

Our data indicate that nearly 66% of women heads of household opened bank accounts at the time of Bhamashah registration. This indicates a huge push towards financial inclusion through the design of the programme (Figure 11.6a). Almost 90% of these accounts have also been linked to Aadhaar (Figure 11.6b). Moreover, most of the women who opened bank accounts are in the bottom three income categories of the survey, indicating that the process of financial inclusion was highly equitable, and covered those women who would have otherwise probably been left out of the formal banking system (Table 11.4). The move towards digital programmes appears to have improved both access and equity in extending the financial system to the hitherto unbanked women of Rajasthan.

Further analysis builds on this finding. Only one-third of all Bhamashah heads of household had bank accounts before the launch of the programme. Designated Bhamashah head of household for BPL families were 18% more likely to have had a bank account prior to Bhamashah registration than non-BPL families. On the other hand, women in landowning families are 15% less likely to have opened a bank account to receive the PAHAL subsidy than those who did not own land. Although women generally are 15%

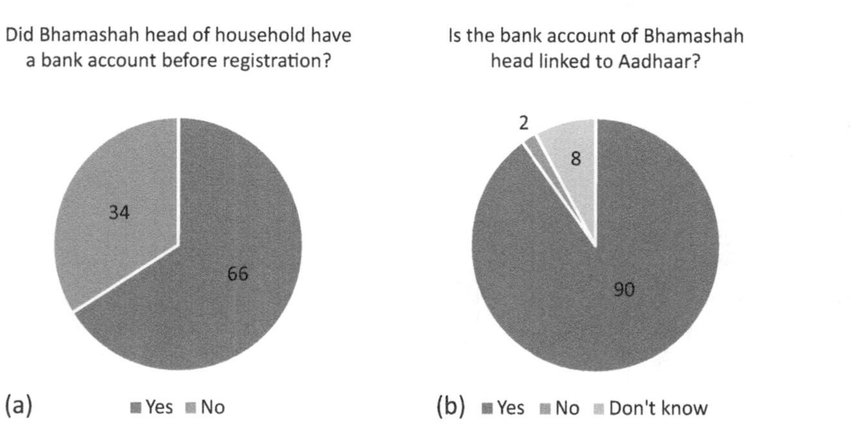

Figure 11.6 (a) Share of new accounts of women head of households. (b) Linkage of Aadhaar with bank account of Bhamashah head of household.

Table 11.4 Income profile of women who opened bank accounts

Monthly family income (INR)	*Women who newly opened bank accounts (%)*	*Percentage of full sample (N = 633)*
< 2,000	7	10
2,000–5,000	39	41
5,000–10,000	47	42
10,000 and above	8	7

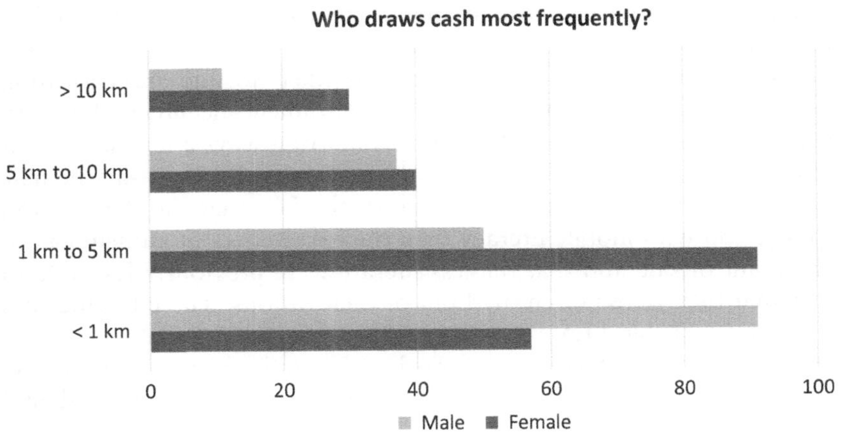

Figure 11.7 How distance affects the gender of cash withdrawers.

less likely to have opened a bank account to receive the PAHAL subsidy, women in BPL families are 15% more likely to say they opened a bank account to receive the PAHAL subsidy. This probably reflects the expansion of cooking gas connections to poorer rural women through the Ujjwala programme, as noted in section 4.2 above.

While it is too early to comment definitively on the impact of digital governance on women's empowerment, our data points to some signs of progress and as well as constraints. Our analysis indicates that women are indeed accessing financial services, with 54% of households reporting that women travel to withdraw cash most often, even more so when the cash point is not very close. However, as the distance to the cash point becomes longer, they are more likely to be accompanied by a male member of the family (Figure 11.7). Responses indicate several reasons why women may be accompanied, including the need for transport as well as the fact that many women are still not familiar enough with banks to transact on their own. Further investigation would be useful to better understand the constraints on women's agency and economic empowerment.

There is still a wide gender gap in digital literacy, taking the ownership and use of mobile phones as an indicator. In our survey, 94% of households possess a mobile phone and 75% reported that the number is mapped to the Bhamashah card. However, only 58% of all households include someone who can read or write text messages and in only 20% of households does the Bhamashah head of family use the mobile phone (Figures 11.8a and 11.8b).

With the shift towards digital delivery of services, digital literacy is becoming a baseline competency for citizens and particularly for women if they are to take control of their finances and reap the full benefit of digital governance. In an increasingly digital environment, owning a mobile phone should be a boon for households. Indeed, our data shows that the families who own a mobile phone are more likely to find authentication easy and to have received the Bhamashah enrolment incentive. However, when the Bhamashah head of household (almost always a female) cannot read messages and make phone calls, they are more likely to say the new PDS system is better. This may be due to the fact that the PDS reform has less to do with mobile literacy than the experiences of authentication at the point of sale and that the less literate were previously less able to ensure that they were not cheated out of their rations. These findings are summarised in Table 11.5.

Digital literacy has therefore emerged as a significant barrier to achieving the goals of women's empowerment in particular and equitable digital

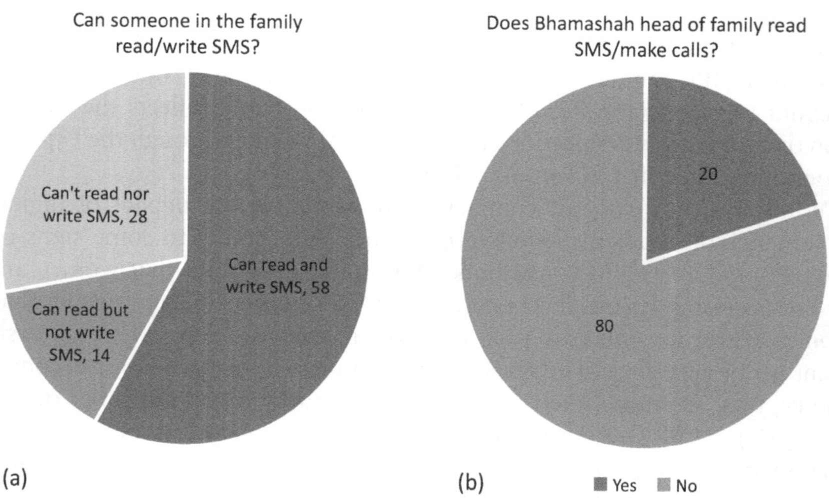

Figure 11.8 (a) Proportion of families with digitally literate members. (b) Proportion of families with digitally literate (woman) head of the family.

Table 11.5 Digital capability and experience of digital governance

Family possesses at least one mobile phone	*Authentication is easy*	*Received Bhamashah enrolment incentive*
Yes	72%	41%
No	54%	20%
Bhamashah head of household reads SMS and makes calls?	**Think the new PDS system is better**	**Takes less time to obtain cash**
Yes	54%	88%
No	67%	74%

governance more generally. While the basic architecture is now in place, the focus needs to shift to remove the constraints that people face in accessing services. This can take the form of changes in the design of programmes as well as their implementation. On balance, and recognising also the problems, survey results suggest that the perception of digital governance in Rajasthan is relatively positive. The challenge will be to maintain support for the programme and further improve the experience of beneficiaries engaged with this new way of interacting with the state.

Conclusion and implications for policy

The reforms in Rajasthan are, of course, only one slice of the remarkable shift towards digitally enabled programmes that is being rolled out across India, combining Aadhaar, financial inclusion and mobile communications. The reforms are on a massive scale, with Rajasthan alone comparable to Germany in terms of area and population. While the LPG programme is at the national level, most programmes are implemented by states, and these are shaping their reforms at different speeds and in somewhat different ways. India is therefore a laboratory for digital reforms of governance and service delivery. There is no guarantee, of course, that Rajasthan's experience will carry over to other states or even survive changes in government, but all evidence is useful, including for the many other countries that are also moving towards the use of digital technology for programme delivery.

Debate on the reforms has been contentious in India, but with still limited empirical evidence there has perhaps been more sound than light. In this study, we have tried to narrow the evidence gap, at least in the area of service quality, by surveying a sample of households in Rajasthan to see whether they consider the new systems to be better or worse and to understand the reasons for their opinions. We did not engage with the state government on possible changes in the fiscal costs of the programmes.

How should we assess the reforms? One criterion could be greater efficiency, as measured by lower fiscal and implementation costs for comparable services. Another could be better service delivery, as seen by the clients of the programmes. There may also be some cross-cutting objectives that are seen as desirable in their own right, such as financial inclusion and women's empowerment. We also need to take into account the transitional costs associated with the shift towards digital programmes, including both pecuniary and societal costs imposed on those who are less able to negotiate the new, digital modes of accessing their benefits.

Our conclusion on reorganisation into digital programmes is that this has not been straightforward. Data errors and inconsistencies need to be resolved and identifiers need to be seeded correctly into beneficiary rolls. Despite these difficulties, the reforms appear to have improved service delivery, which in a narrow sense can contribute to the overall level of "development" if sustained over the long run.

Why did people express these preferences? In the case of PDS and PAHAL the answer is clear – they considered that the new systems gave them greater control over their entitlements and reduced the ability of others to claim their benefits or divert them. Especially considering the inconveniences associated with the new systems – having to travel to banks to collect the PAHAL subsidy and having to be authenticated to receive rations – this confirms that diversion was indeed seen as a serious problem under the old systems by many beneficiaries. The results cannot prove that diversion was actually reduced, but if it was not, or had never existed in the first place, it is difficult to see why respondents answered as they did.

These results are encouraging for the new approaches. They suggest that – as found in other cases – most people welcome technology provided that it is seen to deliver useful services. On the negative side, in addition to transitional costs, the responses confirm some weaknesses in the new systems. Connectivity was also a problem for PDS, though less serious than authentication. The main concern with the LPG programme was the upfront cost of cylinders, a serious issue especially as the programme is rolled out to poorer households through the Ujjwala scheme targeted at poor women in rural areas.

There are clear lessons for other programmes that use technology to deliver public services, subsidies and transfers. More generally, and especially in the context of the COVID-19 pandemic, there is a need to rethink the role of technology in development more broadly. From the efficiency perspective, technology is used to "modernise" government, focusing narrowly on streamlining processes and achieving delivery targets. It does not answer the broader question of reforming administrative rules, objectives and accountability.

From the equity perspective, however, technology assumes a certain set of pre-conditions – everyone having the necessary tools and proficiency – which is often not fulfilled especially in developing countries like India. Technology is neutral – it is the design and implementation of policy and programmes that policymakers and practitioners will be able to narrow existing inequities or exacerbate them. This requires a people-centric approach that preserves elements of post-modernism in the development discourse. As our analysis shows, there is much scope to use technology to facilitate a new, more fruitful interaction between citizens and the state.

Notes

1 This section draws heavily from Gelb, Mukherjee and Navis (2018).
2 A full list of schemes and the current status is available from the official Bhamashah website: http://bhamashah.rajasthan.gov.in/content/raj/bhamashah/en/home.html
3 For a visual description of the Bhamashah process, please see Gelb, Mukherjee and Navis (2018), p. 5.
4 We use the words family and household interchangeably and colloquially refer to the head of the family as the "Bhamashah head of household" in the subsequent discussion.
5 www.microsave.net/files/pdf/171212_Household_Perception_Impact_of_Bhamashah_Digital_Governance_Reforms_in_Rajasthan.pdf
6 Ibid.
7 www.cgdev.org/sites/default/files/Rajasthan_Bhamashah_Questionnaire_Final.pdf
8 For full analysis of PAHAL and Pensions, please refer to: www.cgdev.org/publication/digital-governance-developing-countries-beneficiary-experience-and-perceptions-system
9 The econometric analysis referenced in this chapter utilises univariate ordered logistic regression models to compute linear predictions, and then report marginal probabilities for given ordinal categorical outcome variables (Long & Freese, 1990). We only report statistically significant (at $\alpha = 0.05$) marginal probabilities and apply a Brant (1990) test as a robustness check to ensure that the proportional odds assumption is met, and do not report any linear prediction which fails the Brant test.

References

Alston, P. (2019). Report of the Special Rapporteur on extreme poverty and human rights. *Seventy-fourth session of the United Nations General Assembly*. Retrieved from: https://undocs.org/A/74/493.

Dalberg (2019). State of Aadhaar: A people's perspective. Retrieved from: https://stateofaadhaar.in/download-reports.php.

Demirgüç-Kunt, A., Klapper, L., Singer, D., Ansar, S. & Hess, J. (2018). *The Global Findex database 2017: Measuring financial inclusion and the fintech revolution*. Washington, DC: World Bank. Retrieved from https://doi.org/10.1596/28998

Dreze, J., Khalid, N., Khera, R. & Somanchi, A. (2017). Aadhaar and food security in Jharkand: Pain without gain? *Economic and Political Weekly*, 52(50), 50–59.

Freedom House (2017). Freedom on the net: Manipulating social media to undermine democracy. Retrieved from: https://freedomhouse.org/report/freedom-net/2017/manipulating-social-media-undermine-democracy.

Gelb, A. & Diofasi Metz, A. (2018). *Identification revolution: Can digital ID be harnessed for development?* Washington, DC: Center for Global Development.

Gelb, A. & Mukherjee, A. (2019). *Fuel subsidy reform and green taxes: Can digital technologies improve state capacity and effectiveness?* Policy Paper No. 36. Washington, DC: Center for Global Development Retrieved from: https://www.cgdev.org/sites/default/files/fuel-subsidy-reform-and-green-taxes-can-digital-technologies-improve-state-capacity.pdf.

Gelb, A., Mukherjee, A. & Navis, K. (2018). *Digital governance in developing countries: Beneficiary experience and perceptions of system reform in Rajasthan, India*. Working Paper No. 489. Washington, DC: Center for Global Development. Retrieved from: https://www.cgdev.org/publication/digital-governance-developing-countries-beneficiary-experience-and-perceptions-system.

International Telecommunications Union (2020). World telecommunication/ICT indicators database. . Retrieved from: https://www.itu.int/en/ITU-D/Statistics/Pages/publications/wtid.aspx.

Khera, R. (2011). India's public distribution system: Utilisation and impact. *Journal of Development Studies*, *47*(7), 1–23. DOI: 10.1080/00220388.2010.506917

Khera, R. (2017). Impact of Aadhaar in welfare programs: Social science research network. Retrieved from: https://ssrn.com/abstract=3045235

Mittal, N., Mukherjee, A. & Gelb, A. (2017). *Fuel subsidy reform in developing countries: Direct benefit transfer of LPG cooking gas subsidy in India*. Policy Paper No. 149. Washington, DC: Center for Global Development. Retrieved from: https://www.cgdev.org/publication/fuel-subsidy-reform-developing-countries-india.

Overback, D. (2016). Leakage and corruption in India's public distribution system. *Mimeo*. Retrieved from: https://www.isid.ac.in/~epu/acegd2016/papers/DanielOverbeck.pdf.

Sen, A. & Dreze, J. (1995). *India: Economic development and social opportunity*. Oxford: Clarendon Press.

World Bank. (2016). *World Development Report 2016: Digital Dividends*. Washington, DC: World Bank.

Chapter 12

Organisation structure of family-owned and controlled business groups in India: Some reflections on theories and policies of corporate governance

Mohit Gupta

Introduction

The study of business groups falls within the domain of larger literature dealing with corporate governance. An important subset of this literature deals with the notion of "business groups" in the context of emerging markets. The said literature has put forward various perspectives/views for the emergence of groups in these emerging markets like market imperfections perspective, late industrial development perspective, resource availability view, tunnelling view, value-added view, presence of certain authority structures etc. and also contrasted the business group alongside a standalone "firm" by pointing out some of the important features of the former including a diversified conglomerate character, a multi-company structure, the importance of the institution of family in the business organisation, structures of ownership and control in these groups etc. (Bae, Kang and Kim, 2002; Bertrand, Mehta and Mullainathan, 2002; Claessens, Djankov and Lang, 2000; Ghemawat and Khanna, 1998; Guillen, 2000; Khanna and Palepu, 2000, 2005; Leff, 1978 etc.). Though this literature provides cross-country evidence on groups in emerging markets, yet it is inefficacious in cogently establishing the conceptualisation of economic activity in terms of business groups as opposed to discrete firms. This is largely owing to theoretical weakness in this literature because of its ahistorical approach and certain pre-suppositions regarding particular perspective(s) to be the basis of the existence of a group. In the process, this literature does not situate the emergence of business groups comprehensively, in various spatial-temporal contexts, as being contingent on the interaction of complex factors like a particular country's history, legal systems, politics, law, financial development, wealthy families, institutions, degree of trust etc. (Morck and Steir, 2005).

For instance, in the Indian case, which shall be our focus in the rest of this chapter, it has been argued in this dominant literature that large family business groups persisted because they bridged institutional voids created by

DOI: 10.4324/9781003159940-12

dysfunctional markets and weak economic institutions (Khanna and Palepu, 2005). This "gap-filling" explanation of the dominant theory is based on a "timeless" framework and thus puts forth an inadequate functional theory of the business groups in India (Mazumdar, 2012). A more nuanced discussion on the business group as an important feature of the Indian corporate sector, however, systematically emerged in the decades after independence in response to analysing the problem of concentration of economic power and monopoly in the Indian industrial sector by a few business families (Government of India, 1964, 1965, 1969; Hazari, 1966, 1967). This literature pointed out the phenomenon of control of assets by a few wealthy families in the industrial sector which was done by way of "interconnections" between legally independent entities, a process which was termed as "combinations" in some of the important studies whose emergence was co-terminus with this literature (Mehta, 1952; Mohnot, 1962; Nigam, 1963; Nigam and Chaudhari, 1960). This link between entities which otherwise appear to be independent of each other but in effect are "inter connected" to each other and forms part of a group through the process of "inter-corporate investments" or "inter-locked directorship" has also been traced by studies that emerged on this subject in subsequent decades (Chalapati Rao, 1985; Ghose, 1972; Goyal, 1979; Singhania, 1980). Such inter-linkages allowed the business families that operated through a multi-company structure to spread control with very little direct equity holding. In this entire process of assessing the economic problem of monopoly and concentration in India at that time, one of the main contributions of this gamut of literature was the identification of "group" as a unit of decision-making as opposed to individual companies. A "group" was defined by Hazari in the following manner:

> A corporate group may be defined as consisting of units which are subject to the decision-making power of a common authority ... The group functions as a single organisation, nevertheless, though each of the corporate units under its control is a separate legal entity.
>
> (Hazari, 1966)

Taking insights from this literature on issues of the structure of business groups, identification of the linkages within the group etc. and by building further on other related implications of the group structure; there is an emergence of nascent literature in India in recent times that elucidates how various corporate governance institutions like trusts, Hindu Undivided Family (HUF), partnership firms, companies etc. form part of the family business groups, their deployment in the organisation of convoluted group structure and familial basis of control over large group structure having a plethora of entities with very little direct ownership of family members (Das Gupta and Gupta, 2017; Mazumdar, 2006, 2018). This set of literature falls within the domain of bourgeoning research that critiques the theoretical considerations of dominant literature on business groups discussed above and takes a methodological departure from it. This is because of the multiple shortcomings in the analysis of business groups by dominant literature which includes; eschewing the task of fleshing out complexities in the structure of business groups, following a top-down ahistorical approach, a priori generalisations, constructing models and testing hypothesis which are mostly based on anecdotal observations etc. (Mazumdar, 2012, 2017). All these shortcomings render the mainstream literature incapable of correctly describing the nature, structure and working of Indian business groups. The present study also avoids the methodological subjectivity inherent in the dominant literature on business groups and thereby takes a departure from this existing literature. This is in so far as this study builds on publicly available data to gather detailed evidence that highlights the modalities of operation of a peculiar and relatively contemporary corporate governance entity known as limited liability partnership (LLP) in the organisation structure of a family business group. In this process, it also describes how the lacuna in dominant theories on corporate governance in India results in ineffective policies related to the corporate sector which allows them to engage in peculiar practices that best serve their interest.

The rest of the chapter is organised into four sections. The second section begins by briefly discussing the evolution of the concept of limited liability with corporate governance institutions. In the process, it also dwells on a brief history of the origins of LLP as a unique corporate governance structure distinct from the other existing structures around the world. This section then also points out literature in the Indian context dealing with the business groups and the specificities of inclusion of various corporate governance entities in the group structure. Subsequently, it discusses how LLPs were legally embedded in the Indian corporate governance code. The third section points out the process and modalities of installation of LLPs in the organisation structure of the largest business group in India and how this then served as the vital institution to spread control with very little direct ownership of family members. The fourth section points out the lacunae in two key policy areas, namely, the competition law in India in dealing with group monopolies deploying corporate governance institutions like LLPs and those in the taxation law in India which allows for lower effective tax rate being paid by the group as a whole by avoiding taxes using various entities which are conceptualised as standalone entities in the taxation code. Finally, the fifth section dwells on the gap between theory, policy and practices of the family business groups in India and also some possible suggestions to deal with the peculiar practices of the Indian corporate sector meant to bypass the policies discussed in the chapter, namely, tax avoidance and spreading group control with little direct ownership.

Limited liability and corporate governance structures

The LLP bill was introduced in 2006 in the Indian Parliament and subsequently was notified as a statute in 2009. It was an important and historic piece of legislation. This is because it instated LLP as a new entity in India's corporate governance code and the features of an LLP entailed a combination of the advantages of both of the company as well as that of a partnership firm. At the same time, LLP as a new form of the business organisation got away with the disadvantages of both of these existing forms of business organisation (Sharma and Garg, 2014). To corroborate, on the one hand, unlimited liability and upper ceiling on the number of partners which were disadvantages associated with the partnership were done away in this form while at the same time the privilege of limited liability, which hitherto was an exclusive feature of the company form was provided to it. The other features of this entity are that it requires two partners to begin an LLP, and there is no minimum capital contribution requirement for them. It is a body corporate having perpetual succession and allowed other body corporate like company, other LLPs and partnership firm to be a partner in it. The liability of each partner was restricted to her/his contribution, and she/he was not to be held responsible for the wrongful acts of other partners. The taxation structure of an LLP is similar to that of a traditional partnership and it is subjected to the same rates as the partnership firms. It is not subjected to dividend distribution tax (DDT) and minimum alternate tax (MAT) to which a company is subjected but is subjected to alternate minimum tax (AMT) from 2012. The partners of an LLP are also not taxed on the share of profits received by them on which taxes have already been paid by LLP. The comfort of limited liability, taxation advantages and the opaque disclosures associated with this form; all of which are discussed in subsequent sections makes it a favourable entity to be placed in the complex organisation structure of business groups in India.

LLP was instated in the Indian corporate governance code based on the suggestions of various expert committees that were constituted from time to time with the objective of suggesting reforms in the operations of medium and small scale enterprises in India. These committees suggested the need for LLP to deal with various problems faced by these small enterprises like credit, finance, growth etc. (Nayak Committee, 1992; Abid Hussain Committee, 1997; S.L. Kapur Committee, 1998; S.P. Gupta Committee, 2001). Finally, it was after the recommendations of the J.J. Irani committee report (2005) known as "The Expert Committee on Company Law" report, that the draft bill for LLP was introduced in the Parliament. It suggested that this form would be helpful for various professionals like charted accountants, company secretaries, lawyers, doctors, etc., especially in an era of globalisation for growth and expansion of their firms.

However, the espousal of the principle of limited liability with corporate governance structures is not a recent phenomenon and has evolved with time due to the "depersonalisation of businesses" as against the rights and obligations remaining vested in an individual. In the Roman law, well before the wave of de jure incorporation of enterprises and consequent to *de facto* depersonalisation of business (due to customs, lack of technology for record-keeping and less developed legal institutions) there existed a form of business known as "slave ran business" *(negotiatio per servos communes)*. This form of business was the equivalent of a modern-day corporation in its functioning (Abatino et al., 2011). This evolution of corporate governance structures with limited liability was then followed in the middle ages in the context of maritime trade in Italy where limited liability existed for various alternate forms of partnerships including "Commenda' and 'Societa." The liability of the partners was limited because all the partners were registered with guilds, and the contract entered by one partner was made binding on all others (Mitchell, 1909).

After the middle ages, limited liability emerged with the company form of organisation with the United Kingdom (UK) adopting the Limited Liability Act in 1855 which was repealed in the subsequent year following the fears of being misused. This was because while the legislation was introduced to encourage the private entities to augment the state in financing the infrastructure projects having a longer gestation period (Muchlinski, 2010). However, it was increasingly getting subjected to the problem of moral hazard, that is increasingly reluctant and careless behaviour on the part of shareholders or partners towards the funds of creditors knowing that their own liability is limited (Djellic and Bothello, 2013). Such behaviour is termed as "corporate irresponsibility" in the literature dealing with limited liability and includes dressing of financial statements, concealing of the point of final liability, multiple layers of ownership and control etc. (Ireland, 2010). This calls for a need to examine the implications of limited liability for other corporate governance institutions as well as those that have emerged over time. For instance, in the recent past, the fusion of the limited liability took place with a relatively newer corporate governance structure in the form of an LLP. The LLP form in recent times emerged in the United States of America (USA) in the 1980s following the financial crisis to limit the explosion of financial liabilities of the professional banking firms with Texas adopting it in 1991 which was followed by other states of the USA adopting it (Keatinge et al., 2016). Subsequently, this model was adopted by the UK in 2000 following the demand by professional firms and recently by many other countries like Singapore, Pakistan, etc.

The functioning of a corporation with limited liability has received some attention in the literature. The broad literature dealing with the theory related to a corporation, for instance, views corporation with limited liability, in a myopic way either as a distinct unit or as one having a parent-subsidiary relationship and has limited itself mostly with case law analysis in the international context for the implications of limited liability (Mendelson, 2002). The other dominant theories of corporate governance in literature have also addressed various concerns associated with the functioning of corporations which holds true for corporations with limited liability as well. This includes, for instance, the "agency theory" which describes the classic "principal-agent" relationship between shareholders and managers in a corporation as one which is often conflicting (Jensen and Meckling, 1976; Fama, 1980; Orts, 1998 etc.). Then there is "stewardship theory" which challenges the claims of agency theory because it considers managers as stewards who are trustworthy, efficient and prudent and can maximise the firm value (Donaldson, 1990; Donaldson and Davis, 1991). A more encompassing point of view from this strand of literature can be found in stakeholder theory which argues that there is a need to move beyond the traditional theories that capture the interest of shareholders-managers only and emphasise the need to cater to the interest of all the stakeholders in a firm (John and Senbet, 1998).

However, the inferences drawn by the various theories of corporate governance discussed here are yet again based on discrete "corporations" as the unit of analysis, like the case of dominant theories on business groups discussed in the first section. This brings to light the weakness of these theories because the assumptions derived by these theories do not hold true for analysing the functioning of Indian business group, particularly those that are family owned. This is true because of at least two reasons; one because the boundaries of ownership and control often get blurred in the case of these groups (Das Gupta, 2016; Mazumdar, 2006, 2017 etc.) and hence these dichotomies between a principal, an agent and stakeholders emanating from a firm-level analysis may not hold true for them. Second, as pointed out above, the business groups in India operate through an optimum mix of a plethora of entities (and not just any individual firm) registered under the Companies Act 2013, The Partnership Act 1932, Limited Liability Partnership Act 2008, etc., which legally are independent from each other because of their legal structure defined by provisions of the statutes governing them but in fact, operate as a single unit linked to a centralised control thereby forming part of a "business group." Furthermore, a business group is not a simple aggregate of the firms and hence juxtaposing the analysis of the theories discussed above, which are derived from a firm-level analysis to a group is erroneous. However, the domination of firm-level analysis in the theory of corporate governance and functional theories of business groups has resulted in the fact that in practice, this notion of a "business group" as an entity has not found a place in corporate governance code and taxation structure in India. Both of these identify a firm as a unit of analysis and consider each one of them as a separate unit even when they operate together as a group.

In this backdrop, the study of the inclusion of various entities like LLPs in the convoluted business group structure also requires gauging into the relevant literature dealing with the issue. In the Indian context on the one hand while there is an emerging literature on business groups in India that have fleshed out the interlinks and cross-holdings among various corporate entities which form the part of a business group using their financial statements and have not relied on the usual datasets on business groups because of the limitations of these data sets (Naz, 2016; Mazumdar, 2017 etc.). On the other hand, there is literature in the legal realm that has described the nuances of various provisions of the LLP Act, 2008 like those related to the nature and structure of an LLP, number and contribution of partners, taxation, etc. which has been pointed out above (Sen and Mathen, 2011; Sharma and Garg, 2014; Arora, 2015, etc.).

The first set of literature has not placed LLP as an institution in the structure of the business groups in India perhaps because it is a relatively new concept while it is beyond the scope of the second set of literature to describe the economic impact of provisions of the LLP Act, 2008 on structuring arrangement of a business group. Thus, there has been very little comprehensive engagement in "theory" pointing to the multiple and unique roles of an LLP as a distinct entity in the organisation structure of business groups including facilitating structuring and restructuring arrangements of the business groups, perpetuating familial basis of control, serving as a tax minimising holding structure and providing legal benefits of limited liability (Das Gupta, 2010). Further, the quantitative estimates about LLPs are not available even after a decade of the introduction of LLPs in India in the commonly used databases like PROWESS which provides information on the various financial indicators of entities based on their financial statements. This follows from the contemporary understanding of the operation of firms and LLPs not being a part of a group structure. Thus a lack of information in both "theory" and "data" obscures the questions as to whether or not and how LLP enters into a business group structure. This is our point of entry and for this purpose the financial statements of LLPs that forms part of the promoter group holding of the largest business group in India, namely, the Reliance Group will be examined. This will provide us with insights about the peculiar uses of entities like LLPs by business groups.

This is because the process of organising a convoluted group structure and including seemingly unorthodox entities like LLPs, trusts, HUF within it is not a phenomenon exclusive to the Reliance Group. In fact, the Reliance case discussed here is a microcosm of the organisation practices of the other family-controlled business groups in India. This is in so far as other leading family business groups in India have also included entities like LLPs, HUF or family trusts in their group structure for spreading control. This is evident from Table 12.1 below, which lists out the various entities and their number(s) in the promoter group structure of the flagship company

Table 12.1 Entities in the promoter group structure of flagship company of a few family business groups in India (March 2019)

	Number of Entities in Promoter Group						
Name of flagship company (name of the group)	*Individuals*	*HUF*	*Family trusts*	*LLPs/ partnership firms*	*Companies (domestic)*	*Companies (foreign)*	*Total*
ADANI Enterprise Limited *(ADANI Group)*	2		2	1		4	9
Aditya Birla Fashion and Retail Limited (AV BIRLA Group)	4	1			14		19
TATA Steel Limited (TATA Group)					10		10
GODREJ Properties Limited (GODREJ Group)	8		30	1	4	1	44

Source: Compiled from Shareholding Pattern of Various Companies from Bombay Stock Exchange website.

of some of the largest family business groups in India. In Table 12.1, the first column contains the name of the company along with the name of the group to which it belongs (in parenthesis). The rest of the columns contain the number of entities like individuals, HUF, LLPs, family trusts, domestic and foreign companies that form part of the promoter group of the company listed in the first column. Table 12.1 is for illustration purpose only and contains the details of one company, each of the various family business groups. However, if we take into account the composition of the promoter group structure of other listed companies of these groups as well, then it can be easily shown that the organisation structure of these groups is knitted around a combination of these entities. This establishes the importance of a variety of these entities (like those of LLPs in the case of Reliance Group discussed in the next section) in the group structure.

Complex organisation structure of family business group in India: An illustration

There are several debates and discussions that go around the country's largest business group – The Reliance Group. The group was built by Dhirubhai Ambani and the success of Reliance had been perceived to be built around the exceptional qualities of this individual who started his career as a petrol pump attendant. However, it has been shown that much beyond this impression and many similar myths; the Reliance success was dependent on a combination of particular historical forces (Mazumdar, 2017). This is because while the Reliance Group was an example of the new monopoly capital that emerged between the mid-60s and the end of the 80s, the group as a type was not fundamentally different from the traditional Indian monopoly capital. The success of Reliance had followed the same trajectory as the traditional business groups. It was a family-controlled enterprise (in fact continues to be one), began its history with trading activities as most of the other groups, sourced technology from abroad and finally, the use of state patronage was key to its success (Mazumdar, 2006).

The organisation structure of Reliance, which later turned into a group structure, can be divided into three phases. The period between 1958 and 1966 when they operated through partnership and proprietorship firms, 1966 and 1977 when narrowly held private limited companies became part of its structure, 1977 and 1990 when the flagship company of the group became widely held public company, and there was a proliferation in the number of companies that were added to the group (Mazumdar, 2017).

The undivided Reliance Group broke away in 2005, three years after the death of group patriarch Dhirubhai Ambani in 2002. This happened because of a family feud between the sons of Dhirubhai Ambani after his death. Subsequently, it was decided that Reliance Industries Limited (RIL) which was the flagship company of the group and the largest private company in India by turnover, along with Indian Petrochemicals Corporation Limited (IPCL) will be managed by Mukesh Ambani, the elder son of Dhirubhai. Anil Ambani, the younger son, got the charge of Reliance Infocom, Reliance Energy and Reliance Capital (Hisrich, 2010, p. 467) and operated his group of companies under the banner of Anil Dhirubhai Ambani Group (ADAG). The LLPs that we are dealing with in the present study are associated with RIL, the flagship company of the Mukesh Ambani led Reliance Group.

The said company RIL operates through a plethora of legal corporate entities which is the hallmark of a business group in India. It had 94 subsidiary companies, four associate companies, several LLPs, joint ventures with Limited Liability Companies (LLCs) and other companies abroad, foreign LLCs as subsidiaries, trusts (for instance petroleum trust in promoter holding) etc. The company bears a conglomerate character and is diversified into various areas which include petrochemicals, retail, digital services, entertainment and media, oil and gas exploration etc. (RIL, 2017).

In the present discussion, we are examining the peculiarities in the promoter group holding of RIL, modalities of installation of LLPs in the promoter group and the complexities in the organisation structure of the group subsequent to the insertion of these LLPs. Before delving into the process of changes in the promoter group structure of the company under analysis, it is important to understand the concept of "promoter" and "promoter group." In common understanding, the term promoter or promoter group tends to mean those individuals who have started or promoted a company, but the contemporary lexicon of corporate governance assigns a much broader and a crucial meaning to these terms from the vantage point of "control." The two key legislations that spell out the meaning of these terms include the Companies Act, 2013 and the Securities and Exchange Board of India, (Issue of Capital and Disclosure Regulations) 2018 (hereafter SEBI(ICDR) 2018); both of which deal with publically listed companies among others. The former legislation incorporates the meaning of a "promoter" only, defining it as the controlling authority of a company while the latter legislation defines both a promoter and the "promoter group." Thus it is the "control" over a company rather than ownership only which is important in defining a promoter or the promoter group of a company. This is evident from the definition of "promoter" as per the Companies Act, 2013 and SEBI (ICDR) 2018.

> *Promoter means a person –*
>
> (a) *who has been named as such in a prospectus or is identified by the company in the annual return referred to in section 92; or*
> (b) "who has control over the affairs of the company," *directly or indirectly whether as a shareholder, director or otherwise; or*
> (c) *in accordance with whose advice, directions or instructions the Board of Directors of the company is accustomed to act:*
>
> *Provided that nothing in sub-clause (c) shall apply to a person who is acting merely in a professional capacity;* (emphasis added)

"Promoter group," on the other hand, is referred to as groups of individuals and entities who have a controlling stake in the company. Clearly, the definition of "promoter group" is broader than that of a promoter and includes within its ambit a promoter, her/his relative and other body corporate. The SEBI (ICDR) 2018 defines promoter group in the following way.

> "Promoter Group" includes:
>
> i) the promoter; ii) an immediate relative of the promoter (i.e. any spouse of that person, or any parent, brother, sister or child of the person or of the spouse); and iii) in case promoter is a body corporate:
>
> A) a subsidiary or holding company of such body corporate;
> B) any body corporate in which the promoter holds twenty per cent or more of the equity share capital; and/or any body corporate

which holds twenty per cent or more of the equity share capital of the promoter;

C) any body corporate in which a group of individuals or companies or combinations thereof acting in concert, which hold twenty per cent or more of the equity share capital in that body corporate and such group of individuals or companies or combinations thereof also holds twenty percent or more of the equity share capital of the issuer and are also acting in concert; and

iv) in case the promoter is an individual:

A) any body corporate in which twenty per cent or more of the equity share capital is held by the promoter or an immediate relative of the promoter or a firm or Hindu Undivided Family in which the promoter or any one or more of their relative is a member;
B) any body corporate in which a body corporate as provided in (A) above holds twenty per cent or more, of the equity share capital; and
C) any Hindu Undivided Family or firm in which the aggregate share of the promoter and their relatives is equal to or more than twenty per cent of the total capital;

v) all persons whose shareholding is aggregated under the heading "shareholding of the promoter group"

Thus, the inclusion of various entities in the promoter group is a way of ensuring control over the affairs of the company by members of the family owning the group. The introduction of the LLP Act, 2008 had a significant bearing on the promoter holding of RIL. This is because as soon as the LLP Act came into force in 2009, in the year succeeding to that, there was a major shift in the promoter holding of RIL and several LLPs became part of the promoter group in that year. There were 29 new LLPs added to the promoter group of the RIL during June 2010 and subsequently there was a transfer of shares from companies to these LLPs between June and September 2010. Table A.1 and Table A.2 given in the appendix; contain an extract of the promoter holding of the RIL for the quarter of September 2010 and the previous quarter of June 2010. Table A.1 is an extract of the change in the shareholding of the LLPs during this period while Table A.2 shows the change for the companies and other entities. The last column in both tables shows the change in the shareholding over time. A negative sign indicates a decrease in the number of shares held by an entity. A comparison of these tables shows how the promoter group of the RIL changed after the

LLPs became a part of it in the year 2010 and had acquired significant shares in the promoter group.

There is a need to look at the sequence of the transfer of shares among various group entities and from these entities finally to LLPs, for understanding this change in the promoter holding structure and the reasons for introducing LLP into the promoter group. As evident from Table A.1 and A.2, during the period, June 2010 and September 2010, there was no change in the size of the promoter group holding (number of shares held) of Reliance Industries Ltd. There was also no change in the overall composition of the promoter group. However, 1059170001 shares changed hands within the promoter group – transferred from 14 companies to 29 LLPs (RIL, 2010). This number constituted 72.35 % of the total promoter holding and 34.17 of the total share capital of Reliance Industries at that time. This transfer of 1059170001 shares was an "Inter-Se transfer" (meaning within the group and not involving the public) that took place on 11 August 2010 as evident from the mandatory disclosure on Substantial Acquisition of Shares and Takeover (SAST) Regulations and Prohibition of Insider Trading Regulations, 1992. This transfer was made as an "Inter-Se" transfer to avoid the open market clause in the takeover code. This also seems to be the reason why initially the LLPs were made part of the promoter group in the previous quarter that is in June of 2010 with each one of them acquiring a small number of shares that is only 50 shares each.

Further, to avoid the open market clause in SAST disclosure when they acquired substantial shares in September 2010, the spread of the shareholding among LLPs was done in such a way that none of the LLP individually crossed the 5% threshold of shareholding. This is because otherwise the provisions of the takeover code of SEBI as governed by SAST would have been triggered and an open market offer would be required to be made if an entity crosses the 5% threshold (SEBI (SAST) Regulations, 2011). Even when the individual holding of each LLP that was made part of the promoter group was less than 5% of the shares, together these LLPs had over 30% of the shareholding which is evident from the balance sheet. There were various other entities that were brought under the group control using these LLPs through complex inter-linkages, cross-holdings and overlapping directors and partners. This ensured that there was a group monopoly in terms of a mammoth group structure that was constructed with LLPs serving as a pivotal point. These complex inter-linkages among the group entities and the resultant group structure forms the part of the discussion in the subsequent section along with the inefficacy of the anti-monopoly measures in dealing with this group monopoly.

Another important issue that requires attention is the price at which these shares were transferred to the LLPs. It needs to be examined whether "Inter-Se" transfers or off-market transactions can take place at prices substantially different from market prices without violating any regulations. On

11 August 2010, the low and high prices of RIL shares were INR 980 and INR 988, respectively. The value of the 1059170001 shares transferred on that day should, therefore, have been a minimum of INR 1,03,798 crores, this is far above the value of assets of the LLPs as evident from their financial statements after their acquisition. The answer to this question is also revealed in the next section, which fleshes out the lacunae in governance policies pertaining to business groups in India.

The discussion in this section throws light on how a family business group in India acquires a multi-entity character. This multi-entity character of the business groups is attained by including an optimum mix of entities in the fold of group structure in a particular spatial, temporal and institutional context. One of these entities which is a relatively contemporary institutional form of organising capital, namely LLPs, has found a significant place in the promoter group holding of the Reliance Group. The process of their inclusion and the resultant changes in the group structure are elaborated above. One such crucial change that occurred post-facto the inclusion of these entities is the importance accorded to this unlisted form of business organisation within the promoter group of RIL. The importance of LLPs is evident from the fact that their number and the proportion of aggregate shareholding held by this institutional form of business organisation in the promoter group of RIL remained greater than other forms of entities that formed part of the group at that time including the most common "company" form of organisation. There seem to be some specific reasons for which this form was deployed by the Reliance Group in its organisation structure which are discussed in the next section.

Business groups: Lacunae in governance policies

This section discusses a couple of key policy areas associated with the governance of family business groups in India and the way in which these policies were rendered ineffective in the present case because of underlying weakness in theories on which these policies are premised and also because of peculiar organisational practices of the group that ensured circumvention of these policies. In particular, the discussion here deals with policies for taxation and those related to curbing anti-monopoly practices as governed by the Income Tax Act 1961 and the Competition Act 2002 respectively. Talking about the former, the issue of taxation of family business groups is discussed and elaborated here with the help of tax data for the LLPs that formed part of the promoter group structure of the family group discussed in the previous section.

The statutory rates of taxation applicable to various entities are provided in the form of tax slabs under the Finance Act, which is announced along with the annual budget. The tax slabs contain the details of varied rates of statutory taxes corresponding to various thresholds of income levels that are applicable to different taxable entities. For example, currently, the statutory rate for the LLPs is similar to those applicable to the general partnership that is 30% plus surcharge and cesses.

However, it is important to point out that there is a distinction between the statutory rates prescribed by law and what actually an assessee ends up paying as taxes because of the various legal deductions and exemptions. For instance, there are exemptions available to assesses under various sections of the Income Tax Act 1961 for investment in provident fund, insurance policies, government bonds etc. which lowers their actual tax liability. These exemptions then bring down the actual payment of tax made by them compared to a situation where they would have paid according to the statutory rates prescribed by the law without taking these exemptions. Thus, the actual payment of tax as a proportion of the total declared income of an assessee is called the "effective rate" of taxation which is usually lower than the "statutory rate" of taxation (Bandyopadhyay, 2012; Das Gupta and Gupta, 2017).

This distinction between the statutory and effective tax rate is crucial for our analysis of lacunae in taxation policy governing business groups. The ensuing discussion shows how LLPs provided a mechanism for lowering the effective tax rate (ETR) paid by the business group under study. Table 12.2 provides the data for tax provisions and profit before taxation for LLPs, which became part of the promoter group of RIL in the year 2009 immediately after the LLP Act 2008 came into place. On the basis of the information available from financial statements of LLPs, the average ETR for the years 2012–2017 is computed in Table 12.2 for all these LLPs. It is evident from this table that as the profit before taxes (PBT) increases for the LLPs, the average ETR paid by them decreases. Substantiating this claim from the data in Table 12.2, the LLPs which had a PBT of less than INR 1 crore in our study paid an average ETR of 35.5% between 2012 and 2017. This is

Table 12.2 Average ETR (2012–2017) by range of profit before tax of 30 LLPs in the Reliance Group

S.No	*The range of profit before tax (in INR)*	*Average ETR(2012–2017) (%)*	*Number of LLP in each category*
1	**< 1 Crore**	35.45838	11
2	**1 Crore < 500 Crores**	0.895376	5
3	**500 Crores < 1,000 Crores**	0.785191	3
4	**1,000 Crores < 10,000 Crores**	0.067378	2
5	**10,000 Crores < 20,000 Crores**	0.043051	8
6	**20,000 Crores < 35,000 Crores**	0.000984	1
	Total		30

Source: Author's calculation based on Information from Financial Statements of LLPs forming Part of RIL Promoter Group for the years 2012 to 2017, accessed from Website of Ministry of Corporate Affairs.

close to the statutory rates prescribed for the LLPs, which is 30% plus other cesses. However, as the PBT increases beyond Rs 1 crore, the ETR paid by the LLPs register a huge dip from around 35% in the previous PBT category to a mere 0.89%. This declining trend in the percentage of ETR continues without fail as the range of PBT rises. The LLPs falling in the subsequent PBT categories of INR 500–1,000 crores, INR 1,000–10,000 crores, INR 10,000–20,000 crores and INR 20,000–35,000 crores ended up paying an extremely low ETR of 0.78%, 0.06%, 0.04% and 0.001% respectively. Thus, the moment the PBT crossed the threshold of INR 1 crore in our study all the LLPs ended up paying an effective tax percentage of less than 1% and the tax rate declined with every subsequent higher threshold income level.

The institutional mechanism of LLP, therefore, ensured that the group faced a regressive tax structure and provided a basis for lowering the effective tax payout. However, this finding that LLPs related to a corporate house faces an extremely regressive structure of ETR is not unique. This is similar to the findings that firms and companies in India also show a very regressive structure of effective taxation (Das Gupta and Gupta, 2017). This regressive tax structure exhibited by LLPs in our case (based on the range of income) exists at an aggregate level or cannot be ascertained because of the unavailability of the disaggregated income tax data on LLPs separately.

The significant point that emerges from the data above is how LLPs ended up paying such a low level of ETRs when the statutory rates are similar to a partnership. The explanation lies in a lacuna within the Income Tax Act, 1961 which remained in the act till 2016. Section 10(34) of the Income Tax Act, 1961 provided that any income by way of dividends shall not be included in the total income of the assessee. This provision ensured that up till 2016 (when this provision was amended) the LLPs and other entities (specified assesses) were totally exempted from paying tax on any amount of income earned by way of dividend if the company declaring the dividend had paid the DDT. This seems to be the reason that for all LLPs belonging to the RIL promoter group, income from the dividends of shares of RIL was the only source of income and that too a significant one, during the years 2012 to 2016.

However, this could not be ascertained explicitly because neither the nature of the income earned by LLPs nor the source of financing the investment was clearly reflected in the financial statements of LLPs. The income earned by LLPs was recorded under the head "other income" in the financial statements making it difficult to assess the precise source of this income because of lack of other disclosures. The source of financing the investment in shares of RIL brought by these LLPs and the various complexities in the process of acquiring these shares also were not captured by the financial statements of LLPs.

This is because the aggregate dividend income earned by all the LLPs was disproportionately lower to the total assets of all the LLPs (which was approximately around INR 1,241 crores in 2010) as well as the total partner contribution (approximately INR 13 crores in 2010) including liabilities that might have been used to finance the investments and assets. Further, the value of assets held by the LLPs should have been greater or at least equal to the product of the market price of the share and the number of shares of RIL held by these entities by virtue of their promoter group holding (which comes out to be slightly over INR 103,000 crores). As pointed out in discussion in the previous section, this is certainly not the case, and the total assets (not only investments but the sum of all other assets) held by the LLP as recorded in the financial statements are disproportionately lower than this value (approximately a meagre 1% of the value of investments made by them in shares of RIL).

The sequence of transactions and answers to other complexities of the process of acquisition of shares was revealed by the examination of financial statements of companies of the Reliance Group. These shares were acquired first by the companies and then transferred to the LLPs without payment of any consideration using complex transactions among group entities like mergers, amalgamations etc. For the companies, this transfer could be detected using the disclosures; therefore, we discovered that it was without payment of any consideration. However, for the LLPs, this is not possible given the lack of disclosures. Thus, there is no rise reflected in the assets of the financial statements of LLP pursuant to this investment made by the LLP in RIL shares. The opaque nature of financial disclosures associated with LLPs provides enough room for manoeuvring around and concealing vital information. This is in so far as there are mainly two mandatory financial disclosures – Form 8 (Statement of Account and Solvency) and Form 11 (Statement of Annual Returns) providing information about the financial position of an LLP. However, generally, there are no attachments to the forms containing financial statements of an LLP, providing the details of figures reported under various heads in the main statement like investments, assets etc. This is unlike the case of a company where a detailed attachment is provided with the financial statements namely, "Balance Sheet" and "Profit and Loss Account" of a company. The mandatory attachments to these two statements are detailed compared to the LLPs and include all supporting documents to a balance sheet like schedules, notes, annexure, directors report, auditor's report etc. These attachments, schedules and annexure provide the details of investments made by the company, the nature of the investment, the details of investment and the source of financing it. Thus, in our case, the mystery that the "other income" is the dividend income earned by LLP from investing in shares of the group company that is RIL cannot be ascertained explicitly from the financial statement of LLP but by examining the financial statement of the company.

Coming back to the issues of lacunae in section 10(34) of Income Tax Act, 1961, this remained unaltered till 2016, and it was only after that there was another part inserted to this section 10(34) which provided that "with effect from 1st April 2017 any income exceeding INR 10 lakhs earned by *specified assesses by* way of dividends shall be subjected to an income tax of 10%." Subsequent to this amendment, there was another significant change in the promoter holding of RIL, which helped in yet another favourable tax arrangement. However, the assessment of that is beyond the scope of the present analysis. For the purpose of present analysis what is important is that clearly, this loophole in the taxation policy and the favourable nature of disclosure of LLPs seems to have served as a precursor for the defining shift in the organisation structure of the business group which is evident from the significant change in the promoter group structure discussed in the previous section. In addition to this "particular" loophole in the taxation structure, there is also a more "general" flaw in the direct taxation code which paves the way for the family business groups in India to have a convoluted organisation structure in order to dodge around the actual tax liability. This shortcoming stems from the fact that the direct taxation code in India earmarks various entities as distinct units for the purpose of taxation without taking into account the notion of a "business group" which may consist of a plethora of such "discrete" entities with a common familial basis of control. This focus on a discrete "firm" as a unit of analysis rather than a group which is a complex combination of a multiple of such entities in the taxation policy also draws its genesis from the dominant theories of corporate governance pointed out in the previous section which treats all these entities as separate and distinct units. This shortcoming in a key policy area then provides one of the reasons for the proliferation of these entities. For instance, the multi-entity structure of the group in our case was shaped by virtue of introducing LLPs in its promoter holding. This complex structure along with the lacunae in the taxation policies and the opaque nature of financial disclosures of LLPs allowed the group to have a favourable tax arrangement by diverting the group incomes towards LLPs which enjoyed a favourable tax treatment at that time.

Now, let us turn our attention to yet another crucial policy area and the shortcoming in its applicability to family business groups in India. The Competition Act 2002 and the corporate law through Companies Act 2013 contains anti-monopoly provisions to ensure fair competition and for restricting monopoly practices. We shall see in this section that how both of these legislations were rendered ineffective in dealing with group monopoly created using LLPs. For this purpose, it is important to examine the extremely convoluted structure that was constructed with LLPs as a nucleus and which ensured control over an extremely vast set of entities with interlinkages. The relationship of LLPs which form part of the promoter group of RIL with other group entities is shown in Figures A.1 and A.2 given in the appendix, both of which are sketched out based on information from financial statements of LLPs. In Figure A.1, the box from which the arrow originates shows the entity which is the partner and the box where the arrow is pointed towards shows the entity in which the entity is a partner. An arrow on the top of the box indicates that the originating entity is a partner in all those entities which lie inside the box. If the arrow ends on the side of any box, then it shows that the entity from where the arrow originated, is a partner in only that entity where the arrow is pointed whereas an arrow that goes inside the box refers to all the entities inside the box. The solid lines are for entities and dotted lines for the individuals as partners. Similarly, in Figure A.2, the arrow originates from the boxes containing the name of the LLPs in which the LLP/ the individual towards whom the arrow is directed is a designated partner. In Figure A.2, below the name of every individual at which these arrows are pointed is a box that contains the list of companies and LLPs in which that individual is a director or designated partner. An LLP can have more than one individual as a designated partner who in turn can be a director in several group companies.

The two figures show how control is spread from LLPs to companies with an overlapping set of people as directors, at key managerial positions in the company and partners in other LLPs. This is done without violating the corporate law because Section 165 of the Companies Act, 2013 allows a person to be a director in 20 companies at any point in time. The fact that the Companies Act, 2013 only stipulates the ceiling for the number of companies in which an individual can be a director and does not include partnership firms, LLPs and other entities in its purview makes it easier to bypass the stipulation and establish interlinks among entities for spreading greater control. The LLPs in the promoter group of RIL are inter-related to each other and is evident from the fact that 20 out of the 29 LLPs were registered at one address and several other hundreds of companies were found at this address (Government of India, 2017).

Figures A.1 and A.2 illustrate that using ten individuals (who overlap as directors in group companies and designated partners in LLP), the inter-linkages of the 30 LLPs are established with over 100 group companies. This provides us with an idea of how the LLP is used as a device to spread control over group entities by appointing the same individuals at multiple positions.

There are several reasons for the inefficacy of the Competition Act 2002 in dealing with the use of LLP by business groups for developing complex group structures, spreading control and establish group monopolies. It is important to understand that the "group monopoly" here refers to the structural monopoly of the group (huge group structure) as opposed to market, product or price monopoly usually discussed in dominant economic understanding. The structural monopoly that emanates from the mammoth size of the group gives advantages to a group to operate in various sectors simultaneously and also in new sectors by taking advantage of the existing scale of operation which is not available to new entrants. There are multiple reasons why the anti-trust provisions are unable to regulate this issue.

First of all, there are certain categories of transactions which are not likely to have an adverse impact on competition and thus there is no need to file a notice to the Competition Commission of India in respect of these transactions. These exempted transactions are provided in Schedule I of "The Competition Commission of India (Procedure in regard to the transaction of business relating to combinations) Regulations, 2011" as mentioned in Clause 4. Further, Clause 1 of this schedule provides that

> An acquisition of shares or voting rights, solely as an investment or in the ordinary course of business in so far as the total shares or voting rights held by the acquirer directly or indirectly, does not exceed twenty-five per cent (25%) or more of the total shares or voting rights of the company.

The explanation following this clause which was inserted by the amendment regulations in 2016 further provides that "any acquisition of shares below 10% shall be treated solely as an investment." Now in the case of RIL, discussed above, none of the LLP individually acquired more than 5% shares of RIL owing to the mandatory adherence to stipulations of the SAST Regulations as well. However, taken together the 29 LLPs acquired more than 30% of the shareholding of the RIL. Thus the shares acquired by LLPs fell within the purview of investments and this provision was bypassed by splitting the shareholding among various LLPs.

Further, the subsections (a) and (b) of this clause provides that the acquirer should have the rights similar to an ordinary shareholder and should not be on the board of directors in the acquiring company. These LLPs are body corporate and not individuals, and they were not on the board of directors of RIL. However, the partners in these LLPs and the individuals from companies which are partners in these LLP continue to serve as directors in RIL. Thus the structure of LLP as a "body corporate" allows it to circumvent this provision. However, control of family members and key personals is maintained over group companies by having these LLPs in the group structure.

For our purpose of understanding how LLPs can further circumvent the Competition Act, 2002, it is important to look at two other important clauses in this schedule I (which provides the list of transactions which are exempted from notice) of the regulation. Clause 6 provides that any *acquisition of shares under a bonus issue*, stock split, buyback, consolidation or subscription to rights but not leading to control. Clause 7 provides any acquisition of shares or voting rights or assets by one person or enterprise of another person or enterprise within the same group. This means that an increase in the shareholding under a bonus issue is exempted from serving the notice if it does not lead to control in the acquiring entity and so is any acquisition of shares by an enterprise within the same group. In the case of RIL, there was a bonus issue announced by RIL in 2017 which led to an increase in the shareholding of the promoter group entities like LLP and got exempted from providing notice to the commission because of the above clause. An increase in shareholding in this fashion, however, indeed allowed a higher degree of control over the group entities through LLP.

Next, the Competition Act, 2002 brings in its purview the notion of a group and following from that the definition of control. However, the effectiveness of this definition of a group is diluted because the "group" has to exist in a "relevant market" as per section 4 (e) of the act. The relevant market is further defined in terms of the relevant product market based on the substitutability of the products and the relevant geographical market based on the conditions for the supply of goods. A group has to also satisfy the abuse of the dominant position in a relevant market which is defined as; indulgence in discriminatory or predatory pricing, unfair practices like limiting or restricting access to the market for others. Thus even if the indirect control is acquired through the holding of shares of other enterprises which in turn holds the shares of an enterprise whose control is acquired, even then for entities to qualify for a group needs the satisfaction of certain conditions related to price, market access which are based on a more mainstream understanding of monopoly/anti-competitive practices. This narrow understanding of the abuse of a dominant position (narrow because it addresses only product monopoly and market monopoly which follows from the mainstream economic understanding of monopoly) allowed the business group in our case to create group monopoly using LLP and still satisfy the conditions related to prohibition of abuse of dominant position.

Finally, there is also ambiguity around the definition of control in the Competition Act 2002. According to the definition of the term control, any enterprise or group is said to jointly or singly control another group or enterprise if it is controlling the affairs or management of that group or enterprise. However, the Act fails to objectively and explicitly define the term "controlling the affairs or management." Thus, whether or not an enterprise controls another enterprise depends on a case to case basis. This criterion of "controlling the affairs and management of enterprise" was also a qualifier for the definition of a group and seems ambiguous, thus dependent on the decisions of the commission in various cases.

Conclusion

The family business groups in India have resorted to the peculiar ways of organising their structure which is governed by various considerations – including factors like spreading maximum "control" with little direct ownership, taxation of the group entities, prevailing legal and regulatory policies etc. Based on these varied considerations, a group incorporates an optimum mix of various entities within the ambit of its organisation structure like companies, partnership firms, HUF's, trusts etc. by weighing the above-listed considerations with the advantages offered by these entities. This results in a complex organisation structure with all these entities having a familial basis of control. However, there is no "one size fit all" structure and depending upon circumstances there are variations and mobility in this multi-entity structure in various spatial-temporal contexts.

The present study deals with the contemporary case of a leading family business group that bears such a multi-entity character. Among these multiple entities that form part of a group, the focus here, in particular, is on fleshing out the modalities of incorporating and including a relatively new form of corporate governance entity called LLPs in the organisation structure of the group. The importance of this entity in the present case is highlighted by examining the way in which it served as a nucleus for organising the group structure which was meant to bypass certain policies and the provisions meant to regulate the operations of a business group. A couple of such crucial policies, namely, relating to taxation and anti-monopoly practices in the Indian corporate sector formed the point of discussion in the present chapter, along with the emphasis on lacunae in these policies. The chapter elaborates on how these specific policies are circumvented in the present case using a "peculiar practice" adopted by the business group of knitting an extremely convoluted group structure with inter-linkages and cross-holdings among entities which are distinct from each other for all practical purposes but in effect are under common control. The chapter shows that how despite the policies to regulate the functioning, there were loopholes which ensured that these policies remained good only on paper and could not actually regulate the working of the corporate sector in India. The reason for policies being ineffective stems from the fact that the dominant theories of corporate governance that lie at the helm of designing the policies governing the corporate sector are based on certain flawed premises which fail to capture the true modalities of the operation of business groups in India. This coupled with the adjustments made by the family business groups in their practices of organising a convoluted group structure, as mentioned above, rendered these policies inefficacious.

One of the key lacunae in the policies discussed above is their focus on a discrete "firm" as a unit of analysis which seems to emanate from dominant theories on corporate governance which believes in "methodological individualism" and thus treats each firm and individuals as a distinct unit for its analysis. As we have shown in the chapter using the data from financial statements of the group entities, from a taxation perspective such a policy allowed business group to split up and redistribute their income among entities which are favourable from the perspective of taxation law. Eventually, this allowed business groups to end up avoiding taxes and pay lower effective tax rates for the group as a whole. This highlights the gaps in taxation policies which treats various entities as distinct for taxation purposes and allows the business group to take advantage of this distinct character accorded to entities in theory, but which are all practically part of the group. Similarly, in the case of anti-trust policies, while there are policies for curbing monopoly practices in India as specified in various anti-trust legislations but in reality, they are hardly able to make a difference in preventing mammoth group monopolies created by family business groups. This is again because the anti-monopoly policies are premised on the dominant economic understanding of monopoly and the underlying theories governing this view have a narrow or restricted understanding of monopoly that defines monopolies that exist with respect to a product, price or market etc. and does not delve into the question of monopoly that originates from a gigantic group structure. Such a gigantic structure was deployed by the business group in the case study discussed in the previous section for spreading greater control over entities with little direct ownership. This, as we have shown, was done without inviting the provisions of anti-monopoly policies because the mainstream theories had a narrow conceptualisation of monopoly. Through this detailed discussion about these two policies, the underlying theories behind these policies and the subsequent practice in which the corporate sector indulges into, the present study tries to put forth an important point that has received less attention in literature dealing with this issue – there exists a gap between theory, policy and practices pertaining to the Indian corporate sector.

One of the starting points in order to bridge this gap between theory, policy and practices in the studies pertaining to family business groups in India is to ensure that the notion of a "firm" as a central unit of decision-making needs to be revisited and "business groups" (a combination of firms under common control) needs to be considered as a unit of analysis in policies pertaining to corporate law, taxation and anti-trust law. This should guide the future discussion about the family business groups in India. More importantly, any discussion about business groups in India should go beyond dominant understanding associated with these groups by trying to address among other things; the issues of lacunae in the dominant theories of corporate governance, the policies that are subsequently designed largely based on the analysis put forward by these theories and how the Indian corporate sector which is dominated by "family business groups" indulge in certain specific practices to get around these policies because of various loopholes in these policies. A wider recognition of this inter-linkage between theory, policy and practice as well as of the gap that exists between them will pave the way for further research on this area and will be helpful in developing a more comprehensive approach in dealing with these issues.

Bibliography

Abatino, B., Dari-Mattiacci, G., & Perotti, E. (2011). Depersonalization of Business in Ancient Rome. *Oxford Journal of Legal Studies*, *31*(2), 365–389.

Arora, H. (2015). Limited Liability Partnership-Taxation Issues. *International Journal of Management and Commerce Innovations*, 2(2), 468–474.

Bae, K. H., Kang, J. K., & Kim, J. M. (2002). Tunneling or Value Added? Evidence from Mergers by Korean Business Groups. *The Journal of Finance*, 57(6), 2695–2740.

Bandyopadhyay, S. (2012). Tax Exemptions in India. *Budget Track*, 8(3), 20–23. Centre for Budget and Governance Accountability. Retrieved from http://www.cbgaindia.org/budget-tracks/vol-8-track-3-2012/.

Bertrand, M., Mehta, P., & Mullainathan, S. (2002). Ferreting Out Tunneling: An Application To Indian Business Groups. *The Quarterly Journal of Economics*, 117(1), 121–148.

Chalapati Rao, K. S. (1985). Inter-Connections under MRTP Act in the Context of Asset Limit Hike. *Economic and Political Weekly*, 20(27), 1132–1146.

Claessens, S., Djankov, S., & Lang, L. H. (2000). The Separation Of Ownership And Control In East Asian Corporations. *Journal of Financial Economics*, 58(1–2), 81–112.

Das Gupta, C. (2016). *State and Capital in Independent India: Institutions and Accumulations*. Delhi: Cambridge University Press.

Das Gupta, C. (2010). Globalisation, Corporate Legal Liability and Big Business Houses in India. *Cambridge Journal of Economics*, 34, 895–913.

Das Gupta, C., & Gupta, M. (2017). The Hindu Undivided Family in Independent India's Corporate Governance and Tax Regime. *South Asia Multidisciplinary Academic Journal*, 15, 1–24.

Djelic, M. L., & Bothello, J. (2013). Limited Liability and Its Moral Hazard Implications: The Systemic Inscription Of Instability In Contemporary Capitalism. *Theory And Society*, 42(6), 589–615.

Donaldson, L. (1990). The Ethereal Hand: Organizational Economics and Management Theory. *Academy of Management Review*, 15(3), 369–381.

Donaldson, L., & Davis, J. H. (1991). Stewardship Theory or Agency Theory: CEO Governance and Shareholder Returns. *Australian Journal of management*, 16(1), 49–64.

Fama, E. F. (1980). Agency Problems and the Theory of the Firm. *Journal of Political Economy*, 88(2), 288–307.

Ghemawat, P., & Khanna, T. (1998). The Nature of Diversified Business Groups: A Research Design and Two Case Studies. *The Journal of Industrial Economics*, 46(1), 35–61.

Ghose, A. (1972). Monopoly in Indian Industry: An Approach. *Economic and Political weekly*, 7(5–7) 385–392.

Government of India (2017). *Report of the Director General of Audit (Central)*. Bombay: Indian Audit and Accounts Department.

Government of India (2014). *Securities and Exchange Board of India Act, 1992 [As amended by the Securities Laws (Amendment) Act, 2014*. Retrieved from https://www.sebi.gov.in/sebi_data/attachdocs/1456380272563.pdf

Government of India (2013). *The Companies Act, 2013*.Retrieved from http://www.mca.gov.in/Ministry/pdf/CompaniesAct2013.pdf

Government of India (2011). *The Competition Commission of India (Procedure in regard to the transaction of business relating to combinations) Regulations, 2011*. Retrieved from https://www.cci.gov.in/sites/default/files/regulation_pdf/Combination%20Regulations%202016%20-%20FINAL_0.pdf

Government of India (2008). *Limited Liability Partnership Act, 2008*. Retrieved from http://www.mca.gov.in/Ministry/actsbills/pdf/LLP_Act_2008_15jan2009.pdf

Government of India (2005). *Report of the Expert Committee on Company Law*. New Delhi: Chairman: Jamshed J. Irani, Ministry of Corporate Affairs.

Government of India (2002). *The Competition Act, 2002*. Retrieved from https://www.cci.gov.in/sites/default/files/cci_pdf/competitionact2012.pdf

Government of India (2001). *Interim Report of the Study Group on Development of Small Enterprises*. New Delhi: Chairman: SP Gupta.

Government of India (1998). *Report of the High Level Committee on Credit*. New Delhi: Chairman: SL Kapur.

Government of India (1997). *Report of the Committee on Small Enterprises*. New Delhi: Chairman: Abid Hussain, January 27, 1997

Government of India (1992). *Report of the Committee to Examine the Adequacy of Institutional Credit to SSI Sector and Related Aspects*. New Delhi: Chairman: P.J. Nayak.

Government of India (1969). *Industrial Licensing Policy Inquiry Committee (ILPIC) Report, New Delhi: Department of Industrial Development*. New Delhi: Ministry of Industrial Development, Trade and Company Affairs, Government of India.

Government of India (1965). *Monopolies Inquiry Commission (MIC) Report*. New Delhi: Government of India.

Government of India (1964). *Committee on Distribution of Income and Levels of Living (Mahalonobis Committee) Report*. New Delhi: Planning Commission, Government of India.

Government of India (1961). *Income Tax Act, 1961*.Retrieved from: https://www.incometaxindia.gov.in/pages/acts/income-tax-act.aspx

Government of India (1932). *The Partnership Act, 1932*. Retrieved from: https://www.mca.gov.in/Ministry/actsbills/pdf/Partnership_Act_1932.pdf

Goyal, S.K. (1979). *Monopoly Capital and Public Policy*. New Delhi, Bombay, Calcutta, Madras, Bangalore, Hyderabad: Allied Publishers Private Limited.

Guillen, M. F. (2000). Business Groups in Emerging Economies: A Resource-Based View. *Academy Of Management Journal*, *43*(3), 362–380.

Hazari, R. K. (1967). *Industrial Planning and Licensing Policy*. New Delhi: Planning Commission.

Hazari, R. K. (1966). *The Structure of the Corporate Sector: A Study of Concentration, Ownership and Control*. Bombay: Asia Publishing.

Hisrich, R. D. (2010). *International Entrepreneurship: Starting, Developing, and Managing a Global Venture*. United States and America: SAGE.

Ireland, P. (2010). Limited Liability, Shareholder Rights and the Problem of Corporate Irresponsibility. *Cambridge Journal of Economics*, *34*, 837–856.

Jensen, M. C., & Meckling, W. H. (1976). Theory of the Firm: Managerial Behaviour, Agency Costs and Ownership Structure. *Journal of Financial Economics*, *3*(4), 305–360.

John, K., & Senbet, L. W. (1998). Corporate Governance and Board Effectiveness. *Journal of Banking & Finance*, *22*(4), 371–403.

Keatinge, R. R., Donn, A. G., Coleman, G. W., & Hester, E. G. (2016). Limited Liability Partnerships : The Next Step in the Evolution of the Unincorporated Business Organization. *American Bar Association*, *51*(1), 147–207.

Khanna, T., & Palepu K.G. (2005). The Evolution of Concentrated Ownership In India: Board Patterns and A History Of The Indian Software Industry. In R.K. Morck (Ed.), *A History of Corporate Governance around the World* : Family Business Groups to Professional Managers (pp. 283–321). Chicago: University of Chicago Press.

Khanna, T., & Palepu, K.G. (2000). Emerging Market Business Groups, Foreign Intermediaries and Corporate Governance. In R.K. Morck (Ed.), *Concentrated Corporate Ownership* (pp. 265–294). Chiacgo: University of Chicago Press.

Leff, N. H. (1978). Industrial Organization and Entrepreneurship in the Developing Countries: The Economic Groups. *Economic Development and Cultural Change*, *26*(4), 661–675.

Mazumdar, S. (2018). The Multi-Entity Structure and Control in Business Groups. Retrieved from: https://mpra.ub.uni-muenchen.de/93241/1/MPRA_paper_93241.pdf

Mazumdar, S. (2017). From "Outsider" to Insider: The Case of Reliance. *South Asia Multidisciplinary Academic Journal*, *15*, 1–27.

Mazumdar, S. (2012). The Indian Corporate Structure And The 'Theory'of Emerging Market Business Groups. *History and Sociology of South Asia*, *6*(2), 87–109.

Mazumdar, S. (2006). Business Groups and Concentartion in the Private Corporate Sector in India. PhD Thesis, Centre for Economic Studies and Planning, Jawaharlal Nehru University, Delhi.

Mehta, M. M. (1952). *Combination Movement in Indian Industry: A Study in the Concentration of Ownership, Control and Management in Indian Industries*. Allahabad: Friends Book Depot.

Meiners, R. E., Mofsky, J. S., & Tollison, R. D. (1978). Piercing the Veil of Limited Liability, *Delaware Journal of Corporate Law*, *4*, 351.

Mendelson, N. A. (2002). A Control-Based Approach to Shareholder Liability for Corporate Torts, *Columbia Law Review*, *102*, 1203–1303.

Mitchell, W. (1909). Early Forms of Partnership. Select Essays in Anglo-American Legal History, vol. III. Boston: Committee of the Association of American Law Schools. Retrieved from http://oll.libertyfund.org/titles/schools-select-essays-in-anglo-american-legal-history-vol-3

Mohnot, S. R. (1962). *Concentration of Economic Power in India: A Statistical Study of Concentration and Diffusion of Economic Power in India*. Allahabad: Chaitanya Publishing House.

Morck, R.K., & Steir L (2005). The Global History of Corporate Governance: An Introduction. In R.K. Morck (Ed.) *A History of Corporate Governance around the World* (pp. 1–64). University of Chicago Press.

Muchlinski, P. (2010). Limited Liability and Multinational Enterprises: A Case for Reform? *Cambridge Journal of Economics*, *34*(5), 915–928

Naz, R. (2016). The Conflict between Corporate Governance and Corporate Social Responsibility in India. Paper Presented at Fourth LASSNET Conference, December 12, New Delhi.

Nigam, R.K. (1963). Interlocking of Directorship between Banking and Other Companies In Selected Articles on Working and Management of Corporate Sector in India (pp. 27–39), Research and Statistical Division, Department of Company Law Administration, Ministry of Industry.

Nigam, R. K., & Chaudhuri N.C. (1960). The Corporate Sector in India, A Factual Presentation of Long and Short-Term Trends, Research and Statistics Division, Department of Company Law Administration, Ministry of Commerce and Industry, Government of India, New Delhi.

Orts, E. W. (1998). Shirking and Sharking: A Legal Theory of the Firm. *Yale Law & Policy Review*, *16*(2), 265–329.

Reliance Industries Limited (RIL) (2017). *Annual Return 2017–18*. Retrieved from: https://www.ril.com/InvestorRelations/Downloads.aspx

Reliance Industries Limited (2017). *Q3 2017 Shareholding Pattern of 'Reliance Industries Limited', Corporate Announcements, Bombay Stock Exchange*. Retrieved from: https://www.bseindia.com/corporates/shpSecurities.aspx?scripcd=500325&qtrid=95.00&Flag=New

Reliance Industries Limited (2010). *Q2 2010 Shareholding Pattern of 'Reliance Industries Limited', Corporate Announcements, Bombay Stock Exchange*. Retrieved from: https://www.bseindia.com/corporates/shpSecurities.aspx?scripcd=500325&qtrid=95.00&Flag=New

SEBI (ICDR) Regulations (2018). Securities and Exchange Board of India (Issue of Capital and Disclosure Requirements) Regulations, 2018, SEBI Notification in Gazette of India, 11th September, pp. 1–252.

SEBI (SAST) Regulations (2011). Securities and Exchange Board of India (Substantial Acquisition of Shares and Takeovers) Regulations, 2011, SEBI Notification in Gazette of India, 23rd September, pp. 1–71.

Sen, N., & Mathen, N. (2011). Decoding the New Business Vehicle of India: The Limited Liability partnership. *NUJS LAW REVIEW*, October-December, 669–689.

Sharma, R., & Garg, B. (2014). Limited Liability Partnership in India: Study of Different Aspects for Optimum Growth. *International Journal of Commerce, Business and Management (IJCBM)*, *3*(5), 720–725.

Singhania, V. K. (1980). *Economic Concentration Through Inter Corporate Investments*. Bombay: Himalaya Publishing House.

Appendix

Table A.1 Extract of promoter group of Reliance Indusries Limited (RIL) showing shareholding of limited liability partnerships (LLPs)

Name of entity	*Holding at the end of June 2010*	*Holding at the end of September 2010*	*Change*
Chakradev Enterprises LLP	50	100	50
Chakradhar Commercials LLP	50	100	50
Chakresh Enterprises LLP	50	100	50
Chhatrabhuj Enterprises LLP	50	100	50
Devarshi Commercials LLP	50	100	50
Harinarayan Enterprises LLP	50	100	50
Janardan Commercials LLP	50	100	50
Karuna Commercials LLP	50	100	50
Samarjit Enterprises LLP	50	100	50
Shripal Enterprises LLP	50	100	50
Srichakra Commercials LLP	50	100	50
Svar Enterprises LLP	50	100	50
Tattvam Enterprises LLP	50	100	50
Vasuprada Enterprises LLP	50	100	50
Vishatan Enterprises LLP	50	100	50
Jagdanand Investments and Trading Co. Pvt. Ltd.	100	200	100
Jagdishvar Investments and Trading Co Pvt. Ltd.	100	200	100
Narahari Enterprises LLP	50	616,840	616,790
Kamalakar Enterprises LLP	50	6,370,016	6,369,966
Rishikesh Enterprises LLP	50	60,409,418	60,409,368
Pavana Enterprises LLP	50	61,673,400	61,673,350
Adisesh Enterprises LLP	50	81,099,093	81,099,043
Pitambar Enterprises LLP	50	1,04,900,070	1,04,900,020
Taran Enterprises LLP	50	1,06,373,069	1,06,373,019
Trilokesh Commercials LLP	50	1,24,513,168	1,24,513,118
Abhayaprada Enterprises LLP	50	1,24,514,168	1,24,514,118
Ajitesh Enterprises LLP	50	1,27,041,799	1,27,041,749
Badri Commercials LLP	50	1,27,041,799	1,27,041,749
Bhuvanesh Enterprises LLP	50	1,34,616,811	1,34,616,761
Total	14,63,923,343	14,63,923,343	0

Source: Compiled from shareholding pattern of RIL for the year 2010 available from the Bombay Stock Exchange Website.

DOI: 10.4324/9781003159940-13

Table A.2 Extract of promoter group of RIL showing shareholding of companies

Name of entity	*Holding at the end of June 2010*	*Holding at the end of September 2010*	*Change*
Kshitij Commercials Private Limited	3,10,869,936	100	-3,10,869,836
Nityapriya Commercials Private Limited	2,62,034,165	100	-2,62,034,065
Kardam Commercials Private Limited	2,49,027,336	100	-2,49,027,236
Kankhal Investments and Trading Company Private Limited	3,13,800,540	1,48,490,952	-1,65,309,588
Aavaran Textiles Private Limited	31,716,852	100	-31,716,752
Sanatan Textrade Private Limited	29,956,898	100	-29,956,798
Pams Investments and Trading Company Private Limited	6,369,966	100	-6,369,866
Bahar Trading Private Limited	1,634,510	100	-1,634,410
Bhumika Trading Private Limited	1,634,510	300	-1,634,210
Vita Investments and Trading Company Private Limited	616,790	100	-616,690
Madhuban Merchandise Private Limited	300	100	-200
Synergy Synthetics Private Limited	300	100	-200
Reliance Consultancy Services Private Limited	300	200	-100
Terene Industries Private Limited	300	250	-50
Amur Trading Private Limited	300	300	0
Anumati Mercantile Private Limited	300	300	0
Deccan Finvest Private Limited	300	300	0
Ekansha Enterprise Private Limited	300	300	0
Eklavya Mercantile Private Limited	300	300	0
Farm Enterprises Limited	92,077,290	92,077,290	0
Fidelity Shares and Securities Private Limited	10,715,110	10,715,110	0
Futura Commercials Private Limited	845	845	0

(*Continued*)

Table A.2 Continued

Name of entity	*Holding at the end of June 2010*	*Holding at the end of September 2010*	*Change*
Guruvas Textiles Private Limited	1,580,000	1,580,000	0
Hercules Investments Private Limited	200	200	0
Jogiya Traders Private Limited	300	300	0
Kda Enterprises Private Limited	1,060,000	1,060,000	0
Kedareshwar Investments and Trading Company Private Limited	6,500,623	6,500,623	0
Krish Commercials Private Limited	300	300	0
Master Akash M Ambani	3,363,190	3,363,190	0
Master Anant M Ambani	100,000	100,000	0
Ms. Isha M Ambani	3,364,390	3,364,390	0
Neutron Enterprises Private Limited	825	825	0
Nikhil Investments Company Private Limited	100	100	0
Ornate Traders Private Limited	300	300	0
Petroleum Trust (Through Trustees for Sole Beneficiary-M/S Reliance Industrial Investments And Holdings Ltd.)	1,20,471,003	1,20,471,003	0
Priyash Commercials Private Limited	200	200	0
Real Fibres Private Limited	100	100	0
Reliance Consolidated Enterprises Private Limited	300	300	0
Reliance Industrial Infrastructure Limited	172,000	172,000	0
Reliance Welfare Association	2,505,468	2,505,468	0
Shri.M D Ambani	3,615,846	3,615,846	0
Silvassa Hydrocarbons and Investments Private Limited	300	300	0
Smt.K D Ambani	7,330,454	7,330,454	0
Smt.Nita Ambani	3,398,146	3,398,146	0
Tresta Trading Private Limited	300	300	0

Source: Compiled from Shareholding Pattern of RIL for the year 2010 available from Bombay Stock Exchange Website.

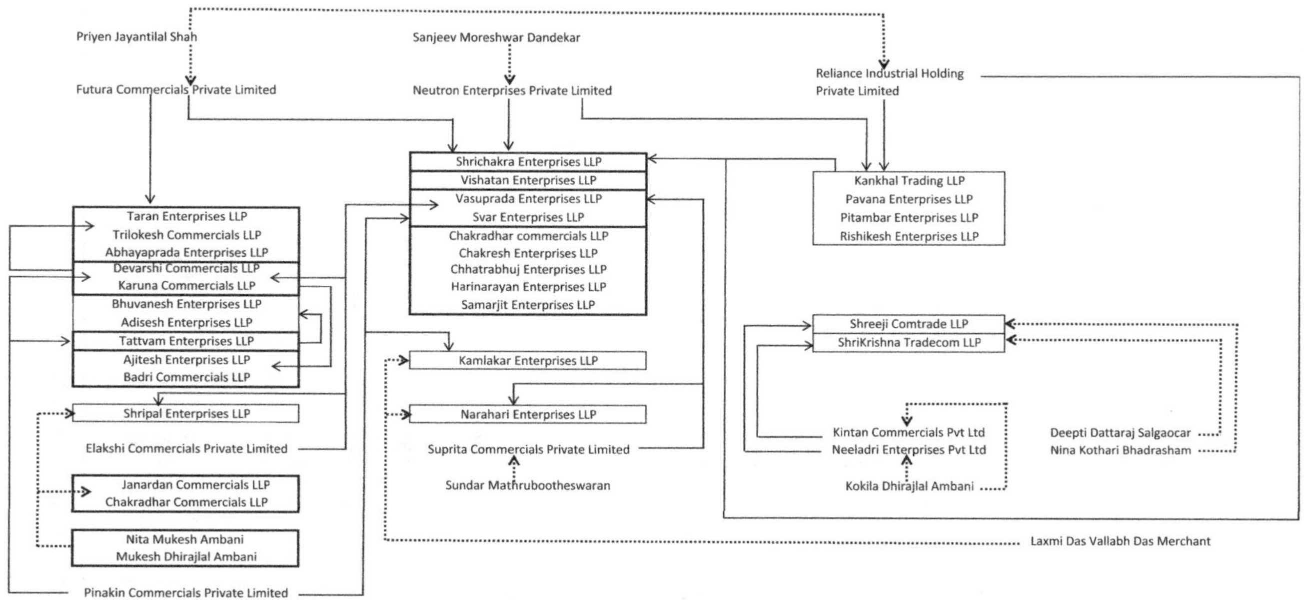

Figure A.1 Complex Structure of LLPs forming Part of the Reliance Group: Group Entities & Individuals Serving as Designated Partner in LLPs. Source: Author's schema based on information from financial statements of LLPs for the year ending 31 March 2017.

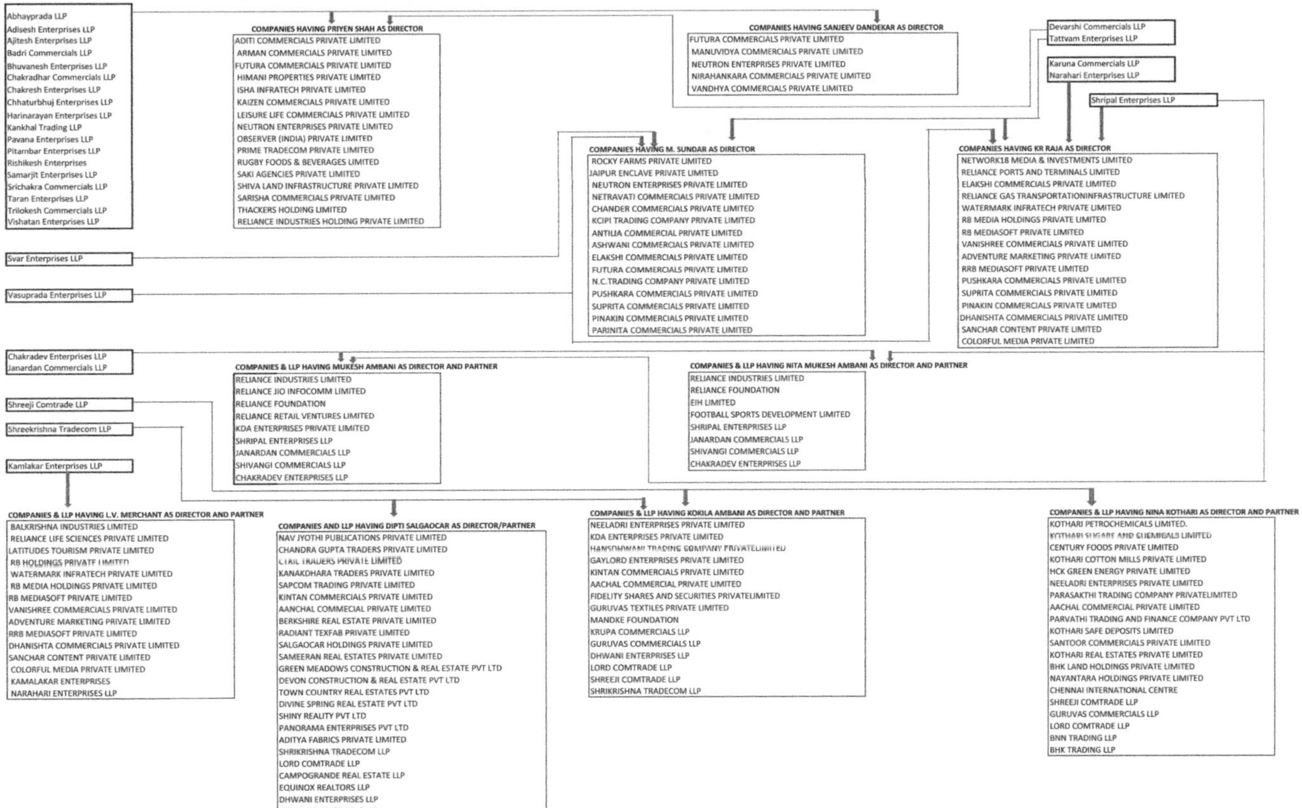

Figure A.2 Designated partners of LLPs as directors in group companies and partners in other LLPs. Source: Author's schema based on information from financial statements of LLPs for the year ending 31 March, 2017.

Index

For Product Safety Concerns and Information please contact our EU representative GPSR@taylorandfrancis.com Taylor & Francis Verlag GmbH, Kaufingerstraße 24, 80331 München, Germany